The Celebration of the Eucharist

Enrico Mazza

The Celebration of the Eucharist

*The Origin of the Rite and
the Development of Its Interpretation*

Translated by
Matthew J. O'Connell

A PUEBLO BOOK

THE LITURGICAL PRESS COLLEGEVILLE, MINNESOTA

A Pueblo Book published by Liturgical Press

Design by Frank Kacmarcik, Obl.S.B.

ISBN 13: 978-0-8146-6170-3
ISBN 10: 0-8146-6170-X

Library of Congress Cataloging-in-Publication Data

Mazza, Enrico.
    [Celebrazione eucaristica. English]
    The celebration of the Eucharist : the origin of the rite and the
development of its interpretation / Enrico Mazza ; translated by
Matthew J. O'Connell.
        p.   cm.
    "A Pueblo book."
    Includes bibliographical references and index.
    ISBN 0-8146-6170-X (alk. paper)
    1. Lord's Supper—Catholic Church—History. 2. Mass—History.
3. Eucharistic prayers—History. I. Title.
BV823.M38613   1998
264'.02036'09—dc21   98-37348
                                                                CIP

Contents

Preface

People accustomed to a liturgy like the one at the Last Supper in the upper room or like the one described in Book VII of the *Apostolic Constitutions* would have trouble getting their bearings at a liturgy such as the one (for example) in the *Pontificale* of William Durandus. The fact is that the eucharistic liturgy has differed in different centuries and different Churches. We must recognize, then, that a work dealing with this eucharistic liturgy must be a historical work.

At no point in the course of the centuries has the eucharistic liturgy been handed on in isolation; it has always been accompanied by the interpretations given to it at various periods, so much so that at times the celebration has been changed to fit better with the interpretation. The interpretation—in other words, the theology of the sacrament—is born of the rite, but as the interpretation changes in the course of time, this is reflected in the liturgy and brings about changes in it. I could not have dealt with the eucharistic liturgy without at the same time dealing with the interpretations given of it down the centuries. In this book, then, readers will find both the facts of the liturgy and the interpretation of them, that is, the theology of the Eucharist, in the course of history.

I deal first with the origin and development of the Eucharist and then with eucharistic theology as found in various authors—Fathers of the Church and medieval writers—whom I have chosen as typical representatives of the major stages in the historical development of thought on the Eucharist. In choosing the thought of one author, I choose to omit that of another; this is inevitable, and I am aware of having excluded authors of the first rank.

What, then, is the Eucharist? The Eucharist is an imitation of the Last Supper, and the latter in turn is a figure and announcement of the passion. These are the two constants in the Eucharistic Prayers of the Church since its beginnings. They guided the thinking of the Church Fathers of the first four centuries. During that period, therefore, theology developed in unison with the liturgy, maintaining the same conceptions and the same interpretive categories. At that period, the claim was constantly made that the conception of the Eucharist was a matter of obedience to the command of Christ: "Do this in remembrance of me," and that the rite imitated the rite in the upper room. In like manner, all the elements of the rite were regarded as an imitation of the various elements present in the celebration in the upper room: the bread, the wine, the Eucharistic Prayer, and even the priest.

"Antitype" (*antitypos*) is the word we find used in the earliest liturgies to describe the bread and wine of the eucharistic supper.[1] To account for this fact and to understand the terminology it is necessary to develop a *typological* interpretation of the eucharistic meal. The reason: the term *antitypos* and its correlative, *typos*, came from the typology that in the period of Christian origins and during the patristic period was the principal systematic tool used in the interpretation of the Scriptures. The terminology came to be used in two different but closely connected contexts: the interpretation of the Scriptures and the description of the liturgy.

The use of "antitype" to describe the bread and wine of the Eucharist means that these elements corresponded to elements of the Last Supper that were their model.[2] Although the terminology was not

---

[1] For example: "We thank you again, our Father, for the precious blood of Jesus, shed for us, and for the precious body, these antitypes of which we bring to completion, since he himself commanded us to proclaim his death. Through him glory be yours through the ages. Amen" (*Apostolic Constitutions* 7.25.4); see M. Metzger (ed.), *Les Constitutions apostoliques. Livres VII et VIII* (SC 136; Paris, 1987) 52. In early examples of the liturgies in Latin, *figura* plays the same role as *antitypos*.

[2] In Christianity, biblical typology was applied in the reading of the Old Testament in order to ensure its unity with the New Testament. The result was a single economy of salvation and a single Savior, Christ. The method was also used by Paul in 1 Corinthians 10:1-4. Success in establishing this unity required finding in the New Testament, or in the liturgy as the case might be, analogies or correspondences with events in the Old Testament. This meant the use of the allegorical method, by which the text of the Old Testament was made to speak authentically of New Testament events, as Jesus says in Luke 24:44: "These are my words that I spoke to you while I was still with you—that everything written about me in the law of Moses, the prophets, and the psalms must be fulfilled." Only because New Testament events fulfilled the ancient promise could they be regarded as saving events authenticated by God; only in this way, indeed, did they correspond to those Old Testament events that brought salvation to Israel.

In this conception, the facts and events of the Old Testament acquired a special function, that of being paradigms of salvation. In order to have this paradigmatic

function, those events were subjected to a process of "standardization" that brought out the characteristics expressing an action of God that was understood as salvific. In later periods, those events would be regarded as salvific that had a certain correspondence with the paradigmatic Old Testament events. Such was the "figural" or "typological" interpretation of the Scriptures; it was applied also to the liturgical rites, thus giving rise to a true and proper *theoria* (in the patristic sense of this word) and "interpretation" of the liturgy in terms of salvation.

There was a difference between straightforward biblical typology and typology as applied to the liturgy. In the latter, the paradigmatic character of the biblical figures was accentuated to the point of assigning them the role of models for the liturgical celebration. "Model" is here understood as referring to two things: (1) the rite, both in its content and in its externals, that is, the succession of the several ritual units; thus even in the succession of its several liturgical units the rite of the Last Supper is the model or type of the Church's Eucharist; (2) the saving efficacy that is described authentically in the Scriptures is attributed also to the Church's liturgical action (Melchizedek and his offering of bread and wine were seen as a "type" of both Christ and the Christian Eucharist; so, too, the gift of manna in the wilderness and, among other instances, David and the loaves of showbread).

In the Gospels, the role of type and therefore of model belongs both to the various stories of the multiplication of loaves and to the meals taken with the risen Lord. In these instances, there was question not so much of ritual "models" (although some elements of them were such) as of events that were paradigmatic in the order of salvation; the connection with the Eucharist was mediated through the fact that these incidents, which were connected with salvation, were also connected with meals.

The bibliography on biblical typology is very extensive. I list here only some classical studies. J. Daniélou, *Sacramentum futuri. Etudes sur les origines de la typologie biblique* (Etudes de théologie historique; Paris, 1950); ET: *From Shadows to Reality. Studies in the Biblical Typology of the Fathers,* trans. W. Hibberd (Westminster, Md., 1960); idem, *Platonisme et théologie mystique. Essai sur la doctrine spirituelle de saint Grégoire de Nysse* (Paris, 1954); H. De Lubac, *Exégèse médiévale. Les quatre sens de l'écriture* (Paris: Aubier, 1959); J. Daniélou, "Figure et événement chez Méliton de Sardes," in *Neotestamentica et patristica. Festgabe O. Cullmann* (Leiden, 1962) 282–92; L. F. Pizzolato, *La dottrina esegetica di sant'Ambrogio* (Studia patristica Mediolanensia 9; Milan, 1978); J. Pépin, *La tradition de l'allégorie. De Philon d'Alexandrie à Dante. Etudes historiques* (Paris, 1987).

On typology as applied to the liturgy: C. Jacob, *Arkandisziplin, Allegorese, Mystagogie: ein neuer Zugang zur Theologie des Ambrosius von Mailand* (Athenäums–Monographies. Theologie Theophaneia 32; Frankfurt, 1990); idem, "Zur Krise der Mystagogie in der Alten Kirche," *Theologie und Philosophie* 66 (1991) 75–89; E. Mazza, "Les raisons et la méthode des catéchèses mystagogiques de la fin du quatrième siècle," in A. M. Triacca and A. Pistoia (eds.), *La prédication liturgique et les commentaires de la liturgie* (Bibliotheca Ephemerides liturgicae, Subsidia 65; Rome, 1992) 154–76; R. N. Fragomeni, "Wounded in Extraordinary Depths: Towards a Contemporary Mystagogy," in M. Downey and R. N. Fragomeni (eds.), *A Promise of Presence. Studies in Honor of David N. Power* (Washington, D.C., 1992) 115–37; P.-M. Gy, "La mystagogie dans la liturgie ancienne et dans la pensée

fixed but fluctuated, the Last Supper was seen as the "type," while the Eucharist of the Church was the "antitype"; antitype corresponded to type. The idea of imitation (antitype–type) was to lead to the development of an interpretation of the Eucharist that used philosophical categories in order to describe the ontological value of the "Sacrament" of the Body and Blood of Christ.

At the center of the patristic treatment of the Eucharist was the Eucharist as "figure" of the Body and Blood of Christ and "figure" of his death. This conception was handed on to later periods that did not correctly understand a sacramental vocabulary based on the language of figure and typology. The idea of figure, now downgraded to allegory, was succeeded by a new conception based on the idea of presence. This new idea, which received a full development in the Middle Ages, became the way par excellence of formulating a eucharistic theology. The theme of presence was taken over in the official teaching of the Church, the climax of which was reached at the Council of Trent.

Vatican II initiated a radical liturgical reform that has drawn upon the sources of the patristic period in composing new Eucharistic Prayers for use in the Missal. At the same time, the category of "re-presentation" has been used in interpreting the eucharistic "sacrifice," although "re-presentation" seems to be simply a variant of "presence" as applied to the events of redemption.

The final question, which I raise in my last chapter, is whether present-day Christians are capable of understanding the Eucharist according to the figural and typological categories of early Christianity, while giving these the same meaning they had at that time: type–antitype, "figure of the body," "likeness of the blood," "figure of his death," "sacrament," and so on. The answer is Yes. Despite the difference in cultural setting and the different philosophical background of that time, biblical scholars have succeeded in interpreting the Last Supper as a figure and proclamation of the passion, while giving this conception an ontological value that is not different from that given it by the Fathers, although it is expressed in a very different way and

---

liturgique d'aujourd'hui," in A. M. Triacca and A. Pistoia (eds.), *Mystagogie: pensée liturgique d'aujourd'hui et liturgie ancienne* (Bibliotheca Ephemerides liturgicae, Subsidia 70; Rome, 1993) 137–43; Ph. De Roten, "Le vocabulaire mystagogique de Saint Jean Chrysostome," ibid., 115–35; E. Mazza, "Saint Augustin et la mystagogie," ibid., 201–26 (this volume is very important for the subject of mystagogy); D. Sartori, "Mistagogia ieri e oggi: alcune publicazioni recenti," *Ecclesia orans* 11 (1994) 181–99.

without using the categories of the patristic age. I have already set forth this biblical interpretation of the Eucharist in my book *The Eucharistic Prayers of the Roman Rite;*[3] readers will therefore find some pages from that book used here.

I have said a great deal about the history of the anaphora in my other publications, but there is no question here of mere repetition, since I have put together researches published at different times and in various reviews and have made connections that may have escaped readers of those older works, since the connections were only implicit. Furthermore, I have endeavored here to give synthesis priority over analysis, while making the exposition more accessible even to readers who are not professional historians of the eucharistic anaphora.

Enrico Mazza
Milan
September 25, 1995

---

[3] *Le odierne preghiere eucaristiche* (Bologna, 1984); ET: *The Eucharistic Prayers of the Roman Rite,* trans. M. J. O'Connell (New York, 1986).

Chapter 1

Introduction

1. A HISTORICAL STUDY OF THE LITURGY: ITS METHOD

In the miscellany published in honor of Arthur Hubert Couratin, Geoffrey J. Cuming presented a review of the most important studies on the liturgy from the work of Gregory Dix[1] to 1977.[2] In it he provided a picture of great interest, since not only did he describe the subjects of the various studies but also, and above all, he focused on the perspective and method of the various writers. About fifteen years later, in a festschrift for Balthasar Fischer,[3] Albert Gerhards published a noteworthy essay on the results of studies on the liturgical sources for the Eucharist in the early Church. In addition, although there is question of a quite specific area, I must mention the Syrian liturgy, for which we have fine specialized expositions connected with the critical edition of the Anaphora of Addai and Mari.[4]

---

[1] G. Dix, *The Shape of the Liturgy* (London, 1945).

[2] G. J. Cuming, "The Early Eucharistic Liturgies in Recent Research," in B. D. Spinks (ed.), *The Sacrifice of Praise. Studies on the Themes of Thanksgiving and Redemption in the Central Prayers of the Eucharistic and Baptismal Liturgies. In Honor of A. H. Couratin* (Bibliotheca Ephemerides liturgicae, Subsidia 19; Rome, 1981) 65–69. Other contributions of the same author may be added: "Four Very Early Anaphoras," *Worship* 58 (1984) 168–72; "The Shape of the Anaphora," in E. A. Livingstone (ed.), *Studia patristica XX* (Kalamazoo–Louvain, 1989) 333–45; *The Liturgy of St. Mark* (OCA 234; Rome, 1990) (published after the author's death by Bryan D. Spinks).

[3] A. Gerhards, "Entstehung und Entwicklung des eucharistischen Hochgebets im Spiegel der neueren Forschung. Der Beitrag der Liturgiewissenschaft zur liturgischen Erneuerung," in A. Heinz and H. Rennings (eds.), *Gratias agamus. Studien zum eucharistischen Hochgebet. Für Balthasar Fischer* (Freiburg–Basel–Vienna, 1992) 75–96.

[4] A. Gelston, *The Eucharistic Prayer of Addai and Mari* (Oxford, 1992); see also B. D. Spinks, *Worship: Prayers from the East* (Washington, D.C., 1993); P. Yousif,

A reading of these reviews provides us with a great deal of information, since the researches being surveyed yielded a wealth of data that has expanded to a remarkable degree our knowledge of the eucharistic celebration. Unfortunately, the information remains unused, since it is locked up in professional journals not usually read except by historians of the liturgy. Our knowledge of the Eucharist has changed radically ever since G. Dix focused his investigation on "the actions of the Last Supper rather than on a conjectural reconstruction of the words uttered"[5] by Jesus on that occasion.

A second methodological advance that complements the first consists in using the Jewish liturgy for a point-by-point comparison with the earliest eucharistic texts of the Church. This method originated in the area of Jewish studies and then, especially due to the studies of Dix, Ligier, Bouyer, and others, became widespread[6] and is now standard. But in the study of anaphoras it is not only a comparison of the anaphoral texts with the Jewish sources but also, and above, a comparison of the texts with one another that has enabled scholars to determine the original form of a text and to draw a kind of map or genealogical tree showing the development of texts and their influence on each other. In this context I cannot fail to mention the names of Botte, Lanne, Engberding, and others.[7]

How do the gains made in these historical and philological studies of the eucharistic liturgy, and especially of its origins, fit into the broader realm of eucharistic studies? Is it possible to construct an organized picture of the data? How is the study of Christian origins related to the study of later developments? These are all questions that call for an answer. It is time, therefore, to go back to writing manuals or handbooks, not so as to neglect area studies but so as to locate them within a broader horizon.

That is what I have tried to do in this book, which takes the form of a manual that has for its subject the rite of the "eucharistic meal" and the understanding of it. If such a manual is to profit from historical studies of the eucharistic liturgy, it must itself follow the historical

---

L'Eucharistie chez saint Ephrem de Nisibe (OCA 224; Rome, 1984); idem, A Classified Bibliography (Rome, 1990).

[5] G. J. Cuming, "The Early Eucharistic liturgies" (note 2, above), 65.

[6] See E. Mazza, L'anafora eucaristica. Studi sulle origini (Bibliotheca Ephemeridies liturgiche, Subsidia 62; Rome, 1992) 7–17. [Henceforth: Mazza, L'anafora.]

[7] See ibid., 7–17 and 363–87 for the writings of the authors cited and for other researches which space does not permit mentioning here.

method; otherwise the conclusions of the studies on which this treatise is based would be distorted.[8]

It seems right to me that theology should profit by the strict historical method as applied to the liturgy, just as in the recent past it has profited from the application of the historico-critical method to biblical studies.

This treatise on the Eucharist is, then, intended as a work on the history of the liturgy, for I am convinced that by following this method we shall attain the best results for the study of the Eucharist.

2. STRUCTURE AND METHOD IN TREATISES ON THE EUCHARIST

After describing the method to be followed in this treatise, I must say a few words on the different way in which a treatise is constructed when the problem is approached using the theological method rather than a philological and historical analysis of the liturgical texts and rites.

A treatise on the Eucharist is usually developed on the basis of a thematic division that came into existence in the scholastic age and was standardized by the Council of Trent. The treatise is divided into three fundamental subjects: the Sacrament of the Eucharist, the eucharistic sacrifice, and Communion. Material on each of these subjects is selected from the tradition of the Church, thus supplying the store of knowledge that is to be systematically divided among the three subjects. The first subject, the Sacrament, is concerned with the true, real, and substantial presence of the Body and Blood of Christ under the appearances of bread and wine. The second has to do with the relationship between the Eucharist and the sacrifice of the Cross. The third subject has very little content, since eucharistic Communion, insofar as it is an eating and drinking, does not lend itself to any extent to a speculative treatment, especially when the method is dependent on Aristotelico-Thomistic ontology; as a result, the subject is removed to discussions of a spiritual kind that are concerned with the fruitful reception of the Sacrament.

---

[8] The texts are treated as texts, and this means with the historico-critical method. Only in a second phase can theologians intervene with their reflections; the two phases and the two roles must not be inverted. I do not believe in a "double truth"; furthermore we should ask ourselves what the theological relevance of history is.

All the elements that do not fit into this basic division are marginalized and relegated to a few notes or scholia, or else they are simply passed over. Think, for example, of the complete lack of attention to the Last Supper as the "model" for the Church's celebration, or the no less total lack of attention to the Eucharistic Prayer, its role, and its content.[9] In addition, we must consider a further fact: The Roman Church, involved as it was in its controversies with Protestantism, could not fail to project its concerns onto the treatise on the Eucharist, thus locking it into an apologetic stereotype that allowed for no real alternatives.

This was the settled position when, at the end of the last century and the beginning of this, a new phenomenon made its appearance: The investigation of sources, which were published and studied with the historico-critical method and gave rise to various treatises on the "history of dogma." These in turn gave rise to a special branch of theology, known as "positive theology."

Theological treatises on the Eucharist were unable to ignore these historical studies, and they acquired a new bipartite structure: a positive theology of the Eucharist and a speculative theology.

3. THE TWO PARTS OF THE TREATISE

Yves Congar provided a theory of this state of affairs, creating a kind of theological program with two phases: the hearing of the faith and the understanding of the faith.[10] As a result, treatises on the Eucharist[11] came in two parts: in the first, the "positive" data were set forth,[12] while in the second there was a systematic explanation of the

---

[9] Because of the methodological approach adopted, only a part of the Church's eucharistic tradition entered these theological treatises, the deplorable consequence being a general impoverishment both of the spirituality of the faithful and of thinking about the celebration. The field was thus left open to devotionalism, which responded better to needs not met by the celebration and its theology.

[10] Y. Congar, "Théologie," *DTC* 15/1 (Paris, 1946) cols. 341–502; ET: *A History of Theology,* trans. and ed. H. Guthrie (Garden City, N.Y., 1968).

[11] G. Colombo has made a careful study of these works in his "Per il trattato sull'Eucaristia," *Teologia* 13 (1988) 95–131; 14 (1989) 105–37. The writings studied there are those published after Vatican Council II. To complete the picture: G. Colombo, "La transustanziazione," *Teologia* 20 (1995) 8–33.

[12] Positive theology, at least for Y. Congar, is already a theological work (see "Théologie," col. 444; ET, p. 275). For this reason, the historical treatment is necessarily different from that of positive theology.

doctrine.[13] For a classic example of this method, we may look at the treatise published by De Baciocchi, which is divided into two parts: (a) Positive and historical data; (b) Doctrinal exposition. The first is subdivided into (1) biblical data, and (2) patristic and liturgical data. The doctrinal exposition contains the data, problems, and developments of the medieval, modern, and contemporary periods, which are distributed under three subject headings: sacrifice, Sacrament, and Communion.[14]

Theological manuals published since Vatican II rely on theological categories supplied by the history of salvation. For this reason they usually begin with an essay on biblical theology, which deals not so much with liturgical celebrations as with "biblical themes" connected with the Eucharist and taken from both the Old and the New Testaments. This section is placed at the beginning of the "positive theology" of the Eucharist and remains rather autonomous and isolated from the rest. Above all, it is not brought into a dialogue with the "systematic" part. It succeeds neither in altering the plan of the treatise nor in supplying a new basis for the systematic formulation of eucharistic doctrine. As a result, the systematic part continues to divide the treatise into sacrifice, Sacrament, and Communion.

4. RECOURSE TO THE CATEGORY OF "MEMORIAL"

Within the framework I have been describing, a degree of renewal has been produced by what has come to be known as "mystery theology," which was developed between the two World Wars by Odo Casel[15] and was based on the practice and theology of the patristic period. "Patristic period" is really too broad a description, since the sources which Casel used were almost exclusively from the fourth century.[16] "The theology of the mysteries" makes use of the

[13] This approach is open to a very severe critique on the score of methodology: (a) the first part is not a truly critical historical investigation; it is already theology and influenced by the data that make up the second part; (b) the second part is subdivided into the same three parts I mentioned above (Sacrament, sacrifice, Communion), independently of the content of the first part.

[14] J. De Baciocchi, L'Eucharistie (Mystère chrétien: Théologie sacramentaire 3; Tournai, 1964).

[15] The most important work to be mentioned is Casel's Das christliche Kultmysterium (Regensburg, 1935²; 4th enl. ed.: 1960); ET: The Mystery of Christian Worship and Other Writings, ed. B. Neunheuser (Westminster, Md., 1962).

[16] See, e.g., O. Casel, Faites ceci en mémoire de moi (Lex orandi 34; Paris, 1942).

conception of rites that was developed in the mystery religions,[17] the vocabulary of which was taken over by the liturgy and by the theology of the Fathers in the fourth century. After Vatican Council II the "theology of the mysteries" underwent a real revival and became the most common way of interpreting the liturgy.

The theology of the mysteries conceives of the rite as being a "memorial" of the redemptive work of Christ, and this view has been seen as in harmony with the theology of Vatican Council II, which is based to a great extent on the history of salvation. Insofar as it is a memorial the eucharistic rite (it is claimed) is a ritual memorial that renders the historical event operative now. It must be said that this teaching is winning ever greater success, since it seems to give the best explanation of the Church's eucharistic doctrine[18] and also allows the patristic data on mystery, as developed by Casel, to be in coherent continuity with the biblical data that have been brought out in some recent studies.[19]

It is, in fact, rather commonly said that in the Scriptures "memorial" signifies mystery in the Caselian sense; this is why when writers speak of "memorial," they usually specify "memorial in the biblical sense." But there is, strictly speaking, no single biblical sense of the term "memorial," since each book of the Old Testament has its own conception and use of the theme "remembrance,"[20] and since, in addition, the cultic use of *zkr* (memorial) in Old Testament sacrifices is

[17] Here is a good summary by Casel himself: "The *Kyrios* of a mystery is a God who has entered into human misery and struggle, has made his appearance on earth (epiphany) and fought there, suffered, even been defeated. . . . This was the way of pious faith and sacred teaching *(hieros logos),* of society in the earliest mythical age. . . . Worship is the means of making it real once more, and thus of breaking through to the spring of salvation. The members of the cult present again in a ritual, symbolic fashion, that primeval act" *(The Mystery of Christian Worship,* 53).

[18] It respects fully the uniqueness of the foundational event and, at the same time, guarantees the efficacy of the sacramental rite.

[19] Max Thurian, for example, has systematically studied the biblical data on the Eucharist in the perspective of the memorial; see his *L'eucharistie. Mémorial du Seigneur. Sacrifice d'action de grâce et d'intercession* (Neuchâtel, 1963); ET: *The Eucharistic Memorial,* trans. J. G. Davies (2 vols.; Ecumenical Studies in Worship 7–8; Richmond, 1960).

[20] I have already discussed this topic in "L'interpretazione del culto nella chiesa antica," *Celebrare il mistero di Cristo. Manuale di liturgia. I. La celebrazione: introduzione alla liturgia cristiana,* ed. Associazione Professori di Liturgia (Ephemerides liturgicae. Subsidia 73. Studi di liturgia. Nuova serie 25; Rome, 1993) 229–79.

quite remote from the eucharistic celebration of the Church. In Old Testament sacrifices, *zkr* designates the best part of the victim, which is offered to God in remembrance. I see no connection between the best part of the victim, which is sacrificed to God in remembrance *(zkr),* and the words of Jesus at the Last Supper: "Do this in remembrance of me." Similarly, I do not see how it can be said that the Eucharist was instituted to remind God to be mindful of us.[21]

5. THE SACRAMENT OF THE SACRIFICE

In the classical theology that was heir to Thomism or, more generally, to scholasticism, the "Real Presence" was treated in ontological terms, while the theme of "sacrifice" was treated in purely symbolic terms according to a figural interpretation. Today this latter aspect of the problem has undergone a radical change, inasmuch as it is generally taken for granted that the "sacrifice" belongs to the same sacramental order as the "Real Presence." In other words, the Eucharist is the Sacrament of the sacrifice of Christ. In the present treatise we shall see the historical origin of this different way of approaching the Sacrament and the sacrifice, the starting point being the unitary approach of the patristic age. On the other hand, the "classical" method followed in the treatise on the Eucharist had its origin in the Western medieval drift in the direction of allegory and away from the typological method of the Fathers of the Church. As we shall see, the historical data on "sacrifice" and "Real Presence" are in agreement with each other and with the remarks of Giuseppe Colombo. Speaking as a theologian about the decisions of the Council of Trent that subdivided the Eucharist into two parts, sacrifice and Sacrament, Colombo says that these parts

"cannot be intended as autonomous chapters that are independent of one another and/or simply juxtaposed. If that is formally the case with the Tridentine decrees—a formality suggested, in fact, not by any rational principle but by historical circumstances—then we must evidently move beyond it to the synthetic understanding of the mystery that theology offers. In other words, real presence/transubstantiation and sacrifice of the Mass do not refer to different subjects; therefore

---

[21] In my discussion, then, I shall take the data of tradition into consideration without giving too much space to the category of "memorial" (understood in its biblical sense), for, when it is not legitimated by the sources, it loses the principal ground on which it was chosen.

they demand to be seen as substantially identical, in the sense that if the Eucharist is the sacrifice of Jesus Christ, it is, in a more complete formulation, the real presence of the sacrifice of Christ."[22]

---

[22] See Colombo, "Per il trattato," 130.

Chapter 2

Old Testament Sacrifices and Ritual Meal

The Old Testament can be used in several ways to shed light on the
Christian Eucharist. These ways are reducible to two different methods, the typological and the historical.

With the help of the typological method it can be shown how the
old law prefigures the new and, consequently, how the old has its
fulfillment in the realities of the New Testament. In this perspective,
even the eucharistic celebration will be seen as a fulfillment of Old
Testament types, such as Melchizedek, the manna, and the various
kinds of sacrifice. This method is particularly suited to shedding light
on the salvific power of the Eucharist.[1]

The historical method enables us to bring out the relationships
between the New Testament liturgy and the Old Testament rites, by
showing how, in what ritual forms and structures, and by what paths
and transformations, the Christian liturgy has descended from the
Jewish.

The Christian Eucharist originated in the Last Supper of Christ,
which in turn drew its character from the ritual setting of Jewish
meals. We must inquire, first, into the ritual aspect of the Jewish meal
and then show the connection between the liturgy of the Jewish meal
and the liturgy of the Lord's supper. The starting point, then, will be
the rite of the Jewish meal, without consideration of the theology attached to it, since the connection is between two ritual structures, and
this connection is independent of theological considerations. The inquiry into the Jewish ritual meal and its origin takes us into the area
of the Jewish sacrifices; we must, therefore, attend chiefly to these.

---

[1] I shall not deal with this approach here because I have already described its
characteristics in my essay: "L'interpretazione del culto nella chiesa antica" (see
chapter 1, note 20).

9

1. THE SLAUGHTER OF ANIMALS IN DEUTERONOMY 12:15

Prior to Deuteronomy every slaughter of animals has a ritual character and therefore falls within the sphere of sacrifice. Only after Deuteronomy 12:20-25 is a distinction made between slaughter for sacrifice and slaughter simply for food. The ritual slaughter is done on the altar.[2]

The second part of the book of Deuteronomy is divided into four sections: (1) worship (12:1–16:17); (2) the organization of the state (16:18–20:20); (3) family law (21:1–23:1); (4) laws of cleanness, social laws, and various other laws. This collection is known as the Deuteronomic Code and forms a unit that is integrated with the remainder of the book. The laws are formulated with theological motifs in mind, such as the gift of the land of Canaan, the blessing promised to Israel, and the deliverance from Egypt. While the theological foundation is clear, any definition or determination of the juridical status of the laws is only approximate, since we are not dealing with a code or even a constitution in the modern sense of these terms. It would perhaps be better to say that this code, "like the rest of the book, is a catechesis, but one ordered to practical applications,"[3] which therefore have also a juridical value.

At first sight, Deuteronomy seems to speak abstractly in reference to an indeterminate period, but if we look more closely, the historical setting is well defined: Israel is a national state like all those that made their appearance in Syria-Palestine at the end of the second millennium: Edom, Moab, Ammon, Phoenicia, Aram, and so on. These states were characterized by a strong sense of nationalism and a democratic organization. The state was monarchical and tended toward a centralization of the country's religious and civic life; everything associated with nomadism tended to disappear and be replaced by the institutions of a sedentary society. Deuteronomy reflects this transitional situation, and this at a time when, for example, the development toward the centralization of worship was not yet complete (12:8-12; 18:1-8).

The ideal planned by Deuteronomy can be summed up in two points: fidelity to the covenant, and unity. In this perspective, the plan becomes concrete when it endeavors to close the gap between religious Israel and political Israel. In fact, the states of Judah and

---

[2] Exodus 20:24-26 authorizes as materials for an altar either stones or mud bricks, which, being simply a raw material, are equated with earth.

[3] P. Buis and L. Leclercq, *Le Deutéronome* (Sources Bibliques; Paris, 1963) 99.

Israel did not have much in common with the tribal league for which the covenants and laws were intended. The Deuteronomic Code had to take on the various civic institutions and put them at the service of its Yahwistic ideal, that is, of the entire history of the People of God. The Code approves new institutions that increase the power of the state at the expense of ancient local autonomies, the purpose being to strengthen the unity of the people and form a solidly organized nation.

This, then, is the perspective that governs the new legislation for worship, an activity that must, for the sake of the goal, be carefully controlled and centralized. The ancient local sanctuaries at which Yahwism had slowly manifested itself and become obligatory will cease to be recognized, and the celebration of "legitimate" worship will be allowed only at the central sanctuary. The latter derives its legitimacy from two characteristics: (a) it has been chosen by Yahweh, and (b) it is exclusive. Beginning with Hezekiah, this single sanctuary could only be the one in Jerusalem. Deuteronomy, however, remains vague, perhaps in order not to confirm the important role which the Davidic dynasty has assigned to itself. The reform of Hezekiah can only be explained by the existence of a prior tradition that was already partially codified (2 Kgs 18:4–22; 2 Chr 31:1). From the eighth century on there existed a current of thought, represented by some of the prophets, that was decisively in favor of a single sanctuary (Amos 4:4-5; Hos 4:13-15) and that explicitly condemned other places of worship.

This lengthy introduction has been necessary if we are to understand the development of sacrificial practice in Israel.

In Deuteronomy's conception of the liturgy, the sacrifice that serves as type is the "communion sacrifice." This consists in the killing of the living animal and its dissection into various parts, some of which are burned on the altar, others are given to the priests, and still others are given to the offerers, to be eaten at a family "sacred meal" that is marked by joy and thanksgiving.[4] The part given to the offerers is the one most consistently mentioned.

---

[4] The communion sacrifice was the one most frequently practiced in the earliest period. It was the typical sacrifice offered by the clans at their various meetings (1 Sam 20:6-28; etc.). It was also offered on the occasion of pilgrimages, which, as we know, were the way in which people traveled to places of worship where the great feasts were celebrated (see 1 Sam 1:21; 2:19). This kind of sacrifice was a joyous one which brought together at a single meal the priest, the offerer, and the people, each of these having their own part of the victim. All the blood, however, was sprinkled, while the fat was burned on the altar.

These points about this sacrifice are important not only theologically but also historically. The communion sacrifice and its ritual showed the usual practice in the slaughtering of animals, but the centralization of worship marked the beginning of a new period in the history of Jewish sacrifice, a period in which the nonritual slaughter of animals made its appearance.

Here is the standard set by Deuteronomy:

"Take care that you do not offer your burnt offerings at any place you happen to see. But only at the place that the Lord will choose in one of your tribes—there you shall offer your burnt offerings and there you shall do everything I command you. Yet whenever you desire you may slaughter and eat meat within any of your towns, according to the blessing that the Lord your God has given you" (Deut 12:13-15).

We can see from this passage how and why the slaughter of livestock became a secular activity that was licit in all circumstances and had no connection with sacrificial rites. The passage also gives us, indirectly,

---

For this sacrifice, too, we have few details that would help us describe the rite. This much can be said: the animal was slaughtered away from the altar; the victim was cut up into several parts; some of these were placed on the altar and burned, that is, offered to God; other parts were given to the faithful to be eaten in the meal that followed the sacrifice. The main concern of the biblical accounts is with the observance or nonobservance of the rules for dividing the victim among those who had a right to share in it. At Shiloh, for example, the sons of Eli were reproached for not observing these rules; they ordered their servant to fish for pieces in the pot in which the meat was being cooked, and, in addition, they claimed a part of the raw meat for roasting before the fat had been offered to Yahweh (1 Sam 2:12-17). In 1 Samuel 9:23-24, Samuel, after sacrificing, offers Saul the thigh and the tail, even though, according to Leviticus 7:32, the thigh was assigned to the priest and, according to Leviticus 3:9, the tail was to be burned for Yahweh.

The communion sacrifice was distinguished by its joyful character and was so frequently practiced that in the historical books it is often signified simply by *zebah*, as though it were the sacrifice par excellence. Of itself the term *zebah* meant every bloody sacrifice that entailed a religious meal; it was also applied to the Passover sacrifice.

The holocaust, which was an exception in early times, became the regular sacrifice in the temple, while communion sacrifices became increasingly rare. The holocaust was primarily an act of homage expressed in a gift. Thus it became the type of the perfect sacrifice, of homage offered to God in the form of a total gift, the Qorbân or sacrifice par excellence (Leviticus 1). The holocaust included the blood rite (Lev 1:4), to which an expiatory power was attributed, as indeed it was to the blood rite of any other sacrifice (Lev 17:11). See R. de Vaux, *Studies in Old Testament Sacrifice* (Cardiff, 1964).

another piece of information: that prior to Deuteronomy every slaughter of livestock, even simply for food, was a sacred action and governed by liturgical rules. In nomadic societies a domestic animal could not be killed and eaten apart from a liturgical action. Every slaughter was a sacrifice.[5] The rite consisted essentially in offering the blood, which was the symbol of life (Deut 12:24), by pouring it out on an altar or just on a stone.[6]

Deuteronomy ordained that there be a single sanctuary. This meant that every family needing meat for food would have had to go on pilgrimage to the sanctuary and have the animal killed ritually. This was obviously not to be envisaged. Two solutions were possible: (a) to prohibit the eating of meat apart from sacrifices at the legitimate sanctuary, as the Holiness Code indeed ordered (Lev 17:3-4); (b) to allow slaughter as a secular act. Deuteronomy chose the second alternative, thereby acknowledging the autonomy of the secular world and leaving behind the nomadic mentality, which by that time was an anachronism. Once the rite of slaughter had been changed into a secular activity, the strictly sacral nature of other actions, which could be performed only at the sanctuary, was reinforced.[7] Readers may usefully consult also Deuteronomy 12:20-27, which repeats, but in a more developed vocabulary, the two earlier passages on the slaughter of animals and the offering of first fruits and vows at the place of worship.

[5] In short: if the meat were to be eaten, the animal had to be slaughtered, and this could be done only in a ritual form. The liturgical rite of slaughter was the only way to have the meat for the meal.

[6] "After they struck down the Philistines that day from Michmash to Aijalon, the troops were very faint; so the troops flew upon the spoil, and took sheep and oxen and calves, and slaughtered them on the ground; and the troops ate them with the blood. Then it was reported to Saul, 'Look, the troops are sinning against the Lord by eating with the blood.' And he said, 'You have dealt treacherously; roll a large stone before me here.'" Saul said, "Disperse yourselves among the troops, and say to them, 'Let all bring their oxen or their sheep, and slaughter them here, and eat; and do not sin against the Lord by eating with the blood.' So all of the troops brought their oxen with them that night, and slaughtered them there. And Saul built an altar to the Lord; it was the first altar that he built to the Lord" (1 Sam 14:32-35). On the implications of Israel's sacrificial worship see C. B. Costecalde, *Aux origines du sacré biblique* (Paris, 1986).

[7] "Nor may you eat within your towns the tithe of your grain, your wine, and your oil, the firstlings of your herds and your flocks, any of your votive gifts that you vow, your freewill offerings, or your donations; these you shall eat in the presence of the Lord your God in the place that the Lord your God will choose,

2. JEWISH MEALS AS RITUAL MEALS

2.1. Was a Ritual Meal a Sacrifice?

As long as the rule was in force that animals had to be ritually slaughtered, every meal was a religious action and connected in some manner with sacrifice. It was the rule about the secular slaughter of animals that created a clear difference between the sacred meal at a sacrifice and the secular meal taken simply for nourishment. But secularizing the slaughter of animals did not mean the loss of the religious character proper to the realm of eating, which is so important from an anthropological point of view. This religious character was not removed but only transferred; the act of slaughter was secularized, but the meal remained a religious action.[8] The result was the rise of the special liturgy of the Jewish ritual meal, which was traced back to the divine command given in Deuteronomy 8:10: "You shall eat your fill and bless the Lord your God for the good land that he has given you."

From this verse we can see that it is not a prayer that sanctifies the meal; on the contrary, the meal itself, being the expression of the divine gift of the land, has its own sacral character that calls for the presence of prayer. The purpose of the prayer is not to change the meal into a "sacred meal," but to acknowledge the gift of God. It is God who is blessed, and not the meal. Since every meal, as such, stems from God's gift, it follows that all meals should be celebrated with prayer.

Since the ritual meal had its origin in the history of Jewish sacrifice, we can say that there is a connection between sacrifice and the liturgy of the Jewish meal. At the same time, however, we must deny that the meal itself had any kind of sacrificial character, since it arose out of the reform in the practice of slaughtering animals, when the distinction between secular slaughtering and sacrificial slaughtering was introduced.

---

you together with your son and your daughter, your male and female slaves, and the Levite resident in your towns, rejoicing in the presence of the Lord your God in all your undertakings" (Deut 12:17-18).

[8] In connection with Israel it is incorrect to speak of either a "sacred meal" or a "profane/secular meal." In Israel a meal was neither sacred nor secular, but religious. This meant that the category of the sacred was transcended and that there was a direct relationship with God. For this kind of interpretation of sacred and profane see J.-P. Audet, "Le sacré et le profane. Leur situation en christianisme," *NRT* 79 (1957) 33–61.

In conclusion: The Jewish ritual meal was one of the stages that structured the history of Old Testament sacrifice, but it cannot be said that the ritual meal was itself a sacrifice or had a sacrificial character, even as a result of the liturgy that accompanied it.[9]

2.2. The Basic Prayer of the Jewish Meal

The rabbis were very clear on the connection between a meal and the prayer of thanksgiving with which it ended, and they asked what the source was of the obligation to recite such a prayer. They found their answer in Deuteronomy 8:10, which came to them as a divine command establishing the Jewish meal. This divine institution gave rise to the theology and juridical obligation of the prayer said at the end of meals. This prayer was the *Birkat ha-Mazon.*[10]

Whenever there is a meal, provided it consist in something more than a medium-size olive, the *Birkat ha-Mazon* is said.

It is extremely difficult to establish the exact original tenor of this prayer, since there has never been a single, normative text which everyone had to follow. According to the rules governing Jewish prayer, every kind of prayer had to follow a pattern, but within the pattern the one praying was free to formulate his or her own prayer,

---

[9] In explaining the source of the sacrificial character of the Christian Eucharist, authors have often had recourse to the sacrificial character of the prayer of thanksgiving that accompanied the Old Testament rites and that accompanies the Christian Eucharist. One who has taken this approach is Henri Cazelles. See his "L'anaphore et l'Ancien Testament," in B. Botte, et al. (eds.), *Eucharisties d'Orient et d'Occident* I (Lex orandi 46; Paris, 1970) 11–22; idem, "Eucharistie, bénédiction et sacrifice dans l'Ancien Testament," *MD*, no. 123 (1975) 7–28. This interpretive approach has been given an original development in C. Giraudo, *La struttura letteraria della preghiera eucaristica. Saggio sulla genesi letteraria di una forma. Toda veterotestamentaria, Beraka giudaica, Anafora cristiana* (AnBib 92; Rome, 1981). This author finds a direct connection between the *Toda* and the Christian anaphora, with the result that there would be a specific continuity between sacrificial rites connected with the covenant and containing a *Toda*, and the eucharistic celebration. For an assessment of this view see "La discussione sull'origine dell'anafora eucaristica: une messa a punto," *Rivista di pastoral liturgica* 32, no. 182 (1994, no. 1) 42–54.

[10] This prayer is also used in the Passover meal, during the ritual of the third cup, which stands out as very important. It was also used in communion sacrifices, as can be seen from the account of Abraham's death in the *Book of Jubilees* 22:1-10. Here again it must have played an important role, since it is cited rather extensively as one of the most important moments in the events surrounding Abraham's death as told in this Old Testament apocryphal work.

thus creating an improvised text. For this reason it is very difficult to find detailed testimonies regarding the *Birkat ha-Mazon*. A further difficulty is that there were specific prohibitions against putting the prayer in writing.[11]

Scholars have made an effort to reconstruct, from the few texts that have come down to us, a text that would serve as a general pattern for the *Birkat ha-Mazon*. Here is the text proposed by Finkelstein.[12]

"(a) Blessed are you, Lord, our God, king of the universe, who feed the whole world in goodness, kindness, and mercy. Blessed are you, Lord, who feed the universe.

"(b) We thank you, Lord, our God, who have given us as an inheritance a desirable land, that we might eat of its fruits and nourish ourselves on its goodness. Blessed are you, Lord, our God, for the land and the food.

"(c) Have mercy, Lord, our God, on Israel your people and on Jerusalem your city and on Zion the dwelling place of your glory and on your altar and sanctuary. Blessed are you, Lord, who build Jerusalem."

We must bear in mind that this pattern is a reconstruction by Finkelstein, who proposes it as a kind of basic model. This text never existed as such and therefore can be used only with great caution. Unfortunately, many make use of the pattern without dealing with actually existing texts, though these are much more interesting because of the parallels they show with the later Christian development of it. One text, among others, is especially important: the *Birkat ha-Mazon* in the *Book of Jubilees* (22.6-9), which was written around 100 B.C.:

"⁶And he [Abraham] ate and drank and blessed God Most High who created heaven and earth and who made all the fat of the earth and gave it to the sons of man so that they might eat and drink and bless their Creator. ⁷'And now I thank you, my God, because you have let me see this day. Behold, I am one hundred and seventy-five years

---

[11] This prohibition would have been one of the rabbinical norms and an element in the rabbinical theology of the prayer. But there is not, of course, always a correspondence of practice to rule. On the subject see J. Heinemann, *Prayer in the Talmud. Forms and Patterns* (Studia judaica 9; Berlin–New York, 1977).

[12] L. Finkelstein, "The Birkat ha-Mazon," *JQR* N.S. 19 (1929) 211–62. [I have not had access to this publication, and have had to backtranslate it from the author's Italian version.—Tr.]

old, and fulfilled in days. And all of my days were peaceful for me. [8]The sword of the enemy did not triumph over me in anything which you gave to me or my sons all of the days of my life until this day. [9]O my God, may your mercy and peace be upon your servant and upon the seed of his sons so that they might become an elect people for you and an inheritance from all the nations of the earth from henceforth and for all the days of the generations of the earth forever.'"[13]

The *Birkat ha-Mazon* tells of the meaning the meal has in Judaism. The land was given to the Jewish people by Yahweh as a pledge of the covenant. In the rite for the contracting or renewal of the covenant, the eating of the produce of the country is therefore, in itself, an acceptance of the covenant. At the end of the meal, these themes are voiced again in the *Birkat ha-Mazon;* we may therefore conclude that in every meal the devout Jew celebrates and remembers the gift of the land that is a pledge of the covenant.[14]

---

[13] "The Book of Jubilees" (Charlesworth 2:97). On the Jewish literary genre of the *Berakah* ("Blessing") see J.-P. Audet, "Literary Forms and Contents of a Normal *Eucharistia* in the First Century," in K. Aland and F. L. Cross (eds.), *Studia Evangelica* (TU 18; Berlin, 1959) 643–62; idem, "Esquisse du genre littéraire de la 'Bénédiction' juive et de l'"Eucharistie' chrétienne," *RB* 65 (1958) 371–99; T. J. Talley, "De la 'berakah' à l'eucharistie. Une question à réexaminer," *MD*, no. 125 (1976) 11–39; idem, "The Literary Structure of Eucharistic Prayer," *Worship* 58 (1984) 404–20; idem, "Structures des anaphores anciennes et modernes," *MD*, no. 191 (1992) 15–43.

[14] The divine blessing that comes down from heaven is matched by an ascending response from the heart of the devout Jew. It is in this way that God saves his people: by placing on their lips a response in the form of a blessing.

Chapter 3

The Origin of the Christian Eucharist

1. THE LAST SUPPER

The Christian Eucharist has its origin in the Last Supper. There, Jesus took bread, blessed God, broke the bread, and gave it to his disciples, telling them to take it and eat of it, because it was his body. In the same way, after they had eaten, he took the cup, gave thanks, and gave it to his disciples, telling them all to take it and drink of it, because it was the cup of the covenant in his blood. At the end he said: "Do this in remembrance of me." With this action he set a model so that we might do the same, that is, do what he himself had done. To celebrate the Eucharist, then, is to obey Christ's command and do what he himself did.

The bread and the wine, which are the elements of this ritual meal, are indicated in the two prayers that accompany them: the blessing for the bread, the thanksgiving for the cup.

These prayers that Jesus uttered at the supper are the origin and model of the Church's eucharistic prayer, or anaphora. These two thanksgiving texts were the starting point of a very complex textual development that leads us to the anaphoras that we find today in the Missal of the Roman Church.

It must be said that our texts today are extremely faithful to the tradition that originated in the upper room. To use an expression that smacks of journalism, we may say that today's Eucharist is like a live broadcast of the Eucharist of Jesus in the upper room.[1]

---

[1] Only an expert, however, can see in today's rite a development of the rite which Jesus celebrated at the Last Supper and can show the presence in it of all the elements making up that rite. Believers attending Mass can see only the Mass, not the rite of the Last Supper. If they have a good education, they can realize that the Mass shows evidence of many cultural influences from various periods and

2. IMPORTANCE OF THE EUCHARISTIC PRAYER

At the Last Supper there were two factors that marked the rite celebrated by Jesus and made it different from any other comparable rite and any other meal, ordinary or profane or religious, at which bread and wine were consumed. I am referring to the explanatory words over the bread and the cup, and to the several prayers of blessing and thanksgiving which Jesus spoke in the upper room.

Christ's disciples received from the master the command: "Do this in remembrance of me," and loyally began to celebrate a meal like that which the master had celebrated. Beginning with the earliest testimonies this liturgy was called a *eucharistia,* a Greek word that means thanksgiving and designates both the prayer of thanksgiving recited in imitation of the prayer of Jesus, and the bread and wine that are the constitutive elements of this meal.[2]

Since the Mass is an act of obedience to the command of Jesus and an imitation[3] of his supper in the upper room, it follows that the Eucharistic Prayer is what determines the very nature of the Church's Eucharist.

Just as the Eucharistic Prayer is an imitation of the thanksgiving offered by Jesus in the upper room, so too the constitutive elements used in our Eucharist, namely, the bread and wine, will be like the bread and wine of Jesus in the upper room, or, to use the technical term, they will be a "likeness"[4] of the bread and wine of the upper room and, consequently, of the Body and Blood of Christ.

---

that in it are seen traces of decisions made by the Church and problems faced by it throughout its history; they cannot, however, see the ritual development of the Last Supper of Jesus. The fact remains, however, that, despite appearances, the rite of the Last Supper is in direct continuity with the Eucharist of the Church, so that in the Mass we see and experience again what Jesus did at the Last Supper, and not something different, not even an ancient and venerable rite of the Church.

[2] See *Didache* 9–10.

[3] Such terms as "imitation," "likeness," "figure," "image," "form," and "act of obedience" are to be understood not in their present-day sense but according to their acceptance by the Fathers. If we had to translate this understanding into today's language, we would have to use the term "sacrament," and it would be an excellent translation. On the meaning and use of this terminology, see my essay, "L'interpretazione del culto nella chiesa antica" (see chapter 1, note 20).

[4] Jesus said of the bread and wine which he gave to his disciples in the upper room that they were his Body and his Blood; we rightly say the same about the bread and wine on our altars. We say that they are the "Sacrament" of his Body and his Blood.

3. CONFORMITY TO THE LAST SUPPER

The command of Jesus at the Last Supper refers to everything he did at the ritual meal; he summed up all these elements in the demonstrative pronoun "this": "Do 'this' in remembrance of me."

We must note, however, that the Eucharist of the Church is quite different from the rite at the Last Supper; the Last Supper was also a meal in the full sense of the word, with the participants taking food as at any other meal. Yet from as early as the second century, there was no longer any connection with a supper, and the eucharistic rite was separated from any meal proper. Moreover, at the supper of Jesus there were two separate and distinct prayers of thanksgiving, one for the bread and one for the cup, whereas in the Mass there is only one, the Eucharistic Prayer or anaphora, which embraces both the bread and the cup, since the rite of the bread has been united with the rite of the cup.

In light of this difference, it is clear that the very early Church reinterpreted the "this." The rite at the Last Supper was reinterpreted by the apostolic Church so as to bring out which elements of the Last Supper were normative and which were not, or, in other words, which elements were essential if the ritual supper of the Church were to be a faithful and effective carrying out of the command "Do 'this' in remembrance of me." This reinterpretation of the Last Supper had already been completed when the New Testament was written. For, in fact, the Supper is not reported with all its ritual details, as in a chronicle, but in a liturgical perspective, that is, as "the model" which Jesus left for others to imitate.

The Last Supper is not simply a model for ritual, but has its own proper role in the life of Jesus, both as a summing up of his work and as an announcement "in action" of the passion and cross. At this point in my discussion, however, I must focus attention on the Last Supper as model for the celebration of the Church, because it is in this perspective that the New Testament shapes and passes on its report of the institution. The New Testament reports describe the actions of Jesus which the Church must repeat, and they are these: (1) he took bread, (2) gave thanks, (3) broke the bread, (4) gave it, (5) while saying; (6) he took the cup, (7) gave thanks, (8) gave it, (9) while saying.

If the Church's celebration, then, is to be an act of obedience to the command of Christ, it must include all these actions belonging to the rite which Jesus gave as a model. These, then, are the parts that have been determined to be essential and constitutive of the rite of the Church.

As a matter of fact, the Eucharist of the Church is "conformed" and "corresponds" to the rite carried out by Jesus in the upper room, and it is such because it consists of the series of actions listed. In the language of the Fathers, the rite performed by Jesus at the Last Supper was a *traditio mysteriorum* ("handing on of the mysteries") and therefore a *typos* ("model") of the celebration which was called a mystery, an antitype, and, using a word more familiar to us, a sacrament.

4. THE RITUAL OF THE LAST SUPPER

4.1. *The Two Traditions about the Last Supper*

The New Testament contains four reports of the Last Supper. These belong to two independent traditions: on the one side, the tradition of Mark[5] and Matthew,[6] and, on the other, that of Luke[7] and Paul.[8] To these may be added a third tradition attested by a sentence in the Gospel of John that reports only the words of Jesus over the bread.[9] From a literary point of view, the text in Paul is the oldest, having been set down probably in the spring of 54,[10] but the eucharistic

[5] Mark 14:22-24: "While they were eating, he took a loaf of bread, and after blessing it he broke it, gave it to them, and said, 'Take; this is my body.' Then he took a cup, and after giving thanks he gave it to them, and all of them drank from it. He said to them, 'This is my blood of the covenant, which is poured out for many.'"

[6] Matthew 26:26-28: "While they were eating, Jesus took a loaf of bread, and after blessing it he broke it, gave it to the disciples, and said: 'Take, eat; this is my body.' Then he took a cup, and after giving thanks he gave it to them, saying, 'Drink from it, all of you; for this is my blood of the covenant, which is poured out for many for the forgiveness of sins.'"

[7] Luke 22:17-20: "Then he took a cup, and after giving thanks he said, 'Take this and divide it among yourselves; for I tell you that from now on I shall not drink of the fruit of the vine until the kingdom of God comes.' Then he took a loaf of bread, and when he had given thanks he broke it and gave it to them, saying, 'This is my body, which is given for you. Do this in remembrance of me.' And he did the same with the cup after supper, saying, 'This cup that is poured out for you is the new covenant in my blood.'"

[8] 1 Corinthians 11:23-25: "For I received from the Lord what I also handed on to you, that the Lord Jesus on the night when he was betrayed took a loaf of bread, and when he had given thanks, he broke it and said, 'This is my body that is for you. Do this in remembrance of me.' In the same way he took the cup also, after supper, saying, 'This cup is the new covenant in my blood. Do this, as often as you drink it, in remembrance of me.'"

[9] John 6:51c: "The bread that I will give for the life of the world is my flesh."

[10] J. Jeremias, *The Eucharistic Words of Jesus*, trans. N. Perrin (London, 1966) 188.

tradition which Paul sets down must have been formed earlier, since he speaks of "what I also handed on to you," an event that occurred probably in the fall of 49, at the beginning of his missionary activity in Corinth. Paul also says that he passed on what he himself had received, but when did he receive it? Perhaps at the time of his conversion. The points of similarity between the Pauline tradition and those of Luke and John suggest that Paul was repeating the Hellenistic tradition of the Last Supper story that was followed in the community of Antioch. This relationship is confirmed by the similarity between the structure of the Last Supper story in Luke 22:17-20 and the structure of the Eucharist that is attested in 1 Corinthians 10:16-17 and *Didache* 9–10.

The Lukan redaction is older than that of Paul; according to Jeremias, it goes back to the forties.

It is supposed that Luke's redaction was preceded by that of Mark, a text full of semitisms and linguistically closer to an original Aramaic/Hebrew redaction of the Last Supper story, while Matthew's version is only a variant that hellenizes Mark.[11] From the linguistic point of view, Mark is a more faithful reflection of the Semitic tradition; its date of composition must therefore have been earlier than that of Luke and is to be located in the first decade after the death of Jesus.[12]

The problem of the chronology of the Last Supper accounts has thus been answered by arguments based on the literary form of the texts and their evolution. However, when it comes to our particular purpose here, which is to achieve a better knowledge of what occurred at the Last Supper, we must deny that because Mark represents the earliest redaction, it is therefore to be given a privileged place. It would indeed have to be given a privileged place if there had existed a single primitive account (an *Urtext*) of the Last Supper and if this single text had been the source of the other narratives that have reached us. In that case, and only in that case, would the text in the form that is earliest from a literary point of view be able to give better guarantees than other texts.

As we know, however, the story of the Last Supper was told by the various traditions in accordance with the kerygma of the various Churches and with their liturgical forms. For the form of the narrative

[11] Ibid., 188–89.
[12] Ibid., 189.

served not only the needs of the kerygma but also its liturgical use; that is, it told the story of the Last Supper in such a way as to account for the development of the Christian liturgy. Luke's is a heavily grecized text, but that does not mean that it is not very ancient. Arguments of a linguistic and literary kind must be supplemented by liturgical arguments, with special attention being paid to the structure of the rites that made up the Last Supper.[13]

If, then, we are to learn which narrative best corresponds to the events of the Last Supper, we must follow a route other than that of purely linguistic considerations; we must consider, above all, the ritual data; that is, we must study the customary Jewish ritual meal and decide which of the New Testament data are most compatible with that usage. It is on the basis of such arguments as these that Luke's account becomes quite uniquely important in sketching the history of the Eucharist in its first moments. Following Heinz Schürmann,[14] I maintain that the text in Luke should be regarded as the earliest redaction of the Last Supper story.

4.2. A Passover Meal?

According to the Synoptic Gospels the Last Supper was a Passover meal, while according to the Gospel of John it was not. In fact, according to John the death of Jesus took place on the eve of Passover, at the very moment when the lambs were being slaughtered in the temple; a meal without a Passover lamb and celebrated before Passover could not have been a Passover meal. Since the Synoptic Gospels used to be regarded as more reliable on historical facts, while John's Gospel was described as more concerned with symbols, scholars gave preference to the Synoptic chronology of the passion over the Johannine. It was the Synoptics that merited credence, and therefore the Last Supper was a Passover meal. But as the symbolism of John's Gospel came to be better understood, scholars realized that John, too, was interested in historical details and, consequently, that his chronology of the passion likewise deserved attention.[15]

---

[13] Mazza, L'anafora.

[14] H. Schürmann, Der Einsetzungsbericht Lk 22, 19-20 (Münster, 1955).

[15] On this basis Annie Jaubert developed a new interpretive hypothesis founded on the fact of two calendars in use in Judaism. Given the two calendars, there is no contradiction between the two chronologies; being based on different calendars, both chronologies could be true. This was an ingenious hypothesis, but it has never been proved, since we cannot know whether the two different calendars

Today's critics have shifted their focus, giving priority to the Johannine chronology, according to which the Last Supper was not a Passover meal.[16] In order to deal correctly with the question of the Passover character of the Last Supper we must distinguish between the theological significance of the Last Supper and its ritual and historical status. From the historical and ritual points of view, the meal taken in the upper room was not a Passover meal; the Synoptic writers, however, realized that the Last Supper was the typological fulfillment of the Jewish Passover and they therefore gave it a detailed Passover character, even to the point of using a chronology that had the Last Supper being celebrated at the very moment of the Jewish Passover. There is therefore a theological purpose at work in this chronology. It is the same theological intention that is at work in the Gospel of John, who has the death of Jesus take place at the same time as the slaying of the Passover lamb.

John gives a Passover interpretation of the death of Jesus, while the Synoptics make the supper a Passover meal. Paul, too, took part in this process of "Passoverization" by interpreting the very person of Jesus in Passover terms: "Clean out the old yeast that you may be a new batch, as you really are unleavened. For our paschal lamb, Christ, has been sacrificed. Therefore, let us celebrate the festival, not with the old yeast, the yeast of malice and evil, but with the unleavened bread of sincerity and truth" (1 Cor 5:7-8).[17] The Passover character was thus a theological given that was applied to the events of the passion and that in time permeated the theology and spirituality of the Church.[18]

This theological datum is a precious golden thread that runs down through history from the New Testament to our day, but it remains a theological interpretation. The historical fact is that the Last Supper

---

were equally widespread so as to have been simultaneously in use in Jerusalem in the time of Jesus.

[16] The question has once again been discussed by G. Visonà; see his "Pasqua quartodecimana e cronologia evangelica della passione," *EL* 102 (1988) 259–315.

[17] On this entire subject see R. Cantalamessa, *L'omelia "In S. Pascha" dello Pseudo-Ippolyto di Roma. Ricerche sulla teologia dell'Asia minore nella seconda metà del II secolo* (Pubblicazioni dell'Università cattolica del S. Cuore. Contributi. Serie terza. Scienze filologiche e letteratura 16; Milan, 1967); idem, *La pasqua nella chiesa antica* (Traditio christiana 3; Turin, 1978).

[18] The high point of this development was reached at the Second Vatican Council which related the liturgy in its entirety to Easter. This is true especially of the Eucharist which is regarded as being simply the "paschal mystery" (*Sacrosanctum concilium,* nos. 5, 61, etc.).

was not a Passover celebration and, consequently, that its liturgy was not that of the Jewish Passover.

4.3. The Course of the Last Supper

The eucharistic rite is described in Mark and Matthew, but these writers do not provide the information needed for an appraisal of the Last Supper in its entirety. Mark says only that while Jesus and the disciples were eating, he took bread and, after pronouncing the blessing, broke it and gave it to them, saying: "'Take, this is my Body.' Then he took a cup, and after giving thanks he gave it to them, and all of them drank from it. He said to them, 'This is my Blood of the covenant, which is poured out for many'" (Mark 14:22-24). Matthew, who depends on Mark, does not add anything.

Luke, on the other hand, is much more detailed and describes the rite in a way that brings out the ritual structure of the Last Supper. The Last Supper has three parts: the introductory rite, the supper in the proper sense of the word, and the concluding rite. The introduction is made up of two elements: the rite of the cup and the rite of the bread, each accompanied by explanatory words.[19] The ritual of the cup comes first and is accompanied by a short eschatological discourse:

"When the hour came, he took his place at the table, and the apostles with him. He said to them, 'I have eagerly desired to eat this Passover with you before I suffer; for I tell you, I will not eat it until it is fulfilled in the kingdom of God.' Then he took a cup, and after giving thanks he said: 'Take this and divide it among yourselves; for I tell you that from now on I will not drink of the fruit of the wine until the kingdom of God comes'" (Luke 22:14-18).

This is followed by the ritual of the bread, which is accompanied both by explanatory words and by the command to repeat the rite in memory of Christ: "Then he took a loaf of bread, and when he had given thanks, he broke it and gave it to them, saying: 'This is my Body, which is given for you. Do this in remembrance of me'" (22:19).

[19] In the German world the term *Deutewort* (word of explanation) became the common designation of the words accompanying the cup and the bread, since the purpose of these words is to explain the nature and function of the bread and wine of the Last Supper. From a literary point of view, the words do indeed have an explanatory function and nothing more. From the viewpoint of western theology they have a further role, which is to "consecrate."

The eschatological words over the cup establish the significance both of the Passover meal and of the rite of the cup, which, by synecdoche, stands for the entire rite (the cup and the bread) that begins the supper. The "fruit of the vine" will not be drunk again nor will the Passover be eaten again until the kingdom of God comes in its fullness. The present time with its imminent darkness is thus already set in the light of the future, so that the image of the kingdom of God is made part of the Last Supper.[20] In the words of Jesus, this meal, which is, theologically, a Passover meal, takes on the value of a "type" and becomes a model for that future meal, that is, the eschatological banquet in the coming kingdom. By this I mean that there will be no further stages between the Last Supper and the coming of the reign of God. The words over the bread, which is broken as it is at the beginning of any meal, establish a clear connection of identity between the bread and the Body of Christ: The bread which Jesus gives his disciples to eat is his Body.

After the introductory rite comes the supper in the ordinary, proper sense of the word. At its end, in keeping with the Jewish custom that I have already explained, the prayer of thanksgiving, the *Birkat ha-Mazon*, is said by Christ while holding the cup that ends the rite. Luke does not explicitly say that the final cup was accompanied by a prayer of thanksgiving; the fact is inferred from the adverb *hôsautôs* ("in the same way") which verse 20 puts in an appositive position in relation to the cup: "the cup *in the same way.*" The point of the adverb is that the actions previously done are done again for the cup. The cup is accompanied by explanatory words that say: "This cup that is poured out for you is the new covenant in my blood" (Luke 22:20). Here the account of the Last Supper ends without a command of repetition, although this was indeed given earlier, at the end of the words over the bread.

This fact, together with the brusque way in which verse 20 is introduced ("in the same way"), without any reference to the prayer of thanksgiving, suggests that verse 20 is an addition which Luke introduced later on as being an important element in one of his sources. In this interpretation, the earliest stage of the narrative in the Antiochene tradition (Luke, Paul) would have contained only verses 17-19.[21]

---

[20] K. H. Rengstorf, *Il vangelo secondo Luca* (Nuovo Testamento 3; Brescia, 1980) 410.

[21] See the discussion in Jeremias, *The Eucharistic Words of Jesus*, 139–59.

We may therefore conclude that according to Luke, the liturgy celebrated by Jesus at the Last Supper had the following structure: the rite of the cup, the rite of the bread, the supper, the final rite of the cup. Each of the three rites was accompanied by its prayer of thanksgiving.

Chapter 4

From the Jewish Liturgy to the Christian Eucharist

1. THE RITE OF THE JEWISH FESTIVE MEAL

After seeing the structure of the Last Supper, we must ask whether there existed a Jewish rite with a structure analogous to that which Luke describes. There was: the Jewish festive meal. This had three stages: it began with the rite of the *Qiddush* ("sanctification"), which introduced the celebration of the feast; when this rite was finished, the meal proper began; at the end of the meal came the concluding rite: the rite of the cup, which was accompanied by the prayer of thanksgiving, the *Birkat ha-Mazon*.

The *Qiddush* in turn had three parts. It opened with the rite of the cup, which began with the story in Genesis 1:31b–2:1-3. After this reading there was a short blessing: "Blessed are you, Lord, our God, king of the universe, who creates[1] the fruit[2] of the vine."[3] To this was added a second blessing for the sanctification of the Sabbath or other feast day in the liturgical calendar. The rite of the cup was followed by the rite of the bread. The father of the family took the bread and placed it on the table after reciting the following blessing: "Blessed are you, Lord, our God, king of the universe, who produces bread from the earth."[4] After the blessing, the father broke the bread and distributed it for the meal, which followed directly.

---

[1] The shift from the second to the third person singular is due to the history of these blessings, which originally contained only what is now the second part and not the first (i.e., "Blessed are you, Lord").

[2] "Fruit of the vine" is the expression Luke uses in 22:17 in referring to the first cup at the Last Supper.

[3] Text in Hänggi-Pahl, 6.

[4] Ibid., 7. For a commentary see L. A. Hoffman, "Rabbinic *Berakhah* and Jewish Spirituality," *Asking and Thanking,* ed. C. Duquoc and C. Florestan (Concilium, 1990, no. 3; London and Philadelphia, 1990) 18–30.

After the meal, on the occasion of which *Zemirot* or ritual hymns were sung, the *Birkat ha-Mazon* was recited, the thanksgiving that was to be said at the end of every meal and that on feast days was one with the rite of the cup. Rabbis had a serious obligation to recite this prayer, an obligation based on the divine command in Deuteronomy 8:10.

2. THE RITE IN *DIDACHE* 9–10

From this description of the rites accompanying a Jewish festive meal and consisting of the *Qiddush* at its beginning[5] and the *Birkat ha-Mazon* at its end, we can see that the sequence of ritual elements is the same as that found in the ritual supper described by Luke. But Luke is not the only instance. From the very early Church we have a document, the *Didache*,[6] which describes the eucharistic celebration and is almost certainly of Antiochene origin. The description is of a celebration that has the same structure as the one I have just been describing and parallels both Luke and the Jewish festive meal. This Eucharist begins with the rite of the cup, accompanied by a short blessing;[7] it is followed by the rite of the bread, which is likewise accompanied by a blessing[8] and to which is added an expansion (known technically as an "embolism") in the form of a prayer for unity.[9] After this rite there is the meal, which is followed by a Christian *Birkat ha-Mazon*.[10] This further rite begins with the rubric: "After eating your fill, give thanks in this fashion";[11] the rubric is based on Deuteronomy 8:10 and indicates the point at which the prayer of thanksgiving is to be said: "after having supped." We should note that the rubric in *Didache* 10.1, says the same thing as Luke: "In the same way, after having supped, he took the cup" (Luke 22:20).

---

[5] I speak of the *"Qiddush"* for the sake of brevity and in order to given a specific name to this rite that begins the meal, even though the identification is not completely accurate, since only at a later time did the *Qiddush* as we know it acquire a fixed form. In the New Testament period, however, there were already in use rites of prayer before meals, which were the origin of the rite of the *Qiddush*. Attestations of these Jewish rites are found not only in the New Testament but also in the Essene communities and in Philo when he speaks of the Therapeutae.

[6] W. Rördorf and A. Tuilier (eds.), *La doctrine des douze apôtres (Didachè)* (SC 248; Paris, 1978).

[7] *Didache* 9.2.

[8] Ibid., 9.3.

[9] Ibid., 9.4.

[10] Ibid., 10.

[11] Ibid., 10.1.

3. THE RITE IN 1 CORINTHIANS 10:16-17

The eucharistic rite of the Church of Corinth is similar to those we have seen thus far. In his first letter to the Corinthians Paul gives us two descriptions of the Eucharist. In the first (10:16-17) we have the eucharistic rite of the Church, while in the second (11:23-25) we have the rite of the Supper of Jesus in the upper room or, in other words, the account of the institution of the Eucharist. The differences between the two passages show how rapid, and of what kind, was the development of the liturgical tradition from the rite of the Last Supper to the rite in Paul's Church. The latter has a eucharistic rite composed of two parts: (a) the rite of the cup, with its blessing; and (b) the rite of the bread broken, to which is linked the theme of unity.

In the *Didache,* too, there is a close connection between the rite of the bread and the theme of unity. In both Paul and the *Didache* the connection takes the literary form of an embolism based on a key word.[12] The Eucharist of Corinth corresponds to that in *Didache* 9: rite of the cup, rite of the bread, embolism for unity.[13] In 1 Corinthians 10:16-17, however, there is a difference from both Luke and the *Didache:* The meal has been eliminated, and if there is no meal, there can be no thanksgiving after the meal and therefore no reference to the *Birkat ha-Mazon* (the thanksgiving after a meal). But a reference is nonetheless made to this prayer when the eucharistic cup is called "the cup of blessing," a phrase that suits the cup over which the *Birkat ha-Mazon* was said at the end of a meal.[14]

4. THE DEVELOPMENT OF THE STRUCTURE OF THE EUCHARIST

The evolution just described brings to term the tendency already discernible in Luke's account: Everything concerning the Eucharist and placed in the rite at the end of the Supper had to be shifted to the rite at the beginning of the meal. This tendency is found in all the texts thus far examined and can be better perceived from the following synoptic outline:

---

[12] In ibid., 9.4, the key word is "this [= bread that is broken]," whereas in 1 Corinthians 10:17 it is "bread."

[13] Observe that 1 Corinthians 10:1-4 shows a knowledge of *Didache* 10.3. See my *L'anafora,* chapter 3.

[14] In Paul this cup is the one that precedes the rite of the bread and therefore does not belong to the rite at the end of the meal.

JEWISH RITE	LUKE	*DIDACHE*	1 COR 12:16-17
Before supper	*Before supper*	*Before supper*	*Before supper*
Rite of cup with blessing	Rite of cup with thanksgiving	Rite of cup with thanksgiving	Rite of cup with blessing
Rite of bread with blessing	Rite of bread with thanksgiving	Rite of bread with thanksgiving Embolism	Rite of bread (with blessing) Embolism
After supper	*After supper*	*After supper*	*After supper*
Rite of cup with thanksgiving	Rite of cup with thanksgiving	— Thanksgiving	— — —

The development of the eucharistic liturgy was guided by the clear intention of combining the rite of the cup, which is a communion[15] in the Blood of Christ, with the rite of the bread, which is a communion in the Body of Christ. Both rites were to be placed before the meal. This development becomes even clearer if we place the New Testament accounts of the Last Supper side by side:

LUKE (long text)	1 COR 11:23-25	MATTHEW– MARK	LUKE (short text)
Before supper	*Before supper*	*Before supper*	*Before supper*
Rite of cup with thanksgiving			
Rite of bread with thanksgiving	Rite of bread with thanksgiving	Rite of bread with blessing	Rite of bread with thanksgiving
		Rite of cup with thanksgiving	Rite of cup (with thanksgiving)
After supper	*After supper*		
Rite of cup (with thanksgiving)	Rite of cup with thanksgiving		

[15] Today, people would say "sacrament," but I prefer "communion" because it is the word used by Paul in 1 Corinthians 10:16 as a technical term for sacramentality.

Due to the elimination of the meal, the rite of the cup is placed immediately after the rite of the bread. As a result of this juxtaposition, the sequence that would prevail and become normal was bread–cup and no longer cup–bread.[16] This juxtaposition of the two rites, which were no longer separated by the meal, would become a union, so that the two prayers of thanksgiving (one over the bread and one over the cup) were merged into a single text that would hold for both the bread and the wine, these being henceforth regarded *per modum unius*, or as a single whole.

It was in this way that the Eucharistic Prayer came into existence as a single text down to the present time.

5. CONCLUSION

In the New Testament tradition of the Last Supper, the points calling for major attention are two: (a) the sequence of rites that make up the Last Supper; and (b) the use of the terms "bless" *(eulogein)* and "give thanks" *(eucharistein)*.

(a) In the Lukan and Pauline tradition, to which the *Didache* also belongs, the Last Supper is composed of three elements that are the direct model of the Church's eucharistic celebration: (1) the rite of the cup, which opens the meal and is accompanied by its blessing; (2) the rite of the bread that is broken, and which is accompanied by its usual blessing; in the *Didache* and Paul there is also an embolism in the form of a prayer for the assembly and for the unity of the Church; (3) after the Supper, there is the customary recitation of the *Birkat ha-Mazon*, which normally accompanies the last cup.

(b) In Mark and Matthew, in accordance with Jewish custom, the prayer over the bread is a "blessing" *(eulogia)* and the prayer over the cup is a "thanksgiving" *(eucharistia)*, while in Luke, the *Didache*, and Paul (1 Cor 11:23-26), the prayer over the bread, like that over the cup, is a "thanksgiving" *(eucharistia)*. This difference between the two traditions is explained by the tendency, proper to the Antiochene tradition, to transfer all the elements found at the end of the Supper and incorporate them into the rite that begins it. For this reason Luke describes as a "thanksgiving," and not a "blessing," both the prayer

---

[16] The sequence cup-bread in texts stemming from the *Didache* was very carefully corrected and changed, as we see in the case of what is known as the "Mystical Eucharist" of the *Constitutiones apostolicae* 7.25–26 (see my *L'anafora*, chapters 2 and 6).

accompanying the first cup (22:17) at the beginning of the meal and the prayer accompanying the bread (which also comes before the meal proper). On the other hand, when he comes to the cup that concludes the Supper and ought to be accompanied by its own "thanksgiving," he does not go into detail but is content with a very generic description, "in the same way" (hôsautôs).

In Paul, too, there is a shifting of the material in the direction of the rite that begins the Supper; in fact, both the Supper and, consequently, the rite after the Supper have completely disappeared. The cup, which the explanatory words identify as the Blood of Christ, has been shifted from after the Supper to its beginning and is in the position occupied by the first cup[17] that begins the Supper, becoming identical with this and replacing it. The Birkat ha-Mazon has undergone an analogous displacement, moving from after the Supper to its beginning and thereby replacing the short blessing over the cup that would have occurred at this point in the rite. As a result, the cup that begins the rite is described as "a communion in the blood of Christ" and is called "the cup of blessing" (1 Cor 10:16)—two descriptions that, as such, were proper to the cup that ended the meal, along with the Birkat ha-Mazon.

The same tendency is already evident in Didache 10. The cup that should have accompanied this Christian Birkat ha-Mazon has already disappeared and been identified with the cup that begins the meal rite in Didache 9. Here another change can be seen: the third strophe of Didache 10, a prayer of petition for the assembly of the Church, is duplicated and, in a slightly shorter form, becomes part of Didache 9. As a result, Didache 9 acquires a tripartite structure: (1) thanksgiving over the cup; (2) thanksgiving over the bread; (3) prayer for the assembly and for unity. This tripartite structure will remain a distinctive trait of the earliest anaphoras.

[17] I am going back to Luke's description of the Supper, since it is closer to the Jewish model that I explained above in speaking of the Qiddush.

Chapter 5

Primitive Anaphoras:
From the *Didache* to the Mystical Eucharist

The Last Supper as reported by Luke is very closely connected with the Jewish rite for a festive meal. Starting with this basic relationship, I have tried to show the origin of the other descriptions of the Last Supper, which show a different structure from that of Luke. The same explanation applies to some other eucharistic celebrations such as the Eucharist of the Antiochene tradition that is attested in *Didache* 9–10, from which was derived the Eucharist of the Pauline community as described in 1 Corinthians 10:16-17.

Our task now is to see what subsequent developments took place, the starting point of which was the well documented Antiochene nucleus of which I spoke in the preceding chapter. The first development is represented by the eucharistic liturgy[1] in Book VII of the *Apostolic Constitutions,* a work composed in Antioch in 380, using previous materials. This celebration depends directly on *Didache* 9–10, by way of an intermediate redaction that has not come down to us. When we set the two texts side by side, we immediately become aware of the great fidelity with which the Mystical Eucharist follows *Didache* 9–10: *Apostolic Constitutions* 7.25, depends on *Didache* 9, while 7.26, depends on *Didache* 10. The paralleling of the texts also shows up in the changes that were introduced having to do with both the structure and the text. In the celebration of the Eucharist in the *Didache,* the main element consists in the rite of chapter 10, that is, in the Christianized

---

[1] For convenience, this liturgy is called "Mystical Eucharist" ("sacramental thanksgiving") in accordance with the title given it in the manuscript tradition. The title is, in fact, a later addition and does not belong to the original redaction of the text.

Birkat ha-Mazon that is recited after the meal. The first change is the elimination of the meal that intervened between the rite in *Didache* 9 and that of *Didache* 10. As a result, the text of *Apostolic Constitutions* 7.26, ceases to be a Christianized *Birkat ha-Mazon*[2] and becomes the thanksgiving after Communion.[3]

This change marks the end of the journey by which the rites at the end of the Supper were transferred to a different position, at the beginning of the meal, and were joined to the rites which opened the meal and with which they were henceforth identified.[4] As a matter of fact, the principal text is not that of 7.26, but that of 7.25, which derives from *Didache* 9, that is, from the rite preceding the ritual meal.

In the Mystical Eucharist this text has already become a eucharistic prayer, more or less as we understand the term today, although it has such markedly archaic traits and shows such obvious traces of the liturgy from which it derives and which still link it quite closely to Judaism, that I hesitate to describe the text as an anaphora; for this reason I prefer to call it a "paleoanaphora" or "primitive anaphora."[5] Because of these changes that move the rites of the end of the meal into those of its beginning, the most important prayer is no longer the thanksgiving at the end of the meal (the *Birkat ha-Mazon*), but the

[2] The relationship of the text to the *Birkat ha-Mazon* is unrecognizable, although its origin can be traced to *Didache* 10, which derives directly from that Jewish prayer.

[3] This fact makes understandable the importance of the thanksgiving after Communion, which has its remote origin in the Last Supper and is therefore not to be understood as a devotional text, comparable to the thanksgiving after Communion as found in medieval devotionalism.

[4] Thus ends the shift from the Jewish rites after the meal to those for the beginning of the meal. This was truly a radical change of position, since in the beginning the rites for the end of the meal were more important than those at the meal's start. At the end of the development, however, the rites for the beginning of the meal clearly had the upper hand. The prayer that came into being as heir of the *Birkat ha-Mazon* henceforth lost its importance, since it was now simply a thanksgiving after Communion. The result was the severing of the link between the *Birkat ha-Mazon* and the developing Christian Eucharist.

[5] I give this name to all those texts that occupy an intermediate position between the Jewish liturgy and the later anaphoras, which were now structured in a clearly theological way, and which clearly distinguished the great liturgical families and have come down to our time almost unchanged. The paleoanaphoral texts go back to the end of the second century and the beginning of the third, while the major anaphoras had their golden age from the middle of the fourth century on.

prayer that precedes it and has its origin in practices that gradually gave rise to the Jewish rite of the *Qiddush*.[6]

The shift I have been describing has further complicated the problem of the structure of these prayers of thanksgiving. In fact, the problem is created by the coming together and superposition of two very similar series of texts, inasmuch as both series have a tripartite structure. The first series depends on the *Birkat ha-Mazon*, and its three strophes are the classical strophes of the Christian *Birkat ha-Mazon*; the second series depends on rites which preceded the meal and which, once Christianized (as in *Didache* 9), are likewise made up of two strophes of thanksgiving and one of petition.

The likeness should not deceive us, since the two series of texts differ from each other both in their origin and in their function. On the one hand, there are the three strophes of the *Birkat ha-Mazon*[7] and, on the other, the three of the rite that began the meal.[8] However, when the two tripartite structures are superimposed, it is no longer possible to decide whether a paleoanaphora or anaphora having a tripartite structure originated in the rites following the meal or in the rites preceding it.

---

[6] This evolution marks the development not only of the Christian Eucharist but also of the Jewish texts themselves, which later on gave an ever-increasing importance to the rite of the *Qiddush*.

[7] (1) Opening thanksgiving for the works God has done and for the gift of food; (2) thanksgiving for the present moment; (3) petition. For this structure see the *Birkat ha-Mazon* in the *Book of Jubilees* 22:6-9 (Charlesworth 2:97).

[8] (1) Thanksgiving over the cup; (2) thanksgiving over the bread; (3) petition.

Chapter 6

Primitive Anaphoras:
Developments of the Eucharistic Liturgy

The texts I have just examined represent a kind of initial nucleus out of which the later anaphoras developed. All of the latter display some kind of relationship—some texts more, others less—with the texts I have been considering; the relationships pertain both to the structure and to the thematic contents. Let us now look at the main families of anaphoras.

1. THE ALEXANDRIAN LITURGY

From the Church of Alexandria comes a very interesting paleo-anaphora that attests to the archaic character of the Egyptian Eucharist; it is the paleoanaphora in Strasbourg Papyrus Gr. 254. This text is important not only because of the archaic character of its structure and because it is the earliest testimony to the Eucharist of this Church, but above all because it enables us to understand the development of the three paleoanaphoral strophes that gave rise to later texts with their more complex theological structure.

1.1. The First Strophe of the Alexandrian Paleoanaphora

The first strophe gives thanks for creation, singling out the light[1] and leaving aside the theme of redemption. At the close of the strophe,

---

[1] The theme is based on two passages of the Bible: "I am the Lord, and there is no other. I form light and create darkness, I make weal and create woe; I the Lord do all these things" (Isa 45:6-7); "O Lord, how manifold are your works! In wisdom you have made them all; the earth is full of your creatures. Yonder is the sea, great and wide, creeping things innumerable are there, living things both small and great" (Ps 104:24-25).

the theme of light is developed along messianic lines, with thanks-giving for Christ, who is the true light of God.

In the case of this text, too, we must go looking for a connection with the Jewish liturgy, especially because the text falls outside the line of development of the Jewish meal liturgy, as we have seen the latter in connection with the *Didache* and the Mystical Eucharist.

1.1.1. Connection with the Yotser

The contact between the eucharistic liturgy and Jewish morning prayers is easily demonstrated; all we need do is compare the first of the three strophes of the Alexandria paleoanaphora[2] with the *Yotser*, the first of the three blessings of the *Shema'*.

In their morning prayers devout Jews recite the *Shema'*, which is preceded by two blessings[3] and followed by a third.[4] This was the basic pattern, but it could be adapted in various ways.

(a) One of these blessings, the *Yotser*, celebrates the creative work of God, which is described more closely as a creation of light, this being a typical theme of morning prayer. In this prayer, the blessing of God for the work of creation is based on a citation from Psalm 103:24;[5] then the prayer turns to a contemplation of the light, with support in a citation from Isaiah 45:7. In the Jewish tradition this theme of light was interpreted along messianic lines, a development attested in the Academies both of Sura and of Pumbedita. The interpretation was thus widespread until Rav Saadja Gaon (A.D. 918–942) censured the messianic interpretation of the light in the *Yotser*, claiming that the light in question is simply the natural light of creation when the sun rises in the morning.[6] This is a specifically sapiential theme.

---

[2] The text is that of Strasbourg Papyrus Gr. 254, which later on would become the first part of the Anaphora of St. Mark. The fragmentary text is in Hänggi-Pahl, 116–19.

[3] The first is the *Yotser*, which celebrates God who creates the light and the entire universe (Isa 45:7) with wisdom (Ps 103:24). The second is the *Ahabhah Rabbah*, which celebrates the mercy and fidelity of God. Texts in Hänggi-Pahl, 36–38.

[4] The *Birkat gh'ullah*, which celebrates redemption by God (text ibid., 38–39).

[5] Psalm 103:24: "O Lord, how manifold are your works! In wisdom you have made them all; the earth is full of your creatures."

[6] L. A. Hoffman, *The Canonization of the Synagogue Service* (Studies in Judaism and Christianity in Antiquity 4; Notre Dame–London, 1979) 25. On the whole question see my *L'anafora*, 213ff.

(b) The first strophe of the Alexandrian paleoanaphora[7] has for its subject the work of creation,[8] which was accomplished through Christ; on the basis of the passage in Psalm 103:24, Christ is identified with the divine Wisdom that presided over the work of creation. Furthermore, at the end of the strophe Jesus is given the titles "true light" and "Savior."[9]

(c) In conclusion, when we compare the Alexandrian paleoanaphora with the *Yotser*, we may say that there is a correspondence between the two texts, even though they differ in literary formulation and in breadth. The strophe and the *Yotser* are in fact identical in content, namely, (a) in the themes of thanksgiving (for creation and light); (b) in the two controlling biblical citations; (c) in the messianic interpretation of the theme of light; and (d) in the sapiential perspective.

This comparison of the two texts enables us to conclude, then, that the blessing known as the *Yotser* was one of the Jewish liturgies that influenced the Christian Eucharist. Once the fact is established, we need to ask how this influence was possible, since the Christian Eucharist was connected with the celebration of the Jewish ritual meal and not with Jewish morning prayer. The answer is not to be found in the history of the ritual meal.

1.1.2. *The Therapeutae*

We may formulate a hypothesis based on the special culture of worship and sacrifice to be seen in a Jewish community in Alexandria: the monastic community of the Therapeutae.[10] In recounting the origin of

[7] Here is the text of the first strophe of the thanksgiving: "To praise, night and day . . . you who made the heaven and all that is in it; you who made man according to your image and likeness, and in your wisdom created all things in your true light, your Son, the Lord, our Savior Jesus Christ" (Hänggi-Pahl, 116–17).

[8] The text is based on Nehemiah 9:6: "You are the Lord, you alone; you have made heaven, the heaven of heavens, with all their host, the earth and all that is on it, the seas and all that is in them. To all of them you give life, and the host of heaven worships you." Later developments of this anaphora will continue to draw on this prayer from the book of Nehemiah.

[9] In this strophe the theme of redemption is present only in the form of these two attributes, inasmuch as the thanksgiving emphasizes only the work of creation.

[10] J. Riaud, "Les Thérapeutes d'Alexandrie dans la tradition et dans la recherche critique jusqu'aux découvertes de Qumrân," in W. Hasse (ed.), *Aufstieg und Niedergang der römischen Welt. Teil II: Principat*, Band 20/2: *Religion* (Hellenistisches Judentum in römischer Zeit, ausgenommen Philon und Josephus) (Berlin–New York, 1987) 1189–1295; idem, "Thérapeutes," *DSp* 15 (1990) cols. 562–70; V. Nikiprowetzky, "Les Suppliants chez Philon d'Alexandrie," *REJ* 122 (1963) 241–78.

Alexandrian Christianity, Eusebius of Caesarea refers to Philo, who describes the community of the Therapeutae, Jewish monks who lived near Alexandria on the shores of Lake Mareotis. Eusebius is not satisfied simply with claiming that the Therapeutae were Christians,[11] but attempts to prove it by extensive citations from the work *De vita contemplativa*, in which Philo describes this community.

Let us look briefly at two rites of this community: the ritual meal and morning prayer. The meals of the Therapeutae[12] ended without the recitation of the *Birkat ha-Mazon*, the Jewish prayer after meals, because the meal ended with the hymn that began a vigil. All stood in the middle of the room and sang, first in two choirs and then in a single choir, in imitation of the song of Moses and Miriam after the crossing of the Red Sea.[13] The vigil lasted throughout the night and ended at dawn the next day, at which time the monks recited morning prayers. Here is how this morning liturgy is described in the *De vita contemplativa*: "They stand with their faces and whole body turned to the east, and when they behold the rising sun, with hands stretched heavenward they pray for a joyous day, truth, and acuity of thought."[14]

The Therapeutae had a very rich and well-organized system of worship, but one that was not, strictly speaking, attuned to the Jewish orthodoxy of the Jerusalem Temple. What, then, was this liturgical practice that, in all its characteristics, was an alternative to the worship practiced in Jerusalem? What was the significance of its

[11] Eusebius speaks of the churches of Alexandria (in the plural), implying thereby that Alexandrian Christianity arose simultaneously at several different points, like the spots on a leopard. He tries to show that the Therapeutae were already Christians, even though they practiced a complete observance of Jewish traditions—something that could be explained by the Jewish origin of the community.

[12] The meal began with a commentary on a passage of the Bible, which was interpreted according to the allegorical method; those present listened with interest and involvement. After the homily, the speaker "rises and sings a hymn composed in honor of the Deity, either a new one of his own composition, or an old one by poets of an earlier age." After him, the others also sing in their proper order; finally, the meal begins (*De vita contemplativa*, 75–81; ET: *Philo of Alexandria: The Contemplative Life, the Giants, and Selections*, trans. David Winston [The Classics of Western Spirituality; New York, 1981] 54–56; citation from 55). The prayer before the meal asks that God may find the meal pleasing to him and that it be according to his will. See also Philo, *De plantatione*, 161–62.

[13] Note the important place given to the typology of the Exodus: The liturgy celebrated by Moses serves as a type of the liturgy of the Therapeutae.

[14] *De vita contemplativa*, 89 (ET: 57).

sacred meal, and what was the nature of its morning prayers? What was the nature of all these observances to which the community of the Therapeutae was so strongly committed?

According to Philo's description, the Therapeutae employed the typological method in interpreting the Scriptures and the entire work of God. The method was based, on the one hand, on an allegorical reading of the texts and, on the other, on the Platonic interpretation of reality, using the category of participation, which was a metaphysical category applied both in the theory of knowledge and in ontology. This interpretation had to use the typological method, because reality itself is by its nature typological.[15] It was to typology that the Therapeutae looked in inquiring into and establishing the nature of the various cultic practices.

The Therapeutae made extensive use of biblical typology and applied it to their own rites. By means of typology they established a connection between their morning prayers and the sacrificial liturgy of the Jerusalem Temple; they applied the same technique to their ritual meals. Because of the connection with the sacrifices in the Temple, the liturgy of the meal and that of morning prayer became two of the most important elements in their worship of God. Consistently with this interpretation of their rites, the Therapeutae had a specifically priestly conception of their community, and this in turn had a direct impact on their conception of worship: the meal and prayer were assimilated to the sacrifices in the Temple.[16]

Since the community of the Therapeutae corresponded typologically to the priesthood of Israel, their prayer and meal corresponded typologically to the sacrifices. Did the Therapeutae regard themselves as priests, or were they in fact priests? And were the rites in question regarded as sacrificial, or were they in fact sacrificial? Because of the typology at work, they really were, and they were so by participation.

Both the meal and the morning and evening prayers were linked to the sacrifices that were offered, morning and evening, in the Jerusalem

[15] For the connection between biblical typology and the liturgy, see my essay, "L'interpretazione del culto nella chiesa antica" (see above, chapter 1, note 20).

[16] Those who presided at the meal were called *ephemereuti,* a term signifying not simply presidency but also the priestly office of those who were ministering that day; see J. Riaud, "Thérapeutes," *DSp* 15:567. Many elements in the meal could be paralleled in the temple ceremony. The very name "Therapeutae" had a priestly meaning and was connected with the sacrificial role of the priest (Nikiprowetzky [note 10, above], 256).

Temple; the typological method ensured that the prayers of the Therapeutae were a participation in the nature of the Temple sacrifices. For the Therapeutae, then, their morning prayers corresponded ontologically to the sacrifices in the Temple.[17] In order to understand this state of affairs fully, we must bear in mind that in Israel the morning and evening sacrifices were a perpetual sacrifice or, in other words, worship par excellence. In fact, according to the midrash, the sacrifice of Isaac was the origin of the later institution of perpetual sacrifice that was offered morning and evening in the Temple, and every time this perpetual sacrifice was offered, God remembered the sacrifice of Isaac.[18]

This explains why, in the eyes of the Therapeutae, morning prayers were a primary element in their system of worship. In fact, since these prayers corresponded typologically to the perpetual sacrifice in the Temple, they did, in fact, for all intents and purposes, have a sacrificial character, since typological correspondence implied ontological correspondence.

1.1.3. Was There a Connection between the Therapeutae and the Alexandrian Liturgy?

I explained earlier the connection between Jewish morning prayer (the *Yotser*) and the Alexandrian paleoanaphora. I then added the hypothesis that this connection originated by way of the conception of the liturgy in the monastic community of the Therapeutae. If we are to advance any further, however, we must not be satisfied with a simple hypothesis, but must offer proof that there was a connection between the Jewish community of the Therapeutae and the later Alexandrian Church.

The link between the two can be found in monasticism, since later Christian monasticism inherited and perpetuated in time the liturgical practices of the Therapeutae. Eusebius compares the monasticism of the first-century Therapeutae with fourth-century Christian monasticism and comes to the conclusion that the institutions, celebrations, observances, and lifestyles of the two were the same.[19]

[17] These prayers were therefore the most important liturgy of the day.

[18] K. Hruby, "La fête de Rosh ha-Shanah," in *Mémorial Mgr. Gabriel Khouri-Sarkis (1898–1968)* (Louvain, 1969) 62 (= *OS* 13 [1968] 47–71).

[19] The point was also made by Jerome, who saw a continuity between the Therapeutae and the monks of the fourth century; see his *De viris illustribus* (PL 23:627). Jerome was following the thesis of Eusebius. For Eusebius, the explanation of such

As a matter of fact, monastic life in the Scete desert displayed many elements quite similar to those found in Philo's description of the Therapeutae.[20] For our argument here it is important to emphasize one particular usage of the monks of the Scete desert: As late as the fourth century they were accustomed to celebrate a vigil, on Saturday evening, which lasted through the night and ended on the following morning at the time of morning prayer. As a conclusion of the vigil the Sunday Eucharist was celebrated, this at the time of morning prayer.[21]

On Sunday morning, then, the eucharistic rite took place at the time of morning prayer, and we know that, in the thinking of the Therapeutae, morning prayer was the principal prayer of the day and was regarded as worship and a sacrifice. I maintain that for that reason the Alexandrian Eucharist was adapted to that particular hour and took over certain themes and characteristics proper to morning prayer in the Jewish tradition, as I have described it. The themes of light, creation, and the Messiah, as well the cultic and sacrificial character of morning prayer, passed from the *Yotser* into the prayers of the Christian Eucharist.

1.2. *The Second Strophe of the Alexandrian Paleoanaphora*

Now that the existence and character of the relationship between the Alexandrian Eucharist and the Jewish celebration of morning prayer have been established, we can broaden our inquiry and see whether the second strophe of the Alexandrian Eucharistic Prayer likewise has connections with Judaism. The answer is positive if we

---

a continuity was the assumption that the Therapeutae were already Christian and had a connection with the Church of Alexandria from its very beginnings. It is not easy to say whether Eusebius was right, but we must surely admit that there must have been some influence at work, since these observances continued to be maintained and to exert an influence.

[20] A. Guillaumont, "Philon et les origines du monachisme," in *Philon d'Alexandrie* (Colloque de Lyons [11–15 septembre 1966]; Paris: Editions du Centre national de la recherche scientifique, 1967) 361–73.

[21] See W. Hauser (gen. ed.), *The Monasteries of the Wâdi 'n Natrûn*, Part II: H.G.E. White, *The History of the Monasteries of Nitria and Scetis* (Metropolitan Museum of Art, Egyptian Expedition; New York, 1932) 207–13. For a picture of the eucharistic celebration in Egypt see U. Zanetti, *Les lectionaires coptes annuels: Basse-Egypte* (Publications de l'Institut Orientaliste de Louvain 3; Louvain-la-Neuve, 1985) 14–21, 133–39, 157–61, 166–75. I am indebted to Father Ugo Zanetti for this bibliography, and I thank him once again.

make our point of reference the Alexandrian Judaism of the Therapeutae and their sacrificial and cultic concept of prayer. As we shall see immediately, all this is fully reflected in the Alexandrian eucharistic celebration; in fact, it is through this paleoanaphora that the conception of the Eucharist as a sacrifice entered the Christian celebration: the thanksgiving proper to the prayer (that is, the Eucharist) participates in the nature of sacrifice and has a cultic character.

The sacrificial and cultic conception of the Eucharist is set down in the text of the anaphora and gives rise to the theme of the second strophe of the Alexandrian paleoanaphora. For proof I need only refer to the constitutive elements of this second strophe: (a) the sacrificial character of the prayer of thanksgiving; (b) the cultic character of the eucharistic celebration; (c) the use of Malachi 1:11 as an account of the institution of the sacrifice and worship that are brought to fulfillment in the Eucharist.[22]

The citation from Malachi 1:11 serves as an account of institution: This is possible precisely because the Eucharist is conceived as being a sacrifice.

Malachi 1:11 foretells that in the last times all human beings will celebrate a perfect sacrifice that is accepted by God: "For from the rising of the sun to its setting my name is great among the nations, and in every place incense is offered to my name, and a pure offering; for my name is great among the nations, says the Lord of hosts." On the basis of this formulation of the account of institution the Eucharist becomes the fulfillment of Old Testament prophecy, that is, it is the perfect sacrifice.[23]

The entire procedure which I have been describing is based on the typological method, and it was thanks to this method that the

---

[22] As conceived according to the Alexandrian anaphora, the eucharistic celebration is worship paid to God, but this cultic character comes solely from the sacrificial character of the prayer of thanksgiving, which was the original nucleus.

[23] It should not surprise us that the account of institution should take the form of a citation from the Old Testament instead of the account of the Last Supper. We should bear in mind that the eucharistic use of this text (Mal 1:11) goes back to the *Didache* 14, and that at so early a time the Old Testament was still the Scriptures from which citations were to be taken. Therefore the account of institution, which by definition is a citation from the Bible, had to come from the Old Testament. The use of Malachi 1:11 to describe the Eucharist was characteristic of the Church from its beginnings to the first quarter to the third century, or from the *Didache* to Irenaeus, Justin, Tertullian, and Origen.

Alexandrian Church was able to think of the Eucharist as a perfect sacrifice and, therefore, as a cultic fulfillment of the ancient economy.

In order to appreciate the importance of the passage in Malachi 1:11, we should bear in mind that the text is also echoed in the Letter to the Hebrews: "Through him, then, let us continually *offer* up a *sacrifice of praise* to God, that is, the fruit of lips that *acknowledge his name*" (13:15).

1.3. The Third Strophe, or the Petition

This part of the paleoanaphora is already rather developed in Strasbourg Papyrus Gr. 254 and will be developed still more extensively in later texts. The third strophe of the Alexandrian paleoanaphora contains intercessions that begin with a prayer for the Church. God is asked for the gift of peace: "We pray and beseech you: be mindful of your one, holy, catholic Church, all peoples, and all your flocks. Bestow upon all of our hearts the peace that comes from heaven, but grant us also the peace of this life."[24] The text continues with a prayer for the king, asking God that the king may himself be concerned for peace: "[Keep the] earthly king [in peace; make him think] of what brings peace to us and to your holy Name." The prayer goes on to include military commanders, the army, princes, and the senate.

We saw that in this Alexandrian Eucharist the prayer of thanksgiving was constructed of themes from the *Yotser*, the first of the blessings before the *Shema'*. The strophe of intercessions likewise derives from Jewish morning prayer and specifically from the second of the blessings before the *Shema'*, the *Ahabhah Rabbah,* which asks God to bring the people back,[25] but instead of asking that they be assembled in unity, it asks that they may be assembled in peace. Here is the text: "Our Father . . . assemble us in peace from the four corners of the earth, and let us enter in freedom into our land. For you are the God who effects salvation and has chosen us from among all peoples and tongues and have led us to your great and holy Name."[26]

The history of Alexandrian Christianity was heavily marked by persecutions, from that of Septimius Severus (202 on) to the disturbances under Philip (249) and the persecution of Decius (250), whose successor, Gallus, while not formally ordering any persecution, did

---

[24] Hänggi-Pahl, 116–17.

[25] "Bring back from the four corners of the earth" is a variant of the theme of "reunion" or "assembly."

[26] Hänggi-Pahl, 37–38.

persecute the saints who were asking God to give him peace and health.[27] Then came the persecutions under Valerian (257), Diocletian (304), and Maximinus Daia (310–312). So great was the Coptic Church's experience of persecutions and need of peace that it began its calendar with the age of the martyrs, which began on August 29, 283, the first year of Diocletian's reign.[28] This may have been the reason why the prayer for the Church took the form of a strong petition for peace and also why this Church prayed that the sovereign would think thoughts of peace. In any case, the felt need found voice in a prayer for peace, which was easily grafted on to the Jewish source that already contained this theme, namely, the *Ahabhah Rabbah,* the second of the blessings that preceded the recital of the *Shema'.*

The theme of peace is followed by intercessions for the various orders making up the Church: the bishop with the entire clergy and various ministers, the king, the living and the dead. The intercession for the living is especially interesting because it immediately becomes an intercession for the offerers and then a *commendatio sacrificii,* that is, God is asked to accept the offering of the faithful and find it pleasing.[29] This is a theme characteristic of sacrificial worship, but completely absent from the Jewish ritual meal; the blessings proper to the liturgy of a meal know nothing of any prayer for offering something to God or of any prayer that he would find the offering pleasing and acceptable.

There is, however, one interesting exception, and it occurs among the Therapeutae, for whom food, as seen in the liturgy for meals, is rich in sapiential references,[30] and whose life is a continual tending

[27] Eusebius, *Historia ecclesiastica* 7.1; ET: *The History of the Church from Christ to Constantine,* trans. G. A. Williamson (Baltimore, 1965) 287.

[28] U. Zanetti, "L'église copte," *Seminarium* 27 (1987) 359; G. Viaud, *Les liturgies des Coptes d'Egypt* (Paris: Libraire d'Amérique et d'Orient A. Maisonneuve, 1978) chapter 3.

[29] Unfortunately, the text of the Strasbourg Papyrus was heavily damaged, so that only the beginning and end of the third strophe are legible. The entire part which I have called the *commendatio sacrificii* is lacking, as is the mention of the heavenly altar, which is an integral part of it. As a result, we cannot be sure whether this section was part of the Alexandrian anaphora at the time of the Strasbourg Papyrus or was added later. However, because of the large space occupied by the now lost text and because of a few words still partially legible, we may think that the *commendatio sacrificii* and the mention of the heavenly altar were already present in this Alexandrian paleoanaphora.

[30] See P. Graffigna (ed.), *Filone d'Alessandria. La vita contemplativa* (Genoa, 1992) 172.

toward wisdom.[31] All this is well expressed in the prayer before the meal, in which God is asked that the meal may be pleasing to him and in accordance with his will.[32] In addition, in the prayer for the acceptance of the sacrifice, the Alexandrian anaphora speaks of how God was pleased with, and accepted, the sacrifices of Abel and Abraham, which are therefore viewed as the model of authentic worship that is acceptable to God. This view is also characteristic of the Therapeutae, who regarded Abel, Abraham, Henoch, and Moses as the true Therapeutae, that is, worshipers of God, the greatest of them having been Abraham. Thus the third strophe of the Alexandrian paleoanaphora likewise shows precise and specific connections with the Therapeutae community.

In conclusion: Of the elements making up the Alexandrian paleoanaphora, there is none that does not have a parallel in the liturgical practice of the Therapeutae as attested by Philo. None of the similarities, taken by itself, is probative, but when all are taken together, they cannot be ignored. This is especially true since the elements of the Alexandrian paleoanaphora are not related to the elements in any of the other families of anaphoras, whereas all of the former do show a similarity to certain special characteristics of the Therapeutae's conception of the liturgy, as well as (as we saw earlier) to the Jewish blessings that precede the recitation of the *Shema'*.

It has been necessary to dwell at length on the Alexandrian paleoanaphora, because it is in it that we find the explanation both of the structure of the Antiochene anaphora and of the Roman Canon, which was the special text of the Roman Church from the patristic age down to the liturgical reform of the Second Vatican Council. I shall now turn to the structure of the Antiochene anaphora and then to the Roman Canon.

2. THE ANTIOCHENE ANAPHORA

The Antiochene anaphora is the one best known because of its structure, and also because the recent liturgical reform in the Roman Church chose the structures of the Antiochene texts as a source of new anaphoras.[33] When I say "Antiochene texts," I am referring, for

---

[31] *De vita contemplativa*, 68 (ET: 53).

[32] Ibid., 66 (ET: 52–53). See also *De plantatione*, 161–62.

[33] The structure of the Eucharistic Prayer in the Missal of Paul VI is typically Antiochene, except for the short epiclesis inserted before the account of institution

example, to the anaphora in the document known as the *Apostolic Tradition* of Hippolytus, the anaphora of Basil in its two forms (the Alexandrian and the Byzantine), and the anaphora of James the Brother of the Lord. These anaphoras are valuable for the harmony and unity of their content, which is developed in a homogeneous way, often on a trinitarian pattern, from the beginning of the thanksgiving to the final doxology.

2.1. *The Antiochene Structure*

This type of anaphora has the following structure: (1) thanksgiving; (2) *Sanctus*; (3) *Post Sanctus*; (4) account of institution; (5) anamnesis; (6) offering; (7) epiclesis; (8) intercessions; (9) doxology; (10) Amen of the people.

This structure is quite different from that of paleoanaphoras, which, as we have seen, are divided into three strophes. The question arises whether it is still possible to see this archaic tripartite structure in the later texts. The answer requires that we first investigate two other matters: (1) the origin of the anamnesis-offering block, which is characterized by the words *mindful-we offer;* (2) the introduction of the account of the Last Supper into the anaphora.

2.2. *The Account of the Last Supper and the Anaphora of Hippolytus*

In order to see how the account of institution became part of the anaphora we must go back to the Eucharistic Prayer of the *Tradition* that is attributed to Hippolytus.[34] I have already shown elsewhere

---

and known as the "first epiclesis." The insertion was made for theological reasons, in order to avoid asking for the transformation of the sacred gifts during the so-called second epiclesis which comes after the account of institution; if the Antiochene structure had been chosen without any change, questions would have arisen about the moment of consecration, which, according to Catholic teaching, is identical with the account of institution. In order to legitimize the creation of the first epiclesis before the bar of liturgical tradition, the reformers had recourse to the Alexandrian anaphoral structure. Indeed, the Anaphora of St. Mark does contain, in the *Sanctus,* an embolism that has an epicletic sound to it, although it cannot be said with certainty that it is an epiclesis that asks for the transformation of the gifts into the Body and Blood of Christ.

[34] This text has three parts: two thanksgivings and a petition. This particular structure can be related to the development of the Christian *Birkat ha-Mazon.* The second thanksgiving has links to some texts belonging within the development of the *Birkat ha-Mazon,* and thus also with the epiclesis, which all the commentators evidently find to be a difficult and troublesome text. I offer the hypothesis that the

how the first part of the anaphora of Hippolytus originated with the introduction into a paleoanaphora of themes and expressions from the celebration of Passover,[35] and I shall therefore not go into this question here.

(a) In the text of Hippolytus the preface of the anaphora becomes, for the first time, a narrative: the development of the history of salvation is described, in a Christocentric fashion, from creation to the passion, resurrection, and descent of Jesus into the world of the dead. In telling the history of salvation, the thanksgiving section of this anaphora draws its material from texts or, better, from the literary genre of Paschal Homilies; the anaphora here consists of a selection, as it were, of the key phrases used in the Paschal Homilies to describe salvation in its historical development. Because of this connection with the paschal texts great emphasis is laid on the death of Christ, to which redemption is attributed, consistently with the concept of "pasch" as passion or suffering.[36]

(b) Because of this close connection with paschal themes[37] that were still alive and seemed suited to giving privileged expression to the faith of the Church, I think it possible to say that the second half of the second century was the most likely period for the composition of the first part of the anaphora of Hippolytus.[38]

(c) The account of the Last Supper entered the Eucharistic Prayer, which in this case was the anaphora of Hippolytus, along with the narrative material from the paschal liturgy. In Hippolytus, the account of institution is part of the preface and is the culminating

---

difficulties in the epiclesis are due to the different strata that make it up. As for the development of the anaphora, I think that the theme of gathering and unity (in the epiclesis) signal a more or less direct connection with texts originating in the Christian *Birkat ha-Mazon.*

[35] See my *L'anafora,* 111–94.

[36] Today, on the other hand, we give a privileged place to the theme of the resurrection, because the concept of "Pasch" has been defined independently of the typology of the lamb.

[37] I am referring to the themes of Pasch = passion.

[38] At this point it will be helpful to recall a notice in the *Liber Pontificalis,* which attributes to Alexander I (105?–115?) the introduction of the *Passio Domini* into the *Praedicatio sacerdotum,* a phrase which signifies the Canon of the Mass; see L. Duchesne (ed.), *Le Liber Pontificalis* I (Bibliothèque des écoles françaises d'Athènes et de Rome; Paris, 1981) 217. The notice in the *Liber Pontificalis* may be accurate, but the attribution to Alexander I is really difficult; the notice becomes more credible if placed after the pontificate of Anicetus (155?–166?).

point, the key point, in the narrative of salvation, that is, in the thanksgiving.[39]

The significance of this fact, namely, the introduction of the account of the Last Supper at the end of the first strophe of the thanksgiving, is very clear: The Eucharist was instituted in order to give believers the fullness of that entire course of Old Testament history that was fulfilled in Christ and, specifically, in the Passover of Christ which was, typologically, the fulfillment of the ancient Passover. Thanks is also given for the Last Supper because it was through it that the prefigurations reached their fulfillment for us.[40]

After showing, on the basis of the texts and a careful synoptic comparison of the anaphora of Hippolytus with the Paschal Homilies, how and why the account of the Last Supper became part of the anaphora, I must still determine whether all this has any connection with the Alexandrian paleoanaphora. As a matter of fact, the insertion of the account could not have been made directly into the anaphora of Hippolytus, because the latter can be read as having two different and irreconcilable structures.[41]

Given the first structure, the text is in the line of development of the Christian *Birkat ha-Mazon*. There is a first strophe of thanksgiving, which runs from the initial thanksgiving to the end of the offering; this is followed by a second that gives thanks for the present moment[42] and has parallels both in the second thanksgiving of the *Birkat ha-Mazon* in the *Book of Jubilees* (ca. A.D. 100) and in the second thanksgiving of the prayer in the *Martyrdom of Polycarp*.[43] The other structure has ties with the Alexandrian anaphora: The first strophe runs to the end of the account of institution, and the second consists of the anamnesis-offering.

Is it possible that this second anaphoral structure arose in Alexandria? Certainly. We need only try to insert the account of the Last

---

[39] In conclusion, we must acknowledge that with the anaphora of Hippolytus the evolution of the text is complete; add a few details, and we have our modern texts. In Hippolytus the thanksgiving becomes a narrative and has for its subject the history of salvation with all its stages, culminating in the death of Christ, his resurrection, and his descent among the dead.

[40] See the *Homily of Pseudo-Hippolytus*, no. 92.

[41] This is another reason why the text of this anaphora is so complex and difficult.

[42] "Thanking you for considering us worthy to stand before you and minister to you."

[43] See my *L'anafora*, 170–77.

Supper at the end of the first strophe of the Alexandrian paleoana-phora. This would be followed by the anamnesis-offering,[44] which arises out of the beginning of the original structure of the second strophe in the Alexandrian anaphora. The hypothesis supposes that the material deriving from the Paschal Homilies entered the Alexandrian anaphora. But this would mean that Alexandria knew and celebrated the Asian Easter. Is that possible? Is there any evidence?

There are two pieces of evidence: (1) When Philo of Alexandria describes the ritual meal of the Therapeutae he makes explicit references to the Jewish Passover. The hymns sung at the beginning of the Therapeutae's vigil are a *mimêma* (copy, image) of the choir which at the Red Sea, with Moses and Miriam leading, had celebrated the events God had brought to pass as he transformed the sea into an instrument of salvation for some and of death for others.[45] On the other hand, when Philo has to speak of the contemplation and manifestation of God, the theme of the exodus and the wilderness becomes a very important one. It is not surprising, then, that he should see the meal and vigil of the Therapeutae in a Passover perspective.

(2) When Eusebius of Caesarea speaks of the Therapeutae,[46] he says that they were wont to follow practices still in use in his time, especially for the feast of the "Pasch";[47] he means by this term the pasch = passion that was characteristic of the Church of Asia, and the rite of which was attested by the Paschal Homilies of the second century. Was there perhaps a connection between the Paschs of the Church of Asia and the Church of Alexandria? The method followed in the Paschal Homilies was simply an application of typology to the Old Testament passages on the Passover, in order to see their fulfillment in the death of Christ, who then rose and ascended to heaven. The typological method was typically Alexandrian, and it was from that city that it spread out.

In our question here, we ought perhaps to change our perspective; instead of asking how the Paschal Homilies of the Church of Asia

---

[44] See section 2.3, below.

[45] *De vita contemplativa*, 85–88 (ET: 56–57).

[46] As I said earlier, Eusebius regards these people as already Christians. For discussion of the problem I refer the reader to my "La structure de l'anaphore alexandrine et antiochienne," *Irén* 67 (1994) 5–40.

[47] Eusebius, *Historia ecclesiastica* 2.17.21 (ET: 89ff.). For text with notes and French translation, see SC 31:77.

could have had an influence on the Alexandrian liturgy, we ought to ask how and in what manner the Church of Alexandria might have brought into being the paschal typology of the Church of Asia.

2.3. The Section Containing the Anamnesis and Offering

This part of the Antiochene anaphora has its remote explanation in the Alexandrian paleoanaphora and, more specifically, at the beginning of the second strophe: "Giving thanks, we offer *(eucharistountes prospheromen)* the spiritual sacrifice, this bloodless worship."[48] The received text of the Anaphora of St. Mark develops the text by eliminating the word "sacrifice" and connecting "spiritual" with "worship": "Giving thanks, we offer *(eucharistountes prospheromen)* this spiritual and bloodless worship."[49] The same sentence occurs in the Greek Anaphora of St. John Chrysostom:[50] here the present participle *memnêmenoi*, which is the subject of the verb *propheromen*, has for its object *ta sa ek tôn sôn* ("what is yours from what is yours"). Immediately afterwards the theme is repeated in this form: "We offer you this spiritual and bloodless worship."[51] This part of the Antiochene anaphora is similar to the Roman Canon: *Unde et memores . . . offerimus de tuis donis ac datis, hostiam puram, hostiam sanctam, hostiam immaculatam* ("Mindful, therefore . . . we offer you, from among the gifts you have given us, a pure victim, a holy victim, a spotless victim").[52]

All these texts display a surprising sameness that transcends the traditional subdivision into liturgical families. I think that the Reverend Dr. Geoffrey J. Cuming likewise saw a certain connection between these texts, since he says: "At a minimum, the words *memores*

---

[48] "Eucharistountes prospheromen tên thusian tên logikên, tên anaimakton latreian tautên" (Strasbourg Papyrus Gr. 254; Hänggi-Pahl, 116).

[49] "Eucharistountes prospheromen tên logikên kai anaimakton latreian tautên" (Hänggi-Pahl, 102).

[50] Ibid., 226.

[51] "Tên logikên tautên kai anaimakton latreian." This phrase occurs at the beginning of the epiclesis and is repeated immediately afterward, at the beginning of the intercessions, but without the word "anaimakton." On the sacrificial character of the beginning of the intercessions see E. Lanne, "L'intercession pour l'Eglise dans la Prière Eucharistique," in *L'Eglise dans la Liturgie*, ed. A. M. Triacca and A. Pistoia (Bibliotheca Ephemerides liturgicae. Subsidia 18; Rome, 1980) 183–208.

[52] *Canon missae romanae. Pars prior: Traditio textus*, ed. L. Eizenhöfer (Collectanea Anselmiana. Rerum ecclesiasticarum documenta. Series minor. Subsidia studiorum 1; Rome, 1954) 34.

. . . *offerimus* recall the *eucharistountes . . . prospheromen* of the Anaphora of St. Mark."[53]

The verbs, which in participial form are the subjects of the verb "offer," may differ, but this is the only difference[54] within a substantial identity of sentences; in the one case, the participle is *eucharistountes,* in the other, *memnêmenoi,* which corresponds to the *memores* of the Roman Canon. It is possible, however, to explain this difference and thus to provide confirmation that the texts cited belong to a single homogeneous bloc because they have a single origin.

In the Alexandrian paleoanaphora the present participle *eucharistountes* is at the beginning of the second strophe[55] and has for its function to describe the cultic value of the immediately preceding action, that is, the action performed in the first strophe: the giving of thanks.

If this present participle is connected with the action just performed and is meant to express the content of the immediately preceding text, then, understandably, it must change, depending on the action expressed in the immediately preceding strophe. Therefore, when there is question of a strophe of thanksgiving, we will have *eucharistountes;* where there is question of remembering the "command" of Christ ("do this in memory of me"), we will have *memnêmenoi* in Greek texts and *memores* in the Roman Canon. But this is not the whole picture, since in the non-Roman Western rites there are other kinds of anamnesis that focus not on "memory" but on the word "do" or, more accurately, on the idea underlying this word, namely, obedience to the command of Christ. Here are some examples: "Haec facimus, haec celebramus tua, Domine, praecepta *servantes"* ("This we do, this we celebrate, Lord, as we *keep* your command").[56] There is a comparable text in the *Missale Gothicum:* "Haec igitur praecepta *servantes* sacrosancta munera nostrae salutis offerimus" (*"Keeping* this command, we offer the holy gifts of our salvation").[57]

---

[53] G. J. Cuming, "The Shape of the Anaphora," in *Studia patristica XX,* ed. E. A. Livingstone (Kalamazoo–Louvain, 1989) 333–45.

[54] The difference is in fact only a seeming one, as we shall see when I explain the origin.

[55] The second strophe of the Alexandrian paleoanaphora expresses a theology of worship: The action just completed is a sacrifice *(thusia)* and an act of worship *(latreia).*

[56] *Feria V in authentica* (Hänggi-Pahl, 453).

[57] Ibid., 492.

In the light of these examples, we understand why when the Alexandrian liturgy took over from Antioch the second part of the anaphora[58] containing the anamnetic formula, it began it with the present participle *kataggellontes* (*proclaiming* the death, we offer) because of the particular Alexandrian formulation of the "command," which was modeled on 1 Corinthians 11:26: "Whenever you eat of this bread and drink of this cup, you *proclaim* the *death* of the Lord until he comes").

In conclusion, I may say that the present participle of which I have been speaking has its referent in the immediately preceding text, and that this reference is primarily of the literary order, since the present participle, which is the subject of "offer," simply cites the action described in the immediately preceding sentence.

We have here a fact that is very important for explaining the genesis of the anamnesis: the term "mindful" (or: "remembering") is a literary datum that is to be seen as simply that and not given a surplus of value by transferring its scope and role to the theological level.[59]

2.4. The Origin of the Epiclesis and the Anaphora of Hippolytus

In the history of the epiclesis, the one in the so-called *Apostolic Tradition* (attributed to Hippolytus) occupies first place, not only chronologically but also morphologically, since it is the simplest form of the phenomenon.[60] For this reason, it must be said that an investigation of the sources of the anaphora of Hippolytus is indispensable for the entire history of the eucharistic anaphora.

The epiclesis in the Anaphora of Hippolytus is in two parts:[61] the first is concerned with the descent of the Spirit "on the offering of the

---

[58] This part includes the account of institution, the mandate, the anamnesis with the offering, the epiclesis (the "second" epiclesis), and the doxology.

[59] What I mean is that the explanation of the present participle, *memores*, should remain a literary explanation and not become a theological explanation. This means that one may not use *memores* as a starting point for extracting an anamnetic conception of the Eucharist or, as one might say today, a theology of the Eucharist as memorial. If we wanted, we could construct other conceptions of the Eucharist (beside the anamnetic conception) on the basis of other present participles that are the subject of the verb *offer*, such as "giving thanks," "proclaiming," "confessing (*homologountes*)," "awaiting (*apekdechomenoi*) his coming," "observing this command," and so on.

[60] B. Botte, "Les plus anciennes collections canoniques," *OS* 5 (1960) 344.

[61] This two-part division is a classical structure and typical of the Antiochene epiclesis, with the first part referring to the holy gifts, and the second to the fruitfulness of the reception of the Eucharist.

holy Church,"[62] while the second asks for the gift of unity and prays that all who share in the holy mysteries may be filled with the Spirit so as to strengthen their faith in the truth.[63] These, then, are the elements of the epiclesis: (1) sending of the Spirit on the *oblatio* (offering) of the Church; (2) the theme of unity; (3) participation in the holy gifts; (4) fullness of the Holy Spirit; (5) ultimate purpose: "to strengthen (our) faith in the truth, so that we may praise and glorify you."[64]

Let me begin with the fifth point. It contains an expression[65] that is found in Irenaeus, where the Holy Spirit is described as "the pledge of incorruption and the strengthening of our faith and a ladder for ascending to God."[66] Shortly afterward and in the same context Irenaeus adds: "The Spirit is truth."[67] His argument here is simple: The Church, and it alone, benefits from the life-giving presence of the Spirit of God; this presence, which is the operation of the Spirit, guarantees the truth of the faith.[68] If the Spirit strengthens faith and is truth,[69] then we are not far from the epiclesis of the *Apostolic Tradition,* in which the Spirit works "to strengthen faith in the truth."

The second part of this epiclesis takes up the theme of unity, which is also present in Irenaeus in connection with the Holy Spirit: "Thus it is that, inspired by the same sentiment *(conspirantes),* the disciples celebrated the praises of God in all languages, as the Spirit was bringing back to unity *(Spiritu ad unitatem redigente)* the scattered tribes and was offering to the Father the first fruits of all the nations."[70]

---

[62] "Et petimus ut mittas Spiritum tuum sanctum in oblationem sanctae ecclesiae."

[63] "In unum congregans, des omnibus qui percipiunt sanctis in repletionem Spiritus sancti, ad confirmationem fidei in veritate."

[64] The words "ut te laudemus et glorificemus" serve as a bridge to the doxology and introduce it; they are, therefore, part of either the epiclesis or the doxology. I prefer to keep them with the epiclesis, since the epiclesis customarily states the purpose of the request it is making.

[65] These words are based on Colossians 2:7: "built up in him and established in the faith"; these words of Paul can be read as "eucharistic," since they are followed by "abounding in thanksgiving *(eucharistia).*"

[66] *Adv. haer.* 3.24.1 (SC 211:472).

[67] Ibid., 474.

[68] See the critique of the text, with commentary, in SC 210:390–93.

[69] Irenaeus is greatly concerned to show the falsity of heretical views; consequently, the title of "truth" which is given to the Spirit is neither accidental nor one title among many; it is part of the reasoning. See also *Adv. haer.* 3.24.2: "having separated themselves from the truth, they are tossed about by every error . . . rather than being disciples of the truth" (SC 211:475).

[70] *Adv. haer.* 3.17.2 (SC 211:331).

In this passage the Spirit is seen as effecting unity,[71] and unity in turn has for its purpose the praise of God. The text is a very interesting one, since in the epiclesis of the anaphora attributed to Hippolytus unity is connected with the work of the Spirit, and its ultimate goal is the praise of God. As far as this text of Irenaeus is concerned, then, our conclusion is a positive one: it shows a set of ideas which it has in common with the anaphora of the *Apostolic Tradition,* and expresses them in identical phrases.[72] Note, too, the general cultic context: The offering to the Father of the first fruits of all the nations.

The remote origin of the theme of unity is in Paul; it is a baptismal theme, in which the action of the Spirit is connected with the building up of the Church, the latter being described as a single body.[73] To understand how the pneumatological epiclesis in the Anaphora of Hippolytus came to be, we must keep in mind the three preceding stages.

The theme of the Holy Spirit is found in both parts of the epiclesis, but in two different ways, since there is no continuity between the two parts and since, in addition, they show differing conceptions of the relation between Eucharist and Spirit. Let us look at these two points in succession.

(a) The first part of the epiclesis says: "And we ask you to send your Holy Spirit on the offering of your Church." This is a pointed request which, when fully formulated, goes on to make explicit the purpose of the descent of the Spirit on the eucharistic species. In this epiclesis, however, the request ends here; it is an end in itself and is not further developed by explaining the purpose of the petition. The purposes of the epiclesis are formulated rather in the second part of the epiclesis, but without any dependence on the first part, as though the latter did not exist. In fact, the second part of the epiclesis begins without any relation to the first and with a petition that is unconnected with what

[71] This unity is to be understood as ecclesiological; it therefore supposes that the epiclesis is read in accordance with the interpretation of it given by B. Botte.

[72] In his *Commentary on Daniel* Hippolytus has an expression that is, from a literary point of view, close to the text of the anaphora; it is part of a prayer: ". . . before you in truth and in faith, with a perfect heart" (*In Dan.* 1.7.4; SC 14:80). But these are only some words similar to those of the anaphora; there is no real closeness of the texts. I maintain, therefore, that the text of Irenaeus is closer and more relevant.

[73] "For by one Spirit we were all baptized into one body—Jews or Greeks, slaves or free—and all were made to drink of one Spirit" (1 Cor 12:13).

has preceded and that can be granted independently of the descent of the Spirit on the offering.

This is a very important point: for if the second part is independent of the first part, complete in itself, and able to exist without the first part, whereas the first part is not equally autonomous, since it demands to be completed by a statement of the purpose of the coming of the Spirit, then I think it can be concluded that the two parts belong to two different redactional stages and that the first part was added to the second part when the latter was already in the form in which we know it today.

(b) In the first part of the epiclesis the theme of the Holy Spirit is primary and stands at the center of the discourse; in the second part, however, the theme of the Spirit is only one of the points made in the petition, and it does not have a central role, a role it ought to have if this second part were a development and continuation of the first. The text of the second part reads: "Gathering [them] into one, grant *(des)* to all those who will partake of the holies [i.e., holy mysteries] that they may be filled with the Holy Spirit, for the strengthening of [their] faith in the truth, so that we may praise and glorify you. . . ."

Conclusion: This comparison of the two parts shows that there is no connection between the prayer for the descent of the Spirit on the offerings and the prayer that God would give the Spirit to those who communicate, so that this Spirit may confirm their faith in the truth. The second part, then, is independent of the first, while the first shows that it belongs to a different order of ideas and therefore to a different stratum of the text of the anaphora.[74]

Just as the account of institution was completed by the anamnesis and offering, so the epiclesis was completed by the addition of the opening sentence: "And we ask you to send your Holy Spirit on the offering of the Holy Church."

The epiclesis of the Anaphora of Hippolytus became the model for the Antiochene epiclesis, which began with that in the Anaphora of Basil and developed into the form that is familiar to us and would become the model for almost all later texts.

[74] I observe, finally, that all the anaphoras dependent on Hippolytus reworked the text, thus showing that even they had some trouble in interpreting it; this group includes the *Testamentum Domini*, which becomes intelligible and recovers its comprehensibility only through the back-translation from Syriac to Greek which B. Botte produced with such critical skill; see his "L'Esprit-Saint et l'Eglise dans la *Tradition apostolique* de Saint Hippolyte," *Didaskalia* 2 (1972) 246.

2.5. Conclusion

Some elements in the structure of the Antiochene anaphora can be explained in light of the structure of the Alexandrian paleoanaphora (for example, the account of the Last Supper, and the anamnesis-offering), while others can be explained in light of the Christian development of the *Birkat ha-Mazon* tradition.

Let me sum up briefly:

(a) If the account of institution is added to the end of the first strophe of the Alexandrian paleoanaphora, we have precisely the structure of the anaphora of Hippolytus: (1) thanksgiving, at the end of which comes the account of institution; (2) anamnesis; (3) offering. The structure is identical even though there is a difference in the choice of the verb (in the present participle) on which the anamnesis is based,[75] for this difference is irrelevant from the viewpoint of the succession of strophes and, therefore, from the viewpoint of the structure of the texts.

(b) The historical development of the account of institution, from its Jewish origin down to the account of the Last Supper in the Antiochene anaphora, may be summarized in this way: the *Birkat ha-Mazon* has, as its account of institution, the citation of Deuteronomy 8:10, while *Didache* 10, which is a thanksgiving derived from the *Birkat ha-Mazon*, retains this citation but adds an embolism showing that the Christian ritual food (the spiritual food and drink) is irreducible to that of the Jewish ritual meal. The Mystical Eucharist, which is derived from the *Didache*, moves the account from the thanksgiving after the meal to the thanksgiving before the meal, with the thanksgiving after the meal becoming simply a thanksgiving after Communion.

In the Mystical Eucharist the connection with the *Birkat ha-Mazon* is henceforth unrecognizable; consequently, there is no longer any trace of the citation from Deuteronomy 8:10. In this document, the account of institution, which has been moved from the thanksgiving after Communion to the earlier thanksgiving, is based on 1 Corinthians 11:16; as a result, the express referent of the account of institution is the Last Supper. In the Alexandrian paleoanaphora, on the other hand, the account of institution consists of Malachi 1:11 (a prophetic announcement of the pure sacrifice which God accepts), and this citation is placed at the end of the second strophe. Deuteronomy 8:10, the

---

[75] In the paleoanaphora we have *eucharistountes* (giving thanks), while Hippolytus has *memores*.

account of institution used in the *Birkat ha-Mazon*, is likewise placed at the end of the second strophe both in that Jewish prayer and in *Didache* 10, which, as we saw, is the Christian *Birkat ha-Mazon*. Even in the Mystical Eucharist, the account of institution (consisting of 1 Cor 11:26) is placed at the end of the second strophe.

From all these paleoanaphoral texts we can conclude that the ordinary place of the account of institution was at the end of the thanksgiving, before the petitions began (third strophe). In the Anaphora of Hippolytus,[76] on the other hand, the account of institution has a different place, being at the end of the first strophe of thanksgiving.[77] This is another reason why the Anaphora of Hippolytus cannot be classified as a paleoanaphora, but is to be regarded as the first anaphora in the strict sense of the term. The different placement of the account of institution, as well as the appearance of the anamnesis, are to be explained solely by the introduction of paschal themes into the first strophe of thanksgiving; among these themes is the account of the Last Supper. Thus there is something completely new, and it is due to the "paschalization" of the anaphora.

2.6. The Alexandrian Anaphora of St. Mark

I shall now speak briefly of the Alexandrian liturgy and describe the evolution which the structure of the anaphora underwent. Strasbourg Papyrus Gr. 254 with its paleoanaphoral characteristics was not bypassed and was not relegated to the bin of outdated texts; on the contrary, it continued to exist as the first part of the anaphora that goes under the name of St. Mark. To the end of the original paleoanaphora was added the entire collection of new anaphoral parts that

---

[76] I mention this text as a good example of the Antiochene structure, but I could cite other texts of this family, such as the Anaphora of St. Basil, the Anaphora of James Brother of the Lord, the Anaphora of John Chrysostom, and others.

[77] In the Anaphora of Hippolytus the second strophe of thanksgiving is very short: "Thanking you for counting us worthy to stand before you and minister to you." This text is in the tradition of the *Birkat ha-Mazon*, as is clear when we look at the second strophe of Abraham's *Birkat ha-Mazon* in the *Book of Jubilees* 22:7: "And now I thank you, my God, because you have let me see this day" (Charlesworth 2:97). The second strophe in the prayer of the martyred Polycarp, which is like a copy of a paleoanaphora, likewise attests to the same model of thanksgiving: "I bless thee for granting me [literally: making me worthy of] this day and hour, that I may be numbered amongst the martyrs" (*Martyrdom of Polycarp* 14.2; trans. Maxwell Staniforth, *Early Christian Writings. The Apostolic Fathers* [Baltimore, 1968] 160).

had been developed in the meantime. The *Sanctus* was added, but in a still archaic form, inasmuch as it ends not with the *Benedictus*,[78] but with a short formula of invocation which turns on the word "full" and asks God to fill with his glory or blessing the liturgy being celebrated. Theologians have been accustomed to describe this text as an epiclesis,[79] but in fact it is simply an embolism in the *Sanctus* and lacks the characteristics proper to an epiclesis.[80]

After the *Sanctus* a whole block of texts was added: the account of institution in the form of an account of the Last Supper, the anamnesis-offering, and the epiclesis. All these texts were imported, for they came from Antiochene anaphoras, which had developed them in the middle of the fourth century and given them the form they have today. The Antiochene structure thus influenced the Alexandrian anaphora and served as a decisive norm. This was true not only of the second part of the Anaphora of St. Mark but also of other texts, the most interesting being the anaphora attributed to Serapion. This text shows a familiarity with the entire anaphoral tradition and reproduces various phases of it, so that it is a valuable collection of the most important stages. The Anaphora of Serapion takes all the material making up the Alexandrian anaphora and redistributes it according to a new structure, namely, the Antiochene. So, too, the various Alexandrian anaphoras in the *Euchologion of the White Monastery* show the characteristics proper to the Alexandrian family, but they are constructed according to the Antiochene structure. In my opinion, this fact bears witness that the Alexandrian anaphoral structure developed in the perspective of the Antiochene structure.

3. THE ROMAN CANON

The Eucharistic Prayer of the Roman Church—the Roman Canon—is attested for the first time in the fourth century, in the *De sacramentis* of Ambrose, bishop of Milan. It is that form of it that we must use in looking for the origins of the Roman Canon.

---

[78] The *Sanctus* without a *Benedictus* is attested as late as the beginning of the fourth century.

[79] The epiclesis is called "antecedent" in virtue of its position in relation to the account of institution; it is called "consecratory" by reason of its supposed function in the eucharistic celebration.

[80] An exception is found in a rather late fragment: the *Dêr Balyzeh Papyrus*, which displays properly epicletic traits.

When we compare this text directly with the other anaphoras of antiquity, we can only feel an exasperating sense of helplessness, for the Roman Canon shows no kinship with any of the structures of the other liturgical families. It is a text different from every other and is not reducible to any of the structures known to us today. At the beginning of the present century, A. Gastoué pointed out some textual links to the Alexandrian anaphora.[81] And in fact there are some prayers of the Roman Canon that are to some extent similar and to some extent identical with a particular section of the Alexandrian anaphora: the *commendatio* or "(re)commendation" of the offerers and the sacrifice, which is located at the center of the intercessions, that is, at the center of the third strophe, if I may continue to use the paleo-anaphoral structure as a model. But, despite the later works of Botte[82] and Jungmann,[83] no one has succeeded in taking the relationship any further.

There was in fact an insurmountable obstacle that did not allow any further comparison with the Alexandrian anaphora; that obstacle was the fact of structure. Because of their different structures, the two texts could not be compared and were irreducible to a common origin. As a result, any kinship the texts presented seemed irrelevant and of no importance for the larger question of the origin of the Roman anaphora.

Today, however, now that the existence and structures of the paleo-anaphoras have been established, the study of the Roman Canon is beginning to yield very promising results. Indeed, both the structure of this text and its possible origin are beginning to emerge. I shall sketch briefly the results thus far obtained.

The similarity of the texts, despite the difference in anaphoral structure, is certainly a problem. To resolve it, we must ask whether the present structure of the two Eucharistic Prayers is original. If it is not, then we must uncover their primitive stage and then try once again to compare them. The present state of the Alexandrian anaphora, that

---

[81] A. Gastoué, "Alexandrie. Liturgie," *DACL* 1, cols. 1189–93. See also A. Baumstark, "Das 'problem' des römischen Messkanons: eine Retractatio auf geistesgechicht-lichem Hintergrund," *EL* 53 (1939) 204–43.

[82] B. Botte, *Le canon de la messe romaine. Edition critique* (Textes et études liturgiques 2; Louvain, 1935); B. Botte and Chr. Mohrmann, *L'ordinaire de la messe* (Etudes liturgiques 2; Paris-Louvain, 1953).

[83] J. A. Jungmann, *The Mass of the Roman Rite: Its Origins and Development (Missarum Solemnia)*, trans. F. A. Brunner (2 vols.; St. Louis, 1951, 1955).

is, the *textus receptus* of the Anaphora of St. Mark, is not the original state; we know in fact that it was originally made up of two parts: (a) the opening part came from the Alexandrian paleoanaphora, the substance of which is well represented by Strasbourg Papyrus Gr. 254; (b) the following part, from the account of institution to the epiclesis (inclusive) came from the Antiochene anaphora. Therefore, to bring the Alexandrian anaphora back to its archaic state means eliminating the entire second part and retaining only the part that corresponds to Strasbourg Papyrus Gr. 254.

An analogous operation must be performed on the Roman Canon. We know in fact that the *Sanctus* was added after Ambrose, and we know that the two prayers *Supra quae* and *Supplices* are not two separate texts in Ambrose's redaction, but a single prayer. We know, further, that today the *Supra quae* precedes the *Supplices,* whereas in Ambrose the text corresponding to the *Supplices* comes first, and then that corresponding to the *Supra quae.* The structure of the text cited by Ambrose corresponds exactly to that of the Anaphora of St. Mark; in the latter, too, the prayer corresponding to the *Supplices* precedes the prayer corresponding to the *Supra quae,* and here again these two prayers are a single text.

From this it is clear that the Roman Canon, too, has had a history involving an evolution, developments, and reworkings. The first step, then, consists in uncovering the earliest formulations of the Roman Canon. The second step will then be to work on this text so as to carry it to the same level of archaism as the Alexandrian anaphora. Otherwise, the two texts will be at different stages of development and cannot usefully be compared.

Such is the method to be used. As applied to our case, it yields the following results: (a) the oldest thanksgiving of the Roman liturgy is made up of two prefaces, very similar to each other, found among Mai's Arian liturgical fragments,[84] and going back to a period before Ambrose. Neither of these prefaces has a *Sanctus,* and therefore we must retain the Alexandrian paleoanaphora without a *Sanctus,* which was in fact added at a later stage of development; (b) since Strasbourg

[84] These two liturgical texts are contained in a treatise that can be dated to the time of Ambrose or very shortly thereafter; the texts are there cited as traditional "authorities," which means that they belong to a period earlier than that of the treatise. See G. Mercati, "Frammenti liturgici latini tratti da un anonimo ariano del secolo IV/V," in idem, *Antiche reliquie liturgiche ambrosiane e romane. Con un excursus sui frammenti dogmatici ariani del Mai* (Studi e testi 7; Rome, 1902) 57.

Papyrus Gr. 254 lacks the account of the Last Supper, we must excise this part of the Roman Canon; (c) once the account of institution is removed, we cannot retain the anamnesis-offering, since this is closely bound up with the account, on which it depends; (d) for other minor points to which the method is applied, I refer the reader to what I have already published on the subject.[85]

After having thus worked out the two texts to be compared, we can set the Roman text and the Alexandrian paleoanaphora side by side. If we thus write the texts out in two parallel columns, we see that there is a complete correspondence between the Roman Eucharistic Prayer and the Alexandrian paleoanaphora.[86] This correspondence holds both for the structure and for the sequence of the various anaphoral themes: (a) the text has three strophes: the first is a thanksgiving, the second is the offering of the sacrifice (the subject of the verb "offer" is a present participle), and the third is the intercession with its *commendatio* of both the sacrifice and the offerers;[87] (b) throughout the anaphora and independently of the function proper to each of the three strophes, there are various themes of thanksgiving and intercession; the sequence of these themes is the same in both texts, with one exception: the position of the memento of the dead is different in the Alexandrian text than it is in the Roman Canon.[88]

We may therefore conclude that the Alexandrian paleoanaphora was the origin of the text and structure of the Roman Eucharistic Prayer, even before giving rise to the connection between the account of institution and the anamnesis in the Antiochene anaphora. The influence of the Alexandrian Eucharistic Prayer on the Roman Eucharist can be dated to the first half of the third century at the latest.

Finally, we must ask why the two texts developed into two such different structures. Everything depended on the point in the prayer at which the block consisting of the account of institution, anamnesis, and offering was placed, once this block had been given its definitive formulation in the Antiochene anaphora. The Roman liturgy took over this block as formulated in the Antiochene liturgy and placed it

[85] See my *L'anafora*, chapter 7.

[86] Ibid. The synopsis is on 296–300.

[87] In both traditions the third strophe is the most fully developed and quite long in comparison with the two preceding strophes.

[88] This difference can be explained by the Antiochene influence to be seen in the Roman formulary of the memento of the dead. Once this difference is explained, the rest of the Alexandrian Eucharistic Prayer corresponds to the Roman text.

at a particular, carefully studied point in the Roman paleoanaphora, namely, in the middle of the *commendatio* of the offerers and the sacrifice, between the prayer *Fac nobis hanc oblationem* and the prayer *Et petimus et precamur.*[89] When, on the other hand, the Alexandrian liturgy took over this same section of the Antiochene liturgy, it did not insert it at a carefully studied point of the anaphora but simply added it on[90] at the end of the third strophe of the paleoanaphora, without concern for the logic of this step.[91]

If we want confirmation of this explanation, we need only take the section consisting of the account of institution, anamnesis, and offering, and transpose it to the end of the Canon, after the intercessions; we will see that we have an anaphora very similar to the Anaphora of St. Mark. Conversely for the Alexandrian anaphora: If we take that same section and place it within the third strophe, at the center of the *commendatio* of the offerers and the sacrifice, we will have an exact replica of the Roman Canon.[92]

4. THE SYRIAN ANAPHORA

This heading is deliberately put in general terms, even though it may be equivocal, inasmuch as the Syrian liturgy may be either Antiochene (West Syrian) or Chaldean (East Syrian). Furthermore, in the West Syrian area a distinction must be made between anaphoras in Greek and anaphoras in Syriac; the Greek Anaphora of James the Brother of the Lord is not completely the same in structure and text

[89] These are the words with which the prayer *Quam oblationem* and the prayer *Supplices* (which is one prayer with the *Supra quae*), respectively, begin in Ambrose's text.

[90] I.-H. Dalmais claims that this is a general trait of the Coptic liturgical style: the Romans and the Syrians constructed "an ordered discourse" (this being the meaning of *Sedro*), while the Copts were satisfied with "juxtaposing rites, acclamations, and prayers." See his essay, "La liturgie alexandrine et ses relations avec les autres liturgies," in *Liturgie de l'église particulière et liturgie de l'église universelle*, ed. A. M. Triacca and A. Pistoia (Bibliotheca Ephemerides Liturgicae, Subsidia 7; Rome, 1976) 120.

[91] In my view, this lack of logic is very important, since it has allowed us to reconstruct the genesis, the stages, and the various passages of the paleoanaphoral structure, up to the final texts that are characteristic of the various liturgical families.

[92] In this entire broad operation I have left aside the second epiclesis of the Alexandrian anaphora, since it originated at a later period. The same holds for the *Sanctus* with its embolism, since this is a problem still too far from a solution.

as the Syriac Anaphora of the same name. The same must be said of other texts, such as the Syriac Anaphora of the Twelve Apostles, which, in many respects, is to be regarded as parallel to the (Greek) Anaphora of John Chrysostom.

If we consider the latter two anaphoras, we will see what the problem is and what the state of the question is for this family of anaphoras. We do not know how the Syriac anaphora came into being nor do we know how it developed. We have only a few points of reference for dealing with this problem; one of them is the connection between the Anaphora of John Chrysostom and the Anaphora of the Twelve Apostles. Recent studies have shown that at least some parts of the anaphora attributed to John Chrysostom were composed by him, but certainly not starting from scratch; he started with an existing text that was completely like, perhaps even identical to, the Syriac Anaphora of the Twelve Apostles, and to it he attached his own material, which enriched the anaphora theologically.

4.1. The Western Syrian Anaphora

Since all the anaphoras had an origin, it is worthwhile for us to inquire into the origin of the pair of anaphoras just mentioned: the Anaphora of the Twelve Apostles and the Anaphora of St. John Chrysostom. It is possible that the Anaphora of the Twelve Apostles and, by way of it, the Anaphora of Chrysostom derived from a common Syrian source that can explain the rise and development of the structure of the anaphoras of this liturgical family. The argument has three steps.

(1) In this pair of anaphoras the *Post-Sanctus* is very interesting; it is identical in both texts[93] and clearly subdivided into two parts: the first repeats the theme of the *Sanctus*, while the second, which consists of a citation of John 13:1, introduces the account of institution.[94] The citation is, then, a transitional and purely redactional bit of text that serves to link the *Sanctus* to the account of institution. The text of the

---

[93] "Together with these powers, O kind and merciful Lord, we too cry out and say: You are holy and completely holy, as is your only-begotten Son and your Holy Spirit. You are holy and completely holy, and your glory is magnificent, you who so loved your world that you gave your only-begotten Son in order that everyone who believes in him may not perish but may have everlasting life" (Hänggi-Pahl, 224: Anaphora of John Chrysostom, and 266: Anaphora of the Twelve Apostles).

[94] In fact, in the Gospel of John the sentence introduces the account of the Last Supper.

Post-Sanctus consists wholly of a citation of what has gone before and an introduction to what follows; it is a text that lacks a theme of its own and is explainable solely by its function. This supposes that the *Sanctus* and the account of the Last Supper preceded the *Post-Sanctus,* which connects them, and that the latter was composed at a second stage, when the *Sanctus* and the account of institution had been set side by side and there was need of connecting them. This means, in turn, that one of the two texts was already part of the anaphora, while the other was introduced later. Which of the two was part of the original structure of the anaphora, and which was added later?

(2) For an answer we must fall back on some patristic homilies on the mysteries that show the *Sanctus* to be already part of the structure of the Syrian anaphora when the account of institution had not yet been introduced. In some mystagogies from the end of the fourth century the commentary on the Eucharist is done in two stages, giving rise to two different homilies. This is the case, for example, with Cyril of Jerusalem, who comments on the account of the Last Supper in his fourth mystagogical homily, while in the fifth he comments on the anaphora, which includes the *Sanctus* but not the account of institution. Something similar is to be seen in the mystagogical homilies of Theodore of Mopsuestia.

Given this fact, we ask ourselves whether this subdivision supposes that the anaphora did not yet contain the account of the Last Supper.[95] If we look only at the homilies of Cyril, the data are not sufficient for resolving the problem, but if we also take into account Theodore's homilies on the mysteries (known also as catechetical or mystagogical homilies), we can reach a positive result. These homilies supply three very important pieces of information: (a) In Theodore's view the rites are a norm which he calls either "law of the Church"[96] or "law of the priesthood" (or of the "pontiff"),[97] depending on whether the liturgical

---

[95] See, e.g., E. J. Cutrone, "The Liturgical Setting of the Institution Narrative in the Early East Syrian Tradition," in *Time and Community. In Honor of Thomas Julian Talley,* ed. J. N. Alexander (NPM Studies in Church Music and Liturgy; Washington, D.C., 1990) 105–14. The most recent writer to deal with this subject is S. Verhelst, "L'histoire de la liturgie melkite de saint Jacques. Interprétations anciennes et nouvelles," *POC* 43 (193) 229–72.

[96] Within this category Theodore distinguishes a "law of the Church from the beginning," when a particular liturgical usage has a positive foundation in the New Testament.

[97] It is the *Ordo* itself that poses the problem in this fashion.

rites are part of the *Rituale* (the liturgical book to be described under point 3, below) or are not part of the *Rituale* but are in force for the liturgy being actually celebrated. In the second case, there is question of rites recently introduced and dependent on a decision of the bishop.[98]

(b) The anaphora does not contain the account of the Last Supper, but there is something equivalent, since within the account of the economy there is mention of the *traditio mysteriorum,* which is the patristic equivalent of the later concept of the institution of the Eucharist. (c) The account of the *traditio mysteriorum* was not fixed, but left to the discretion of the celebrant.[99] I do not think that the presence or absence of a mention of the institution was left to the free choice of the bishop, since it was henceforward part of the anaphora. On the other hand, it was up to each celebrant how to formulate this mention and how to connect it with what preceded and followed.

(3) Our problem—the common root of the Anaphoras of John Chrysostom and of the Twelve Apostles—receives an exact answer when we consider the archaic *Rituale*[100] or *Ordo* which Theodore transcribes for us and which, unfortunately for us here, has never been studied. At the beginning of each of the five mystagogical homilies Theodore cites in its entirety that part of the *Ordo,*[101] the rites of which are to be commented on in the body of the homily.[102] Therefore the *Ordo* existed as a separate document and one that was autonomous

[98] The description "law of the priesthood" is an accurate sign of the fact that a liturgical rite has developed by comparison with its source.

[99] It is possible that in Theodore's text there are also elements belonging to the liturgical text actually being used; as a matter of fact, he says: "It is this, and similar things, that the pontiff says in this sacred liturgy." F. van de Paverd attaches great importance to this passage, and on the basis of it asserts the extreme difficulty of establishing the exact state of an anaphoral formulary at Antioch at the end of the fourth century; see his *Zur Geschichte der Messliturgie in Antiocheia und Konstantinopel gegen Ende des vierten Jahrhunderts. Analyse der Quellen bei Johannes Chrysostomos* (Rome, 1970) 276.

[100] The *Ordo* was a very short text containing only the rites of baptism and the Eucharist.

[101] We ought to call this document an *Ordo,* since this technical term from the Latin liturgy is especially suited to describing the nature and characteristics of the document, which is regarded as a liturgical book. Theodore refers to it as to an authoritative *Ordo,* to the point of calling it "the law of the Church."

[102] Theodore places the relevant text of the Ritual at the beginning of each *Catechetical Homily,* before launching into his mystagogy (as if it was a citation in the proper sense); he introduces it with the caption: "Text of the book." The *Ordo* is thus independent of the homily itself.

in relation to the homily. In the course of the catechesis Theodore successively cites, verbatim, the statements of the *Ordo* having to do with the rite being described and commented on at that point.[103]

If, now, we compare the rites described in the *Ordo* with the rites being described and commented on by Theodore, we find that there is not a complete identity: The *Ordo* tells us of a liturgy older than the one celebrated in the time of Theodore of Mopsuestia. Thus in a homily Theodore comments on the *traditio mysteriorum,* while the *Ordo* says nothing about it.[104] Again, in a homily Theodore comments on a pneumatological epiclesis (described as "law of the priesthood"), which is not present in the *Ordo,* although the source text on the basis of which the epiclesis will be constructed is already identifiable: a petition just before the intercessions.[105] In conclusion, the structure of the anaphora in the old liturgical book cited by Theodore is the following: (a) opening dialogue; (b) praise of God (at the end of which should come the offering of the praise itself[106]); (c) *Sanctus;* (d) epicletic invocation; (e) intercession for the living and the dead. This description shows clearly that there was no account of institution and nothing that would make us think of its existence.

After having established that the *Sanctus* was a constitutive part of this anaphoral structure (the account of institution would enter it only in a second phase, after the epiclesis had taken shape), let us return to the two texts that are our concern: the Anaphoras of the Twelve Apostles and of St. John Chrysostom. I began by noting that the *Post-Sanctus* has two parts, the first connected with the *Sanctus* and the second introducing the account of institution. Theodore also

[103] The complete correspondence between the text of the *Ordo* that is cited before the homily, and the citation of individual phrases from it within the homily, leads B. Botte to say that the text of the *Ordo* is reliable and deserves full trust. He commits himself so radically to this position that, when faced with an occasional discrepancy between the *Ordo* and a phrase from it in the body of the homily, he concludes that there must have been an interpolation; see "Le baptême dans l'église syrienne," OS 1 (1956) 140f.

[104] *Homily* 16, in *Les homélies catéchétiques de Théodore de Mopsueste,* ed. R. Tonneau and R. Devreesse (Studi e testi 145; Vatican City, 1949) 531–33.

[105] The text of the *Ordo* asks only "that the grace of the Spirit may come upon all those who are assembled" (*Homily* 16; Tonneau–Devreesse, 533).

[106] The text of the *Ordo* does not mention this offering, but I think it must have been contained in some stage of the development of the Ritual, since it is an element in the anaphora on which Theodore is commenting, even though his thinking on the subject of offering moves along entirely different lines.

has the *Post-Sanctus,* but it contains only the first part, the one that refers back to the *Sanctus;* the *Ordo,* however, did not have this embolism, but only the diaconal admonition. All of this shows that the account of institution entered this type of anaphora when the *Sanctus* was already present and when the *Post-Sanctus* already existed as a trinitarian embolism. To this would be added the citation from John 13:1 in order to introduce the account of the Last Supper.

Given this state of affairs, we can try to remove the account of institution from the Anaphoras of the Twelve Apostles and of Chrysostom and see what the resultant structure is. The removal of the account of institution (and, of course, the anamnesis–offering) leaves the following structure: (a) opening dialogue; (b) praise of God (at the end of which is the offering of the praise); (c) *Sanctus* with embolism; (d) epicletic invocation; (e) intercession for the living and the dead. This anaphoral structure is the same as that seen in the *Ordo* cited by Theodore, with the addition of some developments found also in the anaphora of Theodore's Church, such as the trinitarian embolism of the *Post-Sanctus.* It is a rather strange structure that has no parallel in any of the other paleoanaphoras I have been studying. Nonetheless, it is a paleoanaphoral structure that was at the basis of the important Syrian family of anaphoras.

In this anaphora, praise of God is thought of as taking the form of the heavenly liturgy, which is described on the lines of Isaiah 6:1-3: The choirs of angels singing the hymn of praise that proclaims the divine name. Here we can see the concept of worship peculiar to this Church: the highest form of worship takes place in the heavens and is carried out by the angelic choirs that celebrate the name of God; consequently, the earthly liturgy possesses cultic value because it participates in the heavenly worship. The introduction to the *Sanctus,* with its description of the angelic choirs, is a very important part of the anaphora because it describes the heavenly assembly and liturgy to which the Church on earth unites itself. The Eucharist is thus conceived as a participation in the angelic liturgy, from which it derives its value as worship.[107] It is for this reason that the *Sanctus* is the central point of these anaphoras and the high point of the celebration.

---

[107] It is important to recall that the Cherubim and Seraphim had also been given a Christological and pneumatological interpretation; see E. Lanne, "Cherubim et Seraphim. Essai d'interprétation du chapitre X de la *Démonstration* de saint Irénée," *RSR* 43 (1955) 524–35.

4.2. The Eastern Syrian Anaphora

The Anaphora of the Apostles Addai and Mari,[108] which belongs to the East Syrian or Chaldean Church, has a peculiarity that has made it famous: it lacks the account of institution in the form of an account of the Last Supper.

The question arises of why this anaphora lacks the account of institution: did it never have it, or did it lose it as a result of the liturgical

[108] E. C. Ratcliff, "The Original Form of the Anaphora of Addai and Mari," *JTS* 30 (1928–29) 223–32; A. Raes, "Le Récit de l'institution eucharistique dans l'anaphore chaldéenne et malabare des Apôtres," *OCP* 10 (1944) 216–26; B. Botte, "L'anaphore chaldéenne des Apôtres," *OCP* 15 (1949) 259–76; idem, "L'épiclèse dans les liturgies syriennes orientales," *SE* 6 (1954) 49–72; H. Engberding, "Zum anaphorischen Fürbittgebet des Ostsyrischen Liturgie der Apostle Addai(j) und Mar(j)," *OC*, N.S. 42 (1957) 102–24; B. Botte, "Problèmes de l'anaphore syrienne des Apôtres Addai et Mari," *OS* 10 (1965) 89–106; W. F. Macomber, "The Oldest Known Text of the Anaphora of the Apostles Addai and Mari," *OCP* 32 (1966) 335–71; B. Botte, "Les anaphores syriennes orientales," in *Eucharisties d'Orient et d'Occident* II, ed. B. Botte, et al. (Lex orandi 47; Paris, 1970) 7–24; D. Webb, "La liturgie nestorienne des Apôtres Addai et Mari dans la tradition manuscrite," in ibid., 25–49; W. F. Macomber, "The Maronite and Chaldean Versions of the Anaphora of the Apostles," *OCP* 37 (1971) 55–84; J. Vellian, "The Anaphoral Structure of Addai and Mari Compared to the Berakoth Preceding the Shema in the Synagogue Morning Service," *Mus* 85 (1972) 201–23; R. J. Galvin, "Addai and Mari Revisited: The State of the Question," *EL* 87 (1973) 383–414; W. F. Macomber, "A Theory of the Origin of the Syrian, Maronite and Chaldean Rites," *OCP* 39 (1973) 235–42; J.-M. Sanchez Caro, "La anafora de Addai y Mari y la anafora maronita Sarrar: intento de reconstrucción de la fuente primitiva común," *OCP* 43 (1977) 41–69; W. F. Macomber, "A History of the Chaldean Mass," *Worship* 51 (1977) 107–20; idem, "The Sources for a Study of the Chaldean Mass," ibid., 523–36; B. D. Spinks, "The Original Form of the Anaphora of the Apostles: A Suggestion in the Light of the Maronite Sharar," *EL* 91 (1977) 146–61; idem, *Addai and Mari—The Anaphora of the Apostles: A Text for Students* (Grove Liturgical Study 24; Bramcote Nottinghamshire, 1980); H. A. J. Wegman, "Pledooi voor een Tekst de Anaphora van de Apostelen Addai en Mari," *Bijdragen* 40 (1979) 15–43; W. F. Macomber, "The Ancient Form of the Anaphora of the Apostles," in *East of Byzantium: Syria and Armenia in the Formative Period* (Washington, D.C., 1982) 73–88; B. D. Spinks, "Sacerdoce et offrande dans les *Koushapè* des anaphores syriennes orientales," *MD*, no. 154 (1983) 107–26; idem, "Eucharistic Offering in the East Syrian Anaphora," *OCP* 50 (1984) 347–71; idem, "Addai and Mari and the Institution Narrative: The Tantalizing Evidence of Gabriel Qatraya," *EL* 98 (1984) 60–67; W. Marston, "A Solution to the Enigma of 'Addai and Mari,'" *EL* 103 (1989) 79–91; J. Vadakkel, *The East Syrian Anaphora of Mar Theodore of Mopsuestia. Critical Edition, English Translation and Study* (Publications of the Oriental Institute of India; Vadavathoor Kottayam, 1989); A. Gelston, *The Eucharistic Prayer of Addai and Mari* (Oxford, 1992); B. D. Spinks, *Worship: Prayers from the East* (Washington, D.C., 1993).

reform by Isho'yab III in the seventh century? We know for certain that the oldest manuscript of this anaphora, the text from Mar Esa'ya,[109] does not have the account of institution, and we can therefore state that the manuscript tradition suggests the absence of this part of the anaphora.

In this Eucharistic Prayer there is the following sequence of parts: (1) praise, confession, adoration, and exaltation of the Name of the Father and of the Son and of the Holy Spirit; (2) introduction to the *Sanctus*, and the *Sanctus* itself; (3) *Post-Sanctus* (with trinitarian development and *apologiae*), recited quietly as a "private" prayer; (4) renewal of the theme of the *Sanctus*, but with a transitional phrase using the word "powers" or "armies"[110] that begins a great thanksgiving addressed to the Son; this becomes a real confession of faith, since it tells of Christ's saving actions; (5) a concluding doxology in which praise, worship, gratitude, and adoration are "offered" to God;[111] (7) within the intercessions there is the offering of the Body and Blood of the Lord; (8) mention of the institution: "as you taught us"; (9) followed by the intercessions; (10) the tradition of the mysteries; (11) a pneumatological epiclesis; and (12) a doxology. This structure is confirmed both by the sixth-century anaphora[112] and by the Anaphora III of St. Peter the Apostle,[113] which is a text paralleling the Anaphora of the Apostles Addai and Mari and is derived from the same source.[114]

4.3. Jewish Origin of This Family of Anaphoras

In order to convey an idea of the structure of the Syrian anaphora I have suggested as its remote source the *Ordo* that is cited at the

[109] Macomber, "The Oldest Known Text" (see note 108).

[110] "And together with these heavenly powers we too, Lord, your weak, frail, and infirm servants, give you thanks" (Hänggi-Pahl, 377).

[111] On the different verbs for offering in these texts see Spinks, "Eucharistic Offering in East Syrian Anaphoras" (see note 108).

[112] British Museum, Add. 14669; see R. H. Connolly, "Sixth-Century Fragments of an East-Syrian Anaphora," *OC* 12–14 (1925) 99–128.

[113] Hänggi-Pahl, 410.

[114] The only difference to be emphasized is the presence of the account of institution, which is placed after the tradition of the mysteries and completed by the citation of John 6:51, followed by 11:26 and 10:10: "and we remember your body and blood, which we offer to you on your living and holy altar, as you, our hope, taught us in your holy gospel and told us: 'I am the living bread that has come down from heaven' in order that 'in me' mortals 'might have life'" (Hänggi-Pahl, 412).

beginning of the mystagogical homilies of Theodore of Mopsuestia. There are, however, differences of structure between the West Syrian and East Syrian families. My view is that the differences are due to the different development of the two families of texts out of the same source, and especially because of the different points at which the pneumatological epiclesis was inserted: before the intercessions at Antioch, and after the intercessions in eastern Syria. Moreover, the difference becomes clearer due to the different points at which the account of institution was inserted: after the *Sanctus* at Antioch, and after the tradition of the mysteries, within the intercessions, in eastern Syria.

Is it possible to go back even further? In other words, is it possible to establish a Jewish source of the *Ordo* that Theodore uses? It is difficult to give an answer, because the *Ordo* is little more than an outline and a list of themes. Perhaps, however, some good result may be reached by applying to the *Ordo* the results of studies of the Anaphora of Addai and Mari. A series of studies, begun by Vellian, has pointed to the Jewish liturgy of morning prayer as a source of this anaphora; in fact, the *Sanctus* of this anaphora is a combination of Daniel 7:10 and Isaiah 6:2, as in the *Qedushah (Sanctus)* of the *Yotser*,[115] that is, the first of the blessings that surround the morning recital of the *Shema'*. But this is not sufficient to assert that the *Sanctus* of this anaphora originated in the *Yotser*, since this Jewish liturgy, as attested by the documents from the Cairo Genizah, lacked the *Qedushah (Sanctus)*.[116] Brian Spinks adds that the celebration of the Name of God in the heavens and on earth, as we find it in the Anaphora of Addai and Mari, echoes the blessings, including the *Qedushah (Sanctus)*, that are characteristic of the *Ma'aséh Merkavah*.[117]

[115] B. D. Spinks, *The Sanctus in the Eucharistic Prayer* (Cambridge, 1991) 60.

[116] A. Gelston, *The Eucharistic Prayer of Addai and Mari* (Oxford, 1992) 70.

[117] Spinks, *The Sanctus* (note 115, above), 60. The Anaphora III of St. Peter the Apostle, which parallels the Anaphora of Addai and Mari, depends on both the *Qedushah* of the *Yotser* and 1 Enoch 61 (Hänggi-Pahl, 61).

Chapter 7

Thematic Developments in the Eucharistic Liturgy

1. THE *DIDACHE*

In this document the themes of thanksgiving are to be found in three successive "Eucharists,"[1] two in chapter 9 and one in chapter 10, the latter being the Christian *Birkat ha-Mazon* and the most important of the texts. On the other hand, there are only two prayers of petition, the first in chapter 10 and the second in chapter 9 (drawn from the one in chapter 10).

Before the meal, in the Eucharist over the cup, thanks is given for the vine of David and, in the Eucharist over the bread, thanks is given for life and knowledge. The thanksgiving after the meal says: "We thank you for your holy Name which you have made to dwell in our hearts and for the faith, the knowledge, and the immortality which you have made known to us through Jesus your servant." The themes of life and knowledge are very close to those of faith, knowledge, and immortality, but I ought to explain briefly the remaining two themes: the dwelling of God in the hearts of the faithful and the vine of David.

1.1. The Vine of David

The devout Jew says a blessing over the cup for the "fruit of the vine."[2] *Didache* 9.2, makes its own the theme of the vine but changes the point of reference: The vine becomes the "vine of David" and is an object of revelation by Jesus. We cannot accept that the "vine of

---

[1] Two before the meal, and one after it.

[2] "Blessed are you, Lord, God of the universe, who createst the fruit of the vine" (Blessing over the cup in the rite of the *Qiddush* at the beginning of the meal).

David" signifies Christ, since in this context the revealer is distinguished clearly from what he reveals. W. Rordorf has shown that in Judaism there was an important "current of ideas that represented the Davidic kingdom in the form of a vine."[3] From this it follows that the great work of God for which thanks is given in *Didache* 9.2, is the kingdom of David or, in other words, the economy of salvation that was carried out in the history of Israel.[4] David had played a decisive part in this economy; it was he who accomplished the works of God and dedicated himself to them with his whole being, and it was for this reason that he was called God's servant *(pais):*[5] "By the hand of my servant David I will save my people Israel from the hand of the Philistines, and from the hand of all their enemies."[6]

In this same strophe of the *Didache* (9.2), Jesus, too, is called *pais,* since it is through the work of Jesus that God has revealed the vine of David.[7] Jesus is the eschatological prophet who is the reality

[3] It is worth recalling here that the vine was one of the most widespread symbols in Jewish art, from coins (see P. Romanoff, *Jewish Symbols on Ancient Jewish Coins* [Philadelphia, 1944] 23ff.) to mosaic paintings (see E. R. Goodenough, *Jewish Symbols in the Greco-Roman Period* [New York, 1964] 79ff.). In Herod's temple, which was destroyed in 70, there was a huge golden vine hanging over the entrance gate. According to Flavius Josephus' description of it, the clusters of grapes were as large as a man and, according to the Mishnah, it took three hundred priests to carry it. Rordorf refuses to admit that the description was a pious fraud. In Judaism the image of the vine expresses the whole messianic expectation of the people. See W. Rordorf, "La vigne et le vin dans la tradition juive et chrétienne," in his *Liturgie, foi et vie des premiers chrétiens. Etudes patristiques* (Théologie historique 53; Paris, 1989) 493–508.

[4] In my opinion, Rordorf's interpretation is better grounded than that which J. Jeremias takes over from R. Eisler: "'for the holy vine of David your servant,' that is, the vine of which David speaks (Ps 80:9ff.)." See J. Jeremias, "Pais Theou," *TDNT* 5:700.

[5] This title is not necessarily messianic (Jeremias, ibid., 680–82); in fact, it is for the most part connected with the activity of any individual who does God's work in a special way; this connection finds expression especially in prayers. Elijah prays as follows on Carmel: "O Lord, God of Abraham, Isaac, and Israel, let it be known this day that you are God in Israel, that I am your servant, and that I have done all these things at your bidding" (1 Kgs 18:36).

[6] 2 Samuel 3:18.

[7] When Jesus is given the title *pais,* he is as it were set beside David as protagonist in God's saving work. The reign of David is seen as a fulfillment of the divine promise of the gift of the land, which is the Old Testament theme par excellence. David is the man *blessed* by God, "and the Lord gave victory to David wherever he went" (2 Sam 8:14). We should note especially that David's conquest is crowned

prefigured by David and his work for the people. In this perspective, Christianity is still a development and unfolding of Judaism, within which it remains.

1.2. *The Dwelling of God in Hearts*

The object of the thanksgiving is the "holy Name" of God which he has "made to dwell in our hearts." This statement is very archaic in tone. E. Peterson asks whether the "name" here is meant to refer to Jesus,[8] inasmuch as the theology of the Name is applied also to Christ in the New Testament.[9] I think, however, that in this case a christological interpretation of the "Name" cannot be sustained. We must take into account what S. Giet says when he connects these words with the following sentence: ". . . You created all things for your name's sake." If the *pais* of the verse we are examining is a christological title, it must follow that God has created everything for his *pais*; but this conclusion is unacceptable, because *pais* signifies the means by which revelation and the divine gifts are given, and not the purpose of creation. On this grounds Giet says he finds it difficult to interpret "name" here as a christological title.[10]

The correct interpretation is different and it emerges from Old Testament cultic usage. The place where God makes his name dwell becomes a temple and place of worship: Here people celebrate the liturgy before God who is present. Deuteronomistic theology teaches that the temple of God is the place in which he has made his name dwell (Deut 12:11) in order that it may be invoked. In this theology "name" stands for "God," but is not fully identical with him. This "name" is, in fact, a kind of hypostasis that is in every way like God but is not completely identical with him.[11] We may say that the role of the "name" is located between God and human beings; it is, however,

---

by the capture of Jerusalem, which will be known as the City of David; thus David and the entire house of Israel form but a single people around their God. Once all this is applied to Christ, it acquires a new meaning and a greater scope, which, however, are neither different from nor opposed to the Israelite economy of salvation.

[8] E. Peterson, "Über einige Probleme der Didache-Überlieferung," in his *Frühkirche, Judentum und Gnosis* (Rome–Freiburg–Vienna, 1959) 179.

[9] See Acts 3:16.

[10] S. Giet, *L'énigme de la Didachè* (Publications de la Faculté des lettres de l'Universitè de Strasbourg 149; Paris, 1970) 211.

[11] T.N.D. Mettinger, *The Dethronement of Sabaoth. Studies in the Shem and Kabod Theologies* (Coniectanea biblica. Old Testament Series 18; Lund, 1982) 130.

something more than a mere intermediary, since the "name," as such, belongs to the realm of the divine. In the Deuteronomistic theology of the name, the sanctuary, the place where sacrifices are offered, becomes a house of prayer (1 Kgs 8:29ff.).[12]

All this information is to be applied to *Didache* 10.2: here, too, God's name dwells, but the place of dwelling is the heart. It follows that the hearts of believers are the place of God's presence, which is mediated by his Name that dwells there, and that in this place a liturgy consisting of prayer is celebrated. This theme will subsequently be developed by Paul, who replaces the theology of the Name with a theology of the Spirit: "Because you are sons, God has sent the Spirit of his Son into our hearts, crying, 'Abba! Father!'"[13]

Didache 10.2, then, is saying that the newness Christ has brought consists in the revelation of a new place of worship and a new liturgy: The temple is no longer a building, but the hearts of the faithful, and the new liturgy consists, therefore, in the invocation of God. In conclusion: Through Jesus, God the Father reveals the nature of Israel and the temple, thereby performing a saving action that has, as its fruit, knowledge, faith, life, and immortality.

1.3. The Prayer of Petition

The third strophe of the *Birkat ha-Mazon* contains a petition; in *Didache* 10, the third strophe likewise consists of a petition: "Remember your Church, Lord, and free it from every evil and make it perfect in your love. And gather it from the four winds as a holy Church, in your kingdom which you have prepared for it. For yours is the kingdom and the glory for ever and ever" (10.5).

The content of this text does not correspond to that of the third strophe of the *Birkat ha-Mazon*: the *Didache* speaks of the Church and the kingdom of God, while the *Birkat ha-Mazon* speaks of Israel, Jerusalem, the Temple which is God's dwelling, the dynasty of David, and the rebuilding of Jerusalem. It is easy to say that there is a theological correspondence between the two texts, since the Church is the new Israel and therefore that the theology of the Church is heir to the theology of the first Israel. This may be true from a theological point of

---

[12] In the Old Testament God assures the people of his presence in the place he has chosen in which to make his Name dwell, and this presence is the way in which he helps and saves his people.

[13] Galatians 4:6f. See also the development in Romans 8:15.

view, but it does not relieve us from the obligation to look for a Jewish source that is close enough to explain *Didache* 10.5. In addition to this methodological argument, I must point out that the passage in the *Didache* is based on the idea of a "gathering" of the Church in the kingdom of God, and this idea is not expressed at all in the texts of the *Birkat ha-Mazon*.[14]

It is still worth our while to look back to the article of L. Finkelstein, for it sheds light on the genesis of our text. That great scholar established that the prayer for Jerusalem was composed during the period of the Maccabean struggle, when the temple and the altar were under pagan control.[15] From the connection between the earliest form of the *Amidah* and Sirach 36:11-14 (RSV numbering), it follows that this prayer was composed during the period between Sirach and the *Book of Jubilees*.[16]

In Sirach 36:10-14, verse 10 speaks of the gathering of the tribes; verse 11 asks for mercy on the people of Israel, whom God calls his firstborn; verse 12 asks for mercy on Jerusalem, the dwelling place of God, and verse 14 asks that the glory of God may once again fill his Temple. The *Birkat ha-Mazon* contains the themes of verses 12-14, while *Didache* 10.5, has only the gathering theme of verse 11. This theme of gathering is also found in the *Amidah* and in the *Ahabhah Rabbah*, the second of the two blessings that precede the *Shema'*. In this second prayer there is no reference to Jerusalem, while the *Amidah* has the themes both of gathering (tenth blessing) and of Jerusalem (fourteenth blessing).

The formulation of the gathering theme that most resembles what is said in the *Didache* is that of Rav Amram Gaon[17] (ninth century A.D.), while the text given by Rav Saadja Gaon (tenth century) is more distant from that of the *Didache*. We know that, generally speaking, the

[14] Even J. W. Riggs, who goes very carefully into the sources of *Didache* 9–10, points to the third strophe of the *Birkat ha-Mazon* as the source of *Didache* 10.5, whereas he had shortly before pointed to the *Amidah* as source of *Didache* 9.4, because of the theme of gathering from the four winds. See J. W. Riggs, "From Gracious Table to Sacramental Elements. The Traditions-History of *Didache* 9 and 10," *The Second Century* 4 (1984) 92–93, 94, 97.

[15] L. Finkelstein, "The Development of the *Amidah*," *JQR*, N.S., 16 (1925–26) 1–43, 137–70.

[16] L. Finkelstein, "The Birkat ha-Mazon," *JQR*, N.S., 19 (1928–29) 220.

[17] "And proclaim our deliverance, so that we may be gathered together from the four corners of the earth" (Hänggi-Pahl, 49).

text of Rav Saadja Gaon has been less reworked and contains a more archaic redaction of the texts, despite the fact that it is from a later time than that of Rav Amram Gaon. The Palestinian redaction agrees with that of Rav Saadja Gaon and not with that of Rav Amram Gaon. The same observation holds for the various redactions of the blessings of the *Shema'*: the version of Rav Amram contains the words: "Lead us back in peace from the four corners of the earth and allow us to enter as free people into our land,"[18] while the shorter Palestinian version does not have them. When there is question of these Jewish texts, it is really difficult to propose dates because the material contained in them may be from a much earlier time[19] and have been in use in prayers that differed from one another.

At this point, and by way of conclusion, it must be said that *Didache* 10.5 has moved away from the *Birkat ha-Mazon* and has drawn on other Jewish prayers, such as the tenth blessing of the *Amidah*, or on the *Ahabhah Rabbah*, the second of the blessings before the *Shema'*. We do not know whether at the time of the *Didache* these texts already had their long form; we do know, however, that the source of this long form of the sentence about gathering was Sirach 36:11, the passage which, in its immediately following verses, was the source of the third strophe of the *Birkat ha-Mazon.* Sirach 36:11 expresses its plea for gathering in this fashion: *"synagage pasas phylas"* ("gather all the tribes"), while the *Didache* prays for the Church: *"synaxon autên apo tessarôn anemôn"* ("gather it from the four winds") (10.5). I can sum up by saying that the third strophe, that is, the petition in *Didache* 10.5, does not go back to the *Birkat ha-Mazon*, but goes back (directly or by way of the other Jewish prayers mentioned) to Sirach 36:11ff. and takes its theme of gathering from there. Sirach 36:11ff. is also the source of the third strophe of the *Birkat ha-Mazon* for the themes other than that of gathering.

In Judaism the gathering of the scattered was already a typical theme in prayer of petition to God, because it was one intrinsically connected with the covenant that was the object of the blessing.[20]

[18] Ibid., 38.

[19] For example, F. Manns gives a series of New Testament texts that parallel phrases and expressions in the *Ahabhah Rabbah;* see his, *La prière d'Israël à l'heure de Jésus* (Studium Biblicum Franciscanum, Analecta 22; Jerusalem, 1986) 138f.

[20] This perspective may also be seen in much later writers, such as Rav Saadja Gaon; see L. A. Hoffman, *The Canonisation of the Synagogue Service* (Studies in Judaism and Christianity in Antiquity 4; Notre Dame–London, 1979) 45.

The third strophe, then, of the Christian *Birkat ha-Mazon,* namely, *Didache* 10, asks for the gathering of the Church into the kingdom of God. This gathering is already a part of salvation, and for this reason the Church thus gathered is called holy. This is the end toward which this petition is moving from its opening words: "Remember your Church, Lord, and free it from every evil and make it perfect[21] in your love." The gathering into the kingdom of God is the response to this petition.

2. THE LITURGY IN 1 CORINTHIANS 10–11

The Pauline texts on the Eucharist do not show any special interest in themes of thanksgiving, even though Pauline theology as such is very interested in these themes. He not only insists that the faithful should give thanks in every place,[22] but he himself gives an example of this practice by beginning almost all of his letters with an abundant prayer of thanksgiving. Some authors have thought that they could determine from these passages what the thanksgiving was like in Paul's own celebration of the Eucharist. In my opinion, that is a road that cannot be successfully traveled, since we do not know what custom Paul followed in the eucharistic liturgy; he does not say that this custom was the same as he followed in his own spirituality of thanksgiving to God.

What we do know with certainty is this: Paul conceives of the Eucharist as the sacrament of unity (to use the terminology of a later time).

2.1. *The Theme of Unity in the Old Testament*

In Jeremiah's "book of consolation" (chapters 37–38) we find the theme of the scattering of the children of Israel and their reunification after the return from exile. Here we have the most direct reference to the connection between the action of scattering, which is the work of wicked shepherds, and the action of gathering, which is proper to God:[23] God will accomplish all this because of his great love. It follows from this that the act of bringing back the scattered and uniting

---

[21] *Teleiôsai* means a complete dedication to the ways of God. See A. Vöobus, *Liturgical Traditions in the Didache* (Papers of the Esthonian Theological Society in Exile 16; Stockholm, 1968) 127.

[22] Here is one passage among many: "Give thanks in all circumstances; for this is the will of God in Christ Jesus for you" (1 Thess 5:18).

[23] D. Marzotto, *L'unità degli uomini nel Vangelo di Giovanni* (Brescia, 1977) 40.

them in the land of Israel is the act by which God saves. The act of gathering or uniting begins to emerge as a saving act. In Ezekiel we have the same promise on God's part, but a new datum is added, the importance of the Name in the work of salvation: It is because of his Name that God will act.[24] He will provide a single shepherd: "my servant David" (34:23). In Deuteronomy, unity has for its condition that the people listen to the voice of God and have life as a result. By his word God is the cause of unity and the source of life: unity and life are parallel; all of this has a direct echo in the Gospel of John.[25]

In Isaiah 60:4, 22, the special contribution of the Septuagint is the understanding of salvation as a gathering together.[26] This contribution is not, however, a deviation or departure, but simply a reinforcement of a theme found elsewhere in the Masoretic text. The purpose of the gathering here is the recognition that God is the Lord who saves. In Isaiah 66:18-21, the theme of gathering is enriched by being placed in a universalist and eschatological perspective and by being given as its ultimate goal the vision of God's glory. The eschatological aspect is further developed in Isaiah 27:12-13: When Yahweh shall have conquered even Leviathan, the symbol of pagan power (27:1), the gathering of the dispersed will be possible.[27]

To all this must be added Jeremiah 39:29-41, which closely links the theme of gathering with the theme of the covenant; the covenant is described as an event that reaches into the interior world, into the human heart, from which will come the following of God's ways. According to Second Isaiah God will manifest his glory by saving his people, that is, by gathering them together from the four corners of the earth: "In chapter 49 this mission is entrusted to the Servant of Yahweh, who will gather people together from every part of the world."[28] In the Book of Micah unity will be assured because it will be the Lord who reigns.

"In the third century the idea of gathering becomes the object of prayer that is based on the ancient promises." And again: "Finally, in the second Book of Maccabees (1:24-29; see 2:7), God is called upon to 'make holy,' 'gather together,' and 'preserve' his 'people,' by freeing

[24] Ibid., 43.
[25] Ibid., 49.
[26] Ibid., 54.
[27] Ibid., 57.
[28] Ibid., 65.

them in all regions of the earth and bringing them to the holy place (see 2:16-18) so that all peoples will 'know' that 'you are our God.'"[29]

The Jewish liturgy regarded all these themes as its own and made them a formal part of prayers which, according to Heinemann,[30] came to be described as "official" and were given authoritative status, even though room was made for creativity in following the model. The tenth of the Eighteen Blessings reads as follows in the *Seder* of Rav Amram Gaon: "Proclaim our deliverance so that we may gather together from the four corners of the earth. Blessed art thou, Lord, who gathers the exiles of his people Israel."[31] The summation in the *Ahab-hah Rabbah* is even more specific: "Our Father . . . Bring us back to peace from the four corners (or: winds) of the earth and enable us to enter freely into our land. For you are the God who works salvation, and you have chosen us among all peoples and languages, and have led us to your great and holy Name."[32]

We have seen that the *Didache* inherited this line of thought and that it conceives of salvation as a gathering of the Church into the kingdom of God in the eschatological times.[33]

2.2. *The Eucharist in 1 Corinthians*

But this was not the final stage of development: It is Paul who brings the theme to completion, and after him there are no important developments.

When discussing food offered to idols, Paul appeals to the Corinthians' experience of the Eucharist. He briefly recalls the liturgical facts that were obviously customary in the Church and on them builds an argument concerning the sacramental nature and therefore the "efficacy" of the liturgical action as such, an argument that must therefore be valid for interpreting the case of flesh sacrificed to idols. It is in this perspective that Paul tackles the theme of unity as this is to be seen in the Eucharist at Corinth. From it he draws a first conclusion: Unity is connected with the sacramental nature and the efficacy of

[29] Ibid., 66.
[30] J. Heinemann, *Prayer in the Talmud. Forms and Patterns* (Studia Judaica 9; Berlin–New York, 1977) 13–36.
[31] Hänggi-Pahl, 49.
[32] Ibid., 37f.
[33] "Just as this (bread), broken, scattered on the hills, and gathered again, became one, so may your Church be gathered from the ends of the earth into your kingdom" (*Didache* 9.4).

the Eucharist. Here is his argument: "Because there is one bread, we who are many are one body, for we all partake of the one bread" (1 Cor 10:17).

The unity of the Church as a body is a familiar idea in the letters of Paul. Initially there was question simply of a comparison and metaphor, inasmuch as Paul was applying to the Church of Corinth the apologue, or moral fable, of Menenius Agrippa,[34] but the image soon took on a quite different meaning. Why is the Church the "body of Christ"? Christians live by the life of Christ himself, and he is present in them; we can say that the faithful participate in Christ. For this reason, since they are united, they form a single body, and this body is the body of Christ; because of their unity, Christians are the body of Christ by participation. "Body of Christ," when applied to the Church, is no longer a mere sociological fact nor a literary image, but a reality that has a precise ontological density, namely, that the mystery of the body of Christ is realized in the Church. In the eucharistic liturgy, unity becomes a reality because the faithful share in the one bread which in turn is a communion in the body of Christ.[35]

In Paul's eyes, the efficacy of the liturgy consists in this, that the Sacrament "effects" what it "is," or, if we may so put it, it effects something like itself. The bread is a communion in the body, and therefore those who eat the bread that is broken become the body of Christ. The bread broken is one; therefore those who eat of it become one body. The reference is to the body of Christ that is the Church, which, because of this basic relationship, is one, that is, has unity as an essential attribute. The Eucharist is thus the sacrament of unity: of the unity of the Church insofar as the Church is the body of Christ. Evidence of this Pauline conception is to be seen in 1 Corinthians 11:17-23,[36] when Paul, on seeing that there are divisions in the Church of Corinth, denies that their celebration is the Lord's Supper.

[34] L. Cerfaux, *The Church in the Theology of St. Paul,* trans. G. Webb and A. Walker (New York, 1959) 243.

[35] In the word "communion" Paul is referring to the relation of sacramentality between the bread and the Body of Christ; "communion" can be correctly translated as "sacrament." The eucharistic bread (which we break) puts us in communion with the Body of Christ, because this bread is itself a "communion" in that body.

[36] "Now in the following instructions I do not commend you, because when you come together it is not for the better but for the worse. For, to begin with, when you come together as a church, I hear that there are divisions among you; and to some

We may not ask here whether Paul is asserting the invalidity or simply the unfruitfulness of the Corinthian Eucharist, since these ideas date from a much later time.[37] In Paul's view, and this is true for a long time after him, the liturgy is the liturgy because it corresponds ontologically to the type which Jesus established. In Christian baptism the type is established by the baptism of Jesus in the Jordan, and in the Eucharist the type is Jesus' celebration at the Last Supper. When Paul says: "When you come together, it is not really to eat the Lord's supper" (11:20), he is saying that the Eucharist of the Corinthians no longer has an ontological correspondence to the type which Jesus passed on at the Last Supper. If the Corinthian Eucharist has lost its correspondence to the type, which is the Lord's Supper, it follows that the Corinthian Eucharist is no longer the Lord's Supper. In saying that division has this effect, Paul is putting negatively what he has said in positive terms in 1 Corinthians 10:16-17, namely, that the eucharistic liturgy is essentially a sacrament of the unity of the Church.[38]

2.3. The Advance in Paul beyond the Didache

According to the *Didache* the one bread is a model of the Church's unity, but the model is only an image; according to Paul, however, the model belongs in the realm of sacramentality, so that those who share in the one bread are one body; thus the bread broken, insofar as it is one, becomes a type of the Church's unity. The sacramental conception of the Eucharist and its efficacy is already fully formulated in Paul.

There is an important difference between Paul's conception of the Eucharist and that of the *Didache*, not only because two different ideas of sacramental efficacy are at work but also because there are two different ecclesiologies. That is why in the *Didache* it is the Church that

---

extent I believe it. Indeed, there have to be factions among you, for only so will it become clear who among you are genuine. When you come together it is really to eat the Lord's Supper. For when the time comes to eat, each of you goes ahead with your own supper, and one goes hungry and another becomes drunk. What! Do you not have homes to eat and drink in? Or do you show contempt for the church of God and humiliate those who have nothing? What should I say to you? Should I commend you? In this matter I do not commend you" (1 Cor 11:17-23).

[37] P.-M. Gy, "La notion de validité sacramentelle avant le concile de Trente," *Revue de droit canonique* 28 (1978) 192–202 = *Mélanges J. Gaudemet*.

[38] It follows that, if unity is lacking, the Church's celebration cannot be an act of obedience to, and a fulfillment of Christ's command: "Do this in remembrance of me."

must be made one, while in Paul it is the assembly itself, which he also describes with a simple "we," the many (1 Cor 10:17).[39] If, through and because of the one bread, Christians are in communion with the person of Christ, which is evidently one, it follows that they are also one among themselves.

Such a shift in ecclesiology has a direct connection with the conception of eschatology, which as a result also changes: The focus changes from the last times as the fulfillment of the reign of God, to the Church in its historical form as this manifests itself in the assembly. The consequence of this is immediately clear: the fruit of the Eucharist will be not so much the eschatological unity of the Church in the kingdom of God, as it is in *Didache* 9–10, but each community's unity in history. Unity becomes not an eschatological gift awaited from God in the last times, but a historical commitment which each Church must carry out in order to be in harmony with the Eucharist which it celebrates or, in other and better terms, in order to correspond to the type handed on by Jesus at the Last Supper. In passing from the *Didache* to Paul, the theological theme of unity moves from the dimension of eschatological gift to the dimension of historical commitment; it does not, however, cease to be a divine gift, since its accomplishment comes not from the social and political activity of human beings but from the one bread of the eucharistic celebration.

3. JOHN

In *Didache* 9–10 there are numerous expressions which in their content are also present in the Gospel of John. Since it is not possible to claim a dependence of the *Didache* on John,[40] the objective closeness of the two texts forces us to accept that both came from the same cultural and theological environment and have the same Judeo-Christian traditions as their source. In assessing the connection between the *Didache* and John we may find help in our examination of the relationship between the first letter to the Corinthians and the Eucharist of the *Didache*. If the eucharistic tradition to which the *Didache* bears witness does not yet know the canonical text of John's Gospel but does belong in the same theological environment, and if this tradition

[39] Paul echoes the words of institution of the eucharistic meal: "for you and for the many."

[40] The *Didache* does not have knowledge of the canonical text of the New Testament; see W. Rordorf and A. Tuilier (eds.), *La doctrine des douze apôtres* (SC 248; Paris, 1978) 84.

precedes the first letter to the Corinthians, it follows that it is also earlier than the Gospel of John.

M.-B. Boismard has this to say in his reconstruction of the stages of formation of John's Gospel: "The interest of John II-B for the Eucharist is shown to the use he makes of the ancient eucharistic prayers in the *Didache:* in 6:12-13a, in 11:52, in 15:5-6, and, finally, in 17:6-26."[41] The theme of unity in John can be clearly seen from Boismard's analysis of the miraculous catch in John 21:1-14.[42] To the mention of the fish John adds mention of the bread, thus making a specific reference to the Eucharist, which is the food of Christians. The meaning is clear: The unity of the Church will be preserved despite the large number of people who will be part of it at various times. In all this there is a certain tension in relation to the eucharistic action that is a manifestation of the risen Jesus. The reference to the Eucharist in the Fourth Gospel is further evidenced by the prayer for unity (chapter 17), which belongs to the literary genre of the last will and testament.

These few points already make it clear that John was very familiar with the theological theme of unity. But we may not stop there, since he makes this theme a central one in his gospel by using it to interpret the salvific function of the death of Christ.

In John's Gospel Jesus three times proclaims his future exaltation (3:14; 8:28; 12:32-34) with specific reference to his death. Isaiah 52:13 had spoken of the Servant of God who was to be highly exalted and glorified, but John rereads that passage in a different key, by anticipating, as it were, the exaltation of Jesus to the Father's right hand and identifying it with the Cross.[43] From the cross, the place of his exaltation, Jesus will draw all to himself (12:32). The verb "draw," which is rare in the New Testament, belongs to the theology of unity that is to be found in Jeremiah: God will draw human beings and a people will be born that is rescued from dispersion. We may therefore conclude that the cross of Christ is the source of unity and that it is life.[44]

[41] M.-E. Boismard and A. Lamouille. *Synopse des Quatre Evangiles* III. *L'Evangile de Jean* (Paris, 1977) 56.

[42] In the commentator's symbolic reading, the fish are the human beings who will be caught by the preaching of Peter and the apostles; Peter pulls to shore the net containing 153 fishes, a number that, as early as Augustine, was a symbol of totality and multitude. If this be the case, then the net must prefigure the Church; consequently there is also a symbolic meaning in the detail in verse 11: "Though there were so many [fish], the net was not torn." See Boismard and Lamouille, 485.

[43] Marzotto, *L'unità* (note 23, above), 44.

[44] Ibid., 150 and 146.

This conception is formally expressed in John 11:51-53: "Jesus was about to die for the nation, and not for the nation only, but to gather into one the dispersed children of God."[45] The New Testament writings are in theological agreement that the death for the people is a saving event and gives life. The Gospel of John shares this view but manages to place it in a quite special perspective, since it locates that death within a theology of unity: the death of Jesus has saving power because it yields the unity of the people. For John, then, to say that Jesus died for our salvation and to say that he died for the sake of unity is to say the same thing in two different ways. John 11:51-53 shows that unity and salvation, unity and redemption, are analogous and almost equivalent concepts. "Unity" is part of the vocabulary of redemption: By dying Jesus will move all to believe in him. In this way he will gather around him all who are scattered, both Jews and non-Jews, and this is the same as making them children of God.[46]

4. THE MYSTICAL EUCHARIST

The Eucharist of the *Didache* is as it were a living text that grows as the community develops. One stage in this development is attested by the Mystical Eucharist. We already know that this liturgy is described in Book 7 of the *Apostolic Constitutions* and that the title "Mystical Eucharist," which is not original but was given it by a redactor, simply means "sacramental thanksgiving."

When we set the texts side by side,[47] we see quite clearly the correspondence between the Mystical Eucharist and the *Didache*, its direct source. There are, however, some variations in the later document; they are very few but are very important, both for the structure, which I discussed earlier, and for the text, with which I shall now deal briefly.

4.1. *The Petition*

We saw earlier (Section 2.3 of this chapter) how Paul changes the ecclesiological and eschatological perspective of the *Didache* into one that is liturgical and historical. That is: whereas the *Didache* asks God to gather the Church into his kingdom, Paul speaks of the unity given

---

[45] John is here commenting on the words of Caiphas and declaring them to be an authentic prophecy: Caiphas, being the high priest, prophesied when he said that one man must die for the people lest the entire people perish.

[46] Marzotto, *L'Unità*, 138.

[47] I give such a synopsis in my *L'anafora*, 56–58, 62–64.

the assembly by the efficacy of the Sacrament, or, in other words, by the eating of the one bread. Now, when the Mystical Eucharist takes over the petition in *Didache* 10, it does so with the new Pauline perspective just mentioned; the prayer for unity no longer envisages the Church in its entirety but the members of the assembly or, to use Paul's language, "us."

Here is what the text becomes in the Mystical Eucharist: "Remember your holy Church . . . and gather *us* all in your kingdom which you have prepared for *us.*"[48]

4.2. The Thanksgiving

After reproducing *Didache* 9,[49] the compiler of the Mystical Eucharist adds a narrative development[50] in which, when speaking of salvation, he describes the role of God the Father as one of "sending," with reference to the incarnation of Christ, and as one of "permitting," with reference to the passion. "The compiler thus presents the Father as the source of redemption and the Son as his servant who acts with complete dependence on 'his God and Father.'"[51] The compiler gives pride of place to the idea of Christ as *mediator,* a title that sums up the others that he gives to the Son: angel, prophet, *pais,*[52] and this idea is very much present in the thanksgiving (text given in note 50).

A more careful examination will show that this text is something more than simply a personal insertion of the compiler; it is to be seen as a confession of faith in the true and proper sense (although limited to the area of christology), one which previously had a life of its own and which the compiler introduces at this point and links to the rest of the text by means of one of his preferential themes: Christ as mediator. He has simply inserted at this point in the thanksgiving some

[48] *Les Constitutions apostoliques. Livres VII et VIII,* ed. M. Metzger (SC 336; Paris, 1987) 56. I have italicized *us* in order to bring out better, even philologically, the shift from a prayer for the Church to a prayer for the members of the assembly.

[49] "We give you thanks, our Father, for the life which you have made known to us through Jesus your servant *(pais)."*

[50] "Through whom you have made all things and provide for all things and whom you sent to become a human being for our salvation, and whom you permitted to suffer and die, and whom you raised up, willed to glorify, and made to sit at your right hand, and through whom you have promised us the resurrection from the dead" (7.25.2-3; SC 336:52f.).

[51] *Les Constitutions apostoliques. Livres III et VI,* ed. M. Metzger (SC 329; Paris, 1986) 21.

[52] Ibid., 29.

elements from the profession of faith of his Church, which we can find already cited in Book 6 of the *Apostolic Constitutions*.[53]

4.3. The Importance of the Term "Antitype"

Another change can be found in the second strophe of the thanksgiving. This strophe, which is derived from *Didache* 9.2, and specifically from the thanksgiving over the cup, is changed by the compiler into a thanksgiving for the precious Blood and the precious Body, at the end of which comes the account of institution.[54] Note, furthermore, that in this paleoanaphora the awareness of the sacramentality of the Eucharist is fully developed, to the point that it is explicitly formulated and brought into the text by use of the technical expression "antitype," which, however, cannot be translated simply as "sacrament" because its meaning is more complex. It will be worth our while if I explain briefly the use of this term.

We have seen how the eucharistic celebration came into being: At the Last Supper Jesus *handed on the mysteries*, since by the words "Do this in remembrance of me," he passed on the model, the *type*, of the Church's Eucharist. The later is therefore an act of obedience to Christ's command and an imitation of the type. The term "antitype"[55] is therefore especially suited to expressing this conception of the Eucharist. In Paul, in the Pastoral Letters, and in the letter of Peter, the word "type" occurs six times with the meaning of a model that shapes the obedience of faith.[56]

"Antitype" is not found in Philo and is attested for the first time in the letter to the Hebrews (9:24). The term was coined precisely as part of the language of worship: On the basis of Exodus 25:40, Hebrews 8:5 conceives of earthly worship as a "copy" of a heavenly "model"; this earthly "copy" is called an "antitype" (Heb 9:5) in relation to the celestial prototype which is described as "the true reality."

During the patristic period, a horizontal typology appears alongside the vertical typology: the actions by which Christ hands on the mysteries are called the type, while the rite of the Church, corresponding

---

[53] Ibid., 6.11.1-10 (SC 329:322–27); 7.42.3-8 (pp. 98–100).

[54] Ibid., 7.25.4 (SC 336:54).

[55] By means of the preposition "anti" the term signifies correspondence to a "type"; the reality involved in "antitype" owes its existence to the relation of conformity with the model.

[56] L. Goppelt, "Typos," *TDNT* 8:250.

as it does to that type, is called an antitype. The relationship between type and antitype was rethought by the Fathers with the help of Platonic categories.[57] The antitype is regarded as participating ontologically in the type; the result is that the type cannot be thought of as remaining external to the antitype, as though the former were a purely external ritual model. Inasmuch as the type is a model that distinguishes, defines, and shapes, it lives on and is present within, and pervades, the antitype. What is true of the type is also true of the antitype, even if only by participation; consequently, there is a real identity of type and antitype.

That is how the Pauline definition of the Eucharist—the Lord's Supper (1 Cor 11:20)—must be understood; the words by themselves designate the Last Supper, while for Paul they must also designate every correct eucharistic liturgy, that is, every Eucharist that corresponds to its model.[58] Between type and antitype there is a relationship of both identity and difference, and it is this fact that founds the patristic conception of the sacraments; only in the fourth century will the conception be expressed in a different vocabulary, namely, a vocabulary drawn from the "mystery" conception of worship.[59]

Given this explanation of the term "antitype," we can understand the importance of its insertion into the paleoanaphoral text which we call the Mystical Eucharist: "We give you thanks, our Father, for the precious blood of Jesus Christ, which was shed for us, for the precious body, and we carry out the antitypes of these, since he himself

---

[57] For further information on the typological conception of worship, see my "L'interpretazione del culto nella chiesa antica" (chapter 1, note 20, above).

[58] Paul says that the Eucharist at Corinth is not "the Lord's supper" because of the divisions there; this is his way of saying that the liturgy of Corinth no longer *corresponds* to the model given by Jesus at the Last Supper.

[59] Odo Casel developed a general interpretation of Christian worship—the "doctrine of the mysteries"—which had abundant recourse to the categories of the mystery cults in order to interpret the Christian liturgy and sacraments. Nowadays this Caselian conception of the liturgy enjoys great acceptance among theologians who study Christian worship, but it must be noted that the sources which Casel studied in evolving his conception of worship never date from before the fourth century. On the other hand, the *typological* conception of worship depends on sources far earlier than the fourth century; this conception, moreover, was still held by such authors as Ambrose, Cyril of Jerusalem, Theodore, and others. For this reason the conception of worship which I expound in the present work differs intentionally from Odo Casel's "doctrine of the mysteries." See also my essay, "La portata teologica del termine 'mistero,'" *Rivista liturgica* 74 (1987) 321–38.

commanded us to 'proclaim his death' (1 Cor 11:26)."[60] In addition to antitype, there are two other terms to be emphasized: *epiteloumen*, which designates the celebration, and *diataxamenos*, which designates the action of Christ in making the type to be the norm of the Church's Eucharist.

[60] "Antitype" is part of the eucharistic vocabulary of the *Apostolic Constitutions*. For example: "He then gave us *(paradous)* the mysteries, the antitypes of his precious body and his blood" (5.14.7); "In your churches and your cemeteries offer the agreed Eucharist, the antitype of the royal body of Christ" (6.30.2).

Chapter 8

The Early Patristic Period

1. IGNATIUS OF ANTIOCH

Ignatius was bishop of Antioch and Peter's second successor in that office; he was condemned to the wild beasts in the reign of Trajan (98–117). In order to suffer his martyrdom he had to travel from Syria to Rome, and on the journey he wrote the seven letters that are our best evidence for the life of the Church in Syria during the sub-apostolic age. Ignatius speaks of the Eucharist only in passing, and is not interested in dealing expressly with the subject; he speaks of it only incidentally when his arguments can be strengthened by a reference to eucharistic practice.

The problems that occupy Ignatius' attention are two: Docetism and divisions within the Church. In dealing with Docetism, he finds it useful to appeal to the Eucharist because it is part of the common faith that the eucharistic bread is the flesh of Christ; from this it follows that if the eucharistic bread is really the Body of Christ, the body of Christ that was born of Mary must be a real body. In dealing with the unity of the Church, he finds it useful to appeal to the eucharistic celebration because the Eucharist is the sacrament of unity; consequently, the eucharistic rite provides various starting points for arguing that there ought not be any divisions in the Church.

In addition to these two concerns, the main theme is that of martyrdom, not because Ignatius is anxious to avoid this fate, but because martyrdom had a very important theological value and can stand as a summation of the entire life of the faithful. Christians are by definition disciples of Christ, but discipleship reaches its full form only in martyrdom. There is therefore a natural tendency of the disciple to achieve martyrdom, precisely in order to be fully a true disciple.

For the reasons given, the information Ignatius supplies on the Eucharist is necessarily fragmentary and incomplete.[1] It would be a mistake for us to try to derive an organized treatise on the Eucharist from the incidental data which he gives us.[2] We must therefore concern ourselves rather with the general framework of Ignatius' thought; only in this way can we bring to the surface the points having to do with the Eucharist.

1.1. "Leave me to imitate the Passion of my God"[3]

Ignatius' entire thought is focused on the experience of martyrdom, with the result that all the ideas expressed in his letters are interconnected and refer to one another. Martyrdom is an imitation of Christ in his passion, which is the climactic moment of his witnessing. It is clear that without martyrdom the imitation of Christ is incomplete, because the high point in the process of being a disciple is missing. Christians are Christians because they are disciples of Christ, and a disciple must imitate Christ in everything. Consequently, Christians are full and complete disciples only through martyrdom.

To imitate Christ is to be a "Christ-bearer" in one's own life; through the works of Christ which believers accomplish Christ is present in their lives and shapes these from within. Ignatius has a real ideology of the imitation of Christ; this is the only way to live. He is so conscious of his way of conceiving Christian life that he

---

[1] As was pointed out as long ago as 1910 by M. Goguel, who was astonished to find that Ignatius does not cite the words of consecration; see M. Goguel, *L'eucharistie. Des origines à Justin martyr* (Paris, 1910) 253.

[2] On this point I distance myself from those who were my teachers in the study of Ignatius and who find in Ignatius elements of doctrine that are definitely from a later time. For example: the Eucharist as a memorial and reproduction of the Lord's supper (P. Th. Camelot in his edition of *Ignace d'Antioche–Polycarpe de Smyrne. Letters–Martyre de Polycarpe* [SC 10; Paris, 1969] 69); the Eucharist as memorial of the passion (J. De Watteville, *Le sacrifice dans les textes eucharistiques des premiers siècles* [Bibliothèque théologique; Neuchâtel, 1966] 57); the Eucharist as linked to the incarnation and as actualization of the redemptive mystery, i.e., death and resurrection (R. Johanny, "Ignatius of Antioch," in W. Rordorf and others, *The Eucharist of the Early Christians,* trans. M. J. O'Connell [New York, 1978] 48–70).

[3] *Romans* 6.3 (SC 10:114), trans. Maxwell Staniforth in *Early Christian Writings. The Apostolic Fathers* (Baltimore, 1968) 105. [I have taken the liberty of modifying this translation at times, or of adding a more literal translation in parentheses, in order to suit the more literal reading of the Greek texts by the author of the present book.—Tr.]

chooses a second name which will symbolize and represent this, a descriptive name which he includes in the opening greeting of all his letters: he calls himself Theophoros, "bearer of God."

This term is not attested as a nickname before Ignatius, and he may have coined it, given the predilection he shows for the vocabulary, even pagan, of worship. In this latter area there were analogies that may have explained his choice of nickname. There were, for example, pagan processions in which the faithful, clad in costly robes, carried sacred objects (these individuals were called *hagiophoroi*), the statue of a god *(theophoroi)*, or a model of a temple *(naos)*.[4] Ignatius transposes this custom to Christian life, giving it a spiritual meaning; he writes to the Ephesians: "You are all pilgrims in the same great procession, bearing your God and your shrine and your Christ and your sacred objects on your shoulders, every one of you arrayed in the festal garments of the commandments of Jesus Christ."[5]

Greek culture, as we can see in Plutarch, had already worked out a heavily spiritualized interpretation of cults and their elements; in Plutarch[6] the *hierophoroi* are those who carry in their souls a faith purified of all superstition.[7]

Ignatius is thus bringing this cultural process to completion by turning the theme of "imitator" into that of "bearer." As a result, the imitator of Christ, of God, becomes a "Theophoros." Ignatius' ideal is to become a complete imitator, and this ideal is expressed in the nickname he gave himself; the name is really an example of *nomen omen* (the name becomes an omen).

Imitation of Christ leads to oneness with him, and this is not possible except within the unity of the Church, which is brought about in the company of the bishop and through obedience and submission to him. The unity of the Church in its turn has a privileged connection with the Eucharist, inasmuch as all the elements making up the rite suppose and create unity: the eucharistic assembly, the prayer of thanksgiving, and the bread and wine which are the Body and Blood of Christ.

---

[4] F. Dölger, "Christophoros als Ehrentitel für Märtyrer und Heilige im christlichen Altertum," *Antike und Christentum* 4 (1934) 73–80.

[5] *Ephesians* 9.2 (SC 10:66; ET: 78).

[6] *De Iside et Osiride*, in: Plutarch, *Iside e Osiride*, ed. D. Del Corno (Piccola biblioteca 179; Milan, 1985) 59.

[7] See Camelot, *Ignace* (note 2, above), 66, note 2.

1.2. The Ministry of the Bishop

A monarchical conception of the episcopate held sway in Ignatius' Church, so that there could be no Eucharist unless the bishop or his delegate presided. In this respect we are far removed from the Church described in the *Didache,* a document that is almost certainly from Antioch. Here it is, above all, the prophets who preside at the Eucharist[8] and, after them, the bishops; in fact, the *Didache* urges that the bishop be held in great respect because he celebrates the same liturgy that the prophets celebrate.[9] Ignatius, too, urges respect for bishops,[10] but the reason for his doing so is quite different: In his view, bishops do not preside at the liturgy in place of prophets, as in the *Didache,* but in the place of God himself.[11] But the discontinuity between the two documents is only seeming, inasmuch as a prophet, by his nature, speaks under the inspiration of God, so that his words are those of God; he too, therefore, stands in the place of God.

My point in referring to all this is to try to locate the thought of Ignatius within the liturgical tradition of Antioch; this makes it easier to understand how he can maintain that when the bishop presides at the Eucharist, he is performing the very actions of God, whereas we know very well that he is performing the actions of Christ at the Last Supper.[12]

---

[8] *Didache* 10.7. Text, French translation, and notes in *La doctrine des douze apôtres (Didachè),* ed. W. Rordorf and A. Tuilier (SC 248; Paris, 1978) 182.

[9] "Choose for yourselves, therefore, bishops and deacons who are worthy of the Lord, gentle, disinterested men, sincere and experienced; they too celebrate for you the liturgy of the prophets and doctors. Do not scorn them, then, for they are honored among you, along with the prophets" (*Didache* 15.1-2; SC 10:192–94).

[10] *Trallians* 3.1 (SC 10:96).

[11] *Magnesians* 6.2 (SC 10:84).

[12] Against this interpretation it may be objected that in the theology of Ignatius Christ is usually called "God," and that therefore, when Ignatius speaks of the bishop carrying out the actions of God, he means the actions of Christ. This is true, but it is not enough to explain how the eucharistic celebration, which imitates the rite of the Last Supper, should be attributed directly to God. It must be noted, furthermore, that Ignatius can distinguish between Christ and God and that in describing the episcopal ministry of Polycarp in the community, he in fact assigns the heavenly episcopal supervision of the Church both to the Son and to God the Father; see the greeting of Ignatius' letter to Polycarp: ". . . to Polycarp, who is bishop over the Smyrnean church—or rather, who has God the Father for bishop over him, together with the Lord Jesus Christ" (SC 10:146; ET: 127). For these reasons I hold that the explanation based on the identification of God and Christ is a further explanation which is grafted on to the preceding and completes it.

The *Didache* concentrates first on the Eucharist and then on the presider; in Ignatius the contrary is true, for the bishop's presidency is the criterion for the "safety" of the eucharistic celebration. The adjective *bebaia* ("solid; safe") is the technical term Ignatius uses to describe the authenticity of the Eucharist.[13] The presidency of the bishop is the first necessary characteristic of the Eucharist: "The meetings they [those who gather apart from the bishop] hold can have no sort of valid *(mê bebaios)* authority."[14] And again: "The sole Eucharist you should consider valid *(bebaia)* is one that is celebrated by the bishop himself, or by some person authorized by him."[15]

The reason why Ignatius speaks of the Eucharist in this way is to be found in his idea of the Church, which (in his view) exists only as gathered around the bishop and the other ministers: "Without these three orders [i.e., bishop, presbyters, deacons] no church has any right to the name."[16] Consequently: "Where the bishop is, there is the community, just as where Jesus Christ is, there is the universal Church."[17]

1.3. A Sacramental Conception of This Ministry

To understand the connection between the theme of discipleship and that of the Eucharist, I must explain what Ignatius means when he identifies union with Christ and unity with the bishop and the Church. If we are to understand the expressions Ignatius uses in speaking of unity, I must go back a step and explain his idea of sacramentality, which is the archaic idea of sacramentality.

The terms Ignatius uses in describing the episcopate are very important. To explain the sacramental nature of this ministry, he says that the bishop is "in the place" of God[18] and is a "type" of God.[19] These words, this language, and this conception have their place in

---

[13] In my view, *bebaios* can be correctly translated as "true" in the sense of "authentic," even if it is more probable that Ignatius uses *bebaios* in the literal sense, meaning that the eucharistic assembly over which the bishop presides is secure or guaranteed, while the assemblies of others are not, or that the bishop's Eucharist "builds," while that of others is not said to "build." I do not think it accurate to translate *bebaios* as "legitimate" or "valid," since these terms reflect a much later theology of the sacraments.

[14] *Magnesians* 4 (SC 10:82; ET: 88).

[15] *Smyrneans* 8.2 (SC 10:138; ET: 121).

[16] *Trallians* 3.1 (SC 10:96; ET: 96).

[17] *To Polycarp* 8.2 (SC 10:138).

[18] *Magnesians* 6.1 (SC 10:84).

[19] *Trallians* 3.1 (SC 10:96).

biblical typology, and Ignatius applies the latter to the liturgy. For evidence of this we may look at some passages in which he speaks of the bishop as the "fleshly bishop," thereby assuming that there is also a spiritual bishop of the community, namely, God or Christ: ". . . Onesimus, a man of indescribable charity, your bishop in the flesh."[20] God is the real bishop, as we see in this passage: "From Ignatius, whose other name is Theophorus. My most cordial greetings to Polycarp, who is bishop over the Smyrnaean church—or rather, who has God the Father for bishop over him, together with our Lord Jesus Christ."[21] We may also cite a thought of Ignatius about the Church of Syria after his death: ". . . the Church of Syria, which in place of me will have God as its shepherd. Only Jesus Christ, and Your Charity, will be its bishop."[22]

For Ignatius, then, the Church exists on two levels: a fleshly and visible, and a spiritual and invisible. The second is the level on which things have their authentic reality, but there is a real correspondence between the two levels, a correspondence regulated by the language of typology: *typos* and also *eis topon*. The correspondence is real; to the invisible bishop there corresponds a visible bishop who authentically exercises episcopacy in a way suited to the episcopacy of God, with the result that if believers disobey or separate themselves from the bishop, they disobey and separate themselves from God. This correspondence is nothing else than the sacramentality of the episcopate.

The sacramental conception of ministry is applied not only to the bishop but also to the presbyters. As the bishop stands in the place of God and Christ, so presbyters stand in the place of the apostles: "Let the bishop preside in the place *(eis topon)* of God, and his clergy in the place *(eis topon)* of the Apostolic conclave."[23] In addition, Ignatius even seems to call the presbyters a "type": "You should also look on the bishop as a type of the Father, and the clergy as *(hôs)* the Apostolic circle forming his council."[24] Ignatius is therefore right in urging: "Defer to your bishop as you would to the Divine Law, and likewise to your clergy."[25]

[20] *Ephesians* 1.3 (SC 10:58).

[21] Opening greeting of the letter to Polycarp (SC 10:146; ET: 127).

[22] *To Polycarp* 9.1 (SC 10:116). [The translator of the Penguin edition seems to have followed a different text here.—Tr.]

[23] *Magnesians* 6.1 (SC 10:84; ET: 88).

[24] *Trallians* 3.1 (SC 10:96; ET: 96).

[25] Ibid., 13.1 (SC 10:104; ET: 98).

Due to this way of conceiving sacramentality, the ministry enjoys such authority that "nobody's conscience can be clean if he is acting without the authority of his bishop, clergy, and deacons."[26] In positive terms: "Follow your bishop, every one of you, as *(hôs)* obediently as Jesus Christ followed the Father. Obey your clergy, too, as *(hôs)* you would the Apostles."[27]

Hôs, a term indicating a comparison, appears often in these passages; it has the same significance as terms which we have already seen: "image" *(typos)* and "in place of" *(eis topon)*. Since the bishop performs the very actions of God, it can be said that he stands "in the place" of God and that, consequently, he is an "image" of God in a real sense. What we have here, according to the thinking of the Greek-speaking Fathers,[28] is a characteristic use of the comparative "as" *(hôs)* to express sacramentality. When Cyril of Jerusalem speaks of the Eucharist in his mystagogical catecheses, he says that "we share as *(hôs)* in the Body and Blood of Christ";[29] this statement parallels the usual assertions that the bread is the Sacrament of Christ's Body. Ignatius, too, makes a sacramental use of the adverb "as" in order to assert the sacramentality of the bishop's role; since there is a relation of sacramentality between the bishop and Christ, Ignatius can conclude that "we must regard a bishop as *(hôs)* the Lord Himself."[30]

1.4. The Eucharist

I said earlier that for Ignatius martyrdom is the most complete and highest exercise of discipleship; imitation is a source of union with the person imitated; there is a kind of identity between the Christian

[26] Ibid., 7.2 (SC 10:100; ET: 97).

[27] *Smyrneans* 8.1 (SC 10:138; ET: 121).

[28] We may not project back into earlier centuries the idea of sacramentality that we will find in the biblical typology which the Fathers of the fourth century apply to the liturgy, using a very technical and sophisticated method. Nonetheless, the fully formed roots of this method may be recognized in Ignatius: On the one hand, there is a strong sense of sacramental realism, to the point of identifying the Sacrament with the reality of which it is the Sacrament; on the other, there is a great lack of terminology, so that he is unable to describe in a univocal way just what sacramentality is. Ignatius uses a vocabulary which in later centuries will be first complemented and later replaced by a technical terminology in the proper sense of the word. But Ignatius' archaic way of thinking of sacraments will not be completely left behind but will survive at least to the end of the fourth century.

[29] *Catecheses mystagogicae* 4.3 (SC 126bis:136).

[30] *Ephesians* 6.1 (SC 10:62; ET: 71).

who imitates Christ, and Christ; in addition, union with Christ leads on to union with God.

The relationship between imitation and unity holds both for everyday life (our "life in Christ") and for the liturgical celebration or, in our case here, the Eucharist. In both cases the idea is the same. In Ignatius' letters the eucharistic celebration is called the "breaking of bread"[31] and also the "Eucharist." The word *eucharistia* occurs four times, and the sense is not constant, because it has a wide range of meanings; it may refer to the prayer of thanksgiving, the eucharistic bread and cup, or the entire celebration. I shall try now to gather together the various elements in the conception of the Eucharist as found in the letters of Ignatius.

1.4.1. *The Eucharist, Thanksgiving, and the Theme of Unity*

The Eucharist is a rite celebrated at regular intervals and presence at it is required whenever it is prescribed. Ignatius rebukes several Churches for neglecting this obligation: "Hold services more frequently."[32] There is but a single Eucharist in which all should take part—the Eucharist at which the bishop or his delegate presides—because this one alone is *bebaia* ("safe, secure").[33] The reasons for this statement are to be found in the conception of sacramentality: It is God himself, and Christ, who, surrounded by his apostles, presides over the eucharistic liturgy through the visible ministry of the bishop and the presbyters.[34]

---

[31] Ibid., 20.2 (SC 10:76; ET: 82).

[32] *To Polycarp* 4.2 (SC 10:148; ET: 128).

[33] "The sole Eucharist you should consider valid [or: secure: *bebaia*] is one that is celebrated by the bishop himself, or by some person authorized by him" (*Smyrneans* 8.1; SC 10:138; ET: 121). "I do not see how people of that kind can be acting in good conscience, seeing that the meetings they hold can have no sort of valid authority [or: can be secure *(mê bebaios)*]" (*Magnesians* 4; SC 10:82; ET: 88).

[34] "Let me urge on you the need of godly unanimity in everything you do. Let the bishop preside in place *(eis topon)* of God, and his clergy in place of the Apostolic conclave, and let my special friends the deacons be entrusted with the service of Jesus Christ. . . . Allow nothing whatsoever to exist among you that could give rise to any divisions; maintain absolute unity with your bishop and leaders, as an example to others and a lesson in the avoidance of corruption" (*Magnesians* 6.1-2; SC 10:84; ET: 88). See also: "Equally it is for the rest of you to hold the deacons in as great respect as *(hôs)* Jesus Christ; just as *(hôs)* you should look on the bishop as a type of the Father, and the clergy as *(hôs)* the Apostolic circle forming his council; for without these three orders no church has any right to the name" (*Trallians* 3.1; SC 10:96; ET: 95–96).

These liturgical gatherings over which the bishop presides are already given the technical name "Eucharist."[35] In the rite itself the bread and wine are called "Eucharist," as is the prayer of thanksgiving, which is described as "thanks (*eucharistia*) and glory (*doxa*) to God."[36]

The prayer[37] is addressed to the Father through Christ, and it is a communal prayer because of the unity of the community that is gathered around the bishop. But even though it is addressed to the Father, it is also described as "singing Jesus Christ." The prayer is communal and is uttered by all as though they formed a single voice, because it is "sung together" about God; using a different terminology, we might say that it is single because it is inspired by God and is in the image of God, who is unity itself. This unity is manifested in the "symphony" of the prayer; for this reason Ignatius judges it to have a salutary value, describing it as useful because it is a "participation in God."[38] He goes even further and, when speaking of the unity of the Church, says that the Eucharist brings about union with God and life in Christ.[39] Union with the Church thus has a sacramental efficacy.

In order to bring home the idea of the sacramental efficacy of unity, I shall once again cite *Magnesians* 6.2, because of its important ending in which the writer says that union with the bishops is the sacramental image of immortality:

"Let me urge on you the need for godly unanimity in everything you do. Let the bishop preside in the place (*eis topon*) of God, and his

[35] "Make certain, therefore, that you all observe one common Eucharist" (*Philadelphians* 4; SC 10:122; ET: 112).

[36] *Ephesians* 13.1 (SC 10:68; ET: 79).

[37] Ignatius is describing the hymns of the liturgy, and the description sums up the nature of liturgical prayer as such. All the more, then, does it hold for the Eucharist.

[38] "Your justly respected clergy, who are a credit to God, are attuned to their bishop like the strings of a harp, and the result is a hymn of praise to Jesus Christ from minds that are in unison (*homonoia*), and affections that are in harmony (*symphônô*). Pray, then, come and join this choir, every one of you; let there be a whole symphony of minds (*homonoia*) in concert (*symphônoi*); take the tone altogether from God, and sing aloud to the Father with one voice through Jesus Christ, so that He may hear you and know by your good works that you are indeed members of His Son's Body. A completely united front will help to keep you in constant communion with God" (*Ephesians* 4.1-2; SC 10:60; ET: 76).

[39] "Every man who belongs to God and Jesus Christ stands by his bishop. As for the rest, if they repent and come back into the unity of the church, they too shall belong to God, and so bring their lives into conformity with Jesus Christ" (*Philadelphians* 3.2; SC 10:122; ET: 112).

clergy in the place *(eis topon)* of the Apostolic conclave, and let my special friends the deacons be entrusted with the service of Jesus Christ. . . . Allow nothing whatever to exist among you that could give rise to any divisions; maintain absolute unity with your bishop and leaders, as an example *(eis typon)* to others and a lesson *(kai didachên)* in the avoidance of corruption."[40]

Unity is the horizon within which Ignatius moves, and it is the explanation of Christian life: The faithful must be united to the bishop *as* the Church is united with Christ and *as* Christ is united with the Father.[41]

The conception I have been explaining applies to the liturgy as such, and therefore it applies all the more to the rite of the eucharistic meal. Ignatius himself draws this conclusion when he says: "Make certain, therefore, that you all observe one common Eucharist; for there is but one Body of our Lord Jesus Christ, and but one cup of union with His Blood, and one single altar of sacrifice—even as also there is but one bishop, with his clergy and my own fellow-servitors the deacons."[42] The oneness of the flesh of Christ and the oneness of the cup point to the oneness of redemption, which is indicated simply by "his blood"; there are not two or more redemptions but a single redemption, and it is expressed by the oneness of the bread and the cup. Ignatius represents a strong sacramental realism, for he identifies the eucharistic bread with the Body of Christ. The Sacrament is not thought of as a ritual "replica" of the body of Christ, a kind of second body; there is only one flesh of Christ, only one redemption, and the Sacrament is identified with it. This is why he insists on the one bread, which is called simply the flesh of Christ, and on the one cup and the one Blood.

After examining all these passages, which have shown that the nature and efficacy of the liturgy are connected with unity, and after seeing that Ignatius situates the Eucharist within a theology of unity, we may conclude that for him the Eucharist is the "sacrament of unity," although this actual expression never appears in his writings. The unity of which he speaks is the unity of the body of Christ.

---

[40] *Magnesians* 6.2 (SC 10:84; ET: 88).

[41] *Ephesians* 6.1 (SC 10:62).

[42] *Philadelphians* 4 (SC 10:122; ET: 112).

1.4.2. The Thanksgiving

It is very difficult to say whether the letters of Ignatius contain any evidence of the thanksgiving that was spoken during the eucharistic celebration. In my opinion, it is not possible to reach any conclusion on the subject, if for no other reason than that the thanksgiving was an improvised composition and therefore could, at least in theory, have been different at every Eucharist.

It is possible, nonetheless, to offer some suggestions, beginning with a passage from the letter of Ignatius to the *Romans*, in which G. Jouassard found a trace of the liturgical cult in honor of the martyrs[43] and which, in my opinion, may also attest to the structure of the paleoanaphora used in the Church of Antioch. I shall proceed by comparing Ignatius' *Letter to the Romans* with the *Martyrdom of Polycarp*, a document composed about forty years later. Both works speak of the martyr as bread;[44] both regard martyrdom as a sacrifice;[45] and both put a prayer on the lips of a martyr.

Polycarp's prayer is quite full; it says in particular: "I bless thee for granting me [or: for having made me worthy of] this day and hour, that I may be numbered amongst the martyrs, to share the cup of thine Anointed and to rise again unto life everlasting, both in body and soul, in the immortality of the Holy Spirit."[46] Ignatius' prayer, on the other hand, is hardly emphasized:

"This favor only I beg of you: suffer me to be a libation poured out *(spondisthênai)* to God, while there is still an altar ready for me. Then you may form a loving choir around it and sing hymns of praise in

[43] G. Joussuard, "Aux origines du culte des martyres. S. Ignace d'Antioche, Rom IV, 2," *RSR* 39 (1951) 362–67.

[44] "Pray leave me to be a meal for the beasts, for it is they who can provide my way to God. I am His wheat, ground fine by the lions' teeth to be made purest bread for Christ" (*Romans* 4.1; SC 10:110; ET: 104).

[45] The "purest bread" is nothing else than the "sacrifice" offered to God. Worship consists in being a disciple, and this worship can be expressed both in the eucharistic rite and in the martyr's death. For this reason, in speaking of his martyrdom Ignatius uses two eucharistic images: "purest bread" and "sacrifice," as can be seen from the following passage: "When there is no trace of my body left for the world to see, then I shall truly be Jesus Christ's disciple. So intercede with Him for me, that by their instrumentality I may be made a sacrifice to God" (*Romans* 4.2; SC 10:112; ET: 104). In his prayer Polycarp says: "May I be received among them [the martyrs] this day in thy presence, a sacrifice rich and acceptable" (*Martyrdom of Polycarp* 14.2; SC 10:228; ET: 161).

[46] *Martyrdom of Polycarp* 14.2 (SC 10:228; ET: 161).

Jesus Christ to the Father, for permitting Syria's bishop, summoned from the realms of the morning, to have reached the land of the setting sun (or: deigning to let Syria's bishop be found [*eurethênai*], summoned from . . . morning to the land of the setting sun)."[47]

"To be found" takes on a cultic meaning when we consider this parallel text: "Intercede with Him for me, that by their [the beasts'] instrumentality I may be made (lit.: be found) a sacrifice for God."[48]

In both cases there is a prayer of thanksgiving to the Father. The motivation for the prayer is formulated in classical fashion as the divine election by reason of which the Father "deigns to make" someone "worthy," that is, deputes someone to fill a specific role, with reference especially to worship. Here are the two formulations: "God has made worthy" in the case of Polycarp, and "God has deigned that I be found" (= "has made worthy") in the case of Ignatius. The object of the thanksgiving is that God has made the bishop worthy of martyrdom. In the *Martyrdom of Polycarp* the prayer is put in the mouth of the bishop, who utters it immediately before being killed, while in the letter of Ignatius to the *Romans* the prayer is placed in the mouth of the community.

The prayer in the *Martyrdom of Polycarp* is part of a more complete prayer that has a complex and organized structure in which everything has its place; it is a tripartite prayer modeled on the structure of the paleoanaphora[49] that was used in the Church of Smyrna, and not there alone. The paleoanaphora had a tripartite structure: a strophe of thanksgiving for the works of God (accomplished in the history of salvation); a second strophe of thanksgiving for the work which God is accomplishing at this precise moment and of which the community is the conscious beneficiary; and a strophe of prayer for the Church and for its unity or peace (depending on the text).

The prayer which I cited from the *Martyrdom of Polycarp*—in its more literal translation: "for having made me worthy of this day and hour, that I may be numbered among the martyrs"—corresponds to the second strophe of the paleoanaphoral structure, that is, to the thanksgiving for what God is doing at the present moment. The prayer of Polycarp, then, has a liturgical origin. But, given the parallelism

[47] *Romans* 2.2 (SC 10:108; ET: 104).
[48] *Romans* 4.2 (SC 10:112; ET: 105).
[49] See Mazza, *L'anafora,* chapter 4, especially 174f.

between Polycarp's prayer and the prayer in Ignatius' *Letter to the Romans*, we must conclude that Ignatius too reflects liturgical usage when he says: "Then you may form a loving choir around it [the altar] and sing hymns of praise in Jesus Christ to the Father in Jesus Christ, for permitting Syria's bishop . . ."[50]

More precisely, Ignatius is alluding to the second strophe of the paleoanaphora, which has for its object the celebration of what God is accomplishing today. This way of conceiving the second strophe had its origin in Jewish practice, as can be seen from the *Birkat ha-Mazon* in the *Book of Jubilees*,[51] one of the few prayers for a ritual meal that has come down to us.

We may therefore conclude that by falling back on a form of prayer characteristic of the paleoanaphora, Ignatius attests that during his time in Antioch there was in use the classical type of paleoanaphora that was descended from the *Birkat ha-Mazon* with its three strophes.

Having ascertained that Ignatius has recourse to liturgical usage, we must ask a second question: Is it possible to identify the liturgy of which Ignatius is thinking when he urges others to sing hymns to God on account of his martyrdom? It is possible that he is urging them to celebrate the martyrdom of the bishop at some kind of prayer meeting, with the singing of hymns on this theme, but it is no less possible that this took place during the eucharistic celebration; in this case, when he says: "you may form a loving choir" (literally: "a choir in love [*agapê*]"), the word *agapê* would signify the Eucharist.[52]

1.4.3. *The Bread and the Wine*

No one has ever doubted Ignatius' sacramental realism. It is clear that in his mind the eucharistic bread is the Body of Christ and the

---

[50] *Romans* 2.2 (SC 10:108; ET: 104).

[51] *Jubilees* 22:7 (Charlesworth 2:97).

[52] The objection may be raised that Ignatius cannot be referring to the prayer of the anaphora, since this was said only by the presider and not chorally by the community. But there is a similar case in the Acts of the Apostles, where Peter alone prays but the prayer is attributed to the entire community, which prays with one heart (*homothumadon*): "When they heard it [Peter's report], they lifted their voices together to God and said, 'Sovereign Lord, who didst make the heaven and the earth and the sea and everything in them . . .'" (Acts 4:24ff.). In this understanding of Ignatius' words, his *choros genomenoi* would be the equivalent of *homothumadon* ("together" = literally, "with one heart") in Acts, and the anaphoral prayer would have a communal aspect even though it was recited by one person, the bishop or his delegate.

cup is his Blood; to show this, it is enough to cite this passage in which the bread and wine are identified with the historical Christ, born, in his incarnation, of the seed of David: "I am fain for the bread of God, even the flesh of Jesus Christ, who is the seed of David; and for my drink I crave that Blood of His which is love imperishable."[53]

This very realistic text on the Sacrament is to be seen alongside another passage of Ignatius, although the latter is regarded as symbolic:[54] "Take a fresh grip on your faith (the very flesh of the Lord) and your love (the life-blood of Jesus Christ)."[55] This is not the place to speak of realism and symbolism, since in Ignatius the two are not opposed; in fact, it is his conception of the sacraments that allows him to use these diverse formulations.

We must recover the archaic idea of the sacraments. The ideal of Christian life is to imitate Christ so as to become like him even in martyrdom. The imitation of Christ takes place both in rites and in life, but in both cases the imitation comes about through faith and love. There is no other way. In order, then, to stress the point that the eucharistic celebration should be a real imitation of Christ (not only in the rite but also in its content), Ignatius combines the terminology of imitation with the terminology of the Eucharist and tells us that *faith is the flesh of the Lord* and that *love is the blood of Jesus Christ.*

In conclusion: The bread and wine are the Body and Blood of Christ, but so are faith and love; in fact, the Body and Blood of Christ, on the one hand, and faith and love, on the other, imply each other.

1.4.4. Medicine of Immortality

The conception of the sacraments as effective for salvation urges Ignatius to a bold effort at inculturation. He calls the Eucharist "the medicine of immortality" and also "the sovereign remedy by which we escape death."[56] T. Scherman has shown that the phrase "medicine

---

[53] *Romans* 7.3 (SC 10:114; ET: 106). Those not having this faith cannot approach the Eucharist: "They even absent themselves from the Eucharist and the public prayers, because they will not admit that the Eucharist is the self-same body of our Saviour Jesus Christ which suffered for our sins, and which the Father in His goodness afterwards raised up again" (*Smyrneans* 7.1; SC 10:138; ET: 121).

[54] See De Watteville, *Le sacrifice* (note 2, above), 55. The use of the word "symbolic" is certainly improper, but it is justifiable, since there is no special technical terminology for expressing the early Church's conception of the sacraments.

[55] *Trallians* 8.1 (SC 10:100; ET: 97).

[56] ". . . United in faith and in Jesus Christ (who is the seed of David according to the flesh, and is the Son of Man and Son of God) . . . in the one common

of immortality" was very common in medical parlance and referred to a kind of ointment supposedly invented by the goddess Isis.[57] By using this description, then, Ignatius is suggesting that authentic salvation, that is, rescue from death, can be obtained through the Eucharist. This, moreover, should be Christians' real concern, rather than the various remedies that throng the marketplaces.

2. JUSTIN

Justin[58] describes two kinds of eucharistic celebration: a Sunday Eucharist and a Eucharist following on a baptism. His testimony is very important because it is addressed to the emperor and is therefore a public record that takes on an official character. What Justin reports should be regarded as a practice customary and traditional among Christians, that is, true to the facts which the Roman administration could easily have verified by an investigation. The *Apology* must, therefore, give us a faithful picture of the eucharistic liturgy at the middle of the second century. Of the various points reported in Justin's writings I shall consider only three: the description of the rite; the probable content of the eucharistic texts; and the conception of the Eucharist as an antitype.

2.1. The Eucharistic Rite

The baptized person[59] is brought to the place where the community is gathered, and a prayer is offered that he or she may be able to practice virtue and receive salvation. After the kiss of peace, bread and a cup of water and wine are brought to the presider.[60] The latter offers a prayer of thanksgiving. At the end of the prayers and the Eucharist the entire congregation says "Amen," a term which Justin is careful to explain. After the prayer the deacons distribute the "eucharistified"

---

breaking of bread—the medicine of immortality, and the sovereign remedy by which we escape death and live in Jesus Christ for evermore" (*Ephesians* 20.2; SC 10:76; ET: 82).

[57] Th. Scherman, "Zur Erklärung der Stelle Epist. ad Eph. 20, 2 des Ignatius von Antiocheia," *Theologische Quartalschrift* 92 (1910) 6–19.

[58] Justin was born in Shechem around A.D. 100 and lived in Ephesus and at Rome, where he wrote his *Apologia* around 150. He describes the rite as if it was the same throughout the Roman Empire.

[59] *Apologia* I 65.1–66.4 (Hänggi-Pahl, 68f.).

[60] Since this was a baptismal liturgy, there were, in all probability, two cups, one containing water and the other wine mixed with water.

bread and wine to the participants and then take it to those who have not been able to attend. These elements are called "Eucharist," and faith and baptism are required in order to receive them; they are not ordinary bread and wine but the Body and Blood of Christ because of a word of prayer that comes from him. In order to demonstrate this, Justin goes on to cite the account of institution at the Last Supper.

The rite celebrated on Sunday is substantially the same.[61] On the day named after the sun all gather in one place, and after the memoirs of the apostles and the writings of the prophets have been read, there is a homily followed by communal prayer. After this prayer bread and a cup of wine and water are brought to the presider. The presider then offers prayers and thanksgivings to God to the best of his ability, and the congregation responds with the acclamation "Amen." The distribution of the eucharistified elements follows, and these are also sent to the absent by way of the deacons.

The *Dialogue with Trypho* also contains two brief discussions of the Eucharist.[62] I think that these should be given careful consideration because of the emphasis placed in them on the sacrificial character of the Eucharist. Malachi 1:11 is cited in both places; this immediately shows the perspective in which the Eucharist is seen: that of sacrifice. It is worth the reader's while to read at least the second passage in its entirety.[63]

This passage shows the same conception of the Eucharist that we found in the Alexandrian anaphora: the Eucharist, understood as a

---

[61] *Apologia I* 67.1-7 (Hänggi-Pahl, 7of.).

[62] *Dialogue with Trypho* 41.1-3; 117.1-3 (Hänggi-Pahl, 72f.).

[63] "God testified in advance that he would be pleased with all those who in his name offer the sacrifices which Jesus Christ handed on to be done—that is, which are offered by Christians in every place in the world in their eucharist of bread and the cup. Those, on the other hand, which you and your priests offer he has rejected, saying: 'I will not accept your sacrifices from your hands. For from the rising of the sun to its setting my name is glorified among the gentiles, but you desecrate it' (Mal 1:10-11). And until now you, in your love of disputes, say the same thing, that God does not accept the sacrifices offered in Jerusalem by its inhabitants, known as Israelites, whereas the prayers of those in the Diaspora are acceptable to him, and that their prayers are called 'sacrifices.' I say that in fact both the prayers and the sacrifices offered by worthy persons are the only ones that reach their fulfillment *(teleitai)* and are sacrifices pleasing to God. And these alone are what Christians have learned to do, even in the memorial of their dry and liquid food, in which they commemorate the passion which the Son of God endured for their sake" (*Dialogue with Trypho* 117.103).

prayer of thanksgiving, is a sacrifice accepted by God, and it is because of the presence of this prayer that the entire action is likewise called a sacrifice, that is, the memorial of the passion that is celebrated in bread and wine. There is another reason why Justin can speak of the Eucharist as a sacrifice: It is related to the Old Testament sacrifice that was to be offered for the purification from leprosy, and the latter is described as a *"type* of the bread of the Eucharist which Jesus Christ said to do *(paredôke poiein)* . . . in memory of the passion."

2.2. Thanksgiving and Petition

We do not know exactly what was said in the thanksgiving and petition parts of the Eucharistic Prayer described by Justin; he does, however, sum up the reasons for thanksgiving, and he could not do more to make known the elements of the celebration, because this was still a period of creativity and improvisation.

In addition to being a prayer and a thanksgiving, the Eucharist is a blessing (rising to God), a praise and glorification of the Father of all things *(Patri tôn holôn)*.[64] The prayer has a trinitarian character because the thanksgiving is offered through the name of the Son and the Holy Spirit.[65] In it, God is praised for the work of creation and for salvation; also commemorated is the incarnation, which, in Justin's thinking, is never separated from the passion.[66] So much for the Eucharistic Prayer; the entire celebration is thus seen as a memorial of the passion and a sanctification of the faithful. The sacrificial character of the rite is ensured by the citation of Malachi 1:10-12.

Finally, we should note that in speaking of the Eucharistic Prayer Justin always uses the plural: prayers *(euchai)*[67] and thanksgivings *(eucharistiai)*; we do not know whether this points to several strophes of thanksgiving and petition, of the kind proper to the paleoanaphoral structure which we examined in the preceding chapter. It would be risky to interpret the use of the plural as signifying a paleoanaphoral

[64] Irenaeus also uses this title for God.

[65] These are elements that appear in both descriptions of the Eucharist, and we may therefore think that they were constants that had to be respected amid the freedom to improvise.

[66] De Watteville, *Le sacrifice* (note 2, above), 77.

[67] The word *euchai* is used either by itself or in conjunction with *eucharistiai.* When it is used alone it refers to prayer in general, whether of petition or of intercession, or to Jewish prayer as opposed to Christian, which, on the contrary, is signified by *euchai* and *eucharistiai* together (De Watteville, 73).

structure; on the other hand, we must acknowledge that the use of the plural is in no way appropriate when referring to a unitary anaphora that was a single block from beginning to end.

2.3. The "Transmission" of the Eucharist

In the *Dialogue with Trypho* Justin says that Christians have learned to do the Eucharist *(parelabon poiein)* and that it was Jesus who handed on the practice *(paredôken Iêsous ho Christos ginesthai)* of offering sacrifices,[68] that is, of celebrating the Eucharist, which in its very substance is a sacrifice.[69] The apostles in turn passed on what had been commanded them *(paredôkan entetalthai)*; this statement is followed by the account of the Last Supper.[70]

The theme of the *tradition,* or handing on or transmission, applies to the eucharistic meal in its entirety, but Justin stresses this element of "tradition" especially in relation to the Eucharistic Prayer. For him, the handing on of the model takes place through the handing on of the Eucharistic Prayer. "Just as Jesus Christ our Savior was made flesh through the word of God and took on flesh and blood for our salvation, so too (we have been taught) through the word of prayer that comes from him, the food over which the eucharist has been spoken becomes the flesh and blood of the incarnate Jesus, in order to nourish and transform our flesh and blood."[71]

In the view of G. Cuming, "the word of prayer that comes from him" is the account of institution.[72] I must disagree with this interpretation, and this precisely for the reason Cuming offers in its favor. Cuming carefully shows that the phrase *di'euchês logou tou par'autou* means a "word" coming from Christ. If the text read simply "a word coming from him," I could accept Cuming's interpretation and say that the reference was to the words of institution; but the text says: "a word *of prayer* coming from him." One thing is certain: The words of the account of institution are not a prayer. We must therefore ask what prayer it is that Jesus has transmitted. In the account of the Last Supper, the Gospels refer to only one prayer: the thanksgiving of Jesus over the bread and the cup.

---

[68] *Dialogue with Trypho* 117.3 (Hänggi-Pahl, 74).
[69] In other words, for Justin the Eucharist is by its nature a sacrifice.
[70] *Apologia I* 66.3 (Hänggi-Pahl, 70).
[71] *Apologia I* 66.2 (Hänggi-Pahl, 70).
[72] G. J. Cuming, "Di'euchês logou," *JTS* 31 (1980) 80–82.

We may conclude that according to Justin the bread and the wine are eucharistified by the prayer of thanksgiving which Jesus uttered at the Last Supper and which he himself passed on in order that we might give thanks as he did.

This is in full agreement with Justin's vocabulary. If the bread and wine become the Body and Blood of Christ by being eucharistified,[73] it follows that it is the "Eucharist" that eucharistifies; the "Eucharist" is the prayer (or word of prayer) handed on by Jesus.

3. THE EUCHARIST IN IRENAEUS:
HEAVENLY ELEMENT AND EARTHLY ELEMENT

In the *Against Heresies* of Irenaeus there are three passages which I shall place in parallel columns so that their close relationship will appear:

The bread taken from the earth	The bread	The grain of wheat fallen to the earth
	prepared	
having received	receives	receiving
the prayer *(epiclêsis)*	the word	the word
of God	of God	of God
is no longer ordinary bread but		
	and becomes	becomes
Eucharist made up of two elements, earthly and heavenly,	Eucharist	Eucharist
		that is,
body		body
of Christ		of Christ.[74]

These three texts complement each other and, taken together, give us the same doctrine as Justin's, which I explained above. In the first column we have "prayer" ("invocation," *epiclêsin*), which in the second

[73] A distant trace of this ancient teaching is still visible today in the practice of calling the bread and wine "Eucharist" because they have been "eucharistified."

[74] The first text is from *Against Heresies* 4.18.5 (SC 100/2; Paris, 1965) 610. The other two are from 5.2.3 (SC 153/2; Paris, 1969) 35.

and third texts becomes "word" *(logon)*. In the same way, Justin combines the two concepts as *euchês logou* ("word of prayer"). Both here and in Justin the result is the same: the bread and wine become Eucharist, that is, the Body and Blood of Christ. Irenaeus is also familiar with the term "eucharistify" and uses it.[75]

Still to be explained is the latter part of the first of the three texts, where the writer speaks of two elements, an earthly and a heavenly. The earthly element is easy to identify, because it is explained by Irenaeus himself: it is the bread taken from the earth. It is more difficult to say what the heavenly element is, as we can see from the discussion summarized by Van Den Eynde.[76] The answer is to be found in the second and third columns of the synopsis above, where it is said that the bread receives "the word of God." Knowing as we do that "heavenly" means "divine," there is no difficulty in claiming that there is a connection between "heavenly element" and "word of God." Van Den Eynde likewise concludes that the heavenly element is the word of God.

The only thing left to explain is how the word of God becomes part of the Eucharist as the second of its two constitutive elements. What is this "word of God"? The final step in my argument is based on the parallelism between the three texts: Since "word of God" is parallel to "prayer *(epiclêsis)* of God," we can say that the phrase in the first text, "the prayer *(epiclêsis)* of God," is the heavenly element in question.

While it is easy to understand that the "word of God" is "heavenly," it is less easy to see how the "prayer of God" can be described as "heavenly." The difficulty disappears if we think of this phrase in the light of Justin's words "word of prayer coming from him," that is, the formula of prayer that comes from Jesus. This is a traditional kind of expression, the meaning being that Christian prayer has its origin in the teaching of Jesus Christ and that the act of praying expresses a fidelity to Christ. Tertullian provides a clear confirmation of this meaning when he describes as "heavenly" the practice of prayer

[75] In translating 4.18.4, Rousseau (the editor and translator) uses "eucharistified" both in his French translation and in his translation back into Greek of the Latin sentence: "Quomodo autem constabit eis eum panem *in quo gratiae actae sint* corpus esse Domini sui" ("How will it be made clear to them that the bread *over which the thanksgiving is said* is the body of their Lord?") (SC 100/2:609). For the justification of the translation see SC 100/1:244f.

[76] See D. Van Den Eynde, "*Eucharistia ex duabus rebus constans: S. Irénée, Adv. haereses* IV, 18, 5," *Antonianum* 15 (1940) 26f.

taught by Jesus: *"Et quid non celeste, quod Domini Christi est, ut haec quoque orandi disciplina."*[77]

Taken together, the passages from Justin, Irenaeus, and Tertullian shed light on one another in a way that suggests the theme was a traditional one. We may therefore conclude that in Irenaeus, as in Justin, the prayer of thanksgiving was something that came from Jesus who, in the upper room, established and transmitted the model (or type) of the eucharistic celebration.

To complete the picture of Irenaeus' thought, there are two further points to be mentioned: (a) he calls the Eucharistic Prayer an "invocation"[78] (Greek: *epiclêsis*[79]) and not "Eucharist," since this term was now reserved for the "eucharistified" bread and wine; (b) the text of the Eucharistic Prayer is still a free composition, although there were

---

[77] *On Prayer* 1.3 (CCL 1, 257). Here is Grossi's translation: "Well, everything about Christ the Lord is heavenly, including therefore this form of prayer as well"; see V. Grossi (ed.), *Tertulliano–Cipriano–Agostino. Il Padre nostro* (Rome, 1980) 43. Compare Ambrose who distinguishes in the Eucharistic Prayer between the words of the priest and those of Christ, and applies the adjective "heavenly" only to the explanatory words: "Do you wish to know what heavenly words effect the consecration? . . . See, up to 'Receive the body . . . the blood,' the words are those of the evangelist; from there on, the words are those of Christ" (*De sacramentis* 4.21 [SC 25bis; Paris, 1961] 114). It is quite clear that for Ambrose the consecratory words as such are the "heavenly words"; their consecratory power derives from their heavenly character. In his understanding, "heavenly" signifies the origin of the words, that is, Jesus insofar as he is God; only their divine character ensures that these words have the same efficacy as the words of creation. Ambrose adds: "By what words does the consecration take place, and whose words are they? They are the words of the Lord Jesus. . . . Of what nature are his words? They are the words by which all things were made. The Lord commanded, and the heavens were made. The Lord commanded, and the earth was made. . . . See, then, how effective the words of Christ are. If, then, the words of the Lord Jesus have such power . . ." (*De sacramentis* 4.14-15; SC 25bis: 108–10).

[78] See also K. Gamber, "Das Eucharistiegebet als Epiklese und ein Zitat bei Irenäus," *Ostkirchliche Studien* 29 (1980) 301–5.

[79] In the disagreement between East and West over whether the consecration is effected by the Lord's words or by the epiclesis, theologians have asked whether Irenaeus is not to be listed among the supporters of consecration by the epiclesis, precisely because of the passage studied above in the text. As we have seen, the question should not be posed in this fashion, since in Irenaeus the word "epiclesis" is not to be confused with the technical term for the prayer that invokes the Spirit in the Eastern anaphoras. For Irenaeus "epiclesis" is a general word for the Eucharistic Prayer in its entirety; his was an age in which the prayer invoking the Spirit for the transformation of the bread and wine did not yet exist.

fairly detailed norms governing it, as can be gathered from the episode of the Marcosians.[80]

In concluding, we must bear in mind that a considerable difference has henceforth been introduced by comparison with the documents examined earlier. It is not the Last Supper that is regarded as a type of the Church's celebration, but only the Eucharistic Prayer. The Eucharistic Prayer is the "element that comes from him." The bread and wine are not an element originating in him, but are simply a material element coming from creation.[81]

4. CONCLUSION

Since the bread and wine are connected with the Eucharistic Prayer and have their meaning determined by it, they too are called "Eucharist." This is the first term used by the early Church to indicate the sacramental character of the bread and wine and of the entire meal as an imitation of Jesus' supper in the upper room. This usage gave rise to a second way of referring to the sacramental bread and wine: "eucharistified." In both cases the intention was to assert a ritual and ontological correspondence[82] between the Eucharist of the Church and the type established by Jesus at the Last Supper. The two cases are not, however, identical with each other, because a certain development has occurred in the meantime. The term "antitype" emphasizes

---

[80] Irenaeus tells the story of Marcus, a charlatan who passed himself off as a prophet and had many followers. He appointed a woman, a faithful disciple of his and a prophetess, to preside at the Eucharist. He also managed, by some trickery, to have the wine in the cup appear to be blood. Irenaeus condemns the use of such devices to give the Eucharist a striking character; he pays no attention to the fact that a woman pronounced the thanksgiving that "made the Eucharist" (*On Heresies* 1.13.2; SC 264/2:192). See J. M. Joncas, "Eucharist among the Marcosians: A Study of Irenaeus' *Adversus Haereses* I, 13, 2," *Questions Liturgiques* 71 (1990) 99–111. A comparable case is reported by Firmilian; writing to Cyprian he tells of a woman who used magical arts to give a stunning appearance to the Eucharist she was celebrating. Firmilian censures the use of magic but is not concerned by the fact that a woman uttered the thanksgiving, which, he says, was "not worthless," that is, was a good thanksgiving, conformed to the tradition (Letter 25.10, in L. Bayard [ed.], *Saint Cyprien. Correspondance* 2 [Collection des Universités de France, Association Guillaume Budé; Paris, 1960] 298).

[81] This fact is very important since it allows Irenaeus to start a theological dialogue between creation and sacrament and in this way to maintain the radical goodness of creation as part of his general attack on heresies.

[82] Thus the conception expressed by "eucharistified" and found in both Justin and Irenaeus is still part of the theology of type and antitype.

the connection between the celebration of the Church and the type, whereas "eucharistified" refers rather to the effect of this connection on the two elements, the bread and the wine. The difference between these two approaches to the Eucharist may seem small, but it is precise and technically well formulated: there has been a shift from the theology of the connection to the theology of the effect of the connection.[83]

For this reason, the interpretation of the Eucharist by Justin and Irenaeus is not to be confused with a theology of eucharistic consecration.[84] In Justin the Eucharistic Prayer plays a decisive role, not because it consecrates but because it ensures the correspondence of the "eucharistified" elements with the "type" established by Jesus at the Last Supper. Irenaeus represents the same conception but at a slightly more advanced stage of development: the "type" has already moved to a less important place and all attention is focused on the "eucharistified" elements.

[83] We have not yet reached the doctrine of consecration, which is later, but we are already on the way to it.

[84] Because of this we cannot say that Justin and Irenaeus attest that the Eucharistic Prayer is consecratory. The reason we cannot make this claim is not because the words of the Lord or the epiclesis are not consecratory, but that the theology of consecration has not yet made its appearance. I must therefore correct my previous way of posing the question, when, not realizing that the theology of the antitype is different from the theology of consecration, I asserted the consecratory value of the Eucharistic Prayer. See my *The Eucharistic Prayers of the Roman Rite*, trans. M. J. O'Connell (New York, 1986) chapter 9, p. 253, and passim.

Tertullian and Cyprian

1. TERTULLIAN

Quintus Septimus Florens Tertullianus (155–ca. 220) is a writer of great importance both for the information he supplies about his times and for the influence he had on later writers. He does not have an organized treatise on the Eucharist, and he speaks of it only occasionally, but he has left enough references to it that we are able to reconstruct both the general outline of the celebration (even if only in broad lines[1]) and his teaching on the subject. In his ideas on the Eucharist he adopts a sacramental realism that is very sure of itself and without problems or uncertainties; it is based on the typological or figural method.

1.1. The Eucharist: Body and Blood of Christ

Tertullian describes the path of ritual followed by one who becomes a Christian; after referring to the baptismal rites, he speaks of the Eucharist: ". . . the flesh feeds *(vescitur)* on the body and blood of Christ in order that the soul may be nourished *(saginetur)* by God."[2] The same idea is expressed in *De pudicitia* 9: ". . . and thus man feeds *(vescitur)* on the richness *(opimitate*[3]*)* of the body of Christ, that is, the Eucharist."[4] In a polemical exhortation directed at those who approach the

---

[1] J. Beran, "De ordine missae secundum Tertulliani *Apologeticum,*" in *Miscellanea liturgica in honorem L. Cuniberti Mohlberg* 2 (Bibliotheca Ephemerides Liturgicae 23; Rome: Edizioni liturgiche, 1949) 3–32.

[2] *De resurrectione mortuorum* 8 (CCL 2, 931).

[3] The allusion is to the fatted calf in the parable in Luke 15:11-32; the banquet for the prodigal son is linked with the Eucharist to which sinners have access when they return to the Church.

[4] *De pudicitia* 9 (CCL 2, 1298).

Eucharist after engaging in the manufacture of idols, Tertullian shows that he has a strongly realistic conception of the Eucharist. He censures their taking of the Eucharist by comparing it to the behavior of the Jews who laid hands on Christ; here is the text: "Reach out *(admovere)* to the body of Christ hands that have given shape to a demon? . . . Only once did the Jews lay hands on Christ; these people assail *(lacessunt)* his body daily. Hands that should be cut off!"[5] What is done to the Sacrament is done to Christ.

In fact, in the passage cited Tertullian is putting the Sacrament on the same level as the historical event experienced by the body of Christ. He can do this because in his eyes there is a real identity between the Sacrament and the historical body of Christ. This is confirmed by following reflection on the eucharistic cup: "There can be no bodily blood unless the flesh is there."[6]

Tertullian's argument is based on the conviction, which he shares with his adversaries, that the eucharistic wine is the Blood of Christ; from this he concludes that if the wine is to be truly Blood, the Body of Christ must be really flesh and not a mere appearance, as Marcion maintained. His argument starts, then, with eucharistic realism and concludes to the truth of Christ's incarnation. There could not be a better demonstration of sacramental realism. This same procedure is used three times. A first is in the passage we have just seen. A second comes in the fifth book of the *Adversus Marcionem*, where Tertullian restricts himself to stating the terms of the question, reminding his reader that he has already dealt with it, and repeating that the Sacrament demonstrates the reality ("truth") of the Body and Blood which Christ assumed in the incarnation: "Thus, from the sacrament of the bread and cup, which is in the gospel, we have already proved the truth of the Lord's body and blood against the fancies of Marcion."[7] The third use of the argument merits separate treatment because of the important phrase it contains: *figura corporis.*

1.2. Figura corporis

In order to prove against Marcion that the incarnation of Christ was not a mere appearance and that the body of Christ was really flesh, Tertullian develops a very subtle argument. He is fully aware

---

[5] *De idololatria* 7 (CCL 2, 1106).
[6] *Adversus Marcionem* 4.40 (CCL 1, 657).
[7] Ibid., 5.8 (CCL 1, 686).

of its significance, since he uses it, as I have said, three times. His starting point is a sacramental realism which he evidently shares with his interlocutors,[8] and his point of arrival is the realism of the incarnation of Christ.

Tertullian uses the technical language of typology, in which the expression *figura corporis*[9] originated. He did not coin the phrase; rather, it comes certainly from the text of some anaphora or paleoanaphora, as the Latin equivalent of *antitypos*.[10] There are, in fact, various testimonies that *figura corporis*, or its Greek and Syriac equivalents, belonged to the text of archaic eucharistic prayers, such as we have seen, at least in part, at the beginning of the present book. In addition, the phrase is also found in the primitive redaction of the Roman Canon to which Ambrose bears witness[11] and in Mozarabic developments of that Eucharistic Prayer.

In using the expression *figura corporis* Tertullian is making clear the sacramental status of the eucharistic bread, in order then to conclude to the reality of Christ's incarnation. The argument begins by recalling that at the Last Supper Jesus clearly said "This is my body," meaning by this that "this is the figure of my body." However, a *figura* exists only in relation to a *veritas* or reality. Therefore, the figural nature of the eucharistic bread necessarily relates to the truth or reality of the incarnation.[12] What is the significance of the word *figura*? At the Last Supper, by saying "This is my body," Jesus turned

[8] This is an important fact that allows us to claim that the sacramental realism attested by Tertullian was commonly held and was not a personal idea of Tertullian's.

[9] For the background of the problem see C. H. Turner, "*Adversaria patristica* III. 'Figura corporis mei' in Tertullian," *JTS* 7 (1906) 595–97; A. Wilmart, "*Transfigurare*," *Bulletin d'ancienne littérature et d'archéologie chrétienne* 1 (1911) 282–92; V. Saxer, "*Figura corporis et sanguinis Domini*," *Rivista di archeologia cristiana* 47 (1971) 65–89; idem, "Tertullian," in W. Rordorf and others, *The Eucharist of the Early Christians*, trans. M. J. O'Connell (New York: Pueblo, 1978) 132–55.

[10] In the Latin and Greek world, the archaic *antitypos–figura* was succeeded by *homoiôma–similitudo*, a term already used in the New Testament to signify sacramentality; in Romans 6:5 it is used of the sacramentality of baptism.

[11] Ambrose, *De sacramentis* 4.5 (SC 25bis, 114). The phrase is also used in Augustine: ". . . in which [banquet, Jesus] transmitted and entrusted to his disciples the figure of his body and his blood" (PL 36:73).

[12] See *Adversus Marcionem* 4.40: "Having said, therefore, that he greatly desired to eat his own passover (it was beneath the dignity of God to desire another's), he took bread and, having distributed it to his disciples, turned it into his body, saying 'This is my body,' that is, a figure of his body. But it would not have been a figure unless his was truly a body."

the bread into the *figura* of his body, and *figura* should therefore be taken in a realistic sense.

Here are the steps in the argument: (1) the body which Christ assumed in the incarnation is called *veritas,* while the eucharistic bread is called *figura;* (2) because of the ontological relationship of *figura* and *veritas,* if the *figura* belongs to the real order, so must the *veritas;* (3) Tertullian concludes that if the *figura* of the Body of Christ (the eucharistic bread) is real, then the body which Christ assumed in the incarnation must also be real. If the latter were not real, the Sacrament could not be called a *figura.*

The term *figura,* then, is used not to signify a purely symbolic interpretation but to show the sacramental realism of the Eucharist. This terminology (*figura, repraesentare,* and so on) is part of the language specific to the interpretation of the Bible and expresses the relationship between the Old Testament and the New, that is, between the announcement and the carrying out of the work of salvation. Biblical typology serves to say that announcement and fulfillment are not two different phases or two different realities of salvation, but are one; the Old Testament participates in the New, and the announcement in the fulfillment.[13] The ontological relationship (of participation) between the event and the prior announcement of it suggested to the early Fathers that they should take over, en bloc, the entire special terminology of biblical interpretation and apply it to the liturgy. We should always bear in mind that the reason for transferring the technical vocabulary of biblical interpretation to the liturgy was that it could ensure the ontological value of the relationship between the two realities, namely, the announcement and the fulfillment. Consequently, since sacramental realism is characteristic of the language of typology—of figure and representation—it is not surprising that Tertullian should apply this language to the Eucharist, thereby staying within a strongly realistic conception of sacramentality.

The expression *figura corporis,* then, is not to be understood as implying a symbolic understanding of the Eucharist that is opposed to realism, for the expression is one of the technical terms of sacramental realism in the original formulation of the latter, that is, the typological formulation. Also to be emphasized is that in the logic of typology

[13] The events in which the fulfillment took place were already present in the announcement of them, even if in a hidden way, concealed inside of others, and that presence was called figural or typological.

the term *veritas* signifies not the Sacrament but the historical body of Christ.[14]

1.3. *The Representation of the Body and Blood of Christ*

Repraesentatio is a technical term in sacramental doctrine, as is *demonstratio*,[15] as we have seen *figura* to be.[16] Does *repraesentare* point to a symbolic or a realistic interpretation of the Eucharist? In his controversy with Marcion Tertullian defends the goodness of created things and maintains this goodness as the basis for the sacramental use of certain elements: the water of baptism, the oil of sacramental anointings, the mixture of milk and honey used at a baptismal Eucharist, and the bread of the Eucharist, which is the Sacrament of the Body of Christ. I must underscore the term used by Tertullian in saying that the bread is the Sacrament of the Body of Christ: ". . . the bread by which he *repraesentat* his body."[17] We saw above the realistic way in which Tertullian views the sacramental character of the eucharistic bread. Since this sacramental character is expressed by *repraesentare* in the short text just cited, we should conclude that this term is to be interpreted in light of Tertullian's sacramental realism, and not of a purely symbolic understanding of the Eucharist, such as this author does not maintain.

1.4. Sacrificiorum orationibus

Since Tertullian was a distinguished man of letters, to the extent of being regarded as the founder of Christian Latin, we must think that

---

[14] In the early Middle Ages, however, the term *veritas* lost the technical meaning it had in typology, and it became part of the vocabulary of sacramental realism; for this reason it was applied to the eucharistic bread, which would not have been possible in typology.

[15] *Adversus Marcionem* 4.40: "He will, he says, wash his robe in wine and his garment in the blood of the grape, showing *(demonstrans)* by robe and garment his flesh and by wine his blood. So now he consecrated his blood in the wine, whereas of old he had made wine a figure of his blood" (CCL 1:657).

[16] In addition to passages already cited, see the following passage in which Old Testament typology also appears: "This wood Jeremias likewise suggests to you, when he foretells what the Jews will say: 'Come, let us put wood in his bread,' that is, into his body. In your own gospel the Lord revealed the same, calling bread his body, so that from this you may understand that he has made the bread a figure of his body; in the past, the prophet had figured this body as bread, while the Lord was later to interpret the bread as this sacrament" (*Adv. Marcionem* 3.19; CCL 1, 553).

[17] *Adversus Marcionem* 1.14 (CCL 1, 455).

he was conscious of what he was saying when he coined the phrase *sacrificiorum orationibus,* meaning "sacrificial prayers." The expression refers immediately to the Eucharistic Prayer, but by extension it refers to the Eucharist as a whole, as is clear from the context.[18] We ought not be surprised that the expression, even though coined to signify the Eucharistic Prayer, should be used for the entire eucharistic celebration. The Greek word *eucharistia* underwent the same development: It referred immediately to the prayer of thanksgiving but from there was extended to mean the bread and wine and the entire celebration.

As Tertullian understood it, the predicate "sacrifice" belonged originally to the Eucharistic Prayer *(sacrificiorum orationibus)* and was extended to the ritual celebration in its entirety *(participatio sacrificii).*[19] He seems to regard the prayer as the element specific to Christian sacrifice.[20]

1.5. The Eucharist and Life

In commenting on the Our Father, Tertullian says that the petition "Give us this day our daily bread" is to be understood as having a spiritual meaning:

[18] See *De oratione* 19 (CCL 1, 267–68): "Similarly regarding Station days, most people think they need not be present at the sacrificial prayers, on the grounds that the Station is replaced by the reception of the Lord's body. Does the Eucharist, then, cancel a service devoted to God or does it not rather link it more closely to God? Will your Station not be more solemn if you also stand at the altar of God? When the Lord's body has been received and reserved, both practices are safeguarded: participation in the sacrifice and the fulfillment of duty" (*De oratione* 19; CCL 1, 267–68). The passage suggests that the eucharistic bread was taken home and Communion was received there after the end of the fast. This is a very early witness to the practice of keeping the Eucharist at home.

[19] Tertullian has an exact idea of the abolition of Jewish sacrifices and a vision of sacrifice as consisting of the contrite heart and thus of prayer. Malachi 1:11 provides him with the basis for his argument, in, e.g., *Adversus Marcionem* 3.22 (CCL 1, 539).

[20] See *De oratione* 28 (CCL 1, 273): "This is the spiritual victim that has done away with the earlier sacrifices. . . . We are true worshipers and true priests, who pray in spirit and in spirit offer the sacrifice of prayer as the victim suited to God and acceptable to him, the victim for which he asked, the victim he anticipated for himself." See also: "And I will not accept your sacrifices, for from the rising of the sun to its going down my name is glorified among the nations, and in every place a sacrifice is offered to my name, a clean sacrifice, namely, the giving of glory, blessing, praise, and hymns" (*Adv. Marcionem* 3.32; CCL 1, 539).

"In fact, Christ is our bread, for Christ is life and bread is life[21] ('I am the bread of life,' Christ says; and just before that: 'The bread is the word of the living God that comes down from heaven'). This is also the reason why Christ's body is located in bread *(in pane censetur):* 'This is my body.' Thus in asking for daily bread, we are asking to abide in Christ and not to be separated from his body."[22]

The Eucharist, then, is life and gives life. Through the following and imitation of Christ, the life that he lived until his death will be manifested in the bodies of his faithful.[23] By bearing the suffering[24] and martyrdom[25] of Christ in their own bodies, believers are to reproduce the life of their master,[26] so that where his suffering is manifested his life also may be manifested.[27]

1.6. The Presidency of the Eucharist

The Eucharist is celebrated at the command of the Lord who at the Last Supper transformed bread into the figure of his body; it can be received during the celebration or be kept at home to be received before a meal.[28] In any case, however, it is to be received only from the one who presides.[29] This directive shows how important the role of the presider is at the eucharistic rite. It seems however that the priestly function was only one of the elements making up the rite, but was not an essential constituent of the sacramental nature of the Eucharist, since at that period a layman could preside at the eucharistic

[21] Augustine tells us that the Punic people, in their own language, called the Eucharist simply "life." In my opinion, this usage may have been common well before the fourth century.

[22] *De oratione* 6 (CCL 1, 261).

[23] *De resurrectione mortuorum* 44 (CCL 2, 980).

[24] Ibid.: "'Always carrying around in our body the dying of Jesus.' What kind of thing is the body, which after being called the temple of God can now be called the tomb of Christ? And why do we carry around in our body the dying of the Lord? In order, he says, that life may be manifested. Where? In the body. In what body? The mortal body."

[25] See, e.g., *De praescriptione haereticorum* 36 (CCL 1, 216): "Peter is made equal to the passion of the Lord."

[26] *Scorpiace* 9 (CCL 2, 1085).

[27] *De resurrectione mortuorum* 44 (CCL 2, 980).

[28] *Ad uxorem* 2.5 (CCL 1, 389).

[29] *De corona* 3 (CCL 2, 1043): "Even at predawn assemblies, and only from the hands of the presiders, we receive the sacrament of the Eucharist, which the Lord ordered to be taken at meals and by all."

celebration in places where the ecclesiastical hierarchy had not yet been established:

"Are we not priests as well as laypersons? It is written: 'He made us a kingdom of priests for God and his Father.' The Church has by its authority established the distinction between hierarchy *(ordo)* and people *(plebs)*, and the hierarchy in turn divides into hierarchic degrees those who are consecrated to God.[30] Where there is no hierarchically organized assembly,[31] you may baptize and preside at the eucharistic celebration and be your own priest; and in fact, wherever there are three, even if they be laypersons, there is the Church."[32]

According to Tertullian, then, the primary requirement for the celebration of the Eucharist is the Church, that is, an assembly of the faithful, within which resides the function of presider, which as such is a priestly function, even when a layman exercises it in utterly exceptional cases. Eucharist and priesthood are thus so intrinsically connected that, in order to explain how a layman can preside at the Eucharist, Tertullian must appeal either to the priesthood of the faithful or to the ecclesial character of the gathered congregation, a character based on the presence of Christ in the assembly.[33] In Tertullian's thinking, the sacramental realism of the Eucharist is based on and originates in its own figural nature, according to which the bread is the Body of Christ because it is the figure of that body. The same holds for the cup in relation to the Blood of Christ and for the relation of sacramentality which the Eucharist has to the passion of Christ. This relation is expressed, indifferently, by either *figura* or *repraesentare*.

2. CYPRIAN OF CARTHAGE
Caecilius Cyprian (ca. 200/210 to 258) does not seem to have known Tertullian personally, but he read the latter's works daily

---

[30] I venture to suggest that the phrase "et honor per ordinis consessus sanctificatos Deo" be translated thus. It is a difficult phrase to restore even for editor E. Kroymann, who proposes the reading "consessum"; *De exhortatione castitatis* 7 (CCL 2, 1025).

[31] Ibid.: "Ubi ecclesiastici ordinis non est consessus."

[32] Ibid. (CCL 2, 1024–25).

[33] On the basis of this position we might say that Tertullian has a lay conception of the Church, but one that is not opposed to the priesthood, since presidency at the liturgy is a priestly action even when performed by a layman.

and referred to him as "master."[34] There was a strong bond between Cyprian and Tertullian despite the fact that they were two very different personalities.

Cyprian's teaching on the Eucharist is contained above all in his Letter 63, "On the sacrament of the Lord's cup," which was addressed to Bishop Caecilius of Biltha in about the autumn of 253. The letter is the only antenicene document to deal exclusively with the Eucharist; in practice it is a real treatise on the subject,[35] the first of its kind, and is of capital importance for us not only because the problem raised is liturgical[36] and because the method used is the typological, but also and above all because it erects a real and proper theory of the Last Supper as the *norma* which the Eucharist of the Church must *imitare*, just as the paleoanaphoras and anaphoras examined earlier had done. In Cyprian, the testimony of a Father is joined to the testimony of the liturgy: the eucharistic celebration must take place in the image of what Jesus did at the Last Supper. If Cyprian had been asked what the Eucharist is, he would have replied as the early anaphoras did: To celebrate the Eucharist is "to follow exactly what the Lord has done,"[37] because "it becomes our clear duty to heed and do only what Christ did and only what He prescribed should be done."[38]

2.1. The Presidency of the Eucharist

Cyprian makes extensive use of typology and applies it to the liturgy. If the eucharistic celebration corresponds to the Last Supper as to its model, it follows that there will be a special correspondence between the "priest," *sacerdos*, that is, the bishop, and Christ who

[34] J. Quasten, *Patrology* II (Westminster, Md.: Newman, 1953) 340.

[35] The Latin text of Cyprian's letters, with a French translation, can be found in the edition of L. Bayard: *Saint Cyprien: Correspondance* (Collection des Universités de France; Association Guilluame Budé; Paris: Les Belles Lettres, 1962ff. Reference here is to vol. 1, p. XXIX. [I shall be using the translation in the Ancient Christian Writer series: *The Letters of St. Cyprian of Carthage.* Volume II: Letters 55–66, trans. G. W. Clarke (ACW 46; New York: Newman, 1986). Cited as: Clarke, with page number.—Tr.]).

[36] The letter deals with the need of using wine with water in the eucharistic celebration, and not water alone, as some had begun to do. The possibility cannot be excluded that this last may have been a very old Jewish Christian practice, which later underwent a significant development. See R. Johanny, "Cyprian of Carthage," in *The Eucharist of the Early Christians* (note 9, above), 160.

[37] Letter 63.18 (Clarke, 109).

[38] Letter 63.14 (Clarke, 107).

presided at the Last Supper. The priest fills the role of Christ: He takes Christ's place and repeats his gestures. This is not simply an external correspondence, for, according to Cyprian there is a real, even if relative, identity between the priest and Christ; the priest can be said to participate in Christ.[39]

In the Greek lexicon of sacramentality this relationship is expressed by the entry *typos–antitypos,* which came into Latin as simply *typus* and is found in the Latin Fathers as well. In Cyprian's thinking, the priest is the *typus Christi*[40] and fills the role of Christ.[41] At times, Cyprian rewords this phrase as *vice Christi.*[42] The meaning is the same: The priest *has the place* of Christ, and he really has it because he is imitating Christ, due to the Holy Spirit whom he has received, so that the actions he performs are the actions of Christ himself, even if only by participation. There is a kind of identification of the priest and Christ, and this is the ultimate reason for the identity of the Church's Eucharist and the Last Supper. For Cyprian, then, the sacramentality of the priesthood is the ultimate explanation of the sacramentality of the Eucharist.

2.2. *The Eucharist an Imitation of the Last Supper*

In the Eucharist "we do . . . exactly what the Lord did,"[43] and his command is not observed unless the same thing is done that the Lord did.[44] At the Last Supper Jesus prescribed and practiced (*praecepit et gessit*[45]) what is to be done when the Eucharist is celebrated. Cyprian

[39] For a proper understanding of the passages from Cyprian that will be cited, we must keep in mind the meaning of the two key terms: *passio* and *sacrificium. Passio* means and refers to the Last Supper and the account of it; at a second level, it signifies all the events of the passion of Christ, Calvary, and the shedding of his blood. The main referent for *sacrificium* is the Eucharistic Prayer but also, by way of this basic meaning, the entire celebration of the Last Supper, the bread and the wine, the events of Calvary, and the eucharistic celebration of the Church.

[40] A modern term to translate *typus* would be "sacrament," although the meaning is not completely the same; in the present case, at any rate, it is correct to say that *typus Christi* means "sacrament of Christ."

[41] See J.-D. Laurance, "Le président de l'Eucharistie selon Cyprien de Carthage: un nouvel examen," *MD,* no. 154 (1983) 151–65.

[42] See Letter 63.14: "That priest truly serves in Christ's place who imitates what Christ did" (Clarke, 107).

[43] Letter 63.10 (Clarke, 103).

[44] Note the emphasis on the verb *facere,* which will play a large part in the Western anaphoras, where *facite–haec facimus* structure the anamnesis.

[45] Letter 63.1 (Clarke, 98).

rebukes those who place only water in the cup instead of water mixed with wine, because they do not "follow the precepts and practices of Jesus Christ our Lord and God, the Author and Teacher of this sacrifice."[46] And again: "You should understand that the warning we have been given is this: in offering the cup the teachings of the Lord must be observed and we must do exactly as the Lord first did Himself for us—the cup which is offered up in remembrance of Him is to be offered mixed with wine."[47] Further on, he says that we are "to offer His cup mixed with wine just as He Himself offered it."[48]

Cyprian sees in the account of the Last Supper[49] an instruction by Jesus, who taught what the faithful are to do: "He has taught us by His own authoritative example that it [the cup] should consist of the union of wine and water."[50] To celebrate the Eucharist, then is simply "to follow exactly what the Lord has done."[51] Cyprian finds it unbelievable that anyone could "depart from the precepts of the gospel,"[52] and he applies the statement of Paul to the tradition regarding the Eucharist: "Even if we ourselves or an angel from heaven should preach to you a gospel different from the one we proclaimed to you, let him be anathema!" (Gal 1:8).

The conclusion is clear: "The Gospel rule and the Lord's instructions are everywhere to be observed."[53] The Eucharist is in the true sense an act of the *sequela Christi,* for "if we are indeed priests of God and of Christ, there is no one I know whom we ought to follow in preference to God and Christ. . . . We ought to follow Christ and to observe His commandments."[54] Cyprian denies that it is possible to follow the custom of a few people when in fact we must follow Christ, and so he sets it down as a principle that "if in the sacrifice which Christ offered we are to follow nobody but Christ, then it becomes our clear duty to heed and do only what Christ did and only what He prescribed should be done."[55]

[46] Ibid.
[47] Letter 63.2 (Clarke, 98).
[48] Letter 63.17 (Clarke, 108).
[49] Matthew 26:28-29.
[50] Letter 63.9 (Clarke, 102).
[51] Letter 63.18 (Clarke, 109).
[52] Letter 63.10 (Clarke, 103).
[53] Letter 63.17 (Clarke, 108).
[54] Letter 63.18 (Clarke, 108).
[55] Letter 63.13 (Clarke, 105–6).

In this way Cyprian establishes the importance of the account of the Last Supper, which provides the model for the Church's celebration. He expresses the same thought in another way when he says that in the celebration of the Eucharist, and especially when it comes to the cup (which was the particular problem he was facing), we must "guard the truth of our Lord's teachings to us."[56] Everything in the eucharistic celebration is connected with the following of the model given by Jesus at the Last Supper: What he did in the upper room is described as *dominica veritas*. The word *veritas* gives theological status to the model that is to be followed.[57]

Because of its correspondence to the truth, the Eucharist of the Church is to be described as *figura* and *repraesentatio*.

2.3. The Eucharistic Prayer

The Eucharistic Prayer is called *Prex* and, in accordance with Cyprian's general teaching on prayer, it calls for a real identification with Christ: "The Father recognizes the words of his Son when we utter the prayer [the Our Father], for he who dwells within our breast is also in our voice."[58] This principle applies not only to the Our Father but on a much broader scale, since Cyprian says: "It was not by words alone but also by deeds that the Lord taught us to pray, for he himself offered prayer and entreaty, thus showing by the witness of his example what we too must do."[59] Finally, let us recall the great principle which Cyprian derived from the Scriptures: "God is one who hears not the voice but the heart," and which he applies to the Eucharistic Prayer: "And when we gather in union with the brethren and celebrate divine sacrifices [the Eucharistic Prayer] with the priest of God [the bishop], we must be mindful of modesty and discipline, not letting our voices wander here and there, as if they were independent of us . . . for God is one who hears not the voice but the heart."[60] On the basis of these statements we can accept the conclusion of John D.

---

[56] Letter 93.19 (Clarke, 109). A little earlier, Cyprian had likewise appealed to the *dominica veritas:* "To drink this cup in the Church of the Lord can indeed bring us joy, but only if, when we drink it, we adhere to the true prescriptions of the Lord" (Letter 63.11; Clarke, 104).

[57] This understanding of *veritas* is the same as that found in Tertullian, and is characteristic of biblical typology as applied to the liturgy.

[58] *De dominica oratione* 3 (CCL 3A, 91).

[59] Ibid., 29 (p. 108).

[60] Ibid., 4 (p. 91).

Laurance: "A priest is one who imitates not only the outward actions of Christ but also his interior attitude of obedience and sacrificial prayer."[61]

Is it proper, however, to fuse the general teaching of Cyprian on prayer with what he says about the Eucharistic Prayer? Well, Cyprian himself links the two in a passage which Laurance describes as short but packed:[62] Cyprian brings together the prayer of Christ at the Last Supper with his prayer in the olive garden: "He prayed and petitioned not for himself . . . but for our sins."[63] Then, after describing what Jesus was asking for in the garden, he adds the climax of Jesus' prayer at the Supper: "I pray not only for them but for those also who through their word will believe in me: that all may be one. As you, Father, are in me and I in you, may they also be [one] in us."[64] Cyprian concludes: "Not satisfied with redeeming us by his blood, he does even more for us, by praying for us as well. And see what his desire was as he prayed: that as the Father and the Son are one, we too might remain in the same unity."[65]

2.4. Old Testament Prefigurations

If we look at the Old Testament prefigurations, only the wine, and not the water, is connected with the Lord's cup and passion; in fact, in the Old Testament, water prefigures baptism,[66] and is not, therefore, a formal constituent of the Eucharist. When Noah drank wine, he became a figure of the Lord's passion, and since he drank not water but wine, he showed forth a type of the truth to come.[67] Cyprian sees the high priest Melchizedek as prefiguring the sacrifice which the Lord offered.[68] Another type of the Lord's sacrifice is shown forth by the Holy Spirit through Solomon as he tells of the banquet of Wisdom,[69] who issues an invitation to eat of her bread and drink of her wine.[70]

[61] J. D. Laurance, *"Priest" as Type of Christ. The Leader of the Eucharist in Salvation History according to Cyprian of Carthage* (American University Studies VII. Theology and Religion 5; New York–Bern–Frankfort a. M.-Nancy: Peter Lang, 1984) 220.

[62] Ibid., 201.

[63] *De dominica oratione* 30 (CCL 3A, 108).

[64] John 17:20-21.

[65] *De dominica oratione* 30 (p. 108).

[66] Letter 63.8-9.

[67] Letter 63.3.

[68] Letter 63.4.

[69] Proverbs 9:1-5.

[70] Letter 63.5.

In addition, the "blood of the grape" in Genesis 49:11[71] refers *(ostenditur)* to the wine in the cup of the Lord, that is, his Blood.[72]

2.5. *Sacrifice and Fulfillment of Figures*

In describing the Last Supper in relation to its prefiguration by Melchizedek, Cyprian says that Jesus offered what Melchizedek had offered, but with this difference, that when Jesus offered his sacrifice[73] to God, he offered bread and wine that were in fact his Body and his Blood. Just as it is not possible to drink wine until the grapes have been trampled and pressed, so it is not possible to drink the Blood of Christ until Christ has been trodden down and pressed in his passion and until he himself drank the cup first in order to incite those who believe in him to do the same.[74] Cyprian develops the connection between the Last Supper and the passion by saying that the Holy Spirit, through Solomon and his description of the banquet of wisdom, "forecasts *(ante praemonstrat)* a type of the sacrifice of our Lord which is to come, referring to a victim offered in sacrifice, to bread and wine, and even to an altar and the apostles."[75] The rite of the Last Supper is sacrificial in character, as is the Cross of Jesus, with which the eucharistic cup has a special figural connection, because in these actions of the passion of Christ the Old Testament prefigurations are fulfilled. In fulfilling and completing the sacrifice of Melchizedek, Jesus offered the bread and the cup of water and wine; thus "He who is Fullness itself fulfilled the truth of that prefigured symbol."[76]

After citing Proverbs 9:1-5, Cyprian concludes that since the Scriptures speak of wine mixed with water, Solomon "prophetically foretells that the cup of the Lord is mixed with water and wine. Hence, it

---

[71] "He shall wash his robe in wine and his garment in the blood of the grape."

[72] Letter 63.6.

[73] Note the great importance of the following passage, which attributes a sacrificial character to the Last Supper of Christ: "In the case of the priest Melchizedek we see foreshadowed in mystery a type of the Lord's sacrifice, as the Holy Scriptures testify . . . and the fact that Melchizedek indeed portrayed a type of Christ is declared in the Psalms by the Holy Spirit speaking in the person of the Father to the Son. . . . And who is more truly a priest of the most high God than our Lord Jesus Christ, who offered sacrifice to God the Father and made the very same offering as Melchizedek had done, viz. bread and wine, that is to say, His own body and blood?" (Letter 63.4; Clarke, 99).

[74] Letter 63.7.

[75] Letter 63.5 (Clarke, 100).

[76] Letter 63.4 (Clarke, 100).

becomes evident that in the passion of our Lord that was accomplished which had already been predicted."[77] The eucharistic sacrifice of the Church is likewise called a sacrifice because of its perfect correspondence with the Last Supper: "How are we going to drink with Christ new wine from the fruit of the vine in the kingdom of the Father if in our sacrifice to God the Father we do not even offer the wine of Christ and if we do not mix the cup of the Lord as the Lord Himself has appointed *(traditione dominica)?*"[78]

2.6. Sacramental Value

The wine in the cup shows forth *(ostendit)* the Blood of Christ[79]—a statement in which the verb *show* has a realistic sense. In fact, the command of Christ regarding the Eucharist concerns "the very mystery *(sacramentum)* of the Lord's passion and our redemption."[80] The Eucharist, which is called a sacrifice, is the passion of the Lord: "And because at every sacrifice we offer we mention the passion of our Lord (indeed, the passion of our Lord is the sacrifice we offer), then we should follow exactly what the Lord did."[81] The effect of the Eucharist is unity, but this theme is developed in a rather weak way, although Cyprian knows that the Eucharist has a special connection with unity, for even he calls it "the sacrament of unity."[82]

The fullest development of the theme of unity is in Letter 63. In his description Cyprian uses the *Didache* tradition, but simply as an image; he looks on it as only a literary theme, and I cannot believe that he knew the *Didache* as a still living liturgical tradition. The theme of unity is brought into play in the areas both of the sacraments and of ecclesiology. Cyprian applies the theme directly to the cup and says that when the water is mingled with the wine, the two, which represent the people and Christ, are combined and united, and then "this spiritual and divine mystery *(sacramentum)* is accomplished."[83] The

[77] Letter 63.5 (Clarke, 100).
[78] Letter 63.9 (Clarke, 102–3).
[79] Letter 63.2.
[80] Letter 63.14 (Clarke, 106).
[81] Letter 63.17 (Clarke, 107).
[82] Among other passages, see Letter 45 and Letter 49.6, but especially the *De ecclesiae catholicae unitate* 6–7, where the author says that it is not possible to have God as our Father if we do not have the Church as our Mother and that it is not possible to approach the Eucharist if we are not united with the Church.
[83] Letter 63.13 (Clarke, 105).

eucharistic bread, being the Body of Christ, is also described in relation to unity. "Under this same sacred image *(sacramentum)* our people are represented *(ostenditur)* as having been made one, for just as numerous grains are gathered, ground, and mixed all together to make into one loaf of bread, so in Christ, who is the bread of heaven, we know there is but one body."[84]

Both the cup and the bread, then, show the unity of the Church. The connection between the eucharistic bread and the unity of the Church is a traditional theme of the liturgy and of eucharistic doctrine, but Cyprian does not succeed in mastering it fully. He says only that the connection exists and that the Sacrament shows the unity of the Church, but although both the Eucharist and the Church are described as the body of Christ, he is unable to say whether there is an ontological relationship, and of what kind, between them. We must wait for Augustine to tackle this question. Cyprian does not have Augustine's competence in either the Scriptures or in philosophy;[85] as a result, this aspect is not taken up, but remains undeveloped, and is set down without being really understood.

2.7. Commemoration of Christ

Cyprian describes the Eucharist as a "remembrance of the Lord,"[86] an expression that originates in the account of the Last Supper and in the mandate: "Do this in remembrance of me." The commemoration of Christ is a commemoration of his passion, and this is why the cup must contain wine, that is, to give expression to the passion of Christ. For Christ said that the wine is his Blood, and if there is no wine, there is no reference to the passion. The sacrifice of the Lord is celebrated only when "the offering and sacrifice we make corresponds with His passion."[87]

[84] Letter 63.13 (Clarke, 195).

[85] It is only these two competences taken together that allow Augustine to identify and formulate in an organized way the ontological relationship between the oneness of the eucharistic bread and the oneness of the Church. According to Paul, the oneness of the bread has the status of an exemplar in relation to the unity of the Church, although we must bear in mind that exemplarity includes efficacy. The Augustinian solution is grounded in the sacramental efficacy developed by Paul, but gives exemplarity a properly philosophical status by drawing on the doctrine of participation that was characteristic of the culture of Platonism.

[86] Letter 63.10 and 2 (Clarke, 103 and 98).

[87] "It becomes, therefore, evident that the blood of Christ is not offered if there is no wine in the cup, and that the Lord's sacrifice is not duly consecrated and

2.8. Conclusions

A study of all these texts shows that since the Eucharist faithfully *imitates* the Last Supper of Christ, it is identical with what is *imitated*. John D. Laurance says that in using this language Cyprian "expresses the fundamental element of Platonic metaphysics, namely, that through the imitation of it *one reality becomes present in another*."[88] I am certain that this is indeed Cyprian's idea of the Eucharist, but I am not certain that it is correct to speak of a *presence*, and still less that it is legitimate to speak of *Platonism*, since what we know of Cyprian's philosophical education does not permit us to say that he is a Platonist, a Stoic, an eclectic, or simply a man of his time, who was able to make use of common and fairly widespread ideas. If we adopt this last perspective, then, without trying to determine whether Cyprian was or was not dependent on Platonism, we can say that he is a good witness to the eucharistic teaching of the early Church. This teaching has numerous elements that reflect a certain culture: a culture and way of thinking that depend on Platonism in its historical development.

In Cyprian's thinking, the relationship of conformity or imitation between the Eucharist of the Church and the Last Supper is the essential constituent of sacramentality. Within this relationship there is first of all the typological relation between the priest and Christ (and his role) at the Last Supper: The bishop takes the place of Christ and acts his role because, prior to doing so, he participates in Christ, being an imitator of him. If the Eucharist is an act of obedience and imitation of the Last Supper, then the bread and wine will be the same as those of the Supper; and, because Christ said that the latter were his Body and his Blood, the bread and wine of the Church will likewise be the Body and Blood of Christ. It is not possible to doubt Cyprian's eucharistic realism;[89] the terms he uses to express the connection between the Blood of Christ and the wine are *ostenditur, intelligitur, manifestum est*. This is the vocabulary of figural and typological interpretation, nor should we be surprised that Cyprian uses it and indeed makes so appropriate a use of it, for he is a true master of typology.

---

celebrated unless the offering and sacrifice we make corresponds with His passion" (Letter 63.9; Clarke, 102).

[88] Laurance, *"Priest" as Type of Christ*, 219.

[89] Think of the passage already cited: "What He [Christ] called blood was wine. It becomes, therefore, evident that the blood of Christ is not offered if there is no wine in the cup" (Letter 63.9; Clarke, 102).

Another reason why the rite of the Church corresponds to the passion of Christ is that in the word "passion" Cyprian includes the rite of the Last Supper; in addition, the blood shed by Christ on Calvary is shown forth *(ostenditur)* by the wine in the cup.[90]

It is in the same unified way and using the same system of figures that Cyprian deals with the Sacrament of the Body and Blood of Christ, the sacrament of his passion, and the *sacerdos* as type of Christ. There is a real identification of the Sacrament of the Body and Blood with the sacrament of the passion, and consequently they are treated in the same way: the figures and the referent are the same. When such a method is followed, the conception of the Eucharist is a strongly unified one. The other elements in the celebration obey the same logic.

Modern readers have great difficulty in entering into Cyprian's thought on the Eucharist. Their conception of the Eucharist is too different from his, since his is completely typological, without any other factors playing a part, and the data on which he reflects are those he has received from earlier tradition. The danger in interpreting him is to confuse the typological-figural method with allegory. The figural or typological method of Cyprian cannot be taken as an exercise in allegorizing: if we look closely at it, we see that sacramental realism underlies the entire treatment and that it is a very solid realism, even though it lacks a cultural and philosophical component that can safeguard the eucharistic tradition in face of problems now arising.

3. EUCHARIST AND MARTYRDOM

(a) The pre-Nicene Fathers assigned a great importance to martyrdom, not only because of the factual situation (many had suffered martyrdom during the persecutions, and martyrdom was still a real possibility for so many), but above all because they conceived of Christian life as a following and imitation of Christ. Imitation of the life of Christ leads to imitation of Christ in his death. Ignatius of Antioch explicitly maintains that he will truly be a disciple of Christ only when he imitates him by martyrdom: He wants to imitate the passion

[90] On the relation between the cup and the blood shed on Calvary, see the passage already cited: "Mention is likewise made to treading and pressing in the wine vat, for just as it is impossible to prepare wine for drinking unless the bunch of grapes is first trodden and pressed, so neither could we drink ourselves the blood of Christ unless Christ had first been trodden upon and pressed, and had drunk before us the cup which He could then pass on to His believers to drink" (Letter 63.7; Clarke, 101).

of his God.[91] The case of Ignatius suffices to prove the point, although citations showing the ideal of martyrdom in the early Church could be multiplied.

(b) Since martyrdom is an imitation of the passion of Christ and since the Eucharist too is an imitation of the passion, it follows that there should be a special connection between the Eucharist and martyrdom. Both belong to the same order of things, with martyrdom imitating the passion of Christ in a fully real way and the Eucharist imitating it in a rite which in turn is connected with the fulfillment of figures.

If the bread and wine, on the one hand, and martyrdom, on the other, are alike participations in the martyrdom of Christ, we can understand the depth concealed in the description of Polycarp's martyrdom: Polycarp was "like a loaf baking in the oven."[92] He was placed on a pile of logs that were beginning to burn, while around him spread a fragrance as of incense or some precious gum. Before the fire was stirred up, he began to pray, offering thanks for his martyrdom, which he understood as the present moment in God's plan of salvation.[93] The text of the prayer follows closely the content and development of a paleoanaphora, with one important change: Instead of the account of institution of the Eucharist there is an account of the institution of martyrdom. Polycarp dies in imitation of Christ, and he dies praying to God in a thanksgiving that imitates the Eucharist.

The martyrdom of Polycarp is linked not only to the Eucharist but to the death of Christ. Here again, the relationship is typological and is expressed by mentioning the day on which the martyrdom takes place: The day is "the Greater Sabbath."[94] Remo Cacitti has shown that the reference is not so much chronological as typological; it is not said that Polycarp died on a Sabbath, but that the day of his death is a typological actualization of the day of Christ's death, of which the Gospel of John says that "that was a great Sabbath day"

[91] *Letter to the Romans* 2–7 (SC 10:126–34).

[92] *Martyrdom of Polycarp* 15.2 (Staniforth, 161).

[93] Martyrdom is therefore a gift from God, for which Polycarp gives thanks in the second strophe of his Eucharistic Prayer. In so doing, he follows the norms governing the structure of the paleoanaphoras: In the second strophe thanks are offered for the present moment, the latter being understood as a moment of salvation or as an act of worship (sacrifice), depending on the period and place to which the various paleoanaphoras belong.

[94] *Martyrdom of Polycarp* 21 (Staniforth, 163).

(19:31).[95] For this reason the death of Polycarp is, typologically, the death of Christ, in the sense that it is Christ who dies in Polycarp; this is why Polycarp is to be called a martyr.[96]

(c) This conception of things led to martyrdom being thought of as having a special sacramental quality of its own, like that of the Eucharist. If Tertullian is indeed the author of the *Passion of Perpetua and Felicity*, then it is he who says that Christ is in the martyr: "Now[97] it is I who suffer what I suffer," Perpetua says; "but then[98] there will be another in me who will suffer in my place *(pro me)*, because I will be undergoing martyrdom for him *(pro illo)*."[99]

This idea, though formulated differently, is also present in Polycarp's thanksgiving for martyrdom: "I bless thee [God] for granting me this day and hour, that I may be numbered among the martyrs, to share the cup of thine Anointed and to rise again unto life everlasting, both in body and soul, in the immortality of the Holy Spirit."[100] The account continues with the death of Polycarp, who is killed with a blow from a dagger: there was "such a copious flow of blood that the flames were extinguished."[101] The death of Polycarp is a figure of the death of Christ, from whose side blood and water flowed.

(d) According to Cyprian, the cup of the Lord prepares men and women for, and makes them worthy of, the cup of martyrdom, because the Lord's cup gives the strength to struggle and to confess the name of Christ.[102] The Eucharist is as it were the model, the type, of the way Christians must face martyrdom. This is why Christians "drink each day the cup of the blood of Christ . . . that they themselves may thus

[95] R. Cacitti, *Grande Sabato. Il contesto pasquale quartodecimano nella formazione della teologia del martirio* (Studia patristica mediolanensia 19; Milan: Vita e Pensiero, 1994).

[96] We have seen that there is a connection between martyrdom and the Eucharist and between martyrdom and the passion of Christ. There is no difference between the two connections; in the final analysis they are the same since the Eucharist is likewise connected with the passion of Christ. It follows that martyrdom is connected with the passion of Christ in two ways: (1) directly, through the shedding of blood; (2) indirectly, through the eucharistic rite inasmuch as this is a proclamation of the passion.

[97] That is, the moment of birth.

[98] The moment of martyrdom.

[99] *Passion of Perpetua and Felicity* 15.6.

[100] *Martyrdom of Polycarp* 14.2 (Staniforth, 160–61).

[101] Ibid., 16.1 (Staniforth, 161).

[102] Letter 57.2.

also be enabled to shed their blood for Christ's sake."[103] According to Cyprian, the profound logic of worship requires that he who performs the sacrifice identify himself completely with this sacrifice; therefore the one who performs the eucharistic action must identify himself with the martyrdom of Christ to the point of becoming himself a martyr.[104]

(e) Summarizing the points here set forth, we can emphasize the fact that martyrdom and the eucharistic celebration are, both of them, imitations of the passion of Christ, martyrdom directly, the eucharistic celebration indirectly through imitation of the Supper. Furthermore, at least for Cyprian, Christian life as a whole is meant to be a martyrdom.[105] This patristic testimony is consistent with the testimony of the anaphoras and paleoanaphoras, as we have seen, and is evidence of a profound harmony between worship and life, between spirituality and liturgy, between eucharistic rite and ethical commitment.

It is not that Christians of that period were better than Christians of other times, as Cyprian's picture of them makes clear.[106] What did differ were the set of interpretative categories applied to the Eucharist, the liturgy, and the ethical commitment of Christian life: the categories of imitation, typology, and following.

---

[103] Letter 58.1 (Clarke, 60).

[104] See the following passage: "Rightly did he [Abel] who took such a part in the sacrifice of God become afterwards himself a sacrifice to God, so that by being the first to exhibit martyrdom he imitated the Lord's passion by his glorious blood" (*De dominica oratione* 24).

[105] S. Deléani, *Christum sequi. Etude d'un thème dans l'oeuvre de saint Cyprien* (Paris: Etudes augustiniennes, 1979) 89.

[106] See, e.g., *De lapsis* 6–7 (CCL 3, 223–25); Letter 4.

Chapter 10

The Fourth Century

1. SOME LITURGICAL TESTIMONIES

Since the Eucharist of the Church had its origin in the celebration of the Last Supper by Jesus and corresponded to it as antitype to type, it followed that every element of the eucharistic celebration was interpreted in terms of its antitypical correspondence to the liturgical rite of the Last Supper. Thus the bread and cup of the Eucharist correspond to the bread and cup of Jesus at the Last Supper;[1] consequently, the bread and wine of the Eucharist are the Body and Blood of Christ in the same way that the bread and wine of the Last Supper were.

The sacramental realism of this conception is very marked and is expressed clearly in both patristic and liturgical texts. Let us look now at some anaphoral texts that convey this way of understanding the Eucharist.

1.1. The Alexandrian Anaphora

The Anaphora of Serapion[2] or, more accurately, of Pseudo-Serapion, introduces the account of institution with an affirmation

---

[1] The Roman Canon very clearly reflects this conception when, in introducing the words of Jesus over the cup, it says that Jesus, "taking into his holy and venerable hands *this* glorious cup [the cup the priest is holding] and again giving thanks, blessed, gave it to his disciples, saying: 'Take and drink of this, all of you.'" There are not two cups, one for the Last Supper and one for the Eucharist of the Church; the cup which the priest has just taken in his hands is the same cup that Jesus took in his hands at the Last Supper.

[2] See my *L'anafora,* chapter 6. The text of the anaphora is in Hänggi-Pahl, 128ff.

of sacramentality that is based on the word *homoiôma*[3] (likeness, figure[4]), after which the account begins with the demonstrative *hoti*.[5] Here is the text:

"It is to you that we have offered this bread, the figure *(to homoiôma)* of the body of your only-begotten Son. This bread is the figure *(to homoiôma)* of the holy body, for *(hoti)* the Lord Jesus, on the night he was betrayed, took bread, broke it, and gave it to his disciples saying: 'Take and eat, this is my body, which is broken for you for the remission of sins.' . . . We offer, too, the cup, the figure *(to homoiôma)* of the blood, for *(hoti)* the Lord Jesus, after the meal, took the cup and said to his disciples: 'Take and drink, this is the new covenant, that is, my blood poured out for you, for the forgiveness of sins.' For this reason we too have offered the cup, using *(prosagontes)* the figure *(to homoiôma)* of the blood."

In this anaphora, the account of the Eucharist is an explanatory expansion of the statement about "the figure,"[6] which is a statement of sacramentality.

This text makes quite clear the function of the account of institution in the Alexandrian anaphora: It accounts for the sacramental character of the bread and wine. If the sacramental character of these elements consists in an antitypical correspondence with the elements at the Last Supper, the account of institution serves to demonstrate this correspondence. This is why the assertion of sacramentality is directly connected with the account of institution.

1.2. *The Anaphora of the Apostles Addai and Mari*
Another liturgical text, in addition to the already cited Anaphora of the Apostles Addai and Mari, that moves along the same lines as the

---

[3] The term *homoiôma* was not coined by Serapion but was imposed on him by an already widespread tradition that can be seen in many writers. The traditional aspect of the usage is confirmed by the fact that in other texts of the *Euchologion* we find not *homoiôma* but *mystêria*. See, e.g., the "Blessing of the people after the breaking of the bread" (*Euchologion* 15.1, in F. X. Funk [ed.], *Didascalia et Constitutiones Apostolorum* [Paderborn: Schöningh, 1905] 2, 178).

[4] For a study of the meaning of *homoiôma* see U. Vanni, "*Homoiôma* in Paolo," *Greg* 58 (1977) 321–45, 431–70. The author studies the word from the biblical viewpoint and limits himself to a passing reference to the patristic period, but the results he obtains are fully valid for understanding the sacramental use of the term.

[5] This is a trait common to the Alexandrian tradition.

[6] Or "analogy," if we follow Nock's terminology.

Anaphora of Serapion is the sixth-century anaphora found in cod. British Museum Add. 14669.[7] In asserting sacramentality, this text uses the Syriac word *demut;* in the Syriac New Testament this word translates the *homoiôma* of Romans 6:5 (which is the source of Serapion 13.13). Another attestation of the use of *homoiôma* as a parallel for antitype is found in chapter 21 of the *Apostolic Tradition* attributed to Hippolytus. After the rite of baptism with its anointings the eucharistic rite is celebrated: The deacons bring the gifts to the bishop, and he "gives thanks over the bread as an image *(in exemplum),* which in Greek is called 'antitype,' of the body of Christ; over the cup of mixed wine, the likeness, which in Greek is *homoiôma,* of the blood that was shed for all who believed in him."[8]

1.3. The Roman Canon

Let us move over to the Latin world. The situation is the same in the Roman Canon, not however in the present-day text, but in the fourth-century redaction that has been handed on to us by Ambrose of Milan in his *De sacramentis.*[9] The sacramental nature of the offering is affirmed in the prayer *Quam oblationem,* just before the account of institution; the Canon asks God to render "approved, spiritual, acceptable" the offering of the Church, and the reason given for this request is the nature of the offering: "because it is the *figura*[10] of the body and blood of our Lord Jesus Christ."[11] This prayer does not contain a request for the change of the bread and wine into the Sacrament or figure of the Body and Blood of Christ. It is right that there

[7] For the Syriac text of the anaphora see R. H. Connolly, "Sixth-Century Fragments of an East-Syrian Anaphora," *OC* 12–14 (1925) 112.

[8] B. Botte (ed.), *La Tradition apostolique de saint Hippolyte. Essai de reconstitution* (LQF 39; Münster: Aschendorff, 1963) 54 and see 55, note 2, for a reconstruction of the clause giving the Greek words of the original text (the clause according to Botte is clearly a gloss of the translator).

[9] Ambrose's version is confirmed by the ancient Spanish Mozarabic or Visigothic liturgy; his prayer is a *Post-Pridie* in the *Liber ordinum* and is also given in the *Liber sacramentorum;* see M. Férotin (ed.), *Le Liber Ordinum en usage dans l'église wisogothique et mozarabe d'Espagne du cinquième au onzième siècle* (Monumenta ecclesiae liturgica 5; Paris: Firmin–Didot, 1904) col. 321; and idem (ed.), *Le Liber Mozarabicus Sacramentorum et les manuscrits mozarabes* (Monumenta ecclesiae liturgica 6; Paris: Firmin–Didot, 1912) col. 641.

[10] In the Mozarabic liturgy *figura* is replaced by *imago et similitudo.*

[11] Ambrose of Milan, *Des sacrements. Des mystères. Explication du symbole,* ed. B. Botte (SC 25bis; Paris: Cerf, 1961) 108.

should not be such a request, since the text explicitly states that the bread and wine are already a figure of the Body and Blood of Christ because of the very rite[12] that is being celebrated.

There is no thought here of a sacramental automatism or, worse, a magic automatism. If the Sacrament is understood as an *imitation* (and therefore a *homoiôma* and *figura*) of the Last Supper, there is no need to do anything else but perform the rite, because it is an imitation. But because the *type* shapes an obedience of faith, and this cannot take place except through grace, that is, by a gift of God, we have a prayer that God would kindly make the offering of the Church spiritual (*rationabilem,* "proper to a rational being"), to our advantage (*scriptam,* "approved"), and acceptable to him *(acceptabilem)*.

Here, in this passage of the Roman Canon, we see an interesting development of the theology of the Sacrament as imitation, for the prayer *Quam oblationem* is a prayer over the bread and wine insofar as these are *figurae* of the Body and Blood of Christ. Later on, after the theology of imitation had been lost from sight, the idea of the "figure of the body" would be eliminated, and the prayer said would be that the bread and wine might become the Body and Blood of Christ. To see this development of eucharistic theology more clearly, I shall set side by side the archaic text in the *De sacramentis* and the received text of the Roman Canon:

Fac nobis	
hanc oblationem	Quam oblationem
	tu Deus
	in omnibus
	quaesumus
	benedictam
scriptam	adscriptam
rationabilem	rationabilem
acceptabilem	acceptabilemque
	facere digneris
quod est	
figura	
	ut nobis
corporis et sanguinis	corpus et sanguis
	fiat
	dilectissimi
	filii tui

[12] The phrase *ex opere operato,* in its original sense, has precisely this meaning.

Domini nostri   Domini nostri
Iesu Christi   Iesu Christi

(Column 1: "Grant us that this offering may be approved, spiritual, acceptable, because it is the figure of the body and blood of our Lord Jesus Christ.")

(Column 2: "We ask you, God, that you would deign to make this offering in every respect blessed, approved, ratified, spiritual, and acceptable, so that it may become for us the body and blood of your Son, our Lord Jesus Christ.")

1.4. The Byzantine Anaphora of Basil

A case analogous to the one just described may be seen in the Byzantine Anaphora of Basil: as in the Roman Canon (of Ambrose) we have a prayer over the bread and wine which are a figure of the Body and Blood of Christ, so in Basil we have a prayer over the gifts set before God, which are described as "antitypes of the holy body and blood of Christ."[13] The prayer goes on to ask that God would bless, sanctify, and show forth[14] these antitypes. In this part, then, the epiclesis has a very archaic character since it regards the bread and wine as antitypes of the Body and Blood of Christ even before the invocation of the Holy Spirit. Since the Spirit is called down upon these antitypes, which are already the Body and Blood of Christ, he is evidently not being invoked to transform the sacred gifts into the Body and Blood of Christ, but only to see to it that they are not a purely material imitation or, in other words, that their correspondence to the action of Christ at the Last Supper is not purely external. In order to prevent that from happening, the prayer asks that the antitypes be blessed, sanctified, and shown forth (as antitypes).

1.5. Conclusion

We may now draw some conclusions from the two cases we have examined. In the Roman Canon, the final redaction of the *Quam oblationem* contains a prayer that the bread and wine may become the Body and Blood of Christ, without any mention of the Holy Spirit, while in the Eastern texts this request is accompanied by an appeal to

[13] Hänggi-Pahl, 236.
[14] I prefer to translate the verb *anadeixai* literally, leaving it its proper meaning, which is to "show, manifest," rather than force its meaning as is done in the usual translations, such as "make" or "consecrate."

the Father to send the Holy Spirit. The prayer that asks for the transformation of the sacred gifts is called an "epiclesis" when it asks for
the coming of the Holy Spirit; but it can be an epiclesis even when it
does not ask for this coming; we must therefore distinguish between
a pneumatological and a nonpneumatological epiclesis.[15] In any case,
theologians interpret the prayer over the sacred gifts as an epiclesis
for their transformation.

The Roman Canon in its Ambrosian form and the Byzantine
Anaphora of Basil are two very important texts because they show
that not every prayer over the bread and wine is to be understood as
an epiclesis for their transformation into the Body and Blood of
Christ, with or without a mention of the Holy Spirit. In fact, in the
Alexandrian liturgy, the Roman liturgy, and the Antiochene liturgy
there is a prayer over the antitypes, which asks that they be blessed,
holy, and spiritual, so that they may be a true imitation of the Last
Supper. The archaic form of the invocation over the gifts, dependent
as it is on an antitypical conception of the Eucharist, is not concerned
with the change of the bread and wine; this problem becomes central
only after this theology that conceives of the Sacrament as an *imitation* of the model (type) established by Christ at the Last Supper has
been left behind. Out of this archaic prayer, then, was to emerge the
nonpneumatological epiclesis of the Roman Canon[16] and the pneumatological epiclesis of the Eastern liturgies.[17]

2. EUSEBIUS OF CAESAREA

The conception of the Eucharist as an antitype is also well attested
outside the liturgical documents, although by reason of the conser-
vatism that is natural to them, the latter remain the principal witnesses
to this conception. Now that we have made sure of this conception in
the liturgy, we can turn to some writers of the patristic period and

---

[15] The *Quam oblationem* attested by Ambrose is not an epiclesis, whereas the
same prayer in the Roman Canon is to all intents and purposes an epiclesis,
though not a pneumatological epiclesis.

[16] ". . . that it may become for us the body and blood of your beloved Son, our
Lord Jesus Christ" (*Quam oblationem*).

[17] "(Let) this bread (become) the precious body of the Lord and God and our
Savior Jesus Christ. Amen. (Let) this cup (become) the precious blood of the Lord
and God and our Savior Jesus Christ. Amen. Which was shed for the life of the
world. Amen" (Epiclesis of the Byzantine Anaphora of Basil; Hänggi-Pahl, 236).

see how they understood the sacramental relation between type and antitype.

Within the antitypical conception of the Eucharist there arose the conception of the Eucharist as *image (eikôn)*. This was a perfectly logical development once we transfer the antitypical conception thus far explained into a framework that is more definitely philosophical or, better, more closely connected with Platonic philosophy. Eusebius Pamphili (ca. 264–340) was not a philosopher but he was surely an educated man who was familiar with the Platonism and Stoicism of his age.[18] His conception of the Logos, for example, is closer to Stoicism than to the Fourth Gospel. If the Eucharist is an antitype of a model, then it is certainly, in Platonic language, an image *(eikôn)* of an archetype.

Eusebius is one of the few writers to have systematically interpreted the Eucharist as an image of the Body of Christ. It is not easy to explain all the passages in which Eusebius deals with the Eucharist, because his thought moves in many directions; it is nonetheless possible to get an idea of his answer to the question, even on a minimal basis, and that is what I shall try to do.[19]

At Caesarea there was a much venerated image of Christ which, it was claimed, was a true image. Constantia, sister of Constantine, wrote a letter to Eusebius, asking to have this true image. Eusebius sent a sharply negative reply[20] and gave a theological reason: There could be no "true image" capable of representing the actual features[21] of Christ. The Son is an image of God, but in this kind of image form and substance go together;[22] Eusebius thus rejects a concept of image as purely material. In his view, an earthly image consists of a form and a substance that are different; it is difference (amid likeness) that

---

[18] F. Ricken, "Die Logoslehre des Eusebios von Caesarea und der Mittelplatonismus," *Theologie und Philosophie* 42 (1967) 341–58; idem, "Zur Rezeption der platonischen Ontologie bei Eusebios von Kaisareia, Areios und Athanasios," *Theologie und Philosophie* 53 (1978) 321–52.

[19] See S. Gero, "The Eucharistic Doctrine of the Byzantine Iconoclasts and Its Sources," *Byzantinische Zeitschrift* 68 (1975) 4–22; idem, "The True Image of Christ: Eusebios' Letter to Constantia Reconsidered," *JTS* 32 (1981) 460–70; H. G. Thümmel, "Eusebios 'Brief an Kaiserin Konstantia,'" *Klio* 66 (1994) 210–22; C. Schönborn, *L'icona di Cristo. Fondamenti theologici* (Saggi teologici 3; Cinisello-Salsamo: San Paolo, 1988) 57–77.

[20] J. B. Pitra, *Spicilegium Solesmense* 1 (Paris, 1852) 383–86.

[21] Ch. Murray, "Art and the Early Church," *JTS* 28 (1977) 303–45.

[22] *Demonstratio evangelica* 5.1.20-21.

characterizes his idea of image. In taking this line he is completely in tune with Platonism.[23] In his view, the true image of Christ is not to be found in a painting but in the Eucharist. Listen to his description of the handing on of the mysteries: "Christ himself handed on to his disciples the symbols of the divine economy of salvation and ordered them to make of these the image of his body."[24]

The position taken by Eusebius had a strong influence on the icono-clastic thought of the eighth century, which developed the doctrine of the insubstantiality of images (icons), since the only true image of Christ is the Eucharist.[25] But it was a position overtaken by events, a position that could not be sustained because the christological debates had strongly influenced the cultural frame of reference, and the Pla-tonic concept of image had been completely eliminated. Let us look briefly at the data of the question. The fundamental problem raised at the Council of Nicaea had to do with the theme of image; the Fathers of Nicaea asked themselves what the meaning was of the statement that Christ "is the image of the invisible God, begotten before every creature" (Col 1:15). In order to convey the authentic meaning of image here,[26] the term *consubstantial* was adopted, thereby establish-ing the truth that Christ is the consubstantial image of the Father. This step was strongly influenced by the thinking of Athanasius, which imposed "the idea of an image that is *equal in essence*, or consubstan-tial, with the original model, and in which the original model is pres-ent 'undiminished.'"[27] This concept of image is certainly far removed from Platonism, according to which the image is the very reality of the original, but in a diminished form.

We must say that the Nicene interpretation, namely, "consubstan-tial image," is completely adapted to the christological problem, but we must also admit that, given this definition of image, it is no longer possible to maintain the archaic conception of the Eucharist as

[23] On this problem see F. Ricken, "L'*homoousios* di Nicea come crisi del platon-ismo cristiano antico," in H. Schlier, et al., *La storia della cristologia primitiva* (Studi biblici 75; Brescia: Queriniana, 1986) 89–119.

[24] *Demonstratio evangelica* 8.1.79-80.

[25] See Gero, "The Eucharistic Doctrine" (note 19, above).

[26] See R. Cantalamessa, "Cristo immagine di Dio," in *La cristologia in S. Paolo* (Atti della 23 settimana biblica; Brescia: Paideia, 1976) 269–87; idem, "Cristo im-magine di Dio nelle discussioni teologiche del quarto secolo," in C. Ghidelli (ed.), *Teologia, liturgia, storia. Miscellanea in onore di Carlo Manziana* (Brescia: Queriniana, 1977) 29–38.

[27] Schönborn, *L'icona di Cristo* (note 19, above), 78.

image of the Body of Christ. This last teaching became outmoded and could be not revived by the iconoclasts of the eighth century, because the cultural frame of reference had been shattered, and for good. It was for these reasons that in the second half of the fourth century the conception of the Eucharist as antitype of the Last Supper experienced an irreversible crisis.

3. THE GREAT MYSTAGOGIES OF THE FOURTH CENTURY

The second half of the fourth century saw the rise of the great mystagogical homilies,[28] which through commentary on the rite construct the theology of the saving event that takes place in the sacramental celebration, and pass it on to the faithful in the form of catechesis. The principal authors are Cyril of Jerusalem, John Chrysostom, Theodore of Mopsuestia, and Ambrose of Milan,[29] but we ought to add the name of Augustine, even though he did not preach sets of mystagogical catecheses in the true and proper sense.

In these homilies, the Eucharist is explained to the neophytes after they have already taken part in it, so that the experience of the rite is the basis for the theological understanding of it. In Cyril, John Chrysostom, Theodore of Mopsuestia, and Ambrose, there are two different and clearly defined ways of asserting sacramental realism. (a) A typological interpretation of the Eucharist is the principal basis on which the entire theology of the rite is built, with the help especially of the biblical figures that are applied to the Christian celebration; the method for using these figures is based on Platonic dialectic. (b) Alongside this first method of interpretation, which I wish to call traditional, there is another, a new one, wholly devoted to expounding sacramental realism; it ends up with a naive and physicist realism: Jesus is incarnated once again, but this time in the bread and wine; in practice, the bread and wine are a new, physical manifestation of the incarnation of Christ. That is what I mean when I speak of a naive and physicist realism.

The first way of affirming and describing the realism of the sacraments belongs to the world of biblical typology and requires a great

[28] For the understanding of mystagogy, see my "L'interpretazione del culto nella chiesa antica."

[29] See E. Mazza, *La Mistagogia. Une teologia delle liturgia in epoca patristica* (Bibliotheca Ephemerides Liturgicae. Subsidia 46; Rome: CLV–Edizioni liturgiche, 1988); ET: *Mystagogy. A Theology of the Liturgy in the Patristic Age,* trans. M. J. O'Connell (New York: Pueblo, 1989).

deal of competence and a refined culture, not only as regards knowledge of the biblical text but also as regards the philosophical categories that can suitably account for both the identity and the difference between the historical event described in the Scriptures and the liturgical rite. The second method, on the other hand, does not use the biblical figures nor does it use philosophical categories, even though it continues to use the sacramental terminology developed by the first method;[30] it restricts itself to asserting the realism of the sacraments in a naive and decidedly rudimentary way, ending in the assertion of a complete physical identity between the bread and the Body of Christ and between the wine and the Blood of Christ.

3.1 John Chrysostom

There is a passage in John Chrysostom that brings out clearly the physicist aspect of eucharistic doctrine at the end of the fourth century. When commenting on the story of the exodus of the Hebrews from Egypt, Chrysostom draws a parallel between the blood of the lamb that was smeared on the doorposts and the Blood of Christ that reddened the mouths of the faithful at Communion time. If the destroying angel had been held back by the type, i.e., the blood of the lambs, all the more will the evil one be restrained when he sees the truth, i.e., the Blood of Christ.[31] True enough, in Chrysostom's work this is but one argument among many, but in order to formulate it he must have lost sight of the typological aspect and have thought of the Sacrament in its physical reality. I do not mean hereby to deny Chrysostom's competence in the area of typology; in fact, he is able to use the typological method very expertly, as is clear from the emphasis with which he distinguishes between the part of the Sacrament that can be seen with the bodily eyes and the part that is perceptible only by faith.[32] I mean to say only that the times had now made it difficult to possess an education in typology which would enable a bishop to communicate with his faithful.

[30] The terminology used is thus still a philosophical terminology, even if the ideas expressed are not.

[31] *Instruction* 3.15. Text and French translation in A. Wenger (ed.), *Jean Chrysostome Huit catéchèses baptismales inédites* (SC 50bis; Paris: Cerf, 1970) 159. ET: St. John Chrysostom, *Baptismal Instructions*, trans. P. W. Harkins (ACW 31; New York: Newman, 1963) 61.

[32] See, e.g., *Instruction* 2.9-11 (Wenger, 139; ET: 46–47).

3.2. Theodore of Mopsuestia

Let us move on to another writer, Theodore of Mopsuestia, and his commentary on eucharistic Communion.[33] The *Ordo* or Ritual prescribed: "Then each of us draws near, gaze lowered and both hands extended."[34] Starting with this rubric, Theodore constructs his commentary on the two prescribed actions (gaze lowered and hands extended): "By looking down, he [the believer] pays a kind of appropriate dues by adoration; he thereby makes a kind of profession of faith that he is receiving the body of the King, of him who became Lord of all through union with the divine nature and who is likewise worshiped as Lord by all of creation." The text continues with a reflection on the hands, which, by receiving the Sacrament, become agents in the action. From the position of the hands Theodore deduces the attitude the person ought to have:

"And by extending both hands, he truly acknowledges the greatness of the gift that he is about to receive. 'It is the right hand that one extends to receive the gift being given, but under it one places the left,'[35] thereby showing great reverence. If the right hand is extended and placed at a higher level, it is in order to receive the royal body which is held out to it, while the other hand supports and guides its sister and companion, thinking it no insult that it should play the part of a servant to that which is its equal in dignity—the reason being that that other hand bears the royal body."[36]

To this passage must be added another description in which Theodore bears witness to a devotional attitude of the time, one that makes quite clear a simple and naive way of understanding sacramental realism:

"When you have received the body into your own hands, you worship it (that is, you acknowledge the power of him who has been placed in your hands), as you recall these words which our Lord, risen from among the dead, spoke to his disciples: *Power has been*

[33] The manner prescribed by the Ritual for receiving Communion (identical with our practice today) becomes an occasion for suggesting an interior attitude.

[34] *Homily* 16.27. Text with French translation in R. Tonneau and R. Devreesse, *Les homilies catéchétiques de Théodore de Mopsueste* (ST 145; Vatican City: Vatican Apostolic Library, 1949) 577.

[35] Theodore is citing the text of the Ritual.

[36] *Homily* 16.27 (Tonneau–Devreesse, 577).

given to me in heaven and on earth (Matt 28:18). With profound and heartfelt love you fix your gaze on it, you kiss it, and it is as if you were offering your prayers to our Lord, the Christ, who is now close to you."[37]

In this passage Theodore talks of the eucharistic bread as if it were physically, and not only sacramentally, the body of Christ, so that to see, touch, and kiss the eucharistic bread is to see, touch, and kiss the body of Christ, and so that when the believer prays to Christ, he prays to him as near, physically near, because he is praying to him in the Sacrament.

3.3. Cyril of Jerusalem

In the homilies of Cyril, too, there is something similar to what we have been seeing. He asserts the opportuneness of offering intercessory prayers for the dead during the eucharistic anaphora, because prayer is more effective when made over the Body of Christ.[38] But along with these bits of naive realism, Cyril is also capable of presenting a eucharistic doctrine based on the strictest typology. Here is an example:

"It is therefore with complete assurance that we share as *(hôs)* in the body and blood of Christ. For it is in the type[39] of bread that the body is given to you and in the type of wine the blood, so that, having participated in the body and blood of Christ, you become a single body and a single blood with Christ. As a result, we become 'Christophers or Christbearers,' since his body and his blood spread throughout our members. In this way we become, as Blessed Peter says, 'sharers in the divine nature.'"[40]

The expressions "in the type" and "as *(hôs)*" bring out very clearly the typological conception of the Sacrament, even while a sure and

---

[37] *Homily* 16.28 (Tonneau–Devreesse, 579).

[38] See *Catechesis* 5.8: "We then pray for the holy fathers and bishops who have fallen asleep and in general for all who have fallen asleep before us, believing as we do that this will be very profitable for the souls in whose favor intercession is made to ascend on high *(deêsis anapheretai)* while the holy and terrible sacrifice is present." Text and French translation in A. Piédnagel (ed.), *Cyrille de Jérusalem. Catéchèses mystagogiques* SC 126bis; Paris: Cerf, 1988) 158.

[39] Since typological terminology was always fluctuating, in order properly to understand this passage we must read "antitype" for "type."

[40] *Catechesis* 4.3 (p. 136).

unhesitating eucharistic realism is maintained, as we see in the clause: "so that, having participated in the body and blood of Christ, you become a single body and a single blood with Christ." A little earlier, after citing 1 Corinthians 11:23-25, Cyril says: "When he himself, then, has declared and said of the bread, 'This is my body,' who will dare hesitate any longer? And when he himself states categorically and says, 'This is my blood,' who will ever doubt and say that it is not his blood?"[41] Cyril also brings up the change of water into wine in order to make credible the truthfulness of the words of Christ at the Supper: "At one time, by his own free will, he changed water into wine at Cana in Galilee, and is he not to be believed when he changes wine into blood? When invited to a bodily marriage, he performed this wonderful miracle. Will we not confess him even more when he gives the companions of the Bridegroom the gift of enjoying his body and blood?"[42]

After affirming sacramental realism through use of the language of typology, Cyril goes on to a figural commentary on the Old Testament types of the Eucharist.

3.4. Ambrose of Milan

In Ambrose too these two types of interpretation are present: the typological and naive realism. In fact, after speaking of the Eucharist in a way that makes thorough use of typology, he moves on, in both the *De sacramentis* and the *De mysteriis*, to statements reflecting a different kind of sacramental realism, one that is more direct and not figural, as though he regarded arguments based on the typological method as insufficient. Let us look at the two different attitudes of Ambrose toward sacramental realism.

The *mystery (mysterium)* is salvation, that is, the content of history as a salvific event, which is made available to human beings by means of the "sacrament" *(sacramentum)*, that is, the liturgical rite. The "explanation of the sacraments" *(ratio sacramentorum)* is the connection between the sacrament and the "mystery"; in short, sacramentality.[43] In some passages Ambrose has a specific word to indicate sacramentality:

---

[41] *Catechesis* 4.1 (p. 134).

[42] *Catechesis* 4.2 (p. 136).

[43] *De mysteriis* 2. Text and French translation in B. Botte (ed.), *Ambroise de Milan. Des sacrements. Des mystères. Explication du symbole* (SC 25bis; Cerf: Paris, 1961) 156.

similitudo ("likeness" or "symbol").[44] Here is a passage of interest to us here:

"But perhaps you may say: 'I do not see the appearance of blood.' But it [the wine] is the likeness of the blood. Just as you have received the likeness[45] of the death, so you drink the likeness of the precious blood, so that there is no disgust evoked by blood and yet the price of redemption produces its effect. You have learned, then, that what you receive is the body of Christ."[46]

The *similitudo* is not the visible element of the Sacrament, which is expressed by the word *species* and which is contrasted with the *similitudo*. The *similitudo* is the invisible element of the Sacrament and can be known only through learning. The *similitudo*, then, is the subject of eucharistic catechesis.

To explain the sacramental realism of the Eucharist Ambrose makes very competent use of biblical typology. Immediately after, however, he undertakes a further explanation, as if, in his judgment, the typological explanation had not exhausted the subject. He asks how the transformation of the eucharistic bread comes about. Here is the passage:

"You may say, 'I see something different. How can you claim that I am receiving the body of Christ?' This is what we must still show. How great are the examples we use to show that this reality [the bread] is not what nature has formed but what the blessing has consecrated, and that the power of the blessing is greater than that of nature, since the blessing changes the very nature itself."[47]

[44] The term *similitudo* has a special meaning when used by Ambrose of the Eucharist: The eucharistic wine does not *look like* blood, but it nonetheless has the *likeness* of blood; the "look" is that to which the senses have access, but the "likeness" is not accessible to the senses. The likeness is rather the invisible aspect of the Sacrament, and sacramentality consists in this likeness and not in the outward appearance in the realm of the senses.

[45] Note the complete identity of the language here with the vocabulary of the Anaphora of Serapion, both in regard to the likeness of the death (which is paralleled with the likeness of the body and the likeness of the blood) and in regard to the origin of the terms used *(homoiôma-similitudo)*, which in both writers is due to the baptismal use of Romans 6:5. The most plausible explanation for this identity is that there was a liturgical tradition in control.

[46] *De sacramentis* 4.20 (SC 25bis:112).

[47] *De mysteriis* 50 (p. 184).

Ambrose goes on to cite a lengthy series of examples from the Bible to show that the transformation of the eucharistic bread is of the order of miracles: Moses with the serpent, the Red Sea, the turning back of the Jordan, the water from the rock, the bitter water of Marah, the axe recovered by Elisha; all these are described as exceptions to the laws of nature.[48]

In using this kind of argument, Ambrose leaves the logic of typology completely behind him; he has established a new way of arguing that is based on the formula of blessing that effects the consecration of the Eucharist. What is the nature of this blessing? He begins his explanation by saying that if the power of a blessing is so great, even when made up of the words of a prophet, which are human words, how much greater will be the power of the "divine consecration [i.e., effected by God], in which the very words of the Lord and Savior are at work? In fact, this sacrament which you receive is brought about (*conficitur*) by the word of Christ."[49] A little further on, he concludes:

"The Lord Jesus himself proclaims: 'This is my body.' Before the blessing with the heavenly words, the eucharistic bread is called by another name; after the consecration it is called the body. He himself says that this is his blood. Before the consecration it is called something else. After the consecration it is called blood. And you say, 'Amen,' that is, 'It is true.'"[50]

The same argument is found in the parallel passage of the *De sacramentis*,[51] where Ambrose distinguishes, within the Eucharistic Prayer, the words of the priest from the words of the Lord, and applies the adjective "heavenly" only to the explanatory words. For Ambrose, the consecratory words as such are heavenly words, and it is clear that their consecratory power comes from their heavenly character.[52]

[48] Ibid., 51 (p. 184).
[49] Ibid., 52 (p. 186).
[50] Ibid., 54 (p. 188).
[51] *De sacramentis* 4.21 (p. 114): "Do you wish to know which heavenly words effect the consecration? . . . Look, all the words are the evangelist's own down to 'Take' (the body or the blood); from that point on, they are the words of Christ."
[52] For Ambrose, "heavenly" signifies the origin of the words in question, that is, Christ as God; only his divine character ensures that his words have the efficacy that is proper to creative words. Here is the passage: "Whose words and utterances effect the consecration? Those of the Lord Jesus. . . . Which utterance of Christ? Why, that by which all things were made. The Lord commanded, the

We can conclude that although Ambrose makes wide use of typology in accordance with the tradition he has learned, and does so with competence, nevertheless, when he wants to give a cogent and conclusive argument for the nature of the Eucharist, he feels compelled to leave aside that method of interpretation and develop another that is patterned on the Old Testament miracles, which show the power of God's word. It is the heavenly words, that is, the words which Christ speaks as God, that work the miracle of consecration.

In summary, we may say that Ambrose gave birth to the doctrine of consecration: consecration is effected by the explanatory words of the Lord ("This is my Body; This is the cup of my Blood") that are cited within the Eucharistic Prayer. That formula brings about the transformation of the bread and wine into the Body and Blood of Christ because the words of the formula are divine words and, consequently, the power of God is at work in them. In this second method of interpretation, sacramental realism is connected not so much with the antitypical correspondence to the model established by Christ at the Last Supper as it is with the efficacy of the formula of consecration.

The difficulty Ambrose has in completely accepting the typological or figural conception of the Eucharist shows also in another way: He coins a new use of the word *figura* in order to indicate the transformation of the bread and wine into the Body and Blood of Christ. We have not yet reached the term "transubstantiation," but we are on the way to it. The vocabulary used is evidence of it: There is a shift from the terms that describe the relationship between type and antitype to words that describe the transformation of the bread and wine into the Body and Blood of Christ.

3.5. Conclusion

A study of these writers shows that the second half of the fourth century was the period of major changes. Although biblical typology was still practiced and applied to the liturgical rite, a new way of doing theology has now emerged that will provide the Middle Ages with their interpretive categories.

---

heaven was made; the Lord commanded, the earth was made. . . . You see, then, how effective the word of Christ is. If then the words of the Lord Jesus have such great power . . ." (*De sacramentis* 4.14-15; pp. 108–10).

4. AUGUSTINE

Augustine follows the mystagogical method in that he speaks to the neophytes about the Eucharist only after they have received the sacraments; it seems even that some of his sermons on the subject were delivered just before Communion and would therefore have been instructions *(didascalia)* rather than homilies. He also describes the eucharistic rite and bases his thoughts on the rite so that the faithful can make their way through it and come to a fruitful participation in the mystery of salvation.

It does not seem that Augustine is to be associated with the writers whom we studied in the previous section: He is not engaged, as they are, in building a cycle of mystagogical homilies, nor is he affected by a crisis in the ambient philosophical culture.[53] In fact, there is no trace in Augustine of either physicism or naive realism. His thinking fully respects the canons of biblical typology as applied to Scripture, but with a sound methodological correction: In dealing with the Sacrament he uses only those texts of the Bible that actually speak of the Eucharist, and not every text that could be made to refer to the Eucharist through an allegorical interpretation. Because of his connection with Neoplatonic culture and because of his typology, critics have often judged his thinking on the Eucharist to be symbolist, in contrast with that of Ambrose, which is judged to be realist. Nothing could be less true, as we shall see at the end of this section.

In two homilies Augustine explains what the eucharistic bread is. Nothing can substitute for reading the text itself, in which when commenting on the stages of Christian initiation, he establishes a full parallel with the process of making bread and reaches this conclusion: "You were made into the Lord's loaf of bread."[54] This conception is central in the works of Augustine; when he has to explain the nature of the eucharistic bread, he refers to the explanatory words which, in keeping with the Lord's command, are uttered at the moment of Communion: "The Body of Christ. Amen." Having derived from them the identification between the bread and the Body of Christ,

[53] See E. Mazza, "Saint Augustin et la mystagogie," in A. M. Triacca and A. Pistoia (eds.), *Mystagogie: pensée liturgique d'aujourd'hui et liturgie ancienne* (Conférences Saint-Serge. XXXIXe Semaine d'études liturgiques; Bibliotheca Ephemerides Liturgicae. Subsidia 70; CLV–Edizioni liturgiche, 1993) 201–26.

[54] "Afterward you came to the water, and you were moistened into dough, and made into one lump. With the application of the heat of the Holy Spirit you were baked, and made into the Lord's loaf of bread" (*Sermo* 229.1; Hill 6, 265).

Augustine goes on[55] to explain what the Body of Christ is that is placed on the altar and distributed to the faithful; to do this, he refers to 1 Corinthians 12:27.[56] With this citation he passes from the eucharistic bread, the Sacrament of the Body of Christ, to the Church, which is also the body of Christ. He concludes: "We too have become his body, and through his mercy we are what we receive."[57] And even more clearly: "It's the mystery meaning you that has been placed on the Lord's table; what you receive is the mystery that means you. It is to what you are that you reply *Amen.*"[58]

Augustine's conception of sacramental realism was developed from within Neoplatonic culture and is therefore based on participation. This philosophical category can explain the eucharistic teaching of the bishop of Hippo. Let us think of Platonic dialectic, which is made up of a whole series of degrees or gradations, each of which participates in the degree above it; each degree or step derives its being through participation in the higher degree. See, now, how this doctrine is applied to the Eucharist. The Church is the body of Christ because it participates in the eucharistic bread, which is the Body of Christ on a higher level or degree of participation. The Church and the eucharistic bread are two different kinds, or two different levels, of participation in the body of Christ, but both are real or, in other words, are ontological.

For that to take place, participation in the body of Christ must be thought of as a synthesis of identity and difference: The eucharistic bread and the Church are ontologically the body of Christ, but they are this body only *in certo modo* ("in a certain way"). In this phrase Augustine expresses the "difference," as is clear from the following passage: "Therefore, just as the sacrament of the body of Christ is in a

---

[55] "As for what your faith asks to be instructed about, the bread is the body of Christ . . ." (*Sermo* 272; Hill 7, 300).

[56] "Now you are the body of Christ and individually members of it."

[57] *Sermo* 229 (PL 38:1247) [not in Hill's translation. Tr.]. "If you want to understand the body of Christ, listen to the apostle telling the faithful, *You, though, are the body of Christ and its members* (1 Cor 12:27)" (*Sermo* 272; Hill 7, 300). And again: "Because he also suffered for us, he also presented himself in this sacrament with his body and blood, and this is even what he made us ourselves into as well" (*Sermo* 229.1; Hill 6, 265).

[58] "So if it's you that are the body of Christ and its members, it's the mystery meaning you that has been placed on the Lord's table; what you receive is the mystery that means you. It is to what you are that you reply *Amen*" (*Sermo* 272; Hill 7, 300).

certain way the body of Christ and the sacrament of the blood of Christ is in a certain way his blood, so the sacrament of faith is faith."[59] This conception of the Eucharist is very solidly grounded and is also taken for granted inasmuch as Augustine uses it as the basis for a doctrinal explanation of the sacrament of baptism.[60] In conclusion I must cite the definition of a sacrament that Augustine very carefully works out; it is a definition of a metaphysical kind, based on *similitudo*, which corresponds to the Greek *homoiôma*: "If sacraments did not have some likeness to the realities of which they are the sacrament, they would not be sacraments at all."[61] Sacramentality, then, consists in this *similitudo*,[62] which refers to that which is not in the realm of the senses.

In order to complete the Augustinian definition of the sacraments, we must consider sacraments not only from the viewpoint of doctrine on the being of the sacraments, in which sacraments are defined as *similitudines*, but also from the viewpoint of Augustine's teaching on knowledge, in which sacramentality is the object not of sense knowledge (*videtur*) but of intellectual knowledge (*intelligitur*): "The reason these things, brothers and sisters, are called sacraments is that in them one thing is seen, another is to be understood. What can be seen has a bodily appearance, what is to be understood provides spiritual fruit."[63] Here is another passage along the same lines: "I have commended a sacrament to you; when understood spiritually, it will give you life. Although it must be celebrated in a visible way, it must be understood as something invisible."[64] Note the difference between the celebration of a sacrament and its fruit, which is the reason why the sacrament exists; the fruit depends on spiritual understanding, that is, on the celebration of a sacrament precisely as a sacrament.

There are three points in Augustine's teaching on the Eucharist that we may emphasize. (1) Augustine is the most important heir to the Pauline conception of the Eucharist as sacrament of unity, not only because he treats this aspect as the primary and formal element of the Eucharist, but above all because he gives a careful theoretical

[59] *Epistola* 98 (PL 33:364).
[60] There is a strong internal consistency in Augustine's thought on the sacraments, to the point where we may speak of a system in the true and proper sense.
[61] *Epistola* 138.7.
[62] This is true also, to some extent, of Ambrose of Milan.
[63] *Sermo* 272 (Hill 7, 300).
[64] *Enarrationes in Ps.* 98 (CCL 39:1386).

justification of the fact. According to Paul the Apostle, a sacrament produces effects that are in conformity with its nature: Since the Eucharist is the Body of Christ, it follows that the community which eats of it becomes "Body of Christ"; since the bread is one, it follows that the community which eats of it becomes "one." The Eucharist, then, inasmuch as it is the Body of Christ is necessarily and by its nature the sacrament of unity. That is what Paul says. The specifically Augustinian novelty consists in the application of a metaphysical principle, the doctrine of participation, to the relation that exists between the Church, which is the body of Christ, and the eucharistic bread, which is likewise the Body of Christ, so that the former participates in the latter. As a result, there is a specific ontological relation between the two, by reason of which they are both identical and different.

(2) There is no automatism at work in the Eucharist. The Eucharist produces its fruit through spiritual understanding of the Sacrament, and this understanding, according to Augustine, requires commitment to God, that is, faith and conversion. Consequently, the moral dimension is not external to the Sacrament but is a constitutive part of it. In other words, the moral dimension is part of the ontological dimension of the Sacrament, as is quite clear from these words: "If you receive them [the Body and Blood] well, you are yourselves what you receive."[65] If the sacrament of unity is to produce its fruit, it is not enough to eat the eucharistic bread and drink from the cup; also needed is conversion, which is the way of eating aright.

(3) Especially when commenting on passages of John, Augustine sees the Eucharist as life, to the point of remarking that Christians who speak the Punic dialect usually call the Eucharist simply "life."[66] The satisfaction Augustine feels in discussing this theme is evident.

In conclusion: After offering even this meager information about Augustine, I cannot allow Augustine to be interpreted as a "symbolist," in contrast to Ambrose, whose thinking is supposedly "realist." Both writers, in fact, identify sacramentality with *similitudo*. In Augustine's view, because of the depth of his ontology that is bound up with Neoplatonism, the category of "likeness" is fully sufficient to explain

[65] *Sermo* 227 (Hill 6, 254).
[66] See *De peccatorum meritis et remissione* 1.24.34 (CSEL 60:33): "Punic Christians are perfectly correct . . . in calling the sacrament of Christ's body 'life.'" ET by R. J. Teske, in *Answer to the Pelagians* (The Works of Saint Augustine. A Translation for the 21st Century, I/23; Hyde Park, N.Y.: New City Press, 1997) 53.

the nature of sacramentality. For Ambrose, on the other hand, "like-ness" is a category which, although in current use, does not exhaust the understanding of sacrament.[67]

The difference between the two writers is due above all to their different competencies in philosophy and certainly not in a different conception of eucharistic realism.

---

[67] It is for this reason that Ambrose has recourse to other categories, such as miracle, thus giving rise to a different conception of sacramental realism.

Chapter 11

The Early Middle Ages

We have seen that the patristic understanding of the Eucharist is based on typology: It uses biblical figures, but with the risk, not always avoided, of descending into allegorism. It also makes use of a particular philosophical culture that is connected with Platonism, in order to ensure the ontological dimension of the interpretive procedure adopted. The foundation of this way of approaching the Eucharist is Pauline, inasmuch as in 1 Corinthians 10:4 Paul uses the typology of the manna in order to claim a relationship of continuity between the book of Exodus and the Christian liturgy. Appreciation of this type of argument requires sharing the culture that produced it. But from the end of the fourth century on, there was a gradual movement away from the typological method. Typology is a strictly unitary procedure in which the biblical figure is in direct relation to the ontological reality of the Eucharist, and this relation is sometimes expressed in properly philosophical language.

Even before the Middle Ages, the culture that supported the typological method had vanished, and the connection or, more accurately, the synthesis of biblical data and the Eucharist was broken, to the point where the two began to lead separate lives, each with its own logic. As a result, the Middle Ages saw the rise of two different ways of dealing with the Eucharist, each independent of the other: The figural method and the method of sacramental realism. (1) The figural method rose out of typology, but after the latter had undergone two changes: It lost its connection with ontology, and it became allegorism. The biblical figures were discussed in themselves and took on a moral value in relation to the eucharistic celebration. This change gave rise to the allegorical commentary on the eucharistic celebration, based on the relation between the Eucharist and the sacrifice of Christ.

(2) Alongside these commentaries there were treatises on the presence of the Body and Blood of Christ in the bread and wine of the Eucharist. In the beginning, these were based on a naive conception of sacramental realism. Only in a second phase was this conception to be given a philosophical status, although it would never lose the traits it had in its prephilosophical stage of naive and exaggerated realism; these traits would survive especially in the devotional conception of the Eucharist.

I shall now follow these two currents of thought, beginning with the relation between the Eucharist and the sacrifice of Christ[1] and then moving on to the matter of eucharistic realism; thirdly, I shall discuss the origin of medieval eucharistic devotion.

1. THE EUCHARIST AND THE SACRIFICE OF CHRIST

From the ninth to the thirteenth centuries in the West a number of authors wrote commentaries on the liturgy, and there was an underlying connection among all of them: In one or other fashion, all of them went back to Amalarius of Metz, who was regarded as the pioneer and had a considerable influence on the whole of medieval eucharistic theology.[2]

1.1. Amalarius of Metz[3]

In the West, the allegorical interpretation of the liturgy developed into an organized system only with Amalarius of Metz, who, at the

[1] The shift from typology to allegorism is already quite visible at the end of the fourth century. One may think, for example, of the mystagogical homilies of Theodore of Mopsuestia. The meanings which this writer finds in the liturgical rites are further developed in later commentaries on the Syriac liturgy and will be the basis for the latter's understanding of the liturgical rites as a collection of gestures and realities, sounds and lights, that symbolize heavenly realities; this is an understanding that will reach its high point in the Byzantine liturgy. Think, for example, of the gesture of waving a piece of cloth, about the size of a napkin, over the bread and cup at the moment of the epiclesis, in order to signify the coming of the Holy Spirit. Limitations of space compel me to pass over the writers of the late patristic period and move on directly to the early Middle Ages.

[2] In terms of liturgical culture, this period is described as the period of allegorism.

[3] Critics are today in agreement that Amalarius of Metz and Amalarius of Trier are the same person. He was born in Metz in 770/75, was bishop of Trier and then of Lyons where he succeeded Agobard; he was Charlemagne's right-hand man and served as his ambassador in Constantinople. When in Rome, he tried to obtain authoritative copies of the Roman Antiphonary in order to reform his own antiphonary back in France. Amalarius is known chiefly for his work on the

urging of Peter of Nonantola, decided to write a comprehensive commentary on the liturgy. After Isidore of Seville (560–636) and his commentary *De ecclesiasticis officiis*, Amalarius was the major heir to the liturgical thinking of the Fathers of the Church, and he would be regarded as the undisputed master until Innocent III (1160/61–1216). His work would then be replaced by the great liturgical commentary of William Durandus (1296).

1.1.1. Amalarius' Method

Amalarius' intention is to investigate each rite for the purpose of grasping both its nature and its origin. He shows that he is interested in both the meaning and the origin of rites, and he thinks he must pursue his investigation in both these directions as though they were one.[4] He represents a new way of making his own and using the liturgical thought of the Fathers. He studies the relationship of a rite to the event of salvation: "What harmony exists between the gospel and the present service?"[5] In his view, in fact, the interpretation of rites is based on their origin.[6] The relationship to the gospel is described thus: "The service is, in part, in continuity with what Christ did corporeally on earth."[7] Amalarius' work is an allegorical commentary and, unfortunately, because of this method, grasps only the meaning of the various rites.

It is a fact that the cultural and religious climate of these four centuries was strongly stamped with the allegorical approach to reality. We must recognize, however, that what Amalarius accomplishes in his commentary is something much deeper and cannot be explained simply by the influence of contemporary culture.

---

antiphonary and for his teaching on the "triform body" *(corpus triforme)*, for which he was condemned at the synod of Quiercy in 838 due to the hostility of Florus, a deacon of Lyons. Amalarius died in 850/53. His liturgical writings are contained mainly in his *Liber officialis*, the *Eclogae de divino officio*, and the more authoritative *Liber de Antiphonario*. For his biography see the critical edition of his works by J. M. Hanssens: *Amalarii episcopi Opera liturgica omnia* (3 vols.; ST 138–40; Vatican City: Vatican Apostolic Library, 1948–50).

[4] "Asking in order why each action is performed" (*Ad Petrum Nonantolanum*; Hanssens 1:230).

[5] *Missae expositionis geminus codex. Codex expositionis. Codex seu scedula prior* 1 (Hanssens 1:263).

[6] It might be better to say that for Amalarius meaning blends with origin.

[7] *Liber officialis* 3.5 (Hanssens 2:281).

Amalarius regards a liturgical action as a global entity in which everything hangs together; each rite participates in the nature of the liturgical action of which it is a part. Consequently, since the Mass is the celebration of the passion of Christ, each of the rites making up the Eucharist must represent a stage in that passion.[8]

The application of this principle means that the Mass is interpreted as a comprehensive dramatization of the passion of Christ. Let us look briefly at one series of rites that show the Mass to be a representation of the passion.

1.1.2. The Mass as Representation of the Passion

The events of the passion are the events of redemption; consequently, since redemption begins with the incarnation, we see Amalarius beginning by describing the first rite of the Mass as representing the entrance of Christ into the world. The beginning of the Mass (the entrance procession) corresponds to the entrance of Christ into the world, and the end of the celebration, the *Ita missa est* ("Go, the Mass is ended"), corresponds to his ascension into heaven.[9] The choir that chants the entrance antiphon (Introit) is the choir of prophets who foretold the incarnation of Christ, and the entrance of the bishop into the Church is the entrance of Christ into the world.[10] The book of the Gospels is placed on the altar, and, lo, the latter represents Jerusalem, the holy city from which the preaching of the gospel went forth.[11] Now the bishop moves over to the right side of the altar; it is not difficult to foresee the symbolism that Amalarius will

---

[8] As a result, when Amalarius comments on a particular rite, he refers to the biblical text not directly but by way of a pre-understanding derived from the nature of the liturgical action of which the rite in question is a part.

[9] "The celebration of this office is such that it shows what part of the passion and burial of Christ was being done at that time, and how we ought to bring to mind, through our service, that which was done for our sake" (*Liber officialis* 3.28.8; Hanssens 2:355).

[10] "To what does the entrance correspond better than to the chorus of prophets who announced that Christ would come into the world and through whom Christ entered the world? . . . For the introduction is openly called 'incarnation'" (*Missae expositionis geminus codex* 1; Hanssens 1:256-57).

[11] "The gospel remains on the altar from the beginning of the service until it is taken up for reading, because from the beginning of Christ's coming gospel doctrine echoed in Jerusalem and went out from there to the wide world, as it is written: 'A light has gone forth from Zion, and the word of the Lord from Jerusalem' (Isa 2:3)" (*Liber officialis* 3.5.31; Hanssens 2:281).

find in this movement: the passage to eternal life, in which the Lord sits at the right hand of the Father.[12] Daily sacrifices used to be offered on the altar of holocausts in the temple; therefore our altar corresponds to the altar of holocausts, since on our altar, at the moment of the offertory, the good thoughts and works—the lives—of the just are offered.[13]

In the rite of the offertory water is combined with the wine in the cup. In this action Amalarius sees the sign of the people being united to Christ.[14] When he comes to the Secret, he does not concern himself with the text of this prayer but only with this moment of the liturgy, that is, the moment that is called the Secret. If there is a moment in the liturgy that is called the Secret, then this action has a special connection with something hidden that occurred during the passion of Christ; lo and behold, the Secret represents Jesus betaking himself to the feast of "Booths, not openly but in a hidden manner as it were."[15] The rite of incensation is performed at the altar. This rite is a sign (*demonstrat*) of how the Father is rendered favorable to us by the Body of Christ; we should not be surprised by this reference to the Body of Christ, since for Amalarius the thurible is a symbol (*designat*) of it.[16]

When the eucharistic celebration reaches the Preface, that is, the hymn of thanksgiving, Amalarius is not concerned with speaking about thanksgiving, but asks instead which episode in the passion of Christ might correspond to this point in the liturgy. Since the hymn is sung before the Canon of the Mass, which *represents* the passion, it follows that the Preface corresponds to the hymns sung by Christ before he suffered. At this moment, then, the altar of the church corresponds to the altar of the sacrifice of incense.[17] The real altar from which the hymn arises is the hearts of the faithful.[18]

---

[12] "I said earlier that the movement of the bishop from the [middle of the] altar to the right side of it signifies the movement from the passion to everlasting life" (*Liber officialis* 3.8.3; Hanssens 2:287).

[13] Ibid., 3.19.17 (Hanssens 2:316).

[14] Ibid., 3.19.27 (Hanssens 2:319). In using this symbolism Amalarius is not clearing new ground, since it is a symbolism that was well known in the patristic period and had already found a place in the Church's prayers.

[15] Ibid., 3.19.15 (Hanssens 2:315).

[16] Ibid., 3.19.26 (Hanssens 2:319).

[17] "At the moment when the hymn before the passion is being celebrated, our altar refers to the altar of incense" (ibid., 3.21.6; Hanssens 2:325).

[18] "This name is to be given to the visible altar, which represents the hearts of the offerers" (ibid.).

These meanings are never precise and univocal, since every liturgical gesture can have various correspondences with the events of redemption.

In the rite, the priest follows the order of the events of the passion.[19] The meaning of the altar, therefore, will change according to the event of the passion that is being commemorated at that particular moment. For this reason, the altar is described as being, at the moment of the Preface, the table in the upper room: The Preface is sung after the *Sursum corda,* and the *Sursum corda* represents the climb to this "upper" room. If the church at this moment is in the upper room, it follows that the altar can only be the table of the Lord there.[20] Amalarius' interest in the altar surfaces again when he comments on the *Te igitur.* During this part of the Mass, our author points out, there are three prayers; this fact is the thing that most attracts his attention, since it is suited to recalling the three prayers of Jesus on the Mount of Olives.

It is important to note that because of this analogy Amalarius can conclude that the rite of the Church is that which Jesus did: "As the Lord did after going out to the Mount of Olives."[21] On the altar there is a napkin that covers the bread and the wine; this "signifies the towel"[22] with which Jesus girded himself when he washed his disciples' feet. Here the altar is the table in the upper room: "the altar is the Lord's table."[23]

Since during Mass we are present at the drama of the passion, which unfolds before our eyes as the rites gradually succeed one another, the *Unde et memores* is seen as the episode of the crucifixion: Jesus ascends the cross.[24] At this point, the altar, too, is necessarily looked at differently and assumes a new meaning: At the *Unde et memores* the altar is the cross.[25] This interpretation of the altar remains unchanged until the end of the *Nobis quoque peccatoribus,* when it becomes the tomb of Christ.[26] After his death Jesus is taken down from

[19] "This is the order that the priest follows" (ibid., 3.21.3; Hanssens 2:324).
[20] "Thus understood, the altar is the table at which the Lord supped with his disciples" (ibid.).
[21] Ibid., 3.23.13 (Hanssens 2:333).
[22] Ibid., 3.24.8 (Hanssens 2:339).
[23] Ibid.
[24] "Just as in what preceded Christ's body was alive in the sacrament of the bread and wine, as well as in my memory, so at this point it ascends into heaven" (ibid., 3.25.2; Hanssens 2:340).
[25] "The altar at this moment is the altar of the cross" (ibid., 3.25.8; Hanssens 2:342).
[26] Ibid., 3.26.13 (Hanssens 2:347).

the cross, and this action is represented by the gesture of the archdeacon who elevates the chalice; it follows from this that the archdeacon represents Joseph of Arimathea, while the priest, in elevating the chalice, represents Nicodemus.[27] If, in Amalarius' way of interpreting the Mass, the altar is the cross, then it is correct to think that the taking of the Body of Christ from the altar in the act of elevating it can signify the taking down of the Lord from the cross.

After the elevation, the chalice is set on the altar once again. At this point, the altar is the tomb of Christ: "He next places the chalice on the altar and wraps it in the shroud."[28] In the text of the Canon at this point there are three prayers; appealing to the number three, Amalarius says that this moment of the Mass signifies the three days of Christ in the tomb.[29]

After the Canon, the rite of Mass calls for the Our Father, a prayer composed of seven petitions; consequently, it is recited as a memorial of the seventh day,[30] which according to Amalarius is the day of the resurrection. As a result, the rite of commingling is seen as referring to the resurrection.

The final rite of the Mass, namely, the rite of dismissal (*Ite missa est*) is connected with the final act in the work of redemption, that is, the ascension.[31]

1.1.3. Scope of the Representation of the Passion

In the description of the rite of the Mass the verb *ostendere* ("show") plays an important role: the Mass "shows" the events of the passion and teaches the faithful how they are to remember[32] those events.

---

[27] "The priest makes two signs of the cross over the cup, signifying that Jesus, who was crucified for the two peoples, is taken down from the cross. The elevation performed by the priest and the deacon shows the taking down of Christ from the cross" (ibid., 3.26.9; Hanssens 2:346).

[28] *Eclogae de Ordine romano* 25.3 (Hanssens 3:257). In this passage Amalarius goes more deeply and makes an explicit reference to the typological method which he has just used: "At this point we identify the deacon with Joseph because he is a suitable type of him" (ibid.).

[29] *Eclogae de Ordine romano* 14 (Hanssens 3:310).

[30] "The Lord's Prayer, which contains seven petitions, is said in remembrance of the seventh day, when Christ rested in the tomb" (*Liber officialis* 3.29.7; Hanssens 2:357).

[31] "The deacon: *Ite missa est.* He speaks to the people as a type of the angels who told the apostles: 'This Jesus, who has been taken up from you into heaven' and so on" (*Eclogae de Ordine romano* 32; Hanssens 3:263).

[32] In this sense the Eucharist is a remembrance of the passion; this conception of sacramental remembrance remains constant throughout the Middle Ages.

Their participation consists in allowing the rite to lead to a review, in memory, of the events of the passion, burial, and ascent to heaven. The liturgy is a kind of sacred drama that has for its function to *represent* our redemption by Christ and the events that make it up. The term *repraesentare* belongs in the realm of *signs,* and our task here is to grasp its scope, for the representation in question is not purely external, since Amalarius is concerned with a real and true *presence* of the events represented. The relation between the Mass and the work of redemption, that is, the passion of Christ, is a real one. Here, for example, is an indication of the real identity between cross and altar: When speaking of the altar, the action taken is related to the cross: "And so he now ascends the cross."[33]

The origin and explanation of this kind of realism is located in the person of the bishop who celebrates the Eucharist. He is understood to be the Vicar of Christ, and this sacramental[34] function is connected specifically with the imitation of Christ,[35] although this finds expression in ritual actions belonging to the visible dimension of the celebration.[36]

Amalarius still uses the archaic language of typology, but he is not in a position to understand it as the Fathers of the Church used to understand it; the sacramental value of the rite as an imitation of Christ has been lost, although not completely.[37] What preserves it, at least partially, is the theology of the minister which Amalarius uses.

---

[33] *Liber officialis* 3.25.2 (Hanssens 2:340).

[34] *Vicarius* translates the Greek *typos,* which belongs to the language of sacramentality; we must translate it as "priest."

[35] Episcopacy involves both apostolic succession and the imitation of Christ, with which the role of "vicar" is to be connected: "We read that Christ in turn appointed the apostles to be his successors in the Church. The successors of the apostles are the bishops, who imitate them" (*Missae expositionis* 1; Hanssens 1:256-57). Imitation, succession, vicarship all belong to the same semantic field and are equivalent each to the others.

[36] In order to explain the responsory Amalarius makes a bold connection between this moment of the Mass and the work of redemption: The responsory is the moment of the call of Peter and the other apostles, inasmuch as they "responded, because they imitated Christ" (*Missae expositionis* 5; Hanssens 1:259).

[37] For example, the description of the altar as a tomb is not to be understood as simply an external image or a mere symbol; in Amalarius' intention it means much more; thus he says that the subdeacon "presents himself with the paten at the Lord's tomb" (*Liber officialis* 3.30.3; Hanssens 2:360).

Since the bishop is the *successor* and *vicar* of Christ, the rites and gestures of the Mass are a true and real *imitation* of the passion.[38] From this it follows that the symbols expressing the relationship between the rite of the Mass and the passion of Christ cannot be taken as purely allegorical, since they express a real relationship that has an ontological significance, although it is not based any longer on the philosophical conception that had been characteristic of the patristic period. The basis now is rather a juridical conception that will henceforth be the keystone of the theology of the Mass.

1.1.4. The Triform Body of Christ

Amalarius never concerns himself with sacramentality as such; that is, he never undertakes a formal discussion of how and why the bread is the Body of Christ. The subject is indeed broached on one occasion, when the author comments on the rite of the breaking of the bread, at which the host is broken into three parts. On this occasion, Amalarius develops his idea of the triform Body of Christ.[39]

Amalarius' doctrine on the Body of Christ as a *corpus triforme* is a very complex one, if for no other reason than that he formulates it in different ways. Properly speaking, it is not a doctrine, but simply a comment on the rite of the fraction, which occurs before the *immixtio* and Communion. The eucharistic bread is broken into three parts: One is placed in the cup, one is placed on the paten and serves for Communion, and one is left on the altar as viaticum, or Communion for the dying. According to the method of interpretation followed by Amalarius, every action must be related to some element of the passion and have a mystical meaning: The division of the host into three parts means a tripartite division of the Body of Christ, since the host is the Body of Christ. Amalarius says that

"the first is the holy and spotless body taken from the Virgin Mary, the second is that which walked on the earth, and the third is that which lies in the tomb. The particle placed in the cup shows *(ostenditur)* the

---

[38] For Amalarius the category of *succession* is the basis of the sacramental realism of the liturgy and therefore of the realism of the relationship between the Mass and the sacrifice of Christ.

[39] The best study of the subject is still H. De Lubac, *Corpus mysticum. L'eucharistie et l'Eglise au moyen âge* (4th ed.; Paris, 1949). See also M. Cristiani, "Il 'Liber Officialis' di Amalario di Metz e la dottrina del 'Corpus triforme,'" in *Culto cristiano— Politica imperiale carolingia* (Convegni del Centro di studi sulla spiritualità medievale, Università degli Studi di Perugia, 18; Todi, 1979) 121–67.

body of Christ already risen from the dead; the part eaten by the priest or the people (shows the body) that still walks on the earth; the part left on the altar (shows the body) that lies in the tomb."[40]

In his *Eclogae* Amalarius says that the fraction recalls the breaking of the bread by Jesus at his meal with the disciples at Emmaus, and he adds that the three parts of the host recall the three participants in that meal: Jesus, Cleopas, and Luke. He goes on to ask why the entire host is not placed in the cup, since it is the entire body of Jesus that rose from the dead; he gives the following answer: "(The body of Christ) in part will rise [he is referring to the dead]; in part it is already living and will not die again [he is referring to the body of Christ that rose and is living in heaven]; in part it is mortal and yet is already in heaven [he is referring to the Church], since the Apostle says: *Our life (conversatio) is in heaven.*"[41]

The idea of the *corpus triforme* is not strictly speaking a doctrine but simply an interpretation of the liturgical rite of the fraction, but an interpretation in the customary allegorical mode of Amalarius that allows several meanings to be given to the same rite, the justification being that the goal Amalarius sets himself is the meaning that is spiritually useful at that point.[42] That is why one and the same rite can have several interpretations, all of which are valid, even if none of them is the true explanation. The idea of the *corpus triforme* needs to be appraised in terms of the author's method of explanation, that is as an interpretation of a rite. On the other hand, the Mozarabic Rite, also known as the Visigothic, already had something similar, inasmuch as the host is there broken into nine parts which are arranged on the paten in the form of a cross and interpreted as signifying nine mysteries of the life of the Christ, from the incarnation to the coming of the kingdom.[43]

In the system established in Amalarius' commentary, the question of the *corpus triforme* is not very important; as I have indicated, the idea is set forth in a few lines and in passing, without the author formally

[40] *Liber officialis* 3.35 (Hanssens 2:367f.).

[41] *Eclogae de Ordine romano* 36 (Hanssens 3:258f.).

[42] According to Amalarius' method the meaning of a rite must correspond to the historical and theological nature of that rite. Any pointer leading to any meaning whatsoever is therefore acceptable.

[43] See the drawing in *Missale mixtum secundum regulam Beati Isidori dictum Mozarabes* (Rome: Typis Joannis Generosi Salomoni, 1755) 1:230.

committing himself to it. It was Florus, deacon of Lyons and a fierce opponent of Amalarius, who turns the latter's comment on the rite of the fraction into a true and proper doctrine, while imputing this to Amalarius along with the accusation of having destroyed the unity of the body of Christ.[44] At the Council of Thionville (835) no condemnation was issued, but at the Council of Quiercy (838) Amalarius was indeed condemned. It must be said that behind the doctrinal problem there lay a political problem having to do with the episcopate of the Church of Lyons, of which Amalarius had become administrator after the removal of Agobard, who had gone into exile for taking sides against Louis the Pious. In his liturgical reforms Amalarius was opposed by important personages of Lyons, among whom Florus the deacon stood out. When Agobard was no longer out of favor, Florus won out against Amalarius when he succeeded in having him condemned for heresy at Quiercy.

The remote origin of the idea of the *triforme corpus Christi* is to be found in Augustine, although the latter could never have used the term *triforme*, since for him there is but one body of Christ, and it has but one form. Both the Eucharist and the Church participate in the physical body of Christ and for this reason are identified with it, even while remaining different. That is the conception of sacramentality that we find in Augustine, and it cannot be transferred to Amalarius' allegorical system without being completely distorted; this is precisely what happened because Amalarius no longer shared the cultural and philosophical setting of Augustine.

1.1.5. Concluding Assessment

(a) Since Amalarius' conception of the liturgy is still dependent on the patristic perspective, he looks at the Mass as a complex of signs that *represent* the work of redemption, that is, the passion of Christ. In his commentary on the eucharistic rite he develops a real theological commentary on the Mass, although one that is very debatable since it depends on the allegorical turn taken by the typological method. Although his intention is to ensure the realism of the relationship between the Mass and the passion, it must be acknowledged that he is unsuccessful except at a purely external level. The relation between the Mass and the passion of Christ is formulated on the basis of the symbolism of the rites, which, performed as they are by the bishop,

---

[44] Florus of Lyons, *Opusculum adversus Amalarium* 1.1, and 2.1 (Hanssens 1:388 and 390).

the *vicar* of Christ, share in a way in the sacramental character of the Eucharist; the absence of philosophical categories, which are replaced by juridical categories, means that the symbols reflect allegory rather than ontology, although Amalarius' intention is decidedly to favor the latter.

(b) The doctrine of the *triforme corpus Christi* is developed using the same method of allegorical commentary that is used in explaining the rites of the Mass. As a result, the connection between the eucharistic bread, the Church, and the historical body of Christ becomes artificial and lacking in sacramental value.

(c) In the following centuries Amalarius' commentary became an obligatory model and an undeniable source of inspiration for anyone desirous of commenting on the eucharistic liturgy. Medieval culture felt quite satisfied with the grandiose framework of allegorical references and did not notice the lack of a valid explanation of the relation between the Mass and the passion.

(d) During almost the same years in which Amalarius was working, Paschasius Radbert gave a very important explanation of the sacramental presence of the Body of Christ. His theology did not arise out of a commentary on the Mass *(Expositio missae)* nor out of a general treatise on the liturgy *(De officiis).* Paschasius produced an explanation of the eucharistic presence that was so realistic as to end in physicism.[45]

1.2. *Commentaries on the Mass after Amalarius*[46]

There is need to distinguish several stages in the development of medieval commentaries on the Mass. Amalarius represents a manifesto

[45] Paschasius' approach depends not so much on the theology of the sacraments as on soteriology.

[46] In addition to the classic work of A. Franz, *Die Messe im deutschen Mittelalter* (Freiburg i. B., 1902), see J. A. Jungmann, *The Mass of the Roman Rite: Its Origin and Development (Missarum Sollemnia),* trans. F. A. Brunner (2 vols.; New York: Benziger, 1951 and 1955), and, above all, M. M. Schaefer, "Twelfth Century Latin Commentaries on the Mass: The Relationship of the Priest to Christ and to the People," *Studia liturgica* 15 (1982–83) 76–86, to be completed by idem, "Latin Mass Commentaries from the Ninth through Twelfth Centuries: Chronology and Theology," in *Fountain of Life: In Memory of Niels K. Rasmussen O.P.,* ed. G. Austin (NPM Studies in Church Music and Liturgy; Washington, D.C., 1991) 35–50. See also T. M. Thibodeau, "Les sources du *Rationale* de Guillaume Durand," in *Guillaume Durand évêque de Mende (v. 1230–1296). Canoniste, liturgiste et homme politique,* ed. P.-M. Gy (Actes de la Table Ronde du Centre nationale de la recherche scientifique, Mende 24–27 mai 1990; Paris, 1992) 143–53.

for allegorical interpretation, while in Florus we have a rejection of symbolism. During the next three centuries commentaries on the Mass follow one another without ceasing; they show greater or lesser originality and a greater or lesser influence of Amalarian allegorism. At the end of this period comes Sicard (ca. 1150–1215), bishop of Cremona, who composes the *Mitrale,* which is the fullest of all the commentaries on the liturgy. The work has some truly original ideas and brings to completion the literary genre of commentary on the liturgy and specifically on the Mass. Innocent III (1160/61–1216) composes a commentary that is closely dependent on that of Sicard but which, partly because its author would become pope, was to have exceptional success and circulation.

The period ends with the *Rationale divinorum officiorum* (1291) of William Durandus. This is a kind of encyclopedia, containing as it does all the elements—normative, juridical, liturgical, spiritual, and allegorical—needed for a proper celebration. The *Rationale* is also a commentary on the liturgy but is not part of the development of this literary genre, which reached its high point in Sicard.

1.2.1. Florus of Lyons

The *Liber officialis* of Amalarius is one of the great fruits of the Carolingian renaissance but not the only one, nor was it accepted without opposition. Florus, deacon of Lyons (d. ca. 850) and an opponent of Amalarius,[47] decided to compose a commentary on the Canon of the Mass that would stick closely to the text and be completely lacking in any allegorical element of the Amalarian kind.[48] Florus' determination to comment on the Roman Canon without using allegory was praiseworthy, but the attempt bore no fruit, since Florus limited himself to a dull paraphrase that often repeated the words of the Canon while simply changing their order.[49] It may be said in summary that there

[47] Florus is the adversary par excellence of Amalarius; not only does he write a work to show how misleading the latter's reform of the antiphonary and his commentary on it were, but he manages to get the man condemned at the Council of Quiercy and have him removed from Lyons where he was bishop.

[48] *De actione missae* (PL 119:15–70). See P. Duc, *Etude sur l'Expositio missae de Florus de Lyon, suivie d'une édition critique du texte* (Belley, 1937).

[49] Florus seems to have been unable to gain much from the text of the Canon on which he is commenting, or from citations from the Bible, or from the citations from the Fathers, of whom he makes quite extensive use. Paradoxical though it may be, he seems not to have been aware of the riches and themes that surface in his commentary. See, e.g., his use of a really valuable biblical text, 1 Peter 2:9, on

is a radical difference in both object and method between the commentary of Florus and that of Amalarius. Florus comments on a text, that is, that which is *written* in the sacramentary, while Amalarius is not concerned with texts but comments on the rites that are performed and are *seen* by priests and faithful during the celebration. As far as method is concerned, Florus tries to be strictly literal, while Amalarius concentrates on the images, figures, and symbols to which allegory gives him access.

1.2.2. The Development in the Commentaries on the Mass

While Jean of Fécamp (ca. 990–1078)[50] cites, almost verbatim, entire sections of the work of Florus, the *Liber de divinis officiis*[51] attributed to Remigius of Auxerre (ca. 840–ca. 908) has a broader horizon, since in some chapters it depends on Florus, in others on Amalarius, citing whole sections from the two authors.

In his *Micrologus de ecclesiasticis observationibus*[52] Bernold of Constance (ca. 1050–1100) chooses to go back to Amalarius, but in a critical way,[53] for he shows his uneasiness with many of Amalarius' applications of symbols, and rejects them. He stresses the point that the actions of the priest are a representation of the actions of Christ, in the sense that the former have a real connection with the latter.

The twelfth century was the golden age of commentaries on the Mass. I may begin with the *Liber de sacramentis* or *De sacramento altaris* of Peter the Painter (Petrus Pictor) (ca. 1100),[54] who harks back to the teaching of Paschasius on the Eucharist and to the allegorical embellishments inspired by Amalarius, although he shows a degree of caution in accepting these. I find it interesting that Peter keeps doctrinal explanation quite separate from reflections of a symbolic kind on the

---

the basis of which he comments on the offering made by the entire Church (clergy and people) as a priestly people.

[50] John of Fécamp, *De corpore et sanguine Domini* (PL 101:1085–98).

[51] PL 101:1246–71.

[52] PL 151:974–1022.

[53] Not only Bernold of Constance but Rhabanus Maurus and Wallafrid Strabo composed non-allegorical commentaries on the liturgy; Florus' work seems to have been at the origin of this genre. We see that it was difficult to compose a literal commentary on the Canon during this period. The commentaries are little more than paraphrases of the text and are therefore disappointingly dry. These are the reasons for the method's lack of success.

[54] PL 207:1135–54.

actions of the priest.[55] In addition, in order to explain the transformation of the bread into the Body of Christ, he lays a heavy emphasis on the analogy between sacrament and incarnation.[56]

In his *Expositio in Canonem Missae*[57] Odo (d. 1113)[58] is a faithful imitator of Florus of Lyons in giving a literal explanation of the Canon and in explaining that the *circumadstantes* are co-offerers of the Mass. The explanation of the account of institution is based on that of Ambrose in his *De sacramentis;* this is a valuable testimony, since the same citation is found in Peter Lombard and is passed on by him to Thomas Aquinas.[59] In the judgment of Mary Schaeffer, Odo is the transmitter of the thought of Florus of Lyons to later commentators.[60]

Rupert of Deutz (ca. 1075–1129) wrote a *De divinis officiis*[61] in which he makes use of both monastic theology and a complex symbology. On the one hand, he draws on the allegorical heritage of Amalarius and on the other he goes back to the eucharistic realism of Paschasius Radbert, which he accepts without seeing any problem in it.

Honorius of Autun (ca. 1075/80–ca. 1156) is a man who had some influence on medieval theology; all that we know of him is what is contained in his writings, for he deliberately concealed any information about himself. In addition to a sacramentary, he has left us a commentary on the Mass that is part of his *Gemma animae;* in this commentary he uses both the symbolic imagery of Amalarius and the method of Isidore of Seville. The Mass is a kind of sacred drama performed by the ministers, but it cannot be reduced to a dramatization pure and simple, since Christ is present and alive in the Sacrament. The conception of the Eucharist as a passion play has a pastoral purpose: to help the faithful remember the suffering of Christ and to

---

[55] This fact is of some importance in explaining how the scholastics came to separate the doctrinal discussion of the real presence of the Body of Christ from the discussion of a symbolic kind that grounds the relationship between the Mass and the passion of Christ. This remark should be linked to what has already been said about Amalarius.

[56] This would be, if one might use the phrase, a "sacramental incarnation."

[57] PL 160:1053–70.

[58] Abbot of St. Martin (Tournai) and bishop of Cambrai.

[59] See P.-M. Gy, "Prière eucharistique et paroles de la consécration selon les théologiens de Pierre Lombard à S. Thomas d'Aquin," in *La liturgie dans l'histoire,* ed. P.-M. Gy (Paris: Cerf–St. Paul, 1990) 211–21 [henceforth: *Liturgie*].

[60] Schaeffer, "Latin Mass Commentaries" (note 46, above), 38.

[61] *Ruperti Tuitiensis. Liber de divinis officiis,* ed. H. Haacke (CCLContMed 7; Turnhout: Brepols, 1967).

imitate it.[62] In Honorius we again meet the two elements: the allegorical and figural, which brings out the connection between the eucharistic celebration and the course of Christ's sufferings, and the properly theological, which deals in a very realistic way with the sacramental presence of Christ.

Ivo of Chartres (1090–1115)[63] does not differ from the preceding authors in his use of the allegorical method, but he does have a touch of originality when he sets up a systematic parallel between the Old and New Testaments, to the point of finding that the first part of the Mass (the Liturgy of the Word) corresponds symbolically to the sacrifices of the Old Testament levitical cult, which were offered on the altar of holocausts, while the second part (the Eucharistic Liturgy) corresponds to the sacrifice of incense offered in the Holy of Holies.

We have little information with which to reconstruct the life and education of John Beleth. We know that he had a first-rate theological formation and was a theologian and master who was esteemed and followed.[64] At Paris, between 1160 and 1164, he wrote his *Summa de ecclesiasticis officiis*,[65] which was very successful. He uses the various liturgical symbolisms but in a very restrained way; it is likely that his thorough theological formation kept him from fully accepting Amalarian allegorism.[66] Properly theological arguments on the sacramentality of the bread and wine are absent from the *Summa*, but this theology is clearly present and taken for granted, to the point that "transubstantiation" is used as a current term; John is the first commentator to use the word.

1.2.3. Sicard of Cremona

Sicard (ca. 1150–1215) was a great canonist, who after having taught in Germany, became a diplomat, a renowned statesman, and bishop of Cremona (1185–1215).[67] He wrote a *Mitrale seu De officiis ecclesiasticis summa*,[68] which depends closely on the *Summa* of Beleth, but also surprises us by the breadth of its treatment and by the wide range of

---

[62] *Gemma animae* 1.36 (PL 172:555).

[63] *Sermones de ecclesiasticis sacramentis* (PL 162:505–610).

[64] P. Masini, "Magister Johannes Beleth: ipotesi di una traccia biografica," *EL* 107 (1993) 248–59.

[65] *Iohannis Beleth. Summa de ecclesiasticis officiis*, ed. H. Douteil (CCLContMed 41A; Turnhout: Brepols, 1976).

[66] Certain points make it clear that John Beleth knew the work of Amalarius.

[67] See G. Picasso, "Sicard de Crémone," *DSp* 15 (Paris, 1990) 810–14.

[68] PL 213:13–436.

sources used: constant citations of the Bible, patristic texts, and medieval commentators. Sicard takes into account the rite in use in Cremona and makes explicit references to what is in the sacramentary, but he has a far wider knowledge of liturgical books and takes into account liturgical usages from other traditions than that of Cremona.

One aspect of his work should be pointed out: for every rite on which he comments he provides the reader with a great many interpretations, one after another, without ever singling out one as better or more meaningful than the others. All the interpretations are logical and are strictly based on one or more passages of the Bible; all are traditional interpretations already developed by other authors, the Fathers or the medieval commentators, and all are equally possible and acceptable.[69] For Sicard, it is a matter of choosing a method, and this is something quite original; no less original is his realization that the method of the four senses, used in interpreting the Scriptures, can be applied also to the interpretation of the liturgy.[70] He has thus grasped clearly, although perhaps unconsciously, a point that is characteristic of the patristic understanding of the liturgy, and he uses it skillfully and with freedom.

Why does Sicard multiply these figural explanations? Is there a reason for the many different explanations of each rite? There certainly is, and the reason is pastoral and catechetical. The pastor of souls is meant to find in the *Mitrale* a collection of information and a source of inspiration for giving the faithful the explanations that he thinks most useful to them and best suited for ensuring a proper participation[71] in the liturgy. Sicard's commentary is concerned with what the faithful or the priest see during the Mass. Although he constantly uses the word "transubstantiation" and is fully aware of its meaning, he is not interested in theology, does not construct a theory of sacramental realism,

[69] This is an oddity that is already present, but to a much smaller degree, in the *Summa* of Beleth and in other earlier commentators. It is not easy to become aware of it in those authors, because it occurs only occasionally; in Sicard it imposes itself on the reader's notice.

[70] Only a hasty reader can think that by choosing his method Sicard intends to apply to the liturgy solely the medieval principle of the four senses of Scripture (historical, allegorical, moral, anagogical). In fact, Sicard mentions this method, but the four senses are present only as four among the many interpretations he gives of each rite. His interpretations range beyond the four senses and much beyond the possibilities available to that method.

[71] Sicard has no equivalent for the modern term "participation"; the use of it within his conception of the liturgy is an anachronism.

does not concern himself with the liturgical texts used in the Eucharist, and is not worried about these texts being understood.[72] In order better to understand his approach, it is enough to read the commentary on the Preface and the Canon of the Mass, in which he comments not on the texts but on the titles of the various parts, the *incipits,* and, above all, on the pictures painted in the Sacramentary.

For Sicard, the function of the Preface[73] is to prepare the mind by means of the devout sentiments required for entering into the mystery.[74] In order to achieve this purpose, he uses, not the text of the thanksgiving, but the *incipit* of the Preface, which consists of the letters *UD.*[75] These letters, appropriately illuminated and larger in size than the text of the Preface, are among the visual elements of the Sacramentary. The same is to be said of the letter "T," the first letter of the prayer *Te igitur* and therefore of the Canon; the letter becomes a cross and the object of the priest's devotion during the recitation of the Canon. Sicard decides that an image of the Crucified should be painted on this cross. When it is thus seen with the eyes of the body, the passion of Christ must impress itself on the heart of the priest, so that he will have the proper interior attitude as he speaks to God.[76] At the *Te igitur* he makes the Sign of the Cross on his forehead and he bows.

These are gestures of devotion toward the images painted in the Sacramentary, namely, the Majesty of the Father and the passion. The image of the Majesty makes "present, as it were," the one who is being invoked; the same applies to the image of the passion.[77] The ritual kiss given to the image is a kind of bridge between the book

[72] This might be described as the approach of Florus of Lyons, but Sicard operates differently; he adopts the approach of Amalarius, who comments on and explains what the faithful or the priests *see* during the celebration, not on the texts *written* in the sacramentary.

[73] The Preface is interpreted in light of its position in respect to the mystery, which is identified with the Canon.

[74] "The Preface is next, that is, a preamble and preparation for the Canon; it prepares our minds for the mystery of Christ" (*Mitrale,* Book 3; PL 213:122).

[75] The letters UD are an abbreviation of *Uere dignum,* but have by this time become a symbol for the Preface.

[76] "Notice that the Canon begins with a tau, a T, which is in the form of a cross; the figure of the Crucified is usually painted on it, so that the passion, the sign of which is before the priest's eyes, may be imprinted also on the eyes of his heart, as he addresses the Father as One present" (*Mitrale,* Book 3; PL 213:125).

[77] "Next the priest kisses the feet of the Majesty and makes the sign of the cross on his own forehead; bowing, he says: *Te igitur,* signifying that they should reverently

and liturgical action or, better, between the priest who read the Sacramentary and the liturgical action. We may therefore conclude that as far as devotional effectiveness is concerned, the liturgical book speaks more through its images than through its texts: The liturgical book is more a book to be seen than a text to be understood, and it has become an object of devotion. This is the extreme consequence of the devotional interpretation of the liturgy.[78]

1.2.4. Innocent III

Lothar of Segni (1160/61–1216) was a student of Sicard and, before becoming pope as Innocent III, wrote a *De missarum mysteriis* (1195–1197).[79] In many respects he is close to Sicard, although he is less concerned with multiplying interpretations of the liturgical rites; in addition, he seems more aware than Sicard is of theological problems as such, as can be seen when he deals with the Sacrament of the Body of Christ or with the priest, who acts *in persona Christi*. In Lothar's view, the eucharistic celebration, in its ritual unfolding, corresponds to the various stages of the passion of Christ, as if it were a dramatization of it: The Eucharist is a memorial of the passion because the various phases of the Eucharistic Prayer (the Canon) recall so many phases of Christ's passion.[80] But we have seen all this already in discussing Sicard.

---

approach the mystery of the cross. In some codices, the Majesty of the Father and the cross of the Crucified are depicted, so that we may look upon, as one present, him whom we invoke, and so that the passion which is represented may be thrust upon the eyes of the heart; in other codices, only the Crucified is depicted. Some priests kiss first the feet of the Majesty and then of the Crucified according to the order in the Canon; others kiss the feet first of the Crucified and then of the Majesty, because it is through the Son that we come to the Father" (*Mitrale*, Book 3; PL 213:124). Something similar is to be seen in Honorius of Autun (1098–ca. 1150): "He says *Te igitur* because he looks on the Lord as present. The Canon begins with the letter T because it has the form of a cross" (*Gemma animae*; PL 172:577).

[78] On the devotional interpretation of the medieval liturgy see my essay "La liturgia nella basilica di Sant'Ambrogio in epoca medioevale," in *La basilica di Sant'Ambrogio. Il tempio ininterrotto*, ed. M. L. Gatti Perer (Milan: Vita e Pensiero, 1995) 1:295–309.

[79] PL 217:763–916.

[80] Here is how Innocent III speaks of the Canon, which is called *Secreta*: "In the *Secreta* [in what is said in a low voice] the passion is remembered, that is, what was done during the week before Easter, from the tenth day of the new moon, when Jesus went to Jerusalem, until the seventeenth, when he rose from the dead" (*De sacro altaris mysterio* 3.2; PL 217:840–41).

1.2.5. William Durandus

"The *Rationale divinorum officiorum* of William Durandus the Elder is undoubtedly the definitive work in a voluminous medieval literature of commentaries on the liturgy." The words are those of Timothy M. Thibodeau,[81] who is repeating a similar judgment by Dom Guéranger. William Durandus was, above all, a jurist[82] and, as such, left works of great importance such as the *Speculum iudiciale*. He follows the same method as a liturgist that he does as a jurist;[83] in fact, the *Rationale,* too, belongs to the literary genre of the *Speculum.*[84]

A first aspect of the *Rationale* that needs to be emphasized is the citations of juridical sources that appear systematically throughout the work. We may legitimately think that it was the *Decretum Gratiani,* along with the *Liber extra* of Gregory IX,[85] that gave easy access to citations from the Fathers. In addition, the *Decretum Gratiani* contains numerous canons on the liturgy and a variety of prescriptions for it.[86]

The *Rationale* draws on four main sources: Innocent III, Sicard of Cremona, William of Auxerre, and Prevostinus of Cremona. In its overall plan, the work follows closely that of the nine books of the *Mitrale;* it is noteworthy that Sicard is one of the few liturgists to whom William refers by name in his treatise.[87] William's allegorical commentary is addressed to educated persons who are capable of using a *Speculum,* and it has for its object the rites of the Mass understood not so much as actions but as juridical norms.[88] At the end of

---

[81] Thibodeau, "Les sources du *Rationale* de Guillaume Durand" (note 46, above), 143.

[82] The age of Durandus was marked by an exceptional development of canon law, which influenced all areas, even the strictly theological, of the Church's life.

[83] Durandus explicitly intends to do so, as he says in the *Rationale* (Prologue, 15).

[84] A *Speculum* is a work of an encyclopedic kind that brings together all the information affecting a question and that reflects the better or more important sources and authors *(auctoritates).* See R. Bradley, "Backgrounds of the Title 'Speculum' in Medieval Literature," *Speculum* 29 (1954) 100–15.

[85] See Thibodeau (note 81, above), 151.

[86] In the section *De consecratione* (dist. 1, c. 70) there are also some short *Expositiones missae.*

[87] See Thibodeau, 147.

[88] Unlike the allegorical commentaries of his predecessors, that of Durandus is addressed to educated persons; this did not, however, mean a limitation on the number of people who used it (as is shown by the work's very extensive circulation); it meant rather that less emphasis was placed on the *pastoral* (and therefore creative) use of the allegorical commentary, to the benefit of a learned use of it for study.

the thirteenth century ecclesiastical rites were understood as laws of the Church, that is, they had passed into the sphere of law[89] and were dealt with as such.

Allegory continues to hold sway, despite the fact that the scholastic method had already been born in the universities of the twelfth and thirteenth centuries. In its content, Durandus' commentary follows closely the complex allegorical symbology that had been passed on from Amalarius to Sicard; but this symbolic approach has been enriched here by a notable broadening of the patristic documentation; Durandus is, above all, an editor who brings together the allegorical explanations inherited from his predecessors, while linking them to the new culture—the juridical culture—that has been developed in the Church of the thirteenth century. The specific element, and the originality, of Durandus consists chiefly in the abundant use of juridical sources and the resultant transformation of the arguments drawn from previous commentaries on the Mass (which serve Durandus as sources) into juridical interpretations; in doing so, he establishes a connection between the juridical status of the liturgical rites and their interpretation.

At this point in its development, the commentary on the Mass has two components, the allegorical and the juridical. Insofar as it is allegorical, the commentary fits well into liturgical practice, since both are connected with value judgments of an existential kind, which as such cannot but be subjective; allegorical commentaries on the Mass thus speak to the soul of the believer. The juridical approach, on the other hand, emphasizes a sphere of objectivity that is not easily combined with the allegorical commentary, and the two inevitably remain simply juxtaposed.[90]

It is a short step from here to a purely rubrical conception of the liturgy. All that is needed is for the characteristically medieval sensitivity to allegory to fade away[91] and, as a result, for the allegorical commentary to disappear. What remains of the commentary on the Mass is a juridical and rubrical understanding of the rite.

[89] See Thibodeau, 152.

[90] It could not possibly be otherwise, because of the deeper logic of any work conceived as a *speculum.*

[91] See, e.g., how in his *The Praise of Folly* Erasmus of Rotterdam criticizes the use of allegory in the interpretations given in homilies.

2. EUCHARISTIC REALISM

We do not find in the early Middle Ages any special discussions of or challenges to eucharistic realism; as a result, the development of ideas about the Eucharist was unmarked by jolts or particular problems. In the patristic period the transformation of the bread and wine into the Sacrament of the Body and Blood of Christ had already been linked to the incarnation in such a way as to lay a heavy emphasis on eucharistic realism. In the Middle Ages this relationship is strongly accentuated, to the point that it becomes the most widespread way of interpreting the Eucharist.

Thus it is said that "Jesus becomes bread,"[92] just as he became flesh in the womb of Mary.[93] It is precisely the unquestioned conviction of sacramental realism that suggests a parallel with the incarnation.[94] The profound difference between patristic thought, with its high point in Augustine, and early medieval theology[95] is made quite clear in two episodes during the ninth century: (1) Paschasius Radbert has to defend his treatise *De corpore et sanguine Domini* against the accusation that it has abandoned the teaching of Augustine; and (2) at the Council of Quiercy Amalarius of Metz is indicted for his teaching on the *triforme corpus Christi*, which, according to Florus of Lyons, ruptures the unity of the (incarnate and risen) body of Christ, the Eucharist, and

[92] See, e.g., R. Falsini, "La 'trasformazione del corpo e del sangue di Cristo,'" *Studi francescani* 52 (1955) 5–57; idem, "La 'Conformatio' nella liturgia mozarabica," *EL* 72 (1958) 281–91.

[93] "If you truly believe that for the incarnation of the Word, flesh was created in the womb of the Virgin Mary by the power of the Holy Spirit and without [human] seed, then truly believe also that what is effected by the word of Christ through the Holy Spirit is his very body taken from the Virgin" (*De corpore et sanguine Domini* 4 [CCLContMed 16; Turnhout: Brepols, 1969] 30).

[94] Note that the statement "the bread becomes the body of Christ" is not the same as "Christ becomes bread." The former is the traditional formulation of the sacramental transformation, whereas the latter derives from the doctrine of the incarnation and, when applied to the Eucharist, implies a second incarnation, which takes place, this time, in the Sacrament. The establishment of so close a connection between the Eucharist and the incarnation pushes eucharistic doctrine in the direction of a more *physicist* concept of the Sacrament. This will be a constant problem throughout the Middle Ages and will continue to be such down to our own times.

[95] Patricia McCormick Zirkel says that the period of patristic discussion of the Eucharist ended at this moment; see her "The Ninth-Century Eucharistic Controversy: A Context for the Beginnings of Eucharistic Doctrine in the West," *Worship* 68 (1994) 3.

the Church. This unity of the body of Christ is a typically Augustinian doctrine;[96] we may therefore conclude that in the second case, too, there is a conflict between Augustinian thought and early medieval thought.[97]

2.1. Paschasius Radbert and Ratramnus

Paschasius Radbert, a monk of Corbie, was the author of the first theological treatise on the Eucharist: *De corpore et sanguine Domini* (ca. 831–833).[98] His theology enjoyed notable success in the Middle Ages, as is evidenced by the broad circulation of manuscripts of his treatise.[99] Paschasius' conception, which is truly innovative from many points of view, is based on the assertion that the Body of Christ which is present in the Eucharist is the very body born of Mary.[100] What is

[96] In the Augustinian tradition, the Church, the Eucharist, and the historical (incarnate and risen) body of Christ are ontologically a single body, but with different levels of participation, as we saw earlier when looking at Augustine; they are not *three modes of being* of the body of Christ. See also my essay, "Saint Augustin et la mystagogie," in *Mystagogie: pensée liturgique d'aujourd'hui et liturgie ancienne* (Conférences Saint Serge. XXXIXe Semaine d'études liturgiques. Bibliotheca Ephemerides Liturgicae, Subsidia 70), ed. A. M. Triacca and A. Pistoia (Rome: Edizioni liturgiche CLV, 1993) 201–26.

[97] Throughout this debate there was a strong sense of the normative character of the patristic tradition, even when the parties realized that they were not in complete harmony with that tradition.

[98] See O. Capitani, "Motivi di spiritualità cluniacense e realismo eucaristico in Odone di Cluny," in *Spiritualità cluniacense* (Convegni del Centro di studi sulla spiritualità medievale; Todi: Accademia tudertina, 1960) 250–57 (complete paper in *Bullettino dell'Istituto storico italiano per il Medio Evo e Archivio Muratoriano* 71 [1959] 1–18); idem, "Studi per Berengario di Tours. Introduzione," ibid., 69 (1957) 71–88; M. Cristiani, "La controversia eucaristica nella cultura del secolo IX," *Studi medievali* 3rd ser., 9 (1968) 167–233; eadem, "Il 'Liber officialis' di Amalario di Metz e la dottrina del 'Corpus triforme,'" in *Culto cristiano—Politica imperiale carolingia* (Convegni di studi sulla spiritualità medievale; Università degli studi di Perugia, 18; Todi, 1979) 121–67; J.-P. Bouhot, *Ratramne de Corbie. Histoire littéraire et controverses doctrinales* (Paris: Etudes augustiniennes, 1976); G. Picasso, "Riti eucaristici nella società altomedievale. Sul significato storico del trattato eucaristico de Pascasio Radberto," in *Segni e riti nella chiesa altomedievale occidentale* (Settimane di studo del Centro italiano di studi sull'Alto Medioevo, 33; Spoleto, 1987) 505–32.

[99] In this respect, there is a political factor at work, since the second edition of the work (843–44) was dedicated to Charles the Bald, who must have sponsored its publication.

[100] See G. Macy, *The Theologies of the Eucharist in the Early Scholastic Period. A Study of the Salvific Function of the Sacrament according to the Theologians c. 1080–c. 1220* (Oxford: Clarendon Press, 1984) 27. For a broader picture see idem, *The Banquet's*

present in the Eucharist is the physical[101] flesh of Christ, which is as
it were "veiled" by the appearances of bread and wine, so that believers will not feel horrified at eating it: The appearances of bread
and wine are nothing but a garment to deceive the senses. If it were
possible to remove this veil, the flesh and blood of Christ would appear in their natural form: Not only is this possible, but it actually occurs in eucharistic miracles.[102] In Communion, the divine-human
nature of Christ is received by the faithful[103] and, through the natural
metabolic process, is assimilated and changed into the flesh and
blood of the recipients.[104] Paschasius explains that it is because of this
process that the eating[105] of the Eucharist becomes a saving act for
the person.[106] The divine-human existence of Christ is thus united[107]

Wisdom: A Short History of the Theologies of the Lord's Supper (New York: Paulist,
1992).

[101] "And therefore the sacrament that gives life has within itself that which it
gives to those receiving it worthily. And if it contains life, then it is the flesh and
blood of him who is truly alive and in whom everlasting life truly is" (Paschasius,
Epistola ad Fredugardum; CCLContMed 16, p. 146).

[102] Guitmund of Aversa (d. ca. 1095), in his *De corpore et sanguine Domini in veritate* (PL 149:1449–50), bases his treatment of the Eucharist on miracles that occur
during the liturgical celebration.

[103] "Thus Christ remains in them corporeally by reason of this sacrament" (*De
corpore et sanguine Domini* 9; CCLContMed 16, p. 55).

[104] "Believe and understand that through this sacrament he remains concorpo-
rate with us just as we are in him through the man he assumed" (*Epistola ad Fredugardum*; CCLContMed 16, p. 173).

[105] "So that in this visible sacrament of communion the divine power, exercising
its invisible might, as though from the fruit of the tree of paradise, sustains us for
immortality by the taste of wisdom and by virtue; made thereby immortal in
soul, as long as we receive the sacrament worthily, we will at last be transported
to a better condition and carried into the world of immortal things" (*De corpore et
sanguine Domini* 1.1; CCLContMed 16, p. 19).

[106] This teaching of Paschasius had a strong influence on subsequent writers,
precisely because of its utter simplicity, and we find it word for word in, e.g.,
Hervé of Bourg-Dieu (d. ca. 1150), who says that "the real substance of the flesh
that is in Christ passes into us, because that same sacrifice that was on the altar
passed into those who ate of it" (PL 181:918); the effect was a "concorporateness"
with Christ (ibid., 919) that produces the salvation of the person (ibid., 936).

[107] This theology, too, speaks of "unity," but with a meaning different from that
which we saw in Paul. In the teaching of the early Christian centuries there is
question of the unity of the body of Christ which is the Church; now it is a question of the union of Christ and the believer. There has thus been a shift from an
ecclesiological and communitarian perspective, that is, from the perspective of
the assembly, to the perspective of the individual in personal dialogue with

"naturally"[108] with the Body and Blood of the faithful who receive Communion.[109]

Some conclusions may be drawn from this brief exposition: (1) the sacramental presence and sacramental efficacy are both explained in a "natural" way or, to use a term more familiar to us, in a "physicist" way; (2) the salvific function of the Eucharist is closely linked to sacramental realism of a physicist kind;[110] (3) The complete identity of the body of Christ born of Mary with the flesh of Christ present under the eucharistic veil makes it possible to assimilate the Eucharist to the incarnation[111] and therefore to transfer to the Eucharist all the attitudes of faith, spirituality, and devotion that people have to the incarnation.

Paschasius Radbert[112] is the key to understanding the development of eucharistic doctrine in the Middle Ages.

Ratramnus[113] also wrote a work entitled, like that of Paschasius,[114] *De corpore et sanguine Domini*. It was composed in reply to Charles the Bald, who had asked him to explain the doctrine of the Eucharist by answering two questions: (1) Is what the faithful receive in Communion the body of Christ *in mysterio* or that body *in veritate*? (2) Is the body they receive the body that was born of the Virgin Mary, the

---

Christ. The theology of unity (of the body of Christ) has been replaced by a theology of union (with the body of Christ).

[108] "He is truly communicated in the sacrament, in order that he may remain in us naturally, as we remain in him" (*Epistola ad Fredugardum*; CCLContMed 16, p. 172). The "divine" flesh of Christ is assumed by the believer, who is thereby divinized, that is, saved.

[109] Macy, *The Theologies of the Eucharist* (note 100, above), 27.

[110] If it is by a physical process that Communion with Christ and its saving effect takes place, the conception of the Sacrament will inevitably develop increasingly along physicist lines.

[111] The change of the bread into the Body of Christ is effected by the same Holy Spirit who was at work in the incarnation (*De corpore et sanguine Domini* 3; CCLContMed 16, p. 27).

[112] We must, however, avoid interpreting the eucharistic teaching of the early Middle Ages in terms of later controversies. In fact, in dealing with Paschasius the problems that will emerge later in the debate with Berengarius do not arise (see McCormick Zirkel, "The Ninth-Century Eucharistic Controversy" [note 95, above], 2).

[113] Ratramnus was a monk of Corbie who was assigned to teach within the monastery.

[114] In both authors, everything comes down to a definition of two phrases: *in mysterio* and *in veritate*; to this pair must be added another: *in figura* and *in veritate*.

body that suffered, died, was buried, rose, ascended to heaven, and sits at the right hand of the Father?

There was no controversy between the two authors (both belonged to the same monastery), and, if we may judge by the testimony of the *Consuetudines* of the Abbey of Corbie, there was no connection between this theological problem and the life of the monastery in the area of the eucharistic liturgy or eucharistic spirituality. And yet the difference between the positions taken by the two men is very clear and surfaces in their divergent understandings of *figura* and *veritas*.

Paschasius takes his definition of a sacrament from Isidore of Seville; the *figura* is the visible appearance, or in other words, what came to be called the "species." The *veritas*, on the other hand, is "that which must be said" about the Sacrament or, in short, what is taught: the truths of faith about the Eucharist.

Ratramnus, however, takes his definition of a sacrament from Augustine, with whose writings he has a more direct and immediate contact. The meaning of *figura* is difficult to describe; at times it seems to signify the nature of things, and in this usage the *figura* is internal to the reality, while at other times it seems to be a kind of external designation. The *veritas* is the deeper reality: the presence of Christ in the Eucharist. Ratramnus' conception of the Eucharist is radically different from that of Paschasius, even if it is difficult to give a formal description of the difference; in fact, we are dealing with two men who live in the same cultural environment and therefore adopt very similar formulas. I think it can be said that the major difference is this: the thinking of Ratramnus is reducible to that of Augustine,[115] while that of Paschasius is not.

According to Paschasius, the change of the bread into the Body of Christ takes place in a physical manner, while according to Ratramnus it occurs in a figural way. In Ratramnus' view, *in figura* signifies a real change, but one that does not belong to the physical world and is even opposed to it. He makes clear his conviction that those who maintain a physical change are not in agreement with the writings of the Fathers. But it is not easy to say more specifically and exactly what the expression *in figura* means.

In answer to Charles the Bald's question about *in veritate* or *in mysterio*, Ratramnus says the first need is to change the question, since it is not possible to oppose *veritas* to *mysterium*. The eucharistic Body of

[115] Although some problems of interpretation arise.

Christ is a Sacrament of his historical body, which was subjected to suffering and death, but it is not his identical historical body, otherwise the one could not be the sacrament of the other. The historical body of Christ must be distinguished from the Body on the altar: the latter is a figure because it is a Sacrament.[116]

It must be noted that this ninth-century affair remained limited to the group of those directly concerned: Paschasius, Ratramnus, and Charles the Bald,[117] along with a few friends of Paschasius. The disagreement ended without any condemnations, since nothing was declared heterodox. The work of Paschasius enjoyed greater success and wider circulation, one reason being the clarity and simplicity of the sacramental realism he proposed, even though it ended in physicism.

2.2. After Paschasius Radbert

Anselm of Laon (ca. 1059–1117), known as "the Chancellor," is one of the most important representatives of the School of Laon, others being Abelard, William of Champeaux, William of Saint Thierry, and Gilbert de la Porrée. Anselm's teaching on the Eucharist survives only in fragments and is contained chiefly in his comments on 1 Corinthians and the Gospel of John, comments which became part of the *Glossa ordinaria*.

In a comment on John 6:29,[118] Anselm sets down the central points of his teaching: The beginning and end of every good action is to be found in the faith that works through love,[119] and when one does not succeed in doing good, the desire to do it is enough. All this is applied to the Eucharist, with the consequence that the true reception of the Eucharist consists in receiving it with the faith that works through love. This conception denotes a radical change from the soteriological approach that underlies the eucharistic teaching of Paschasius and that continued to develop and in fact received its fullest formulation precisely during these same years.

The Body of Christ that is received in the Eucharist is the same one on which the angels in heaven feed through contemplation; but since

[116] Ratramnus, *De corpore et sanguine Domini* 94 (PL 38:1246).

[117] McCormick Zirkel, "The Ninth-Century Eucharistic Controversy," 2–23, assigns great importance to the presence of the king in the affair.

[118] "Jesus answered them, 'This is the work of God, that you believe in him whom he has sent.'"

[119] "For in Christ Jesus neither circumcision nor uncircumcision counts for anything; the only thing that counts is faith working through love."

we are not able to use this spiritual mode of nourishing ourselves, the Word made flesh has provided us with a food more in keeping with our possibilities.[120]

Another major representative of the School of Laon is William, bishop of Champeaux (1113–1121), whose teaching followed in the path of Anselm. He went beyond Anselm, however, in emphasizing to a greater extent the presence of the whole Christ, body, soul, and divinity, in each of the two species.[121] Also important is his disagreement with Rupert of Deutz: While William maintained that the true reception of the Eucharist requires the faith that works through love, together with the (sacramental) participation in the passion of Christ, Rupert held that faith is necessary and sufficient for the salvation of believers, thus leaving the sacramental action in the shadow.

In two collections, *Dubitatur a quibusdam* and *Sententie Anselmi*,[122] the *res* of the Eucharist is described as both "the true body and blood of Christ" and the "heavenly bread" on which the angels feed; the first *res*, the Body and Blood of Christ, is a sign of the second, the "heavenly bread."[123] Since all who receive the Eucharist receive the true Body and Blood of Christ, it follows that only the good receive the "heavenly bread"; these persons, then, are saved because they are united to Christ through faith and love. The *Sententie Anselmi* speak analogously of two ways of receiving: sacramental reception and real reception. Sacramental reception refers to all those who eat and drink the Body and Blood of Christ, while real reception applies only to those who receive the Body of Christ with the faith that works through love.

[120] On all this see Macy, *The Theologies of the Eucharist* [note 100, above], 73–74.
[121] Ibid., 75.
[122] Anonymous collections of an uncertain date; they express the thought of the authors of the School of Laon.
[123] "For each is a sign of something sacred: the visible species is a sign of the body, while the body is a sign of that heavenly, spiritual food on which the angels live and which entered this assumed humanity so that human beings too might live by it" (*Sententiae "Dubitatur a quibusdam,"* in *Das Schrifttum der Schule Anselms von Laon und Wilhelms von Champeaux in deutschen Bibliotheken*, ed. H. Weisweiler [BGPTM, 33/1–2; Münster, 1936] 350). The thought is completed by this passage: "For his body, which is said to be, from different points of view, visible and invisible, is the object of the visible sacrament; it is in turn the sacrament of the heavenly and invisible bread on which the angels live" (*Sententie Anselmi*, in *Anselms von Laon systematische Sentenzen*, ed. F. Bliemetzrieder [BGPTM 19/2–3; Münster, 1919] 116–17).

The primary interest of the *Sententie* is obviously in the real reception that produces a spiritual union with Christ. The *Sententie* go on to speak of three kinds of reception: sacramental alone, sacramental and real, and real alone. This last refers to the just who receive the heavenly "bread" and are united to Christ by the faith that works through love, even when they do not receive the real Body and Blood in the Sacrament.[124] It is clear at this point that union through faith and love is the element that really ensures the salvific effect of the Sacrament.[125] This explains why the practice of spiritual Communion appears in the *Sententie;* this is the first attestation of the practice.[126] Salvation, which consists in union with God, is not produced directly by the presence of Christ in us, but by the faith and love of the believer: This is the "spiritual" reception of the Eucharist. In this perspective, William of Saint-Thierry makes a clear distinction between the bodily and the spiritual eating of the Body of Christ.[127] According to the School of Laon, a mere eating is an imperfect reception.

Hugh Metellus, another follower of the School of Laon, argues very consistently in reaching the position that what takes place on the altar is a sign and not the object of a sign; he thus anticipates Berengarius. He contrasts "sacramental eating" with "spiritual union, that is, non-sacramental eating; the object of the sacrament, not the sacrament; the power and efficacy, not the sacrament."[128] Gilbert of Nocent takes the same position and emphasizes even more that the Sacrament, which is the true Body and Blood of Christ, is only a sign of the mystical union of Christ and the believer through faith and love.[129] This approach to the problem explains how it is possible to receive the fruits of the Eucharist even without the sacramental eating.

The School of St. Victor[130] follows the thinking of the School of Laon and affirms the value of spiritual Communion when it is not

[124] "Yet by faith and love they eat the heavenly bread and are in harmony with it. Therefore Augustine: 'Why do you prepare tooth and stomach? Believe, and you have eaten'" (*Sententie Anselmi,* in Bliemetzreider, 119).

[125] We are far removed from the theology of Paschasius, which maintained the natural efficacy which the Sacrament has simply by being eaten, since eating produces the presence and assimilation of Christ in us.

[126] *Sententia* 381.

[127] William of Saint-Thierry, *De corpore et sanguine Domini* (PL 180:352–53).

[128] Hugh Metellus, *Epistola* 26 (cited in Macy, *The Theologies of the Eucharist,* 119, note 49). The distinction, it is claimed, goes back to Augustine.

[129] Macy, *The Theologies of the Eucharist,* 82.

[130] See the *Speculum de mysteriis ecclesiae,* which depends on both the *De sacramentis* of Hugh of St. Victor and on the *Summa sententiarum* (Macy, 85).

possible to receive the Sacrament.[131] This position is explained by the fact that the Eucharist is the ritual representation of saving union with Christ through faith and love.

2.3. Berengarius

The controversy over Berengarius' views was the great unsettling event of the eleventh century. Berengarius had real difficulty in understanding eucharistic realism; as a result, his opponents were led to think of it in physicist terms. In Rome Berengarius had to accept a profession of faith drawn up by the Roman Synod of 1259; the author of the profession was Cardinal Humbert of Silvacandida. The formula says that after the consecration the bread and wine on the altar are not only the Sacrament but the real Body and Blood of Christ; in other words, the Body of Christ is present in the Sacrament not only sacramentally but *sensualiter*, so that it is in the realm of the senses. The profession goes on to say that in the Sacrament the Body of Christ is in contact with the hands of the priest and is chewed by the teeth of the faithful.[132]

Thomas Aquinas describes Berengarius as the inventor of a heresy that "maintains that the body and blood of Christ are present in this sacrament only as in a sign."[133] Indeed, throughout the Middle Ages Berengarius was regarded as not only a heretic but as a heresiarch, that is, as founder of a heresy that was perpetuated through time.

And yet, although he was a respected teacher who had friends and bishops who took his side, it does not follow that he established a school of followers or a popular movement that could be described as

---

[131] In modern authors, "spiritual Communion" has a precise meaning: It refers to the union of the soul with "Jesus Eucharist," not through actual reception of the Sacrament, but through the desire for this reception. I take this definition, including the debatable phrase "Jesus Eucharist," from L. De Bazelaire, "Communion spirituelle," *DSp* 2, 1294–1300. This devotional practice has a specific method and technique, and aims at obtaining the fruits of the Sacrament without actual reception of the Sacrament but through the faith and love that accompany the desire to receive the Eucharist. We will recall that William of Saint-Thierry distinguishes clearly between the bodily eating and the spiritual eating of the Body of Christ (in his *De corpore et sanguine Domini*; PL 180:352–53).

[132] For the text of the profession of faith drawn up by the Roman council of 1059, see J. De Montclos, *Lanfranc et Béranger. La controverse eucharistique du XI siècle* (SSL 37; Leuven, 1971) 171–72.

[133] *Summa Theologiae* III, q. 75, a. 1.

Berengarian.[134] If we look closely at his thought, we have to say that "during his life and immediately after it he was accused of having taught things which he had never taught, or, at least that his teaching was unduly exaggerated"; furthermore, his teaching was too often "associated with that of heretical groups with which he had had no connection either historical or theological."[135]

After these initial remarks and qualifications we can now ask what in fact Berengarius thought. The documentary material is very extensive,[136] and it is impossible here to take every aspect into account. Following Guitmund of Aversa,[137] we can simply say that there were four positions regarded as those of Berengarius: (a) the Body and Blood of Christ are not really present, and the sacramental signs are simply figures; (b) the sacramental presence is a kind of "impanation" (it seems that Berengarius actually maintained this view); (c) the bread and wine are partly changed, partly not; (d) if an unworthy person receives Communion, the species turn once again into bread and wine.[138]

The problem that lies behind this controversy is the same as the one we saw Ratramnus facing: Is the presence of the Body and Blood of Christ a presence *in figura* or a presence *in veritate*? But the answer given is different: Ratramnus realized that *figura* and *veritas* cannot be opposed, and he rejected this way of posing the question,[139] whereas Berengarius did not grasp the meaning of the *figura–veritas* pair, accepted that they were opposites, and came down in favor of *figura*, thereby disuniting the pair, as did all of his contemporaries. In his *Rescriptum*, Berengarius justifies himself by saying that there are many places in the Scriptures in which Jesus speaks in metaphor: He is the cornerstone, the lion, the lamb; it is in the same way that the priest

[134] G. Macy, "Berengar's Legacy as Heresiarch," in *Auctoritas und Ratio. Studien zu Berengar von Tours,* ed. P. Ganz, R.B.C. Huygens, and F. Niewöner (Wiesbaden: Harrassowitz, 1990) 48.

[135] Ibid., 67.

[136] See De Montclos, *Lanfranc et Béranger* (note 132, above).

[137] Guitmund of Aversa, *De corporis et sanguinis Christi veritate in eucharistia* (PL 149:1430).

[138] Macy, "Berengar's Legacy," 50.

[139] As we have already seen, Ratramnus, too, did not share the patristic culture; as a result, though he still asked the question in the right way, he was unable to give Charles the Bald an answer that was in continuity with the thought of Augustine.

says during the Mass that the bread is the Body of Christ.[140] The archaic patristic categories, *figura* and *veritas*, were now outdated and could no longer be used precisely because they were outdated; on the other hand, categories originating in Aristotle and based on the real distinction between substance and accidents were not yet ready at hand.

3. EUCHARISTIC DEVOTION

Eucharistic devotion was closely connected with the doctrinal development, part of which we have been examining, and was heavy with original growths that would in the end become popular and even influence theological thought. Elements and practices of devotion were also used in asserting eucharistic doctrine against such heresies as Catharism,[141] which was considered to be Berengarian, without regard for the historical accuracy of such an attribution.

Devotion to the Eucharist originated, by way of devotion to the Cross, in devotion to the humanity of Christ. Devotion to the humanity of Christ is one of the characteristics of medieval spirituality, although it cannot be said to have begun in the Middle Ages. There were already signs in the patristic age that a personal relationship with Christ cannot fail to bring into play the whole world of affectivity.[142] But in the patristic period it was all controlled by a strong christological approach in which Christ was seen as Mediator, as Logos, as Lord. The relationship with Christ, especially in the Fathers who came from a Hellenistic background, such as Origen and Gregory of Nyssa, was always set within the relationship to the Father, to whom ultimately believers made their way through contemplation.[143]

In the Middle Ages, on the other hand, devotion to Christ became devotion to the humanity of Christ and was accompanied by a strong affective component. I think Edouard Dumoutet is correct when he says that it is in the veneration of the cross during the Good Friday

[140] *Rescriptum contra Lanfrancum*, ed. R.B.C. Huygens (CCLContMed 84; Turnhout: Brepols, 1988) 73–74.

[141] G. Grant, "The Elevation of the Host: A Reaction to Twelfth-Century Heresy," *Theological Studies* 1 (1940) 228–50.

[142] The foundation for this is already in Paul, who says: "I am hardpressed between the two. My desire is to depart and be with Christ, for that is far better" (Phil 1:23).

[143] See the description of this way in Ch. Kannengiesser, "Humanité du Christ. B) La contemplation de l'humanité du Christ," *DSp* 7, 1043–49.

liturgy[144] that we are to see the first manifestation of devotion to the humanity of Christ.[145] If this be so, then the root of the development is to be found in the Holy Week rites in Jerusalem as reported by Egeria, who describes in a touching way the strong emotional involvement of the participants in the Holy Friday ritual: the whole atmosphere was one of deep feeling stirred by the sufferings of Christ.[146] It needs to be emphasized that all this took place in the Holy City, where the surrender to grief and deep feeling was much easier.[147] Such celebrations served to bring the events of the passion alive, both in dramatic form and interiorly, so that the participants experienced what Christ had experienced and therefore felt as he did and with him. We are in the presence of a very natural feeling, which led the citizens of Jerusalem to try to relive, for their pious consolation, those events of the life of Jesus that had the city as their setting.

Very soon (Dumoutet continues) this movement of devotion to the humanity of Christ became part of the daily life of the faithful; devotion to the crucifix and devotion to the Lord's wounds would become extremely popular in the Middle Ages.[148] In conclusion, then, we may say that devotion to the mysteries of Christ gave birth to devotion to the humanity of Christ.[149]

3.1. In What Does Devotion to the Humanity of Christ Consist?

The dramatic evocation of the passion linked the sensibilities of the faithful to the more human and more fraternal side of their Savior,[150] since what was being emphasized in the humanity of Christ was that which was most human about him: his virtues and feelings, his joys and his sufferings.[151] This approach led to a feeling of union with

[144] The development of the rite of "Veneration of the Cross" has been studied, after M. Andrieu, by D. Sartore, "L'Adoratio crucis' come esempio di progressiva drammatizzazione nell'ambito della liturgia," in *Dimensioni drammatiche della liturgia medioevale* (Atti del 1° Convegno di studio del Centro di studi sul teatro medioevale e rinascimentale, Viterbo, 31 maggio, 1–2 giugno 1976; Rome: Bulzoni, 1977) 119–25.

[145] E. Dumoutet, *Le Christ selon la chair et la vie liturgique au Moyen-Age* (Paris: Beauchesne, 1932) 205.

[146] *Ethérie. Journal de Voyage,* ed. H. Pétré (SC 21; Paris: Cerf, 1948) 232–38.

[147] Dumoutet, *Le Christ selon la chair,* 13.

[148] Ibid., 205.

[149] Ibid., 7.

[150] Ibid., 43.

[151] Ibid., 54.

Christ, in a kind of projection onto him and identification with him. In this respect, though not only in this respect, the humanity of Christ was the object of a real kind of contemplation. People meditated on the mysteries of Christ, and their meditation on the mysteries led to deep emotion. Meditation thus became one of the key devotional rituals.

The passion and humiliation of Christ was symbolized by the crucifix; people venerated the crucifix and contemplated it because it showed the mystery of the passion to them in a moving way, like a rite being constantly celebrated. Contemplation of the crucifix and the kissing of the five wounds were widespread monastic practices, and Aelred of Rievaulx describes the crucifix as extending its arms and inviting us to a delightful embrace.[152] The crucifix had become a fixed point of reference.[153]

Everything formed a whole: devotion to the humanity of Christ was connected with devotion to his mysteries, and this in turn found expression not only in devotion to the crucifix but also in rituals of devotion to the five wounds.[154] There is a final point we should consider: devotion to the wound in Christ's side, to which there was a strong attraction, so much so that people debated its size and wanted to kiss it and drink deep from it. There was an ineffable sense of intimate love in certain devotional gestures, such as bending tenderly over the wound in Christ's side, in order there to gain a foretaste of everlasting blessedness.[155] So important did this become that in the last three centuries of the Middle Ages devotion to the wound in Christ's side became immensely popular along with eucharistic devotion.[156] A miniature in the Sacramentary of Drogo is an interesting witness that combines devotion to the wound in the side with the Eucharist: the Blood that pours from the wound is going directly into the chalice and filling it.[157] It is also a powerful testimony[158] to a

[152] Ibid., 24.

[153] Richard of Verdun was accustomed to recite daily, before the crucifix, prayers whose initial words added up to an invocation: "Adoro te, Christe, in crucem ascendentem et benedico te" (ibid., 20). In addition, devout people made a series of genuflections and recited appropriate prayers at each genuflection.

[154] Bernard says that through devotion and meditation we can enter into the wounds of Christ. This idea would become classic.

[155] Dumoutet, *Le Christ selon la chair*, 29.

[156] Ibid., 30.

[157] Cited ibid., 115.

[158] Other testimonies on the subject can be found in L. Gougaud, *Devotions and Ascetic Practices in the Middle Ages*, trans. G. C. Bateman (London: Burns Oates

eucharistic realism that moves in the same physicist direction we saw in a theology influenced by Paschasius.

3.2. *Devotion to the Body of Christ*

Paschasian theology taught a eucharistic realism of a physicist type: There is present in the Sacrament the same flesh of Christ that was born of Mary.[159] From this it followed that devotion to the humanity of Christ, as explained above, could be directed to images or the crucifix, and much more to the flesh of Christ that was "naturally" present in the Sacrament.[160]

The Eucharist thus became the primary object of devotion to the humanity of Christ. This explains the great desire to see the host.[161] People wanted to gaze on the Body of Christ with their own bodily eyes, for, even though veiled by the appearance of bread, it was always the Body of Christ that was before the eyes of the faithful. It followed that the very host, thus hastily identified with the humanity of Christ, became the object of affection and feeling. There was a sensible and affective contact with the humanity of Christ, because to see the host was to see the Son of God with one's bodily eyes.[162] The need to see the host produced a real movement of devotion that led to the rite of the elevation of the eucharistic bread at Mass, immediately after the words of consecration.[163] The sight of the host at the elevation was as it were the consoling fulfillment of a long-cultivated dream, that of being able to look upon the humanity of Christ so near

---

and Washbourne, 1927).

[159] See Paschasius, *Epistola ad Fredugardum:* "There is the same blood in the cup that there was in the body, just as with the body or flesh in the bread" (CCLContMed 16, p. 154).

[160] Paschasius, *De corpore et sanguine Domini* 9: "How can Christ legitimately be thought not to remain naturally in us, when God made man assumed inseparably our natural flesh and combined his natural flesh with his eternal nature in this sacrament of his flesh to be given to us?" (CCLContMed 16, p. 56). *Naturaliter* is a term peculiar to Paschasius' theology and is a novelty; see O. Capitani, "Studi per Berengario" (note 98, above); idem, "Motivi di spiritualità cluniacense" (note 98, above). The term signifies the realism of the physical presence of Christ's Body in the Eucharist.

[161] See E. Dumoutet, *Le désir de voir l'Hostie et les origines de la dévotion au Saint-Sacrement* (Paris: Beauchesne, 1926).

[162] Dumoutet, *Le Christ selon la chair* (note 145, above), 128.

[163] See the discussion of the intervention of Eudes of Sully (bishop of Paris, 1196–1208), in Dumoutet, *Le désir de voir l'Hostie,* 41ff.

to us in his sufferings. In addition, the sight of the host was put on a level with receiving Communion;[164] its importance was therefore beyond discussion. Only beginning with Alexander of Hales will the matter be clarified by the distinction between Communion through eating and Communion through seeing.[165]

The liturgy was no longer able to satisfy a medieval piety that was henceforth connected with the humanity of Christ. As a result, the liturgy made room for this devotion and accepted its demands, which had, of course, a solid foundation in the theology of Paschasius. In order to satisfy the demands of devout souls, the medieval liturgy had to offer sensations and impressions belonging to the realm of feeling. Given these theological premises, and once the elevation of the host was introduced, devotion to the Blessed Sacrament appeared in the form of rites outside the Mass.[166]

There was a felt need of realistic evocations of the humanity of Christ, and the medieval liturgy tried to satisfy this need, even if it meant making sacred drama part of itself. The *Concordia regularis* (965–975) describes this dramatization for us: The altar becomes the tomb of Christ; this is followed by a second dramatization which we might call a liturgy of resurrection. We also see the appearance of a dramatization of Christmas, accompanied by a more human devotion filled with tender love. Devotion to the passion of Christ takes on more varied tonalities; devotion transfigures everything, to the point that people spoke of the sweetness of Christ as he bows his head in death.[167]

All these factors and influences reached their culmination in the sight of the host at the elevation. On the other hand, if indeed the saving value of eucharistic Communion was due to sacramental realism

---

[164] M. Rubin, *Corpus Christi. The Eucharist in Late Medieval Culture* (Cambridge: Cambridge University Press, 1991) 147ff.

[165] Ibid., 64.

[166] Devotion to the Blessed Sacrament came to be known later as "adoration," a term canonized by the Council of Trent at its Session 13 (1551; Decree on the Most Blessed Sacrament of the Eucharist, Chapter 5; text in *COD*, 695; translation in *The Christian Faith in the Doctrinal Documents of the Catholic Church*, ed. J. Neuner and J. Dupuis [rev. ed.; Staten Island, N.Y.: Alba House, 1982] no. 1520, p. 417). In the process there was a shift from the conception of the Eucharist as the offering of thanksgiving and praise to the Father (and therefore adoration of the Father) to a conception of the Eucharist as a rite for producing the Sacrament (the Body of Christ) which the faithful may adore.

[167] Dumoutet, *Le Christ selon la chair*, 29.

as Paschasius understood it, that is, to the fact that the Eucharist was the flesh of Christ in a physical sense (the humanity of Christ that was born of the Virgin[168]), then the desire to see the humanity of Christ was not really alien to the nature and logic of the Sacrament.

---

[168] "And, more wonderful still, this flesh is not different from that which was born of Mary and suffered on the cross and rose from the tomb" (Paschasius, *Epistola ad Fredugardum*; CCLContMed 16, p. 15).

Chapter 12

The Scholastic High Middle Ages

1. THOMAS AQUINAS

Thomas deals with the sacramental presence of the Body of Christ from the viewpoint of the metaphysical nature of being. He "endeavors to reconcile the teaching of the Church on the Eucharist with Aristotelian ontology,"[1] and in this way definitively to eliminate all danger of eucharistic physicism, because his conclusions are not the fruit of occasional reflections but of the metaphysical system that is his reference point.[2]

1.1. The Use of Scripture

A file of the biblical texts that most influence the thinking of Thomas has been compiled by Ronald Zavilla in his University of Toronto dissertation and summarized by Pierre-Marie Gy:[3] (a) unlike Urban IV and the majority of theologians Thomas does not accept Matthew 28:20[4] as having a eucharistic meaning; (b) on the other hand, he lays a strong emphasis on Deuteronomy 4:7;[5] (c) 1 Kings 19:6-8[6] never appears in the commentary on the *Sentences*, but is found in the Office of Corpus

---

[1] R. Imbach, "Le traité de l'eucharistie de Thomas d'Aquin et les averroïstes," *RSPT* 77 (1993) 181.

[2] See P.-M. Gy, "Avancées du traité de l'eucharistie de s. Thomas dans la 'Somme' par rapport aux 'Sentences,'" *RSPT* 77 (1993) 219–28.

[3] Ibid.

[4] "And remember, I am with you always, to the end of the age."

[5] "For what other great nation has a god so near to it as the Lord our God is, whenever we call upon him?"

[6] "He [Elijah] looked, and there at his head was a cake baked on hot stones, and a jar of water. He ate and drank, and lay down again. The angel of the Lord came a second time, touched him, and said, 'Get up and eat, otherwise the journey will be too much for you.' He got up, and ate and drank; then he went in the strength of that food forty days and forty nights to Horeb the mount of God."

Domini and in the Third Part of the *Summa Theologiae;* (d) finally, attention must be called to the eucharistic use of Psalm 110 (109):4.[7]

To these points that are specific to Thomas two general remarks must be added: (a) all medieval theologians took as the scriptural basis of their discussion of the Eucharist, not the sentence: "Do this in memory of me," but the words "This is my body" and "This is my blood."[8] (b) In the twelfth century there was an important shift of emphasis in the choice of biblical texts that describe the relationship of Christians and the Eucharist: Previously, the key text had been John 6:53,[9] whereas beginning in the twelfth century 1 Corinthians 11:28-29 came to predominate.[10]

1.2 The Development of Thomas's Thought and the Office of Corpus Christi

Some twenty years passed between the fourth book of St. Thomas's commentary on the *Sentences*[11] and the Third Part of the *Summa Theologiae,*[12] and during that time Thomas's thinking evolved to some extent. The difference between the two works is not very great, since that thinking remained essentially fixed, but something did change; a sign of the change is the fact that the term "transubstantiation" occurs eighty-eight times in the commentary on the *Sentences,* but only four times in the *Summa Theologiae.*[13] Meanwhile, between the commentary on the *Sentences* and the *Summa* Thomas wrote three works that greatly influenced him: (a) the Office of Corpus Domini;[14] (b) the fourth book of the *Summa contra Gentiles;* and (c) the commentary on the *Prima Decretale.*[15]

[7] "The Lord has sworn and will not change his mind, 'You are a priest forever according to the order of Melchizedek.'"

[8] Gy, "Avancées," 220.

[9] "Very truly, I tell you, unless you eat the flesh of the Son of man and drink his blood, you have no life in you."

[10] "Examine yourselves, and only then eat of the bread and drink of the cup. For all who eat and drink without discerning the body, eat and drink judgment against themselves."

[11] Taught between 1252 and 1254 and given its final form in 1257.

[12] The questions on the Eucharist are to be dated to 1273, in Naples.

[13] After mentioning this fact, Gy speaks of a growing reserve of Thomas with regard to this term; see "L'Eucharistie dans la tradition de la prière et de la doctrine," *MD,* no. 137 (1979) 96.

[14] The Office was composed at the request of Urban IV in 1264.

[15] That is, on the profession of faith issued by Lateran Council IV; see M. F. Johnson, "A Note on the Dating of St. Thomas Aquinas' 'Expositio super primam et secundam decretalem,'" *RTAM* 59 (1992) 155–65.

Pierre-Marie Gy points out that there is a set of convergent indicators showing that Thomas constantly intensified his contact with the Scriptures, expanded his patristic and conciliar documentation, and, as the Third Part of the *Summa Theologiae* shows, studied the rites of the Mass according to the allegorical method typical of his age.[16] For the Fathers and the councils there are two dossiers: that of the *Catena aurea* and that of the section *De consecratione* in the *Decretum Gratiani*. For the liturgy we must go back to Lothar of Segni's treatise *De sacro altaris mysterio*, since that is the main source on which the liturgical commentary in Question 83 of the *Summa Theologiae* (Third Part) relies.

In addition, Thomas displayed a quite special relationship to the patristic heritage, particularly when, at the invitation of Urban IV, he composed the liturgical formularies for the two offices for the feast of Corpus Domini (the attribution of these to Thomas is today regarded as certain[17]). This work was decisive for the development of his thought. The Office of Corpus Domini is in fact a very original composition; unlike the other offices of the time it is not in rhyme; it is profoundly affective and possesses a high degree of theological exactness, while being formulated on the basis of biblical typology and the patristic heritage. Thomas brings the Old Testament figures onto the scene in an expansive way and compares them with the New Testament realities, showing that the latter are the fulfillment of the former.[18] However, unlike the typology of the Fathers, that of Thomas lacks any metaphysical component and remains purely descriptive. In addition, the conception of the Sacrament as a memorial of the passion involves a remembrance that is subjective and psychological and thus quite different from that described in present-day eucharistic theology.[19]

[16] Gy, "Avancées" (note 2, above), 219.

[17] P.-M. Gy, "L'office du Corpus Christi, oeuvre de Saint Thomas d'Aquin," in *La liturgie dans l'histoire*, ed. P.-M. Gy (Paris: Cerf–St. Paul, 1990) 223–45 [henceforth: *Liturgie*].

[18] The remarks about the determining influence of patristic categories reflective of typology apply also to the *Adoro te devote*, which reads, in its original form: "Adoro te devote latens *veritas*/Te qui sub his *formis* latitas." The attribution of this hymn to Thomas is not certain. See J.-P. Torrell, "L'authenticité de l'Adoro te devote,'" *RevSR* 67 (1993) 79–83.

[19] Gy, "Avancées" (note 2, above), 225. This author asks a very legitimate question: Is Thomas's conception of *memoria–memoriale* better founded in the sources than that of contemporary theologians? His question is obviously a rhetorical one.

1.3. Beyond Physicism

In order to frame the problem of physicism, let me follow the synthesis provided by Pierre-Marie Gy. Starting with Hugh of St. Victor, the theologians began speaking of the corporeal presence[20] of Christ in the Eucharist; quite soon, they saw in this presence the substantial fulfillment of Matthew 28:20,[21] as the Fathers had not done. The new idea of connecting Matthew 28:20 with the corporeal presence, though still not found in St. Bernard, was taken up by the Cistercians in the last quarter of the twelfth century and was accepted by both Innocent III and St. Francis of Assisi.[22] Thomas plays a decisive role in this development, since only in him does theology really and truly move beyond the theological approach of Paschasius Radbert and his views on the *corpus naturale* of Christ in the Eucharist.

In Thomas's system there is no room for a corporeal presence of Christ in the Eucharist. Edouard-Henri Weber explains: "The substance, as determinative of an actually subsisting subject, is of its nature prior to the accidental determination by dimensive quantity; from this it follows that in his body Christ is not subject to the quantitative dimensions of the sacramental species."[23]

This point emerges more clearly in the following two examples, which have to do with the relationship between the body of Christ and surrounding bodies: (1) Because of his philosophical conception of transubstantiation Thomas excludes the possibility of the sacramental presence being a "presence in a place"; in his view, this notion depends on the concept of "localization" and therefore of one of the accidents listed by Aristotle, whereas the Body and Blood of Christ are in the Eucharist "after the manner of a substance."[24] From the commentary on the *Sentences* down to the *Summa* Thomas is unmoved in his aversion to physicism,[25] and so he can conclude that

[20] The expression "real presence" appears for the first time in the Bull of Urban IV that established the feast of Corpus Domini; see P.-M. Gy, "Doctrine eucharistique de la liturgie romaine dans le haut moyen âge," in *Liturgie* (note 17, above), 202, note 49.

[21] "And remember, I am with you always, to the end of the age."

[22] P.-M. Gy, "La relation au Christ dans l'Eucharistie selon S. Bonaventure et S. Thomas d'Aquin," in *Liturgie*, 249.

[23] E.-H. Wéber, "L'incidence du traité de l'eucharistie sur la métaphysique de S. Thomas d'Aquin," *RSPT* 77 (1993) 206.

[24] Gy, "La relation au Christ" (note 22, above), 264.

[25] "The body of Christ is not in the sacrament in the way in which a body is in a place to which it is made commensurate by its own dimensions; it is present in a

"the substance of the body of Christ is related to this place by way of the dimensions of something else [i.e., the bread]. . . . Therefore in no sense is the body of Christ present locally in this sacrament."[26] It follows that space "is filled not by the substance of Christ's body . . . but by the species of the sacrament."[27]

(2) Thomas applies the same logic to the question of eucharistic apparitions or miracles, in which flesh or the child Jesus or the crucified Christ appear in place of the host. Thomas's answer begins with the premise that it is the accidents that have an influence (*immutare*) on the faculty of vision and, on the other hand, that in the case of the Sacrament the accidents of Christ's body are present "by way of the substance; as a result, the accidents of Christ's body have no direct relationship either with this sacrament or with surrounding bodies."[28] Since "the substance as such is not visible to the bodily eye and is not accessible to any of the senses or the imagination but only to the intellect, the object of which is the essence of a thing . . . [it is therefore perceptible] only by the intellect, which is called a spiritual eye."[29] Consequently, neither the angels nor the demons can see the body of Christ in the Sacrament: "The body of Christ, as present in this sacrament, cannot be seen by any bodily eye."[30]

Well, then, what is being seen in eucharistic apparitions and miracles? Thomas answers that since the substance does not fall into the domain of the senses, what is seen is not the substance of Christ's body. "It is forbidden to think that Christ appears in his own semblance";[31] therefore "the proper semblance (*propria species*) of Christ is not seen, but an appearance (*species*) formed miraculously."[32]

All this is far removed from the teaching of Paschasius, according to which it would be enough to remove the veil of the bread and wine in order to see the Body and Blood of Christ as they really are. In the teaching of Thomas, there is no room for this naive conception

---

special way that is peculiar to this sacrament. Therefore we say that the body of Christ is on various altars, not as if it were in various places, but as it is in the sacrament" (*Summa Theologie* [henceforth: *ST*] III, q. 76, a. 3).

[26] *ST* III, q. 76, a. 5.
[27] *ST* III, q. 76, a. 5, ad 2.
[28] *ST* III, q. 76, a. 7.
[29] Ibid.
[30] Ibid.
[31] *ST* III, q. 76, a. 8.
[32] *ST* III, q. 76, a. 7, ad 2.

of eucharistic realism. The Body of Christ contained in the Eucharist is not visible to any bodily eye, because visibility applies to the order of accidents, not of substance. The application of metaphysics is the means that enables Thomas to move beyond Paschasian physicism without falling into the symbolism of Berengarius.

1.4. Philosophy and Theology

The real distinction between substance and accidents is the philosophical datum that makes possible Thomas's treatment of the Eucharist. Were this distinction eliminated, the whole of Thomas's eucharistic theology would collapse, since it is based on a change of substances, with the accidents of the bread and wine remaining unchanged. These accidents do not become the accidents of Christ, because they are not involved in the *conversio substantialis,* and this noninvolvement is in turn possible only because the substance is really distinct from the accidents and therefore separable from them. The entire philosophical system of transubstantiation is based on this principle.

Where did this philosophical principle come from, since it is not in Aristotle and was not part of the common thinking of Thomas's contemporaries? The real distinction between substance and accidents was the fruit of Thomas's theological thinking, for it was precisely the theological problem of transubstantiation that led him to modify his ontology.[33] In his commentary on the *Metaphysics* of Aristotle he deals with substance and accidents apart from any theological concern, and he says calmly that substance can exist without accidents but not accidents without a substance.[34] An accident cannot exist without a subject because by definition it inheres in a subject; according to the Philosopher, in fact, an accident should not be described as "being" but rather as "belonging to a being."[35] Consequently, the problem debated by philosophers was: Can an accident exist "without a subject"?

When he takes up this question in itself, Thomas says No, but when he is pressed by the problem of transubstantiation, he changes

---

[33] Imbach, "Le traité de l'Eucharistie" (note 1, above), 184. See also the important discussion in Wéber, "L'incidence du traité de l'Eucharistie" (note 23, above), 195–218.

[34] *In Metaphys.* VII, lect. 1, nos. 1257–59, and XII, lect. 1, no. 2419. According to Ruedi Imbach, there are also passages in the *Summa Theologiae* that say the same, e.g., I, q. 45, a. 4 (see Imbach, "Le traité de l'Eucharistie," 184, note 29).

[35] *ST* I, q. 45, a. 4.

his ontology and says Yes. The accidents of the bread and wine do not inhere in the substance of the Body and Blood of Christ as in a subject, both because it is impossible for the substance of a human body to be affected *(affici)* by such accidents and because it is impossible that the substance of the body of Christ, which is glorified and impassible, should be changed so as to receive such qualities. Only one conclusion, then, is possible: that "in this sacrament" the accidents of bread and wine "remain without a subject" in which to inhere.[36] This is the first change Thomas makes in Aristotelian ontology.

Let me turn to the second change. It is not easy to maintain the separability of substance from its accidents. To do so, Thomas had to change the definition of either substance or accident, since the Aristotelian definition did not permit a real distinction between the two realities. The Aristotelian concept of accident says that the latter inheres in the substance as in a subject *(ens in subjecto)*. Thomas proposes to add *competit* to the definition; the resultant formula is "it *belongs to* the essence of an accident to exist in a subject."[37] The conclusion: Once an accident is defined not by its inherence in a subject but by the fact that it *ought to* so inhere, it becomes possible to assert the real distinction between substance and accidents. Given this distinction, it can be said that in the Eucharist the accidents of bread and wine remain without a subject in which to inhere. Only thus is it possible to avoid a contradiction.

To this second change in ontology a third had to be added. Thomas designates dimensive quantity as the subject of the accidents of bread and wine. Quantity behaves like a substance with respect to the other accidents, while it behaves like an accident (which it really is) in regard to the substance.[38] After this final change we see that it is not all the accidents of bread and wine that are without a subject, but only the accident of dimensive quantity, in which the other accidents inhere.

But a problem remains if transubstantiation is not to be a contradiction from a philosophical point of view: How is it possible for the accident of dimensive quantity to remain without a subject and to

[36] *ST* III, q. 77, a. 1.

[37] "The definition of 'substance,' therefore, is not 'a being of itself without a subject,' nor is the definition of accident 'a being in a subject'; rather it belongs to the quiddity or essence of substance to have being not in a subject, while it belongs to the quiddity or essence of accident to have being in a subject" (*ST* III, q. 77, a.1, ad 2).

[38] *ST* III, q. 77, a. 2.

serve as subject for the other accidents? Thomas gives a lapidary answer: "And this can come about through the power of God."[39]

For Thomas, then, the ultimate explanation of transubstantiation as a philosophical problem is to be found in God's powerful intervention, that is, in a miracle.[40] Ruedi Imbach continues his discussion by citing some writers contemporary with Thomas who do not share his interpretation; among these I will mention only Siger of Brabant, who, after saying that "the first cause cannot produce the effect of a second cause without using that second cause," adds: "Some argue plausibly but fallaciously when they claim that natural reason clearly shows the first cause able to make an accident exist apart from its subject."[41] Siger inverts the entire philosophical argument of Thomas, who maintains that since God can work miracles, miracles can play a part in a philosophical explanation. According to Siger, who is clearly opposing Thomas here, miracles cannot be accepted as philosophical explanations, even though miracles are acceptable from the viewpoint of religious belief. I find interesting the following summary by Pierre-Marie Gy:

"From Paschasius Radbert to the Berengarian crisis (and at levels well above popular devotion) eucharistic miracles serve as an argument in favor of the real presence . . . and it is not unlikely that the miracle at Bolsena played a part in the institution of the feast of Corpus Domini. . . . In the thirteenth-century theologians, referring to the distant catechetical arguments of St. Ambrose, it is henceforth the eucharistic change that is regarded as miraculous."[42]

I shall end with a statement of Ruedi Imbach: "The Thomist solution takes the form of an effort at mediation that attempts to reconcile the demands of dogma with the demands of reason,"[43] to the point even of altering ontology to make it compatible with transubstantiation.

---

[39] "And therefore it is left to say that in this sacrament the accidents remain without a subject. This is possible by the divine power" (*ST* III, q. 77, a. 1). And again: "When therefore by divine fiat an accident is allowed to exist of itself, it can also of itself be the subject of another accident" (*ST* III, q. 77, a. 2, ad 1).

[40] It is not a religious question that is to be resolved by a miracle, but a philosophical question; the miracle enters into Thomas's metaphysical system as an element required in order to avoid a contradiction.

[41] *Quaestiones super Librum de causis*, q. 2.

[42] Gy, "Avancées" (note 2, above), 220.

[43] Imbach, "Le traité de l'eucharistie" (note 1, above), 193.

1.5. Thomas's Systematic Treatment of the Eucharist

Although Thomas succeeds in moving beyond eucharistic physicism to a metaphysical solution of the problem, he does not manage to break away from the statement of the problem as established by earlier theologians. In fact, it is from the Berengarian controversy that he receives the data and the statement of the problem, namely, whether the Sacrament should be regarded as the true Body of Christ or only a figure of that body.

To the question of whether the Eucharist is the Body of Christ *in figura* or *in veritate*, Thomas answers that the Eucharist is the true Body of Christ.[44] The following are the data to which he applies his metaphysical approach.[45]

The metaphysical perspective is applied to the bread and wine (and to the minister) since these alone are beings to which a hermeneutical system based on the four causes can be applied.[46] Thomas's discussion is in fact based on the four causes excogitated by Aristotle: two internal (material and formal) and two external (efficient and final). The matter of the Eucharist is the bread and the wine; the form is the Lord's words over the bread and the wine; efficiency is the category used to explain the action of the priest who consecrates the bread and wine; final causality is used to interpret the fruits of the Eucharist.

Because of the methodological decision to consider the Eucharist in the perspective of the metaphysics of being,[47] the Thomist analysis precludes the possibility of getting at other aspects of the Eucharist, namely, the Eucharist as a celebration, and the relationship of the Eucharist with the Last Supper. Let us look more closely at some points. (1) In the patristic and liturgical traditions, the word Eucharist can signify three things: the Eucharistic Prayer, the entire celebration, the

[44] Among many possible citations, see *ST* III, q. 75, a. 1: "I answer that the true body and blood of Christ are in this sacrament."

[45] Thomas bases his metaphysics on Aristotelian categories, not on those of the Fathers, which derive from Platonism.

[46] This interpretive method is applied rigorously to everything having to do with the Sacrament. It is applied, for example, to eucharistic miracles, but not to devotions, which then, as today, continued to reflect a sacramental physicism; nor is it applied to the relationship between the eucharistic celebration and the passion of Christ, an area in which we find the kind of allegorical interpretation typical of the age of Thomas.

[47] Or of being as such. This approach is sometimes described as "reification," but I cannot accept so incorrect a term for the metaphysical option exercised in Thomism.

bread and wine. In Thomas, on the contrary, it signifies only one of these three, namely, the bread and wine which are the Sacrament of the Body and Blood of Christ, and it is with this alone in mind that the treatise is developed. The importance of the Eucharistic Prayer is lost, and the mandate of Christ, "Do this in memory of me," is also lost from sight.

(2) In addition, precisely because there is no room in the Thomist system for a theology of the prayer of thanksgiving, the unity of the Eucharistic Prayer is lost from sight, for Thomas succeeds in understanding only the function of the words of consecration, since these alone have a role in a system based on the four causes. (3) The assembly, too, regarded as so important in the patristic period, has no role to play in the Thomist theological system, because the ordained minister is the complete subject of the celebration.[48] (4) There is also a shift in dealing with the fruit of the Eucharist. Early documents speak of the Eucharist as sacrament of the unity of the Church. In the medieval approach the Eucharist changes from sacrament of unity (of the Church) to sacrament of union (of the believer with Christ). This fact, which is coextensive with the entire medieval period, takes on a special importance when it comes to the ontological approach which Thomas takes to the Sacrament of the Eucharist.[49]

1.6. Cause and Sign

According to Thomas, the sacraments are a kind of signs;[50] consequently, he must deal with the question of whether they cause what they signify.[51] It might seem, therefore, that cause and sign are being

[48] In light of this position we can understand the medieval shift of emphasis from the sacrament of baptism to the sacrament of orders.

[49] Thomas does, however, retain the memory of the fact that in the tradition the Eucharist is the sacrament of unity, and he appeals to this when he has to explain why the sinner cannot approach the Sacrament of the Eucharist. Even here, however, while the theme of the *unity* of the Church is remembered, it is subordinated to the theme of *union* with Christ, and the latter becomes the principal theme. Thomas says that sin separates from Christ and also from the Church; the sinner therefore acts deceitfully if he approaches the Eucharist: "Anyone, then, who receives this sacrament signifies by that very fact that he is united to Christ and incorporated among his members. This union and incorporation, however, are accomplished by a formed faith, which no one has who is in mortal sin. It is therefore obvious that anyone receiving this sacrament while in mortal sins acts deceitfully against the sacrament" (*ST* III, q. 80, a. 4).

[50] *ST* III, q. 60, a. 1.

[51] *ST* III, q. 62, a. 1, ad 1.

208

put on the same plane, but this is not the case.[52] In Thomas's eyes, the aspect of cause is more important than the aspect of sign.[53] In Part III of the *Summa Theologiae* the very title of Article 1 of Question 75 treats *figura* and *signum* as equivalents, in contrast to *veritas*.[54] Thomas establishes that, although the Sacrament belongs to the genus of signs and although the body of Christ is present as in a sacrament, it cannot be concluded that his body is present as in a sign. It is present in a manner that is peculiar to this sacrament[55] and that is evidently different from presence in a sign. From other parts of Thomas's teaching we know that he is speaking of a presence *ad modum substantiae*, a presence which belongs to the order of causality and not to the order of sign.[56]

At the end of this examination of the evidence let me return again to Pierre-Marie Gy, who points out Thomas's abandonment of the terminology of *ex opere operato*[57] in favor of the vocabulary of instrumental causality. I think that this is a very important observation, since *ex opere operato* is part of the patristic heritage of "imitation," which in turn belongs to biblical typology in its application to the liturgy.

In summary, we may say that by abandoning the idea of *ex opere operato* Thomas makes it clear that causality is the real root of sacramental efficacy. It is in the same perspective that we must see the shift from transubstantiation to *conversio*, a term that is more at home in the vocabulary of causality. The phrase *in persona Christi*, which is also a reflection of biblical typology as applied to the liturgy, is used in a different context and becomes part of the vocabulary of causality.

[52] In *ST* III, q. 62, a. 1, ad 1, Thomas cites a saying: "As is commonly said, they effect what they figure," but in his argument he seems to want to correct this when he says that the sacraments act "not only in the manner of signs but also in the manner of causes."

[53] "They not only signify but they cause" (*ST* III, q. 62, a. 1).

[54] "Whether the body of Christ is in this sacrament truly *(secundum veritatem)* or only figuratively or in a sign *(secundum figuram vel in signo)*."

[55] "We do not, therefore, understand Christ to be there only as in a sign, although the sacrament belongs to the sphere of signs; but we understand the body of Christ to be there, as I said, in the way proper to this sacrament" (*ST* III, q. 75, a. 1, ad 3).

[56] The transformation of the substance is effected by the divine power that works a miracle. The latter is worked by bringing into play the four causes, which act not as beings but as principles of being and therefore require the (miraculous) intervention of the first cause.

[57] The phrase occurs twenty-three times in the commentary on the fourth Book of the Sentences, and not at all in the *Summa Theologiae*.

In fact, the phrase *in persona Christi* is connected with the power to consecrate,[58] so much so that the *virtus consecrativa* consists not only in the words but also in the power conferred on the priest;[59] the effectiveness conveyed in the expression *in persona Christi* is transferred to the *potestas* which is sufficient to explain the consecration.

1.7. The Consecration

Thomas maintains that the consecration takes place due to the efficacy of the Lord's words, autonomously and independently of the Eucharistic Prayer which contains them. In taking this position, he follows to the end the path taken first by St. Ambrose. He also breaks up the unity of the Eucharistic Prayer[60] and unduly absolutizes the words of consecration; but, as Pierre-Marie Gy has shown, he is an isolated case, and his position is not shared by his contemporaries.[61]

Thomas's understanding of the consecration makes the Eucharistic Prayer superfluous, so to speak, since he assigns it a purely devotional role. It is a conception that will find its logical conclusion in the liturgical reform put in place by some Evangelical Churches, which have done away with the Eucharistic Prayer and kept only the words of consecration.

1.8. The Eucharistic Rite as Figure of the Passion of Christ

Thomas says that there are some parts of the rite, such as the separateness of the bread and wine, that serve to represent the passion of the Lord.[62] What is the significance of this representation? Are we to understand this last word as "presence" and therefore as belonging to the order of sacramentality, or as a true "representation" and belonging to the order of symbolization?

---

[58] "This sacrament . . . is not confected except in the person of Christ. But anyone doing something in the person of another must do it by means of a power given by that person. As the power to receive this sacrament is given to a baptized person by Christ, so the power to consecrate this sacrament in the person of Christ is given to a priest when he is ordained" (*ST* III, q. 82, a. 1).

[59] "Therefore the consecratory power does not reside in the words alone but also in the power given to the priest by his consecration or ordination" (*ST* III, q. 82, a. 1, ad 1).

[60] P.-M. Gy, "Le 'Nous' de la prière eucharistique," *MD*, no. 191 (1992) 7–14.

[61] P.-M. Gy, "Prière eucharistique et paroles de la consécration selon les théologiens de Pierre Lombard à S. Thomas d'Aquin," in *Liturgie,* 211–21.

[62] "To represent the passion of Christ in which the blood was separated from the body" (*ST* III, q. 76, a. 2, ad 1; see also III, q. 79, a. 1).

The theme of representation occurs not simply occasionally but constantly in Thomas, who in fact devotes to it the whole of Question 83: "The Rite of This Sacrament." This very title is a valuable pointer that directs us in our interpretation of the concept of representation.

In Thomas's system the sacramental nature of the Eucharist is reached through a metaphysical analysis of being as applied to the bread and wine, so that knowledge of the Sacrament as a sacrament is obtained through the real distinction between substance and accidents. The rite, however, is not a being but an action. Consequently, the metaphysical analysis of being in terms of substance and accidents cannot be applied to the rite, that is, to the eucharistic celebration. From this it follows that the relationship of the eucharistic rite to the passion of Christ must belong to another order than the sacramental.[63] Here is what Thomas says: "Thus the celebration of this sacrament, as I said earlier, is a kind of image representing the passion of Christ, which is the real sacrifice."[64] The real or true sacrifice, then, took place on Calvary, and the eucharistic celebration is an image of that sacrifice. Thus, when speaking of the bread, the Sacrament of Christ's Body, the adjective "true" is applied to the Sacrament, but when speaking of the ritual celebration, which represents the passion, the adjective "true" is applied to the historical event and not to the rite. This differing application of terms seems to me decisive in understanding Thomas's thought on the subject.

Let us see now how Thomas interprets the various rites; at the end I shall return to the question, which I now leave hanging, of the ontological value of the image that represents the passion.

According to Thomas, the value of the Eucharist is contained entirely in the consecration, which is effected by the words of Christ; everything else, gestures and prayers, was added, Thomas says, out of a need to prepare the people to receive the Sacrament.[65] However, the Mass contains not only the consecration but many other elements as well, and therefore he distinguishes between what is done as a representation of the Lord's passion and what is done "out of reverence[66]

[63] Thomas does not discuss the representation of the passion when he is dealing with sacramentality in terms of substance and accidents, but rather when he deals with the rite, which, as such, is accessible through external observation and not by a metaphysical analysis of being.

[64] *ST* III, q. 83, a. 1.

[65] *ST* III, q. 83, a. 4, ad 1.

[66] For example, the material of which the cup is made has been decided by motives of reverence (*ST* III, q. 83, a. 3, ad 6). This approach to the question is not to

for this sacrament in which Christ is truly contained and not simply as in a figure."[67] In these remarks Thomas introduces a criterion which serves to restrain the allegorical interpretation, so typical of the Middle Ages, by proposing an objective principle. And indeed there was need of some objective principle that would operate within the general framework of allegorical interpretation; Thomas applies the principle both in explaining the gestures and rites of the Mass and in explaining the text of the Canon.[68]

Article 5 of Question 83 is very important, for in it Thomas determines the relationship between the various phases of the eucharistic celebration and the passion of Christ. Here is the principle on which everything rests: The succession of the phases of the celebration[69] must correspond to the successive stages of the passion. At that time, there were nine points in the Roman Canon at which the priest made Signs of the Cross over the bread and wine. Since the Sign of the Cross points to the passion, Thomas chooses these nine points in the eucharistic liturgy and establishes a correspondence with nine stages of the passion.

The first stage of the passion is the betrayal of Jesus (Christi traditio); since the betrayal was threefold—by God, by Judas, and by the Jews—the traditio is represented by the three Signs of the Cross made at the words Haec donae, haec munera, haec sancta sacrificia illibata.[70] The second stage of the passion is the selling of Christ, and it is connected with the three Signs of the Cross at the words benedictam, adscriptam, ratam. The two Signs of the Cross at the words ut nobis corpus et sanguis are added to signify Judas, who sold Christ. The third stage: During the consecration of the bread and wine, at the word benedixit, two Signs of the Cross are made, referring to the prediction of the passion during the Last Supper.

---

be regarded as entirely a marginal one, since Thomas uses the argument of reverence to justify the fact that in some Churches it has been prudently decided to distribute Communion no longer under two species but only under the species of bread (ST III, q. 80, a. 12).

[67] ST III, q. 83, a. 3. There are also other elements that represent the effect of holiness coming from the passion of Christ.

[68] The explanation of the Roman Canon is given in ST III, q. 83, a. 4, which takes the form of a kind of Expositio missae.

[69] Thomas limits the correspondence solely to the eucharistic liturgy, whereas the Amalarian tradition also included the liturgy of the word and even began with the entry of the priest as he approached the altar.

[70] ST III, q. 83, a. 5, ad 3.

Fourth stage: At the words *hostiam puram . . .* , five Signs of the Cross are made, representing the five wounds, while (fifth stage) at the words *corporis et sanguinis sumpserimus* the crucifixion of the body, the shedding of blood, and the fruit of the passion are represented. The sixth stage consists in the three prayers uttered by Jesus on the cross, and so we have three Signs of the Cross at *sanctificas, vivificas, benedicis.* The three hours during which Jesus hung on the cross form the seventh stage and are connected with the three Signs of the Cross at the *Per ipsum.* The ninth and final stage is the resurrection of Christ, which is represented by the three Signs of the Cross at the *Pax Domini sit semper vobiscum.*

There are other phases of the Mass, and other objects, that are put in a relation to the passion. "Since the celebration of this sacrament is an image representing the passion of Christ the altar represents the cross on which Christ was sacrificed in his proper mode of being *(in propria specie)."*[71] Even the time of the celebration is interpreted according to the same method: "Since the passion of the Lord took place from the third hour to the ninth hour, it is during this period of the day that this sacrament is regularly celebrated in solemn fashion in the church."[72] The same kind of remark applies to Good Friday, to which Thomas applies the *figura–veritas* pair, while establishing a clear opposition between the figure (and type) and the reality: "When the truth comes, the figure ceases. This sacrament is an image and type of the Lord's passion, as I have said. Therefore, on the day on which the passion is remembered as it really happened *(realiter gesta est)* there is no consecration of this sacrament."[73]

We have seen the sense in which the eucharistic celebration is an image representing the passion. Now we must ask what ontological value is to be assigned to this systematic representation of the Lord's passion or, in other words, of Christ's sacrifice.[74] As far as an *imago passionis* is concerned, Thomas says, this could be had even in the figures

---

[71] *ST* III, q. 83, a. 1, ad 2. See also: "For the same reason, the priest too bears the image of Christ, since it is in Christ's person and by his power *(in cuius persona et virtute)* that he pronounces the words of consecration. . . . Consequently, in a way the priest is also victim" (*ST* III, q. 83, a. 1, ad 3).

[72] *ST* III, q. 83, a. 2.

[73] *ST* III, q. 83, a. 2, ad 2.

[74] As sacrifice, the *mystery* is offered; as sacrament, it is consecrated and received (*ST* III, q. 83. a. 4).

of the Old Testament;[75] the eucharistic celebration cannot, therefore, claim to have, by its nature, a special relationship with the sacrifice of Christ that is different from that of the Old Testament; in other words, a relationship of a sacramental type. But, after explaining that Sacrament and representation are two different things, we must add that they do meet in the rite of the cup. For the Sacrament of Christ's Blood signifies the passion in a special way ("the blood is more especially an image of the Lord's passion"[76]), because the blood, being consecrated separately from the body, expressly represents the passion.[77]

It is, then, the consecration of the blood, insofar as it is a separate action, that represents the passion.[78] This means that for Thomas, while the figural relationship to the sacrifice of Christ cannot be defined as sacramental, it nonetheless belongs in the realm of sacramental realism, because it is based on the consecration and is brought into existence by it.[79]

In the system adopted by Thomas, no other conclusion is possible, given the starting point of his reflection on the Eucharist; he does not manage to move beyond the problem as stated for him, namely, whether the Body of Christ is in this Sacrament *in veritate* or only *in figura*.[80] Since he is unable to get beyond this distinction, he is not able to grasp the sacramental character of the relationship between the Mass and the passion of Christ, although he does succeed in eliminating a purely figural approach and in reaching, *quodammodo* ("in a fashion"), an ontological dimension of a kind. In fact, Thomas says that through this Sacrament the faithful participate in the fruits of the passion, but he is unable to assert a participation in the passion itself.[81]

[75] *ST* III, q. 83, a. 1.

[76] *ST* III, q. 83, a. 2, ad 2.

[77] *ST* III, q. 78, a. 3, ad 2. See also *ST* III, q. 76, a. 2, ad 1.

[78] *ST* III, q. 80, a. 12, ad 3.

[79] The various commentaries on the Mass and the other medieval theologians who preceded Thomas likewise sought to ensure a certain ontological value for this relationship, but use of the allegorical method did not produce a valid result in this area. Thomas obtains a valid result, even though he uses the allegorical method, since in fact he bases the Mass–passion relationship directly on the consecration, which, in his metaphysical system, is an action that *causes* the substantial change of the bread and wine. Despite this, however, Thomas's solution takes us only as far as the *Christus passus* and not to the sacramentality of the Mass–Cross relationship.

[80] *ST* III, q. 75, a. 1.

[81] *ST* III, q. 83, a.1.

2. ST. BONAVENTURE OF BAGNOREGIO

John of Fidanza, later known as Bonaventure, was born in Bagnoregio in about 1217 and died at Lyons during the work of the council in 1274. He was born into a well-to-do family and was able to attend the School of the Arts in Paris, where he had for mentors Alexander of Hales and John of La Rochelle and, after their deaths, Odo Rigaldi and William of Melitona. He taught in Paris until he became minister general of the Franciscan Order. He worked in Paris at the same time as Thomas Aquinas, and there were disagreements between the two men that are reflected in the *Commentary on the Sentences* which each wrote.

In 1215 the Fourth Council of the Lateran used the term transubstantiation, which henceforth became standard and was accepted by all. In the middle of the thirteenth century the theologians were in agreement that the key point in eucharistic doctrine was transubstantiation, and the interpretations they gave of it were pretty much alike.[82] Bonaventure makes extensive use of the word,[83] but he nonetheless prefers to speak of a substantial change, even if less evidently so than Thomas.

2.1. Theology and Devotion

We saw that Thomas does not accept the eucharistic interpretation of Matthew 28:20; Bonaventure, on the other hand, accepts it completely, because the basis of his conception is "the concrete eucharistic Christology of St. Francis,"[84] with its complete identification between the Sacrament and the person of the historical Jesus. Given this perspective, the Eucharist is a visitation of the Son of God, who humbles himself by coming in the Sacrament, just as he humbled himself by coming in the flesh. The Eucharist is a kind of incarnation. We must not imagine that in Bonaventure's eyes the realities of devotion with their affective charge are confined to a secondary area; on the contrary, he incorporates them directly into the theological treatise which he taught in the university.

[82] Gy, "La relation au Christ" (note 22, above), 254.

[83] For both Thomas (*In IV Librum Sententiarum*, d. 8, q. 1, a. 2, quaestiuncula 1 ad 3) and Bonaventure (*In IV Librum Sententiarum*, d. 8, p. 1, a. 1, q. 1, arg. 3) transubstantiation is one of the most difficult tenets of the faith.

[84] See Gy, "La relation au Christ," 254. For a more complete study of Francis see A. Gerken, "Die theologische Intuition des heiligen Franziskus von Assisi," *Wissenschaft und Weisheit* 2 (1982) 2–25; and also R. Falsini, "Eucaristia," *Dizionario francescano* (Padua: Edizioni Messagero, 1983) cols. 519–48.

In his view, the eucharistic species are as it were the garment or veil that covers the Body and Blood of Christ.[85] When he takes up the subject of Communion,[86] he speaks of nourishment and also of the welcome given to a guest,[87] of the sacrament of union,[88] and of a burning coal.[89] Father Gy asks whether we must say that the ideas of presence and of the reception of a guest place limits on the idea of nourishment.[90] In any case (he adds) we must bear in mind that the honor given to a guest provides norms for access to Communion; Bonaventure gives two examples from the gospel: Zacchaeus and the centurion.[91] The worth required for honoring a guest excludes not only mortal sin but tepidity and a lack of devotion.[92] The fundamental attitude to the Eucharist, which Bonaventure inherits from St. Francis, is respect combined with a sense of unworthiness, which makes one remain before it in reverent adoration.[93]

The burning coal is the body of Christ in his passion, and it is in this sense that Bonaventure defines the Eucharist as a memorial: The Eucharist is as it were a burning coal that sets on fire those who remember the passion, because in so doing they have a kind of affective experience of the passion. But depictions or stories of the passion play the same role and therefore belong in the sphere of memorials. The difference between the two kinds is that the Eucharist is a living memorial, whereas pictures are, so to speak, dead memorials, and narratives of the passion are partly dead and partly alive memorials because they are a living memorial in the heart of the preacher. The Eucharist is a living memorial because Christ himself is present in it.[94]

For Bonaventure, then, the fruit of Communion is, in addition to grace, always linked to contemplation of the passion and has for its

---

[85] *In IV Librum Sententiarum*, d. 10, p. 2, a. 2, q. 2, arg. 2 et ad 2.

[86] Gy, "La relation au Christ," 257.

[87] This idea is also present in Thomas's early teaching (see *In IV Librum Sententiarum*, d. 12, q. 1, a. 3, quaestiuncula 3, arg. 2).

[88] *In IV Librum Sententiarum*, d. 12, p. 2, a. 1, q. 3. By means of an elaborate argument on the sacrament as sign, Bonaventure is able to conclude that the true Body of Christ, that is, the Eucharist, cannot fail to be a sacrament of unity (*In IV Librum Sententiarum*, d. 8, p. 2, a. 2, q. 1).

[89] *In IV Librum Sententiarum*, d. 12, p. 2, a. 1, q. 1, arg. 3.

[90] Gy, "La relation au Christ," 257.

[91] *In IV Librum Sententiarum*, d. 12, p. 2, a. 1, q. 1.

[92] *Breviloquium* 6.9.

[93] Gy, "La relation au Christ," 260.

[94] *In IV Librum Sententiarum*, d. 12, p. 2, a. 1, q. 1.

setting an affective and devotional rapture than can reach the point of ecstasy.

2.2. *The Sacrament as* Corpus verum

According to Bonaventure, the true Body of Christ is contained in the Eucharist. He speaks of the Sacrament of Christ's Body simply as *corpus verum* or *secundum veritatem*,[95] as if the phrases could be taken for granted. As in Thomas, the choice between *figura corporis* and *corpus verum* is made in favor of *corpus verum*, and it could not have been otherwise since, as we have already seen, after the question raised by Berengarius medieval orthodoxy could only be expressed by the phrase *corpus verum*.

Nevertheless, Bonaventure's philosophical approach is more flexible than the distinction just made might suggest; in fact, he speaks of a third reality that is half-way between *figura* and *veritas*. This is another kind of *figura* that has *veritas* connected with it.[96] In this sense, the Eucharist is *veritas* and *figura* at the same time, by reason of the connection between the two.[97] Bonaventure maintains this position even though he is conscious of the difference between the two. It cannot be denied that this conception echoes to some extent the Neoplatonic conception of identity-in-difference.[98]

2.3. *Is the Sacrament a Sign?*

In the *Breviloquium* there is no discussion of the Eucharist as sign and figure, although this subject is dealt with extensively in the commentary on the *Sentences*. Consequently, even though this aspect of

---

[95] Ibid., d. 10, p. 1, a. 1, q. 1, concl.

[96] This approach enables Bonaventure to show the likelihood that the Sacrament of the Eucharist was prefigured; at the end of the argument he concludes by accepting the Old Testament figures as valid for the Eucharist and relevant to an understanding of it.

[97] "That sign has the reality *(veritatem)* connected with it; therefore it is not only a sign but by reason of the link it is the reality *(veritas)* as well; and because it can be a sign and figure of the reality, it can therefore be a sign and figure of the sacraments of the new Law, and especially of this one" (*In IV Librum Sententiarum*, d. 8, p. 1, a. 1, q. 1, ad 1).

[98] There can, in fact, be no *figura* that is, as such, identical with the *veritas*: "It is not necessary that the reality correspond in all respects to the figure, because no figure can be so like the reality that it is not in some way unlike it" (*In III Librum Sententiarum*, d. 22, q. 3, ad 1). See also: "The figure is one thing, the reality another" (*In IV Librum Sententiarum*, d. 24, p. 1, a. 2, q. 3, concl.).

the Sacrament greatly engaged Bonaventure's interest, he regards it as secondary and of lesser importance when he discusses the Eucharist as it is regularly celebrated and attended. The question is nonetheless of great importance precisely for the particular conception Bonaventure has of sign and figure. His starting point is the adage which we have already seen Thomas citing and which Bonaventure also cites as an opinion common among other theologians: "And therefore they say that the sacraments of the New Law are causes of graces and effect what they figure."[99] He goes on to inquire into the relationship between cause and sign,[100] and concludes that this terminology is to be interpreted in a broad sense,[101] for in fact a sacrament is an *ordinatio ad aliquid*; the efficacy is not in the sensible cause but in the divine institution. As a result, if a sacrament is to be in fact efficacious, it must be received *precisely as a sacrament*.

There is in Bonaventure (it comes to him by way of Hugh of St. Victor) a vestige of Augustinian thought, which he shows when he says that there must be a relationship of sign between the sacrament and the reality into which it is changed.[102] Another point that links

[99] *In IV Librum Sententiarum*, d. 1, p. 1, a. unicus, q. 3, concl.

[100] The question of the connection between cause and sign is given extensive treatment because latent in it is the difference between the sacraments of the old Law and those of the new Law: the former are only signs, the latter are causes as well. It is important to cite the statement of Peter Lombard that is the basis for the commentary of various authors: "The sacraments were therefore instituted not simply in order to signify but also in order to cause. Things instituted solely in order to signify are only signs and not sacraments" (*In IV Librum Sententiarum*, d. 1, p. 1, cap. 4).

[101] "We grant, therefore, that the sacraments of the new Law are causes and that they effect and dispose, in the broad sense (as they say), and that so much can safely be said; whether they do something more, I refuse to assert or deny. Following this last method the answers to all the questions are obvious" (*In IV Librum Sententiarum*, d. 1, p. 1, a. 1, q. 4).

[102] "The bread is changed precisely into that to which it has a likeness; for the institution is based on this likeness, and the sanctifying words are added. Because, then, the bread has a likeness only to the body, it was therefore instituted to be changed only into the body, and the sanctifying words, 'This is my body,' signify that it is changed into the body; the bread is not changed into the divinity or into the soul or into the blood. Nonetheless the body is not present in the Sacrament without these other realities, but they are present not because of the change but because of their inseparable connection or indivisibility. The blood is there because of its commingling (with the body), the soul by reason of its conjunction (with the body), and the divinity by reason of the (hypostatic) union" (*In IV Librum Sententiarum*, d. 11, p. 1, a. 1, q. 4, concl.).

him to the patristic past is his conception of causes. Instead of the four Aristotelian causes, he has three, since he combines the exemplary and formal causes. The importance of this position becomes clear when we realize that the area of its application is the resurrection of Christ: Bonaventure makes Christ both the *exemplum* and the *forma* of the resurrection of other human beings.[103] This conception of causality also holds for the sacraments, since Bonaventure applies it to marriage,[104] but we cannot say more than this, since it does not seem to me that he makes a formal application of it to the Eucharist.

However, despite these echoes of the Fathers, Bonaventure's general approach to the theology of the Eucharist is neither Augustinian nor patristic. I say this even though I am well aware of another doctrine of Bonaventure which denies that the sacramental *sign* is to be understood as the *cause* of an effect.[105] Instead of causing, a sign represents the reality of which it is a sign.[106] In face of the adage that the

---

[103] "A double cause of our resurrection, namely, efficient and formal, is to be found in Christ. The efficient cause in turn is twofold: Christ is both first principle and instrument. The efficient cause that is the first principle is Christ according to his divinity and the entire Trinity; the efficient cause that is the instrument is the voice of Christ at whose utterance and call the dead arise. There is likewise a twofold exemplary cause: one in which the reality is known and provided for, and here it is the Son of God in his divine nature and the entire Trinity; another in which the reality is inaugurated and exemplified, and this is the resurrection of Christ; for, as Augustine says in his *The City of God*, 'our bodies will be like the body Christ showed in his resurrection.' His resurrection, then, was as it were the exemplar in which our resurrection was begun, as of the members in the head, as is said in Ephesians 2: he made us alive and raised us along with Christ" (*In IV Librum Sententiarum*, d. 43, a. 1, q. 6).

[104] Ibid., dd. 26–42.

[105] In dealing with this subject he says that: (a) a sign as a sign implies a relation to the reality of which it is a sign; (b) this signified reality is (ontologically) prior to the sign which represents it; (c) therefore the sign depends on the reality of which it is a sign and is not to be confused with the cause that makes the reality exist.

[106] "To the objection that by human agreement a sign gives rise to knowledge and spiritual affections, they say that it does so only as a disposing factor and as an occasion but does not effect the knowledge; on the contrary, it is the soul that by consulting with itself gives rise to the knowledge and affections, as is clear from an obvious example: some people grow afraid at the sight of a gallows, while others do not. But it cannot thereby be shown that the sacrament is the efficient cause of grace" (*In IV Librum Sententiarum*, d. 1, p. 1, a. 1, q. 4, ad 4). "To the objection that Christ is more powerful when it comes to the good, they say that this is true enough, but that it does not follow from the fact that Adam passed on his sin through the flesh, that Christ transmits grace by means of the Sacrament,

sacraments *efficiunt quod figurant*, Bonaventure struggles for an interpretation and says that the sacraments have a causality in the broad sense. They dispose for grace, and this is the way in which they cause;[107] such a causality is rightly said to be a causality only in a broad sense. This represents keen thinking on Bonaventure's part, for despite ideas inherited from the Platonism of the Fathers, he is a man of his age, and when it comes to the treatise on the Eucharist, he does not depart from the classical approach of his time, which distinguishes between *corpus Christi in figura* and *corpus Christi in veritate*.

This does not mean that Bonaventure is to be assimilated to Thomas, since despite all that they have in common, there is a notable difference between them, as we shall see in the next section.

3. WHAT DOES THE MOUSE EAT? *(QUID MUS SUMIT?)*

What does a mouse eat when it eats the eucharistic bread? Does it eat the Body of Christ or only the species? Is it possible to eat the species without thereby eating the Body of Christ?

Nowadays, this is an old-fashioned problem that, if anything, brings a smile to our contemporaries, but for the medieval thinkers it was a genuine problem from both a pastoral and a doctrinal standpoint, and its resolution brought into play all the theological and metaphysical principles at work in their teaching on the Eucharist.[108] The first to raise the theological question was Berengarius of Tours in response to his objectors. If the physicist realism inaugurated by Paschasius and professed by Lanfranc of Bec and Humbert of Silva Candida were true, this conclusion would follow logically: The physical presence of the Body of Christ would be subject to the digestive processes not only of human beings but of animals and birds.

The question was an interesting one, and Guitmund of Aversa was the first to attempt an answer. He says that the true Body and Blood

---

since that would be a disorder. Furthermore, just as a creature cannot receive the power to create, neither can it receive the power to give grace" (ibid., ad 6).

[107] "Everything that effects or disposes or stirs the disposer or effecter to action, can be said in some sense to effect and cause" (*In III Librum Sententiarum*, d. 11, a. 1, q. 3, concl.).

[108] See Y. de Montcheuil, "La raison de la permamence du Christ sous les espèces eucharistiques d'après S. Bonaventure et S. Thomas," in idem, *Mélanges théologiques* (Paris: Aubier, 1946) 71–82; U. Betti, "La ragione della permanenza di Cristo nell'eucaristia: una soluzione teologica dimenticata," *Studi francescani* 50 (1953) 151–68; G. Macy, "Of Mice and Manna: 'Quid mus sumit' as a Pastoral Question," *RTAM* 59 (1992) 157–66.

of Christ remain in the Sacrament even when this is eaten by an animal. He was not the only one to maintain this position, and Gary Macy tells us of other authors of that period who held it.[109] Stephen Langton was the first to think that there would be a reverse transubstantiation, that is, that the bread would return at the moment when the mouse eats the Sacrament.[110] The School of Laon, including William of Champeaux and William of St. Thierry, held that the mouse would eat only the eucharistic species and not the substance of the Body of Christ.[111] Thomas Aquinas, on the other hand, maintained that what the mouse eats is the Body of Christ, because as long as the accidents of the bread remain incorrupt, they are a sign of the substance of the Body of Christ, and where the accidents are, there the substance of the Body of Christ likewise is (by way of the accidents).

Bonaventure held the opposite of Thomas's view and, adopting a completely personal position, said that Christ is present under the species of this Sacrament only to the extent that the Sacrament is ordered to human use. Since its eating by a mouse cannot be described as coming under the use prescribed by Christ, it cannot be maintained that the mouse eats the Body of Christ.[112] Thomas rejects this view outright as derogating from the truth of the Sacrament,[113] while Bonaventure in response says that whatever be the value of Thomas's opinion, his arguments do not prevent pious ears from refusing to listen to it being said that the Body of Christ is in the stomach of a mouse; he asserts that his opinion is the more common one and certainly the most appropriate and the most conformed to reason.[114] Bonaventure was correct in saying that the more common opinion

[109] Macy, "Of Mice and Manna," 159.

[110] Ibid., 160.

[111] Ibid.

[112] If the Body of Christ is to be eaten, the Sacrament must be eaten as a Sacrament, something possible only to human beings.

[113] *In IV Librum Sententiarum,* d. 9, a. 2, quaestiuncula 3, and later in *ST* III, q. 80, a. 3, ad 3.

[114] "There is therefore another opinion according to which the body of Christ does not by any means enter the stomach of the mouse. The consideration that moves those holding this view is that Christ is present in the sacrament only inasmuch as the sacrament is ordered to human use, that is, to human eating; but when the mouse gnaws at it, it renders the sacrament unsuited to that purpose, and so the sacrament ceases to exist and the substance of bread returns, as Innocent says. . . . This opinion is the more common one and certainly the more becoming and reasonable one" (*In IV Librum Sententiarum,* d. 13, a. 2, q. 1–2).

was that the mouse did not eat the Body of Christ; his personal contribution—the ordering of the Sacrament to human use—was a strong theological argument in favor of that opinion.

G. Macy calls attention to another fact that can explain the interest of the theologians in this obscure problem. Heretics, and especially the Cathars, used this question to prove that the Church's teaching on the Eucharist was erroneous. The result was the rise of a current of thought which, in order to combat the heretics, maintained that the Body of Christ was not eaten by the mouse and did not descend into its stomach.[115] In light of this finding of G. Macy we must admit that the response given at the end of the twelfth century and the beginning of the thirteenth was one that met a real pastoral problem: the defense of the faith against the Cathars.

The answers of Thomas and Bonaventure are more properly theological solutions, derived in each case from their systems and from the metaphysical principles on which their eucharistic teaching is based. It is worth noting that this minor question of the mouse enables us to see with greater clarity the difference between the eucharistic teaching of Thomas and that of Bonaventure: the former is more objectivist and more closely linked to the metaphysical analysis of being, while the latter is more closely linked to a personalist perspective that is based on the institution of the Sacrament by Christ, namely, that the Eucharist is for a human use, namely, for eating, and that this intended purpose determines the very nature of the eucharistic bread, inasmuch as a nonhuman use (eating by a mouse, for example[116]) causes the cessation of sacramentality and the return of the substance of the bread.

4. CONCLUSIONS

There is a great difference between the theology of imitation–following, characteristic of the patristic period, especially in regard to the eucharistic rite, and the approach of Paschasius, which is accurately expressed by *naturaliter,* the adverb describing how the Body of Christ is contained in the Eucharist. The two different approaches are not simply two stages or phases in the development of eucharistic theology; they are two different theologies, because they are based on two different conceptions of salvation. In my opinion, the importance

[115] Macy, "Of Mice and Manna," 165.
[116] Another example: The placing of the Sacrament in a latrine, thus making its eating by human beings impossible, would cause the cessation of the sacramentality of the bread, so that the bread would no longer be the Body of Christ.

of G. Macy's studies consists precisely in their having brought out the soteriological origin of Paschasius' teaching on the Eucharist. Without this fact it would not have been possible to understand how it differs from the patristic approach, even though the difference had already been clearly shown by the studies of Ovidio Capitani.

In Paschasius' theology, the salvific efficacy of the Eucharist is connected with a sacramental realism of a physicist kind, to the point of being identified with it.[117] For as a result of eucharistic Communion the Body and Blood of Christ are *naturaliter* present in the believer, and it is through their assimilation by the natural digestive metabolism that they become the source of salvation. Given these premises, the Eucharist takes on the realism of the physical presence of Christ, both as regards the nature of the Sacrament and as regards its efficacy.

Devotion to the humanity of Christ, the origins of which have not been completely explained, found expression in devotion to the passion of Christ and his sufferings and in devotion to the crucifix, to the five wounds, to the wound in the side, and so on. This devotion, which was the source of a profound spirituality, could not but fit in with a eucharistic doctrine of the Paschasian kind and could not but become identified with it. For in this conception, the eucharistic Sacrament was nothing else than the physical body of Christ, not visible now but veiled by the species of the bread. Once the Paschasian interpretation of the Eucharist was put in place, devotion to the Sacrament was seen as a development of devotion to the humanity of Christ.[118]

Despite the position taken by Ratramnus, which was a more or less successful retrieval of patristic views, we must wait for the School of Laon, in the first decades of the twelfth century, before we see a real reversal of Paschasius' ideas. At Laon and later at St. Victor, the importance of the faith that works through love was emphasized in explaining the salvific efficacy of the Eucharist. The principle was correct, but it did not explain the Eucharist. For if the source of salvation is the faith that does the works of love, why is it any longer necessary to receive the Eucharist? What the emphasis on active faith did lead to, and very successfully, was the practice of "spiritual Communion,"

[117] ". . . The flesh of the body of Christ, by which Christ remains in us, so that we are transformed by it into him who became nothing else than God made flesh by his own condescension" (*De corpore et sanguine Domini* 1; CCLContMed 16, p. 19).

[118] At the beginning of the twelfth century there was a real explosion of devotion to the Sacrament, and it was precisely during those years that Paschasius' views received their fullest formulation.

which consists in arousing the sentiments of faith and love without actually receiving sacramental Communion.[119]

The facts thus far mentioned show that the two main areas of eucharistic devotion—devotion to the Sacrament in its objectivity[120] and spiritual Communion as an intimate personal conversation—are closely connected with the two currents of theological thought which we saw earlier: that of Paschasius and that of Laon. The two kinds of devotion were born of those two theologies.

We may therefore conclude that medieval eucharistic devotion possessed a fully theological status, since it fitted coherently into the soteriological framework of the eucharistic theology to which it referred. When thus endowed with an organic link to a soteriology, "devotion" becomes itself a theological datum. It represents a theology which, when its ultimate implications are brought out, gives rise to a particular ritual system and to devotional celebrations that need not be connected with popular piety.[121]

We have seen that Thomas Aquinas played an important part in eucharistic theology, because with his explicit recourse to Aristotelian metaphysics he succeeded in ensuring sacramental realism while avoiding physicism. In this way he explained the nature of the eucharistic bread and wine, but not the nature of the eucharistic celebration as an act of obedience to the mandate of Christ, "Do this in memory of me." Nor was he able to explain the relationship between *figura* and *veritas* in this Sacrament. But, despite having a theology different from that of Thomas, the other great medieval theologians, such as Bonaventure, found themselves in the same position and are subject to the same criticism.

[119] The theory and practice of spiritual Communion (despite the doctrine of the *votum eucharistiae*) are a good proof of the difficulty of explaining the necessity of sacramental Communion.

[120] The Sacrament was hastily interpreted as a manifestation of the humanity of Christ, in complete parallelism with the incarnation. It is on this line that the expressions "Jesus Eucharist" and "Jesus Sacrament" are to be interpreted.

[121] We can therefore conclude that "devotion" is not simply a private, emotionally colored attitude toward the eucharistic reality, since "devotion" already carries within it all the constituents of a real theological system. The characteristics of various devotions can be traced back to the theological systems that gave rise to them and that, through the devotions, remain present and continue to be influential today even though they have been left behind and definitively abandoned in the development of theology in recent centuries. Devotions thus outlive their causes. Even today they have a life of their own that is independent of the fate of the theologies and soteriologies that gave birth to them.

Chapter 13

The Eucharist and the Relics of the Saints

It was customary in Christian antiquity for altars and, later, basilicas to be built over the tombs of the saints; then it became the custom, in fifth-century Africa,[1] that altars, to be considered legitimate, had to contain some of the relics (Latin *reliquiae*) of the martyrs. It was this local phenomenon that gave rise to the general usage of connecting the altar with the relics of the martyrs, even in noncemeterial basilicas.

In the ritual for the consecration of an altar[2] relics of the saints were placed beneath the altar. It is easy to imagine this rite if we think of what the altars of the sixth century were like: Under the altar was the *confessio*, which was sunk into the ground and emerged from it in the form of a small miniaturized tomb; this was surrounded by small columns which supported the altar table, or else it was protected by four walls that served as an enclosed base for the altar. The relics were placed in the *confessio*, to which access was had through a small opening or hole that was protected by an ornate ironwork grill on the forward side of the altar.

---

[1] Sixth Council of Carthage (September 13, 401). We do not have the complete records of this council, but its concerns were taken up again in the Council of Carthage that was held on February 5–6, 525. See *Concilia Africae A. 345-A. 525*, ed. C. Munier (CCL 149; Turnhout: Brepols, 1974) 266. They also reappear in the *Registri Ecclesiae Carthaginensis Excerpta*, ibid., 204.

[2] For the use of relics in the consecration of an altar see N. Herrmann-Mascard, *Les reliques des saints. Formation coutumière d'un droit* (Société d'histoire du droit. Collection d'histoire institutionelle et sociale, 6; Paris: Klincksieck, 1975) 146–68.

The *confessio* tended to disappear because it tended to merge with the altar; the result was the altar-tomb. In this case, the relics were placed inside the altar and closed off by a little slab called a "seal" (*sigillum*); the altar table (*tabula* or *mensa*) was placed over this structure and served as a cover. In a later period and for practicality, the relics were placed in a little hole or chamber cut out in the center of the altar table.

According to the *Ordines,* and especially according to the medieval religious mind, it was not possible to consecrate a fixed or immovable altar unless relics were inserted into it. Moreover, if the *sigillum* of an altar were tampered with, or if it were lost, it was necessary to consecrate the altar again and, with it, the entire church.[3] The Carolingian Renaissance brought an extensive development of religious life and of the building of churches, especially monastic churches. This was a further reason why, from the Carolingian period on, there was a great demand for relics, a demand which was satisfied in various ways. Along with relics, or in the absence of relics, consecrated hosts were inserted in the *confessio* or in the altar table. This latter usage was codified, as a documented practice, in legal documents, in liturgical books, and in commentaries on these, during the period from the eighth century down almost to Innocent III (1160/61–1216). The norm or principle lasted even longer and remained in the liturgical books until the fifteenth century.

I turn now to an examination of this development and shall try to see whether the Eucharist and the understanding of it were influenced by it or, more simply, how they were related to the idea and cultivation of the relics of the saints, which played so important a part in the Middle Ages.

The earliest testimony is in *Ordo XLII,* which is a rite for the placing of relics in an altar[4] and is Roman in origin, as is shown by its connection with the Gregorian Sacramentary.[5] The composition may go back to the eighth century;[6] it was later included in the collection of *Ordines* that began to circulate in France at the beginning of the ninth century.

[3] Sicard of Cremona, *Mitrale seu de Officiis ecclesiasticis summa* 1 (PL 213:37).

[4] *Les Ordines romani du haut moyen âge* 4, ed. M. Andrieu (SSL 28; Louvain, 1965) 393. For an updating on the problems connected with the *Ordines,* see A.-G. Martimort, *Les "Ordines," les Ordinaires, et les Cérémoniaux* (Typologie des sources du moyen âge occidental, 56; Turnhout: Brepols, 1991).

[5] *Les Ordinaires Romani* 4, 385–86.

[6] Ibid., 394.

Even though there was a fuller Ceremonial, especially for the consecration of an altar, this ritual already existed in outline in the letters of the sixth-century popes.[7]

According to *Ordo XLII*, the bishop places the relics on the new altar and, before they are enclosed in the *confessio*, he anoints the four corners of the aperture with chrism, in the form of a cross. "Then he places in the *confessio* three particles *(portiones)* of the body of the Lord,[8] three (grains) of incense, and the relics are then enclosed in the *confessio*."[9] This usage spread throughout the entire West, as is attested by various councils, among them the Council of Chelsea (July 816):

"When a church is built, it is to be consecrated by the bishop of the diocese; he himself blesses water and then sprinkles it. . . . Then the Eucharist, which has been consecrated by the same bishop, is to be placed by another minister in a small box, along with the other relics, and to be preserved in the same basilica. And if other relics cannot be found, this action can be supremely profitable because it is the body and blood of our Lord Jesus Christ."[10]

At a later period, *Ordo XLII* was merged with *Ordo XLI*, which arose in France, almost certainly in the setting of Pepin's liturgical reform.[11] The Sacramentary of Drogo of Metz (826–855) combines the two *Ordines* in its ritual for the dedication of a church. After speaking of the bishop's entrance behind the curtain that has been hung before the altar, the text says that he prepares some mortar, using blessed water; thus even the lime used for walling in the relics is blessed by reason of its very composition. The bishop next sprinkles the *confessio* with blessed water and anoints its four corners with chrism. "Then the relics, along with the three particles of the Lord's body and the three grains of incense, are placed in the *confessio*, while the antiphon 'Under the altar,' is sung."[12]

---

[7] Ibid., 393.

[8] Either three fragments of a consecrated host or three hosts.

[9] *Ordo XLII* 10–11, in *Les Ordines romani* 4.400.

[10] A. W. Haddan and W. Stubbs, *Councils and Ecclesiastical Documents Relating to Great Britain and Ireland* 3 (Oxford, 1871) 580.

[11] *Les Ordines romani* 4.336.

[12] *Zur Ikonographie und Liturgie des Drogo-Sakramentars (Paris, Bibliothèque nationale, Ms. Lat. 9428)*, ed. F. Unterkircher (Interpretationes ad codices, 1; Graz: Akademische Druck-und Verlagsanstalt, 1977) n. 465, p. 60.

To understand why it was so necessary to consecrate the altar and in doing so to use things as holy as the Lord's Body, relics, chrism, and so on, we must realize how the altar was looked upon in that culture. Listen to the language of Drogo's Sacramentary in the blessing of the corporal: "Deign to sanctify it by a heavenly blessing, in order that it may be fit for your holy altar, for on the altar the body of our Lord Jesus Christ is to be confected *(ad conficiendum super illum corpus domini nostri ihesu christi)."*[13] In this understanding, the Sacrament of the Eucharist is equated with the consecration of the Body of Christ, and the covering of the altar must be sanctified if it is to be worthy of so great an event.

The product of the fusion of the two *Ordines* is to be clearly seen in the so-called *Romano-Germanic Pontifical,* which was compiled at Mainz in 950. Rubric no. 40 of this Pontifical, which has to do with the placing of the Lord's Body in the *confessio,*[14] is taken verbatim from *Ordo XLII* and is preceded by a rubric from *Ordo XLI,* which prescribes that a curtain be hung between the altar and the people, in order that the people may not see the rite of the burial of the relics in the altar; the rubric is a sign of how sacred this rite was considered to be. From that point on, the two rubrics remained combined.

This norm in the liturgical books was in fact observed and became the custom. On March 10, 1296, Urban II consecrated the abbey church of Marmoutiers and placed in the altar the Body of Christ, relics of the saints, and a piece of the cross of Christ.[15] Benedict VIII followed the same practice, as is attested by a letter of his to Boniface of Mantua: In granting the latter permission to erect a church in honor of Simeon the Hermit and to consecrate its altar, the pope says that "relics of ancient saints and the most holy body of our Jesus Christ" are to be placed in the altar, "and then, finally, the divine mysteries are to be celebrated."[16]

Under the Ottos, after the *renovatio Imperii* (962), the liturgy reflected in the *Romano-Germanic Pontifical* was installed without difficulty in Rome,[17] chiefly at the wish of Otto, who wanted to halt the

[13] Ibid., n. 477, p. 61.

[14] *Le Pontifical romano-germanique du Xème siècle* 1, ed. C. Vogel and R. Elze (ST 266; Vatican City: Vatican Apostolic Library, 1963) 88.

[15] *De dedicatione ecclesiae Maioris monasterii* (PL 151:275).

[16] Benedict VIII, *Epistulae* XXXV (PL 139:1633).

[17] *Le Pontifical romano-germanique* 3: *Introduction générale et Tables,* ed. C. Vogel and R. Elze (ST 269; Vatican City: Vatican Apostolic Library, 1972) 5.

decline of the Roman liturgy. Furthermore, Gregory V (996–999) asked the Abbey of Reichenau to provide liturgical books, which obviously could only be those of that locale, that is, hybrid forms of a liturgy of the Romano-Germanic type.[18] Beginning in the time of Emperor Henry III (1039–1056), a whole series of German bishops became popes, "and it is evident that these bishops used the liturgical books to which they were accustomed."[19] The *Romano-Germanic Pontifical* thus became a liturgical book of the city of Rome and was used even by Gregory VII, although it was with this pope that the liturgical renaissance of Rome began.

In subsequent liturgical developments, the common background to which everyone referred remained the *Romano-Germanic Pontifical,* and it was on the basis of this book that the new Pontificals of the twelfth century were compiled. We have to bear in mind that in the stages of development I have been describing no liturgical book was simply and abruptly replaced by another; rather there was an osmosis, an amalgamation, that occurred peacefully[20] and slowly.

This brief excursus into the history of the Pontifical has been necessary if we are to understand the subsequent development of the rubrics for the burial of relics in the altar, along with the Body of Christ.

The *Roman Pontifical of the Twelfth Century,* which was based on the *Romano-Germanic Pontifical,* had two main editions: an older and shorter one, composed in France, and a more recent and more complete one which was "the collective work of the Roman liturgists of the twelfth century"[21] and of which only a single copy remains, the *Pontifical* of Apamea. The two editions differ more in spaciousness than in the content proper; one difference in content occurs precisely in the rubric for the placing of the Lord's Body and the saints' relics in the altar. The older text, composed in France, says: "After a curtain has been drawn between the people and altar, the bishop places the relics in a little case and also places in it three particles *(portiones)* of the Lord's body[22] and three grains of incense."[23]

---

[18] Ibid., 49.

[19] Ibid., 50, note 95.

[20] Ibid., 55.

[21] *Le pontifical romain au moyen âge 1. Le Pontifical romain du XII siècle,* ed. M. Andrieu (ST 86; Vatican City: Vatican Apostolic Library, 1938) 116.

[22] Either three fragments of a consecrated host or three hosts.

[23] *Le pontifical romain du XII siècle,* XVII, 48 (p. 186).

The more recent, Roman edition, on the other hand, speaks only of relics and deletes the mention both of the incense and of the Lord's Body.[24] The two different editions of the *Pontifical* continued, however, to live on side by side, without causing too many problems, and both were the source of the thirteenth-century pontifical: the *Pontifical according to the Custom and Usage of the Roman Curia (Pontificale secundum consuetudinem et usum romanae curiae)*, the first edition of which goes back to the pontificate of Innocent III (1160/61–1216). This *Pontifical* says that a small container is to be made ready, containing relics of the saints, but does not mention either grains of incense or the Lord's Body.[25] At the point when the relics are to be placed the rubric says:

"After a curtain has been drawn between the clergy and the people, the bishop, standing before the altar, uses his thumb to put chrism into the *confessio*, that is, the tomb in the altar into which the relics are to be placed; he puts chrism into the middle and the four corners, in the form of a cross. . . . Then he reverently deposits the relics and the three grains of incense that are to be put into the box holding the relics."[26]

Mention is made here of the three grains of incense, although these had not been mentioned earlier when speaking of the preparation for the rite; but there is still no reference to the Body of the Lord.

Let me look back for a moment. Between the *Roman Pontifical* of the twelfth century and that of the Roman Curia, which was compiled under Innocent III, there was the important testimony of Sicard, bishop of Cremona (1118–1215), a very renowned lawyer and outstanding commentator on the liturgy, and a teacher of Innocent III. In his commentary on the liturgy, Sicard refers, with exact citations, to a *Pontifical* that was very like the older and shorter edition of the twelfth-century *Roman Pontifical,* although not completely identical with it. This should not surprise us, since the various Roman Pontificals compiled in the twelfth century are so different among themselves that scholars have excluded the possibility of their deriving from a common archetype. These varied Pontificals were always and

[24] Ibid.
[25] *Pontificale secundum consuetudinem et usum romanae curiae* XXIII, 1 = *Le pontifical romain au moyen âge* 2. *Le pontifical de la curie romaine au XIII siècle,* ed. M. Andrieu (ST 87; Vatican City, 1940) p. 422.
[26] Ibid., XXIII, 55–56 (p. 434).

simply numerous reworkings of the *Romano-Germanic Pontifical.* The various Roman churches within the borders of the ancient *Italia suburbicaria* compiled their own Pontificals as they had need of them.[27] That is what we see in the case of Sicard of Cremona.

Sicard discusses the rite for the consecration of an altar first descriptively and then "morally." He says that "the body of the Lord and relics of the saints are placed in the altar so that we may keep in mind the Lord's commandments and the examples of the saints."[28] This shows that Sicard was quite familiar with the rite of placing in the altar relics of the saints and the Body of the Lord. However, just a little earlier, when describing the rite of placing relics in the altar, after speaking of the curtain drawn between altar and people and after commenting on this rite, he adds: "Put chrism in the four corners of the *confessio* in the form of a cross. . . . Then place three pieces *(portiones)* of incense. . . . And afterwards the relics are sealed in the tomb."[29] Here there is no reference to the pieces of eucharistic bread.

A possible explanation: There was a slow evolution in liturgical practice, so that the new liturgical books no longer contained the rubric about placing the Body of the Lord in the *confessio;* meanwhile, however, commentaries continued to mention the latter practice, since altars consecrated at an earlier date still contained the Body of the Lord. Like other relics, the Body of the Lord ensured the holiness of the altar and its fitness for the celebration of the divine mysteries.

In the *Synodal Constitutions* of Eudes of Sully, bishop of Paris (1196–1208), it is prescribed[30] that "if the blood of the Lord falls on the corporal, the latter is to be torn up and preserved in the place[31] of the relics. If the altar cloth is stained with it, let the section be torn up and be preserved as[32] a relic."[33] From this it can be seen that there is a certain analogy between the preservation of the Sacrament of the

[27] Vogel and Elze (note 17, above), 51.

[28] Sicard, *Mitrale* 1.10 (PL 213:36).

[29] Ibid., 1.8 (cols. 33–34).

[30] Eudes of Sully (Odo de Solacio), *Synodicae constitutiones,* Communia praecepta, can. 23 (PL 212:65). See also canon 16 of the Council of Oxford (1222), in *Councils and Synods,* ed. F. Powicke and C. Cheney (Oxford, 1964) I, 111.

[31] *In loco reliquiarum* may mean either "in the place" in which the relics are kept, or "in place" of the relics, that is, "as if" a relic.

[32] *Pro reliquia.*

[33] The practice codified by Eudes became authoritative and is observed even today in the preservation of the remains of so-called eucharistic miracles. It is a practice to which no objection has ever been raised.

Eucharist and the preservation of the relics of the saints. The analogy was given prominence especially at this synod, which enjoyed great authority and was imitated throughout the Middle Ages. In addition, we must take into account that Eudes of Sully was a not unimportant personage in the history of eucharistic devotion, since it was he who gave the impulse to devotion to the Sacrament and to the actual rite of elevation of the Eucharist at the moment of consecration.

We have seen what the practice was from the eighth century down to the *Roman Pontifical* of the twelfth century and the period of Sicard of Cremona. We must now inquire why the rubric was changed in the thirteenth-century *Pontifical of the Roman Curia*. If this last-named Pontifical was compiled under Innocent III, then everything suggests that this pope, responding to a new sensibility which was then arising, played a decisive role in eliminating the rubric that called for the placing of a consecrated host in the altar. Here is how Nicole Herrmann-Mascard puts it:

"Hostiensis[34] had asked the pope for a judgment on the question. After the pope had consulted with his entourage, he condemned the practice but did not give a reason for his answer. A century later, John d'Andrea[35] suggested a reason for the prohibition: The Eucharist is the food of the soul and it is not fitting that a different use be made of it than that for which it was instituted."[36]

If this reconstruction by Mrs. Herrmann-Mascard is correct, it is consonant with the data we have on the liturgical relationship between Innocent III and the thirteenth-century *Pontifical of the Roman Curia*.

But the matter does not end there; we must bear in mind that in the Middle Ages the compiling and use of liturgical books was not the same as today.

About seventy years later, a great canonist, William Durandus (ca. 1230–1296), compiled a Pontifical that was to be immensely successful. In composing his book he used as his immediate source the *Pontifical of the Roman Curia* and, as secondary sources, the *Roman Pontifical of the Twelfth Century* and the *Romano-Germanic Pontifical*.

---

[34] Canonist Henry Bartolomei, author of the *Summa aurea;* he was also known as Henry of Susa and died in 1271.

[35] A decretalist, a commentator on Durandus; he died in 1348.

[36] Herrmann-Mascard, *Les reliques des saints* (note 2, above), 167.

Despite the fact that his direct source had eliminated the rubric calling for the placing of the Lord's Body in the altar along with the relics, Durandus reintroduced it, even if in a slightly altered form: "On the evening before the day of dedication, the bishop is to prepare the relics of the saints to be placed in the altar that is to be consecrated; he is to put them in a suitable, clean container of glass or of copper or some other material, along with three grains of incense, or, if relics are lacking, he is to place in it the body of the Lord."[37] Normally, then, only relics of the saints are to be placed in the altar, but if it is not possible to obtain such relics, the lack can be compensated by placing in it the Body of the Lord. Thus in the consecration of an altar the Body of the Lord serves the same function as relics.

In later rubrics, too, no distinction is made between a container holding relics of the saints and a container that, if need be, holds the Body of the Lord; the reference is always to "relics." The placing of the container with the relics in the altar calls for great reverence and, in keeping with the tradition in which the practice originated, the rite is equated with a burial.[38] And in fact at the moment when the stone slab covering the container is set in place, the bishop intones the traditional antiphon: "The bodies of the saints are buried in peace, and their names shall live forever."[39] This practice is followed even if the container placed in the altar holds only the Body of the Lord and not the relics of the saints.

Why did William Durandus not simply accept the rubric of his direct source, the *Pontifical of the Roman Curia,* and return instead to earlier sources? The answer is simple: Durandus was a lawyer, and a lawyer does not base his opinions solely on the immediately preceding written source but on custom, which, as such, has normative value. But even this would not have been sufficient if William had not also had the mentality of a *speculator* (writer of "Mirrors"), and indeed he was known by that title, the *Speculator,* because he has composed a *Speculum iudiciale* ("Mirror of the Law") between 1271 and 1276. In composing a work in this literary genre, the compiler would make use of all the legal positions or opinions transmitted by the sources, and would compare them among themselves. William used the method of

[37] *Pontificalis ordinis liber* II, II, 4, in *Le pontifical romain au moyen âge 3. Le Pontifical de Guillaume Durand,* ed. M. Andrieu (ST 88; Vatican City, 1940) 456.

[38] This is why the relics (or the Body of the Lord) were accompanied by three grains of incense: these represented the perfumes used in an entombment.

[39] *Pontificalis ordinis liber* II, III, 33 (*Pontifical romain* 3:485).

the *speculum* even in composing his *Rationale divinorum officiorum* (1921), in which he worked as a compiler; as we saw earlier, this work was a commentary on the liturgy but also had juridical and rubrical value. In this work, as in his *Pontificale*, he prescribed that if there were no relics, the Body of the Lord, along with three grains of incense, should be placed in the altar.[40]

In order correctly to evaluate this medieval custom of placing a consecrated host in the altar, we must look closely at what William Durandus, the *Speculator*, did. He was guided by his method as a lawyer and therefore made a choice that respected the sources both canonical and liturgical. Despite the new line taken by the *Pontifical of the Roman Curia*, Durandus was unable to forget that earlier custom had been different; therefore, as an expert compiler, he looked for a middle way and prescribed that the relics of the saints and three grains of incense were to be placed in the altar, but also, that if there were no relics, the Body of Christ was to be placed there instead.

It was during the Avignon period of the papacy, at the end of the thirteenth century, that the third edition of the *Pontifical of the Roman Curia* entered into competition with the *Pontifical* of William Durandus. After various reciprocal interactions the *Pontifical* of Durandus won out[41] and became simply the *Roman Pontifical* without any qualifications. It remained in use until the fifteenth century, when it was revised with a view to printing it.

The *Roman Pontifical* that was printed in 1485 was modeled directly on the *Pontifical* of Durandus, with a few corrections, and continued in force until the reform inaugurated by Vatican Council II. What became of the rubric ordering the placing of a consecrated host in the altar if relics were lacking? The printed edition of 1485 eliminated it, and it left no trace and gave rise to no discussion. Innocent VIII had charged John Burckard (or Burchard) of Strasbourg, a prelate and papal master of ceremonies, to revise the Pontifical, and the latter took as his model the Pontifical then in use, that is, the Pontifical of William Durandus. The rubric in question had been rendered obsolete by history, due to the development of eucharistic piety, and therefore it disappeared.

[40] "Thus the consecration of an immovable altar is not possible without relics of the saints or, if these are not available, without the body of the Lord" (*Rationale divinorum officiorum* I, VII, 23 (CCLContMed 140, p. 90).

[41] *Le Pontifical romano-germanique* 3 (note 17, above), 5.

Burckard was a simple master of ceremonies who revised both the Pontifical and the *Ordo missae* (1502), with a noteworthy emphasis on eucharistic doctrine, but his historical fortune was unusual. He is the one who introduced into the *Ordo missae* the genuflections at the consecration. His *Ordo missae* was well designed and would be taken over into the reform missal of Pius V in 1570, in keeping with the norms set down by the Council of Trent. Burckard's work thus became normative for the universal Church and remained so, as did his Pontifical, until Vatican II.

It is time to end this chapter on the rubric that gave the Eucharist the role of a relic in the consecration of the altar. The rubric was given a theological assessment by Francisco Suárez (1548–1617), who knew it through the *Rationale* of William Durandus. Here is his opinion of it: "And so he [Durandus] thought that when relics are lacking, a particle of a consecrated host should be enclosed in the altar to be consecrated. But this seems to me unfitting *(indecens)* and improbable, as Pope Innocent is said to have replied according to Torquemada and others."[42]

I think it was important, given the purpose of the present volume, to discuss this concept of the Eucharist as analogous to a relic and able to exercise the function of a relic. The question is clearly a marginal one, but it has some importance, since the concept remained operative in one or other fashion for seven centuries, from the eighth to the fifteenth, but not for this reason alone. There is another consideration: Beginning in the Middle Ages some special rites were devised for the showing, the processional conveyance, and the adoration of the most Blessed Sacrament.

These rites were not, however, peculiar to the Eucharist; there were comparable rites for the showing, the processional conveyance, and the veneration of the relics of the saints. These rites, with the liturgical display and furnishings that accompanied them, arose out of devotion to the relics of the saints. This development took place within a devotional culture that celebrated the religious feast of a saint with a public reading of his deeds (and possibly his martyrdom[43]) and with the rite of the exaltation and triumph of his body.[44] Among these rites

---

[42] F. Suárez, *De sacramentis*, Pars Prima, Quaestio 83, Articulus 3, Disputatio 81, Sectio 5 (in *Opera omnia* [Venice, 1747] 860, 2.

[43] Or simply the account of the translation of his body or his relics.

[44] On this cult see A. Frolow, *La relique de la vraie croix. Recherches sur le développement d'un culte* (Archives de l'Orient chrétien, 7; Paris: Institut français d'études byzantines, 1961); idem, *Les reliquaires de la vraie croix* (Archives de l'Orient chrétien, 8;

the showing of his relics was very important. There were ordinary showings and extraordinary showings, and one of the latter was the showing of the relics by hanging them over an altar to be consecrated and offering them for the veneration of the faithful beginning on the vigil of the day set for the consecration.

I deliberately draw no conclusion from all the information I have given. I wish only to call attention to the problem of whether in the western Church there has been a connection between the conception of relics and the conception of the Eucharist.[45]

Paris: Institut français d'études byzantines, 1965); P. Brown, *The Cult of the Saints: Its Rise and Function in Latin Christianity* (Chicago: University of Chicago Press, 1981); P. J. Geary, *Furta sacra. Theft of Relics in the Central Middle Ages* (Princeton: Princeton University Press, 1990); J. Dubois and J.-L. Lemaître, *Sources et méthodes de l'hagiographie médiévale* (Collection Histoire; Paris: Cerf, 1993).

[45] In the Western Church the cult of relics is analogous to, and has had the same function as, the cult (I prefer not to speak of "spirituality") of icons in the Eastern Church.

Chapter 14

The Reformation and the Council of Trent

1. THE REFORMATION

1.1. Luther

Luther's treatise *The Babylonian Captivity* (1520) contains a harsh challenge to the medieval conception of the Eucharist. The Eucharist (it says) is held prisoner by three doctrinal positions: (a) the reception of Communion under a single species; (b) transubstantiation; (c) the Eucharist as a "good work." In Luther's view, the Church's refusal to give the laity Communion under both species lacked a biblical basis and was to be considered a sin. As a result, the Reformation adopted Communion under both species as a general practice, making this its banner, so to speak, as the Hussites had done in the fifteenth century.[1]

Consider now the question of transubstantiation. William of Ockham had said that consubstantiation is a much more logical position but that he accepted transubstantiation out of fidelity to the Church; in dependence on Ockham, Luther first repeated the same criticism, but then abandoned the doctrine of transubstantiation[2] in favor of consubstantiation. This is the key point in Luther's explanation of the Eucharist, an explanation that allows the substance of the bread and wine to "co-exist" with the substance of the Body and Blood of Christ. Luther wanted to establish a direct connection, an exact analogy, between the Sacrament and the Hypostatic Union: two natures "co-existing" in the one person of Christ. According to Luther, the

---

[1] A. E. McGrat, *Il pensiero della riforma. Lutero, Zwingli, Calvino, Bucero* (Piccola biblioteca teologica, 24; Turin: Claudiana, 1991) 131.

[2] The Lutheran criticism of transubstantiation broadened into a wide-ranging criticism of the use of Aristotelianism in theology.

important thing is the real presence of Christ in the Eucharist, and not the theory by which this presence is explained.[3]

Luther's teaching on the real presence met with lively opposition from other Reformers. To Zwingli's objection that Christ is seated at the right hand of the Father and that therefore he cannot be "present" in the Eucharist, Luther answered that the right hand of the Father is not to be understood as a place[4] but as a way of describing "God's sphere of influence" and "God's government."[5] Therefore, as present at the right hand of the Father, Christ is everywhere present because the power of the Father reaches to every place and is present everywhere.[6]

The doctrine of the sacrificial character of the Eucharist, based on the fact that the sacraments are "good works," was likewise the object of radical criticism because it was not founded on Scripture. The forgiveness of sins is to be obtained through faith in the divine promise, and not through the celebration of a "good work," the Mass.[7] From this alone we can see that Luther understood the Mass in a very one-sided way, due to the fact that his thinking was completely conditioned by the teaching and practice which had developed in the Middle Ages.

While, as we saw, the medieval conception of the sacraments was connected, on the one hand, with the categories of sign and cause and, on the other, with the faith that works through love, Luther's conception of it was connected, on the one hand, with the concept of promise and, on the other, with faith as a necessary response to the promise. In his view, therefore, the sacraments have for their effect to rouse faith in those who participate in them.[8]

---

[3] Luther, *La cattività babilonese della chiesa*, ed. G. Panzieri Saija (Turin: UTET, 1949) 250: "For myself I am unable to say how the bread is the body of Christ; nevertheless I want to make my reason prisoner of obedience to Christ by simply holding fast to his words and firmly believing not only that the body of Christ is in the bread but that the bread is the body of Christ."

[4] In contrast to the sacramental presence, this too being understood as presence in a place.

[5] McGrat, *Il pensiero della riforma*, 139.

[6] This doctrine is known as Lutheran "ubiquitarianism."

[7] "You see, then, that what we call the 'mass' is a promise of the forgiveness of sins from God, a promise confirmed by the death of the Son of God" (*La cattività*, note 3, above, p. 254).

[8] As a rite, the sacrament mediates the word of God, which gives rise to a response of faith.

Luther did not restrict himself to doctrinal reflection but effected a liturgical reform in the true and proper sense. His aversion to the sacrificial character of the Mass led him to undertake a revision of the Roman Canon, since this frequently uses sacrificial language. Initially[9] he asked priests to avoid all language of a sacrificial kind, but later on he undertook to change the Canon, both in the *Formula missae* (1523)[10] and in the *Deutsche Messe* (1525/26).[11] The prayers of the Canon were critiqued one after another and rejected almost in their entirety.[12] What remained was the account of institution, the words of which were to be proclaimed as a gospel message, aloud and in a solemn chant; this was followed by the Communion service.

In the liturgical plan of the *Formula missae,* the structure of the liturgy of the word remained unchanged by comparison with its Roman counterpart. The eucharistic liturgy, however, was reduced to the offertory, the dialogue before the Preface and the Preface itself, and the account of Last Supper, which was followed by the singing of the *Sanctus* and the *Benedictus,* while the bread and wine were to be elevated (but this was optional) so as to be quite visible to the faithful. The Our Father was followed by the Communion service. The prayers which preceded and followed Communion and were meant as a private preparation and thanksgiving, could still be recited, provided that the priest replaced the first person singular (I, me, my) with the first person plural (we, us, our), so as to bring out the communal value of these prayers. The Communion chant was accepted, but the Postcommunion prayer was eliminated because of its sacrificial character. This entire reform strongly emphasized Communion, to which Luther was very attached, while there was no grasp of the importance of the Eucharistic Prayer, or Roman Canon, of which the only part regarded as important was the consecration.

In the *Deutsche Messe (German Mass)* the changes made were more radical, beginning with the fact that German replaced Latin, so that the real agent of worship was the community, which participated primarily through singing.[13] Luther had a very well-defined plan for the

[9] *Of the Two Ways of Receiving This Sacrament* (1522).

[10] The text is translated in *Prayers of the Eucharist: Early and Reformed,* ed. R.C.D. Jasper and G. J. Cuming (3rd rev. ed.; New York: Pueblo, 1987) 191–95.

[11] Ibid., 195–99.

[12] H. Grass, "Luther et la liturgie eucharistique," in *Eucharisties d'Orient et d'Occident,* ed. B. Botte and others (Lex orandi 46–47; Paris: Cerf, 1970) 1, 138.

[13] Ibid., 146f.

participation of the community in the divine service of the holy Supper: After the sermon came the liturgy of the Supper, or the eucharistic liturgy, which began with a catechetical paraphrase of the Lord's Prayer[14] and an exhortation to receive the Sacrament.[15] These were followed by the words of consecration in the Lukan-Pauline form.[16] Immediately after the words over the bread came the Communion in the Body of Christ; then the words over the cup were recited, followed by the Communion in the Blood of Christ. The account of institution was sung in a gospel tone. The elevation was kept, and during Communion appropriate songs were sung, among them the *Sanctus* and *Agnus Dei* in German. At the end came an *Oremus* that was a reworking of a Roman Postcommunion.

In this reform by Luther the Canon was for practical purposes eliminated,[17] and the Preface was replaced by the paraphrase of the Our Father and an exhortation to receive the Sacrament. Why this substitution? It is understandable only if the Preface was being understood not as a thanksgiving (in imitation of Christ's thanksgiving at the Last Supper) but as a prologue or introduction to something. But this was the conception of it among the medieval writers; Luther did not have to invent anything. As understood at that time the Preface was simply an introduction; this being so, it cannot be denied that Luther's choice ought to be viewed positively. Unfortunately for Luther, the Preface is not an introduction, as we saw at the beginning of this book.

In Luther's reform, the entire eucharistic liturgy seems to be reduced to these two elements: the words of institution or the divine testament, as Luther calls it, and the distribution of the Sacrament.[18] The medieval heritage, which, following Ambrose, distinguished between the divine words and the human words in the Eucharistic Prayer, is quite visible in the treatise on the liturgy by Lutheran Peter Brunner. He says that the words of institution and the Communion that is directly connected with them stand apart in solemn grandeur

[14] Luther sought by this novelty to resist a purely ritual recitation of the Our Father.
[15] When the faithful receive the Sacrament, they must with real faith receive the testament of Christ and, above all, the words with which he offers his own Body and Blood (Grass, "Luther et la liturgie eucharistique," 147).
[16] The Lukan-Pauline version was chosen because of the phrase "given for you," which was not in the account of institution in the Roman Canon.
[17] Th. Süss "L'aspect sacrificiel de la sainte Cène à la lumière de la tradition luthérienne," in *Eucharisties d'Orient et d'Occident* (note 12, above), 1, 154.
[18] Ibid.

from the rest of the liturgical celebration. Their power and majesty do not allow them to stand in proximity to any human prayer.[19]

But is there then no longer any prayer of thanksgiving like that of Christ? Strictly speaking, the answer is No: There is no longer any Eucharistic Prayer. It cannot, however, be claimed that praise of God is lacking or thanksgiving to him, which, as Peter Brunner points out, is present in the Communion songs.[20] He is echoed by Hans Grass: "To put it in a somewhat one-sided and extreme way, we can say that in Luther's *Deutsche Messe* the Eucharistic Prayer consists of the community's songs of praise."[21]

1.2. Calvin

Let us turn now to another great Reformer, John Calvin, an author who is certainly not easy to interpret, for "the theology of the sacraments in the Reformers is highly nuanced, especially in Calvin."[22] Calvin has a wide knowledge not only of the biblical data but also of the Fathers of the Church, of whom he makes extensive use. Since he uses the language of the Fathers and the Scriptures, it is very difficult to decide whether or not his thought still reflects Catholic orthodoxy. The obscurity is due to the fact that the Fathers are not discussed from a historical point of view; as a result, when their statements are isolated from the historical setting in which they were made, they can be interpreted in different and even opposite ways. Thus de Baciocchi considers Calvin's position to be definitely irreconcilable with the Catholic position,[23] whereas Thurian sees important convergences, to the point where the differences between the two positions are reduced to mere differences of emphasis on one datum or another.[24] Jean de Watteville adopts a third view when he says that Calvin's greatness consists in the method which he taught and applied: a return to Christian origins by way of the thought of the Fathers. He can therefore

[19] P. Brunner, "Zur Lehre vom Gottesdienst der im Namen Jesu versammelten Gemeinde," in *Leiturgia. Handbuch der evangelischen Gottesdienstes* 1 (Kassel, 1954) 343.

[20] Ibid., 344.

[21] Grass, "Luther" (note 12, above), 150.

[22] J. de Watteville, *Le sacrifice dans les textes eucharistiques des premiers siècles* (Bibliothèque théologique; Neuchâtel: Delachaux et Niestlé, 1966) 211.

[23] J. de Baciocchi, *L'Eucharistie* (Le mystère chrétien. Théologie sacramentaire 3; Tournai: Desclée, 1964) 50f., 88f.

[24] M. Thurian, *The Eucharistic Memorial*, trans. J. G. Davies (Ecumenical Studies in Worship 7–8; Richmond, Va.: John Knox Press, 1960–61) 2, 108ff.

conclude: "What does it mean to be faithful to the Reformation, if not to return to the Reformers! And what does it mean to return to the Reformers, if not to return to the Fathers of the Church!"[25]

Calvin opposes the concept of transubstantiation and, in his great respect for the mystery of God, is unwilling to take a position on the "how" of the real presence. He maintains a strong sacramental realism which he thinks of as half-way between Luther[26] and Zwingli,[27] who hold the opposed extremes on this question and represent two theses which Calvin regards as equally unsatisfactory. He himself maintains what he calls a "spiritual realism," because he refuses to localize the Body of Christ in the bread and in the wine. The Sacrament is the promise of communion with Christ and of his presence: if the faithful accept this promise with faith, the word of God is fulfilled and believers are in real communion with Christ. Here is a fine passage of Calvin in which he rejects the identification, supposedly Augustinian in origin, of eating with the act of faith:

"As it is not the seeing but the eating of bread that suffices to feed the body, so the soul must truly and deeply become partaker of Christ that it may be quickened to spiritual life by his power.

"We admit indeed, meanwhile, that this is no other eating than that of faith, as no other can be imagined. But there is the difference between my words and theirs: for them to eat is only to believe; I say that we eat Christ's flesh in believing, because it is made ours by faith, and that this eating is the effect of faith. Or if you want it said more clearly, for them eating is faith; for me it seems rather to follow from faith. This is a small difference indeed in words, but no slight one in the matter itself. For even though the apostle teaches that 'Christ dwells in our hearts through faith' [Eph 3:17; cf. Vg.], no one will interpret this indwelling to be faith, but all feel that he is there expressing a remarkable effect of faith, for through this believers gain Christ abiding in them. In this way the Lord intended, by calling himself the 'bread of life' [John 6:51], to teach not only that salvation

---

[25] de Watteville, *Le sacrifice* (note 22, above), 220.

[26] Calvin considers Luther's conception (consubstantiation) to be equivalent to the Catholic (transubstantiation).

[27] Zwingli's conception is purely symbolic: If sacrifice involves a bloody immolation, then only the Cross can be a sacrifice, and the Mass is not in any sense a sacrifice. The Mass only stimulates and feeds faith, since it is a figure of the death of Christ.

for us rests on faith in his death and resurrection, but also that, by true partaking of him, his life passes into us and is made ours—just as bread when taken as food imparts vigor to the body."[28]

In the logic of the medievals the affective and devotional aspect of the Sacrament was very important; this traditional conception likewise finds a place in Calvin, who says that we must "now receive him so that the efficacy and fruit of his death may reach us."[29]
In the 1554 edition of the *Institutes of the Christian Religion* Calvin points out that in the Old Testament there were sacrifices of thanksgiving and praise; he therefore allows that these two sacrificial categories are to be applied to the Eucharist, but he is forced to deny that the Eucharist can be regarded as an expiatory sacrifice. He is opposed to the concept of the representation and repetition of the sacrifice of the Cross because, in his great respect for the Cross, he wants to safeguard its uniqueness, which allows for no derogation: "To what purpose is the Mass, which has been so set up that a hundred thousand sacrifices may be performed each day, except to bury and submerge Christ?"[30]
We must bear in mind, finally, the way in which Calvin, basing himself on the Scriptures, describes the purpose of the Sacrament: "Here again the purpose of the Sacrament is made clear, that is, to exercise us in the remembrance of Christ's death."[31] As we have seen, this conception is part of the medieval way of understanding Christ's command to "do this in remembrance of me."[32]
Calvin, too, undertook a reform of the liturgy.[33] The Eucharist was to be celebrated only four times a year; Sunday worship was to consist

[28] J. Calvin, *Institutes of the Christian Religion* 4.17.5, ed. J. T. McNeill, trans. F. L. Battles (Library of Christian Classics 12–13; Philadelphia: Westminster, 1960) 2, 1365.
[29] J. Calvin, *Catechism of the Church of Geneva*, in *Calvin: Theological Treatises*, ed. and trans. J.K.S. Reid (Library of Christian Classics 22; Philadelphia: Westminster, n.d.) 136.
[30] Calvin, *Institutes* 4.18.3 (2, 1432).
[31] Ibid., 4.17.37 (2, 1414).
[32] de Watteville, *Le sacrifice* (note 22, above), 212, draws upon the patristic conception, so-called (O. Casel), and the biblical conception, so-called (M. Thurian), of memorial, and in the name of this criticizes Calvin, saying that his "reasoning lacks clarity, gives the impression of ambiguity and even of contradiction."
[33] Text in *Coena Domini* I. *Die Abendmahlsliturgie der Reformationskirchen im 16./17. Jahrhundert*, ed. I. Pahl (Spicilegium Friburgense 29; Freiburg Schweiz: Universitätsverlag, 1983) 355–62.

of the reading of God's word and a sermon, with the expectation that catechesis would enable the faithful to take part in the holy Supper in the proper way. In 1542 Calvin published at Geneva *The Form of Prayers and Manner of Administering the Sacraments and Blessing Marriages according to the Usage of the Ancient Church.*[34]

It was provided that at the end of the liturgy of the word, after the sermon, the pastor should utter a lengthy prayer of intercession, after which, if the holy Supper was to be celebrated, a prayer was to be added that prepared for the reception of the Sacrament.[35] The Mass contains neither Preface nor *Sanctus,* and the prayer formulas are completely new.[36] There is a fine, very devout prayer that combines good theology and piety, but it can in no sense be regarded as a Eucharistic Prayer. Calvin has in practice eliminated the Eucharistic Prayer from the Lord's Supper and replaced it with an introductory prayer that is followed by the Pauline account of the Last Supper from 1 Corinthians.

Calvin replaced a liturgical text with a biblical text. He obviously thought that he had to make choices out of fidelity to the Scriptures, and that he had to use biblical categories. Yet none of that happened. Unfortunately he was simply dependent on the conception of the Canon peculiar to the medieval theologians.

2. THE COUNCIL OF TRENT

The council's intention was not to compose its own comprehensive and complete treatise on the Eucharist, but only to give answers to the problems raised by the Reformers. It would therefore be a mistake to regard the Tridentine decrees as the synthesis and summa of Catholic teaching on the Eucharist.

The council's treatment of the Eucharist was not a very unified one, due partly to historical circumstances, partly to the way it handled the problems in question. It dealt with three subjects: the Sacrament of the Eucharist (Session 13; 1551), Communion under both species and the Communion of children (Session 21; 1562), and the eucharistic sacrifice, together with a doctrinal defense of the Roman Canon (Session 22; 1562). Discussion of the decree on the Sacrament of the Eucharist

[34] John Calvin, *Opera quae extant omnia* (Brunschwig, 1863–1903) VI, 174. It should be clear that the references to the early Church are out of place.

[35] See *The Manner of Celebrating the Supper,* in *Prayers of the Eucharist* (note 10, above), 215–18.

[36] See J. Cadier, "La prière eucharistique de Calvin," in *Eucharisties d'Orient et d'Occident* (note 12, above), 1, 171.

lasted from 1547 to 1551, starting with a broad collection of statements by the Reformers, although it cannot be said that the theologians who made the collection reported faithfully the thought of the Reformers.[37] During the Bologna period the Council engaged in a very interesting doctrinal discussion, which did not, however, lead to the publication of the canons decided on. The discussion was renewed at Trent and the canons from Bologna were taken into account, but the material was reworked; in addition, the canons were composed before the chapters (the "teaching"), so that the chapters are to be regarded as a broader explanation of what is said in the canons. As a result, there is not a perfect correspondence between the material set down in the canons and the material in the chapters. It is the canons that contain the definitions, and not the chapters, which in some cases were discussed only at the last moment and in a summary way.

2.1. A Note on the Theological Method of the Tridentine Decrees

It is worthwhile to say a few words about the method which Trent followed in composing its decrees. We may begin with the question of the adoration, in the strict sense of the term *(cultus latriae)*, that is to be paid to the Sacrament. In his study of Chapter 5 of Session 13, Anton Gerken points out that

"the Council recognizes that the primary purpose of the eucharistic celebration, and therefore of the real presence as well, is not adoration of Christ present, but the reception. . . . In its context, however, the statement that 'it was instituted by Christ the Lord to be consumed' *(ut sumatur)*[38] sounds like a concession and therefore is not to be taken as the point of departure for a true and proper eucharistic doctrine."[39]

The Council of Trent adopts the same procedure in dealing with other questions on the Eucharist, as, for example, Communion under

[37] For a commentary on the several redactions see E. Schillebeeckx, *The Eucharist,* trans. N. D. Smith (New York: Sheed & Ward, 1968).

[38] See *Decree on the Most Holy Eucharist* (1551), chapter 5: "For it [the holy Sacrament] is not less worthy of adoration because it was instituted by Christ the Lord to be consumed. For we believe that the same God is present therein of whom the eternal Father declared when introducing him into the created world, *Let all God's angels worship him.*" Text and translation in *Decrees of the Ecumenical Councils,* ed. N. Tanner (2 vols.; London: Sheed & Ward, and Washington, D.C.: Georgetown University Press, 1990) 2:695.

[39] A. Gerken, *Teologia dell'eucaristia* (Teologia 14; Alba: Edizioni paoline, 1977) 164f.

both species. In the first Chapter of Session 21 it maintains the Roman usage that denied the cup to the laity, and it justifies this position doctrinally by saying that there is no divine precept obliging the laity to receive the Sacrament under both species.[40] It then turns for a moment to the Last Supper and describes what happened there in the form of a concessive clause: "For, though Christ the Lord instituted this revered sacrament at the last supper and gave it to the apostles in the forms of bread and wine. . . ."[41]

After dealing with the legitimacy of Communion under only one species in light of the institution of the Sacrament, the council turns to its legitimacy in the light of history. Here the council asserts, above all else, the power of the Church over the sacraments, "provided their essentials remained intact" *(salva eorum substantia),* and then goes on to look at the different practice of the early Church. The council acknowledges, while minimizing the importance of the fact, that in the early Church there was Communion under both species. This acknowledgment is, however, put in a subordinate concessive clause: *"Although* from the beginning of Christian worship the use of both kinds was common, *yet* that custom was very widely changed in the course of time; and so holy mother church, acknowledging her authority over the administration of the sacraments. . . ."[42] The chapter ends by saying that the change was decreed by the Church for "good and serious reasons." The change that succeeded the old way is therefore held to be more binding and normative than the original practice.

This way of proceeding was justified by the very purpose of the Council of Trent, which was convoked in order to defend the teaching and practice of the Roman Church against the accusations of the Reformers. Present reality and the need for self-defense made the Roman Church suspicious of a past that was seen to be rich and partly different, but whose meaning was not well understood; as a result, it did not know how to interpret it so as to integrate it into the present. This situation explains why Trent formulated its responses on the basis of Church practice and not of the institution by Christ. But this was not

---

[40] *Teaching on Communion under Both Kinds and of Children* (1562), chapter 1: "Hence this holy council, taught by the holy Spirit . . . and following the judgment and custom of the church itself, declares and teaches that laity, and clergy who are not consecrating, are under no divine command to receive the sacrament of the eucharist under both kinds" (*Decrees of the Ecumenical Councils* 2:726).

[41] Ibid.

[42] Ibid., chapter 2 (p. 727).

the only reason: We must add that the method of Trent was, above all, dependent on the medieval heritage of which the council was the trustee.

2.2. The Council of Trent and the Council of Constance

The Council of Trent was heavily dependent on the Council of Constance, which had condemned 260 articles from the writings of John Wyclif (1320–1384).[43] Wyclif was a pure Aristotelian,[44] who could not accept a eucharistic doctrine that was in opposition to the Aristotelian system.[45] For philosophical reasons,[46] therefore, Wyclif found himself compelled to abandon transubstantiation, embrace the views of Berengarius, and say that Christ's Body is present only figuratively.[47] By its condemnation of Wyclif the Council of Constance thus effected in practice a canonization of the Aristotelianism of Thomas Aquinas, which became the standard of orthodoxy.

2.3. Aristotelianism

The Council of Trent was less concerned with the philosophical aspect than the Council of Constance had been, but the mental horizon and cultural background of the bishops and theologians of Trent was decidedly Aristotelian. As an example I may cite the preparation at Bologna of the canon which at Trent would become canon 1 of Session 13, the canon which defines that after the consecration the substance of the bread and the wine are changed respectively into the substance of the Body and of the Blood of Christ, while the appearances (*species*)

[43] See E. Gutwenger, "Substanz und Akzident in der Eucharistielehre," *ZKT* 83 (1961) 257–306.

[44] He was therefore unable to accept the approach of Thomas Aquinas, who had altered the ontology of Aristotle.

[45] Aristotle's metaphysical system is unable to give an ontologically correct explanation of transubstantiation, which becomes contradictory.

[46] Wyclif strongly denied that an accident could exist without a subject: "The fruit of this madness whereby it is pretended that there can be an accident without a subject is to blaspheme against God, to scandalise the saints and to deceive the church by means of false doctrines about accidents" (Council of Constance, Session 15). Text and translation in *Decrees of the Ecumenical Councils* 1:422.

[47] "The consecrated host . . . is true bread naturally and Christ's body figuratively" (Article 1). The meaning of "figure" is to be seen in Article 4: "Just as John was Elias in a figurative sense and not in person, so the bread on the altar is Christ's body in a figurative sense. And the words, *This is my body,* are unambiguously figurative, just like the statement 'John is Elias.'" Text and translation in *Decrees of the Ecumenical Councils* 1:422.

remain unchanged. In Bologna, at the general meeting *(congregatio generalis)* on Wednesday, May 17, 1547, the bishop of Ascoli proposed that "the second canon should read 'accidents' instead of 'appearances.'"[48] The records of the meeting of the theologians *(congregatio praelatorum theologorum)* on Friday, May 17, 1547, report on the interventions on this subject: three in favor of "appearances," three in favor of "accidents," and two saying that "accident" is just as good as "appearance." Because of this balanced set of views "it was decided to keep 'under the appearances of bread and wine' in the second canon."[49] Because of this equivalence it can be concluded that in Trent's use of it, *species* is equal to *accidens,* even though "appearances" is not a philosophical term; thus the Tridentine interpretation of the Eucharist remained bound up with the scholastic interpretation.

Even though the bishops of Trent were aware of the difference between theology and philosophy, they were unable to think out the doctrine of the Eucharist except in the framework of Thomist Aristotelianism. Despite this, it cannot be claimed that the Council of Trent defined anything in regard to the philosophy to be used in interpreting the eucharistic celebration. All that we can conclude is that the Council of Trent found in Thomas's Aristotelianism a theological system capable of interpreting the eucharistic doctrine that had matured, and been formulated during, the controversies and discussions of the Middle Ages.

2.4 *The Connection with the Middle Ages*

If we take the three Tridentine decrees on the Eucharist and look at the subjects treated, we see that they are the same subjects typical of medieval treatises. The one exception is the theme of the Eucharist as a sign of unity, a theme characteristic of the patristic tradition and one that, as we saw, found its loftiest formulation in Augustine. In Trent, this theme is unfortunately introduced, not in the theological perspective of Augustine, but in a moral perspective.[50] The Council of Trent

---

[48] T. Freudenburger, *Concilii Tridentini Acta,* Pars III, Vol. 1: *Acta Concilii bononensia a Massarello conscripta* (Concilium Tridentinum. Nova collectio. Edidit Societas Goerresiana. Tomus VI, Actorum Pars III, Vol. 1; Freiburg i. B.: Herder, 1950) 157.

[49] Ibid., 161.

[50] See *Decree on the Most Holy Sacrament of the Eucharist,* chapter 8 (Session 13; 1551): The council exhorts "that each and all who are marked by the name of Christian should now, at long last, join together and agree in this sign of unity, this bond of love, this symbol of harmony" and be "mindful of the so great

deals with the theme of eating—sacramental or spiritual or sacramental and spiritual—but does not achieve the clarity of Bonaventure's language on eating the Sacrament as sacrament. In Trent, the word "sacrament" is sometimes synonymous with the "appearances," that is, it refers to what falls within the scope of the senses; it is in this sense that the sinner is said to eat only sacramentally, whereas eating "spiritually" refers to spiritual Communion, and eating "spiritually and sacramentally" refers to Communion received with the proper dispositions.[51]

The principal subject, the one that recurs most frequently, is the theme of the "true" Body. At times, indeed, the adjective "true" is intended only to assert the truth of a statement, but more often it acquires the technical medieval sense: "It has at all times been the belief in the church of God that immediately after the consecration the *true* Body of our Lord and his *true* Blood exist along with his soul and divinity under the form of bread and wine."[52] Again: "It is surely a most intolerable and shameful deed . . . to twist them [the words of institution] to false and imaginary meanings that deny the reality (*veritas*) of Christ's flesh and blood, against the universal understanding of the church."[53] In parallel with this assertion about the true Body there is a denial of a (purely) figural presence of the body of Christ: "If anyone . . . says that he [Christ] is present in it only as in a sign or figure or by his power: let him be anathema."[54]

In order to describe the relationship between the Eucharist and the sacrifice of Christ, the Council of Trent falls back on the term *repraesentatio*,[55] the same word that Thomas used, but it does not oppose

---

majesty and surpassing love of our Lord Jesus Christ." Text and translation in *Decrees of the Ecumenical Councils* 2:697. See also Session 13, chapter 2 (ibid., 693) and Session 13, Introduction (ibid., 693).

[51] *Decree on the Most Holy Sacrament of the Eucharist,* chapter 8: "They [our fathers] taught that some, being sinners, receive it [the Sacrament] only sacramentally; others receive only spiritually, namely those who have the desire to eat the heavenly food that is set before them, and so experience its effect and benefit *by a lively faith working through love;* the third group, who receive both sacramentally and spiritually. . . ." Text and translation in *Decrees of the Ecumenical Councils,* 696.

[52] Ibid., chapter 5 (p. 695); italics added.

[53] Ibid., chapter 1 (p. 694).

[54] Ibid., canon 1 (p. 687).

[55] *Teaching and Canons on the Most Holy Sacrifice of the Mass* (Session 22; 1562), chapter 1: "In order to leave to his beloved spouse the church a visible sacrifice (as human nature requires), by which that bloody sacrifice carried out on the

repraesentatio to *veritas.*[56] But despite this difference, the thinking of Trent is completely reducible to that of Thomas. For both the sacramental presence and the sacrificial nature of the Eucharist the Council of Trent makes its own the solutions developed by Thomas Aquinas.

---

cross should be represented, its memory persist until the end of time, and its saving power be applied to the forgiveness of the sins which we daily commit; therefore, at the last supper on the night he was betrayed . . ." Text and translation in *Decrees of the Ecumenical Councils,* 733.

[56] Ibid., chapter 2 (p. 733): "In this divine sacrifice which is performed in the mass, the very same Christ is contained and offered in bloodless manner who made a bloody sacrifice of himself once for all on the cross. Hence the holy council teaches that this is a truly propitiatory sacrifice."

Chapter 15

The Liturgical Reform of Vatican Council II

One of the principal concerns of Vatican Council II was the liturgy and, within the latter, the Eucharist took first place. The council had little interest in constructing a doctrinal treatise and chose to operate on the pastoral level, its desire being that the faithful should participate actively, consciously, and devoutly in the eucharistic celebration and should no longer be "outsiders or silent onlookers."[1] No one thought that this was an unimportant undertaking, even if not everyone realized that it involved the entire pastoral activity of the Church. There was question, in fact, of moving the faithful from the preceding situation[2] to an entirely new one.

---

[1] Vatican II, Constitution on the Sacred Liturgy (*Sacrosanctum concilium*), no. 48. Text and translation in *Decrees of the Ecumenical Councils* 2:830. [References henceforth will be to *SC* with paragraph number and page number.]

[2] The preceding situation was characterized by a marked passivity: The Mass was considered to be an action of the priest at which the laity were present; it was celebrated in Latin, in a low voice, and with the priest's back to the people. The sacred silence was broken by some devotional songs or by the recitation of the rosary (during the Liturgy of the Word morning prayers were recited, and at the end of them the rosary was begun and continued throughout the Eucharistic Liturgy); the recitation of the rosary was interrupted during the consecration in order to allow the faithful, at the sound of the bell, to look at the host and chalice in silent adoration or while reciting some ejaculatory prayers. The spirituality of those present at Mass was strictly individual; each person withdrew and gave himself or herself to personal practices of piety, with great concentration and devotion. The possible use of a missalette to follow the ongoing rite did not greatly change the situation, although it represented very great progress in comparison with the recitation of the rosary or other prayers. Instead of participation, there was devotion to the Mass and it was common for devout persons to hear two Masses on Sundays and even on weekdays. People preferred that the two Masses followed one upon the other so that during the second Mass they could make a

In the older situation, pastoral practice had had two primary goals: first of all, to persuade the faithful to receive the Sacrament, and then to prepare them for its reception by means of appropriate devotional exercises of piety. Thus pastoral care stopped at the point where the celebration of the Sacrament began, the reason being that the Sacrament would produce its effects *ex opere operato* in the properly disposed faithful. In this theological approach, there was no room for active participation; a devout reception was enough.

The new situation was characterized by the connection between ecclesiology and liturgical celebration: There had come to maturity an awareness that the liturgical assembly was to be described as "Church" in the proper sense[3] and that this assembly was the "integral subject"[4] of the liturgical action.[5] This is why a devout reception is not enough and why active participation becomes necessary: because the assembly is a celebrant. The assembly is called together to hear the word, to pray, to sing of God's works, and to obey the command of Christ, who said at the Last Supper: "Do this in remembrance of me." For this to be possible, the faithful had to be able to understand the mystery of faith through the rites and the prayers.[6] Only in this way would they be able to participate actively, consciously, and devoutly.[7] To achieve results, a few adjustments to the

---

thanksgiving for the Communion received at the first. The latter, in consequence, served as a preparation for Communion. It is easy to see that Communion was thought of as a reality distinct from the Mass. The custom also grew up of not receiving Communion during Mass, but at the beginning or end of it, or even in a suitable rite independent of the eucharistic celebration. In some cathedrals or sanctuaries to which large crowds came, Communion was distributed every half-hour or quarter of an hour at the altar of the Most Blessed Sacrament, independently of and without being coordinated with the Eucharist being celebrated at the main altar.

[3] In keeping with what is already done in 1 Corinthians 11:17ff.

[4] It had to be made clear that the faithful should not remain apart from the eucharistic celebration, the rite of which was supposedly advancing through the action of the priest, independently of the action of the faithful, but that instead they should enter into the rites in a way that would show the entire celebration to be a communal action.

[5] On this entire subject see Y. Congar, "L'Ecclesia' ou communauté chrétienne, sujet intégral de l'action liturgique," in *La liturgie après Vatican II. Bilan, études, prospective* (Unam sanctam 66; Paris: Cerf, 1967) 241–82.

[6] See SC 48 (830).

[7] Not as the result of a doctrinal pre-understanding of the rite, but through the rites and prayers themselves.

rites would not be enough; a general reform of the liturgy would be needed. That is what Vatican Council II set out to accomplish.

1. TWO POINTS OF DOCTRINE

The council followed in the footsteps of Pius XI, who had planned a liturgical reform and had already begun it by reforming the rites of Holy Week and the Easter Vigil. The same persons who had worked on this undertaking of Pius XII were called upon to prepare the text of the Constitution on the Sacred Liturgy, known by its first two Latin words as *Sacrosanctum concilium*. To this base text were later added the *altiora principia*, that is, the general principles that would supply the theological framework needed if the individual reforms were to have a careful objective foundation and avoid the danger of being extempore decisions. The logic of building a reform on the basis of *altiora principia* resulted in the reforms of the eucharistic rite having a clear theological dimension and in their having to take eucharistic theology into account.

There were two points of special interest in this approach. (1) The true, real, and substantial *presence* of the Body of Christ was set in a broader context, inasmuch as it was related to other modes of Christ's presence in the eucharistic celebration, namely, his presence in the assembly and in the person of the minister. In this way, the entire celebration was interpreted by means of the category of the *Real Presence* of Christ in the various visible aspects of the celebration; and Christ's presence under the appearances of bread and wine was said to be *real*, not by exclusion, but by its superiority over the other two modes of presence just mentioned.

(2) The connection between the eucharistic celebration and the sacrifice of Christ on the cross was described by means of the category of *repraesentatio*, which was understood no longer in a purely figural sense but in an ontological sense; in understanding this ontological sense recourse was had to the particular theology developed by Odo Casel between the two World Wars,[8] the "theology of the mysteries," as it was known, in which *repraesentatio* is rooted in the sacramental *presence*.[9]

---

[8] The primary organized exposition of this doctrine is in O. Casel, *The Mystery of Christian Worship and Other Writings*, ed. B. Neunheuser (Westminster, Md., 1962).

[9] In the liturgical celebrations of the mystery religions the rite represented an event in the life of the divinity, and that event was made present anew by means of the representational liturgical action.

Repraesentatio is the term used to name the eucharistic celebration insofar as it is the Sacrament of the Cross of Christ, but it is never used to describe the Body and Blood of Christ. In order to signify the sacramentality of the bread and wine the classical term is *presence*, and this is now regarded as the technical term par excellence, despite the fact that it lends itself to too many meanings and interpretations and is therefore fundamentally ambiguous. Precisely for this reason, when an effort is made to bring out the fact that *repraesentatio* signifies sacramentality, it is located in the category of *presence* and translated not as *representation* but as *re-presentation*. In the same way, the idea of the Eucharist as *memorial* of the saving event is reduced to the category of presence: To remember is identical with to make present;[10] in fact, remembering even makes present.[11]

The success of Casel's doctrine and of the procedure by which *memoria* and *repraesentatio* are reduced to the category of *presence* makes it evident that the time is not yet ripe for understanding the figural, typological conception of the Eucharist maintained in the early patristic period and in some passages of the New Testament, especially in Paul and John.

2. A CHANGE OF MENTALITY

We saw earlier, in speaking of the Council of Trent, that the prevalent attitude was one of defensiveness, because the usages, especially the liturgical usages, of the Church of that period needed to be safeguarded. The necessity of such a defense made the Council of Trent suspicious of everything that was not part of the Church's way at that time, even though it might have been part of it during the patristic period, to which, however, Trent consistently looked for a legitimation of the present. The Church grasped the very great importance of dialogue with the patristic age, but this dialogue was difficult because the Church of the Tridentine period did not possess the key for reading the Fathers, and it did not know how to interpret the Fathers so as to make them relevant to that particular historical conjuncture and to integrate their teaching into it.

[10] At Vatican II, therefore, the term no longer had the meaning it had had in Thomas Aquinas and at the Council of Trent.

[11] The patristic basis of Casel's doctrine is open to criticism, as I have shown in "La portata teologica del termine 'mistero,'" *Rivista liturgica* 74 (1987) 321–38, and especially in "Tempo, memoria, liturgia. Alcuni dati di epoca patristica," ibid., 77 (1990) 414–34.

In the Roman Church down to Vatican II, the problem of its relationship to the early Church was not much different from the description just given of it. At Vatican II, however, two new and very important factors made their appearance and provided the basis for the reform that followed. There was an awareness, first of all, of what a rich store of documentation was available on the early Church; secondly, there was an awareness of the change of mentality that had occurred since the time of Trent: The felt need of defense was replaced by an attitude of great confidence. The results achieved by the biblical movement, patristic and historical studies, and the liturgical movement justified this new outlook. Research into Christian origins had provided and made attractive a great mass of information that could enrich the life and spirituality of the Church; there was therefore no longer any reason to adopt an attitude of suspicion.[12]

This new attitude found expression in a return to the sources and in a recovery of the original structure and meaning of the rites, on the basis of what the Church's tradition has handed on to us. Here is what the council decided in this area: "Duplications which have come in over the course of time should be discontinued, as should the less useful accretions. Some elements which have degenerated or disappeared through the ill effects of the passage of time are to be restored to the ancient pattern of the fathers, insofar as it seems appropriate or necessary."[13] This principle implicitly says that the historical development of the liturgy and therefore also of the Eucharist has not necessarily been a positive development to something better; instead of an evolution there may be have been a devolution, and then a reform is

---

[12] There had been a quite different attitude only a decade earlier. Citing a page of his diary, Henri de Lubac reports that when he, together with Jean Daniélou, wanted to start the collection of patristic sources known as "Sources chrétiennes," he had to overcome some obstacles in his own surroundings because there were some who thought that "the holy Fathers might foster a 'false spirituality.' . . . Once it is clear that the Spiritual Exercises are completely orthodox and traditional, they can only be in harmony with the teaching of the gospel and the holy Fathers. But there is no way in which this teaching of the gospel and the holy Fathers should have to *be made to agree* with the Spiritual Exercises. The very idea of such an effort would imply the hypothesis of a possible disagreement, which orthodoxy rejects." See de Lubac's "Souvenirs (1940–1945)," in *Alexandrina. Hellenisme, judaïsme et christianisme à Alexandrie. Mélanges offerts au P. Claude Mondésert* (Patrimoines; Paris: Cerf, 1987) 13.

[13] SC 50 (831).

required that will restore things according to the ancient patristic standard.[14]

3. SOME DECISIONS OF GREATER MOMENT

The council issued a series of minor and major provisions, all of which had a notable importance and influence on the success of the liturgical reform. The kiss of peace among the faithful was revived, and the universal prayer or prayer of the faithful[15] was restored: Both of these were minor elements in the overall framework of the eucharistic celebration, but they had and continue to play an important role. Another minor element was the removal of the altar from its position against the wall in order to restore its appearance as a table; as a result, the table of the celebration became once again the most important furnishing and ceased to be simply the shelf behind the altar on which candlesticks, vases of flowers, tabernacle, crucifix, and relics were placed.

These minor changes had a major influence on the celebration, since they played a decisive role at the level of the participation of the faithful.[16]

A very important decision was to restore eucharistic concelebration,[17] a rite which though not directly connected with the active

[14] A reasoned judgment had to be made on changes that had taken place in the past, so as to assess their greater or lesser accord with the nature of the rite and with the *altiora principia*. Then, and only then, could reforms be made "insofar as seems appropriate or necessary."

[15] See J.-B. Molin, "La restauration de la prière universelle," in *Liturgia opera divina e umana, Studi sulla riforma liturgica offerti a S. E. Mons. Annibale Bugnini in occasione del suo 70 compleanno*, ed. P. Jounel, R. Kaczynski, and G. Pasqualetti (Bibliotheca Ephemerides Liturgicae. Subsidia 26; Rome: CLV–Edizioni liturgiche, 1982) 291–306. For the historical data see P. De Clerck, *La "Prière universelle" dans les liturgies latines anciennes. Témoignages patristiques et textes liturgiques* (LQF 62; Münster: Aschendorff, 1977); idem, *"Lex orandi, lex credendi.* Sens originel et avatars historiques d'un adage équivoque," *Questions liturgiques* 59 (1978) 193–212.

[16] For this reason it can be said that paradoxically it was the minor provisions that made the liturgical reform of Vatican II more credible.

[17] See A. Franquesa, "La concelebración a los 16 años de su restauración," in *Liturgia opera divina e umana* (note 15, above), 291–306. E. Mazza, *The Eucharistic Prayers of the Roman Rite*, trans. M. J. O'Connell (New York: Pueblo, 1986) chapter 1, "Excursus: Concelebration and the Anaphora" (29–35). See also S. Madeja, "Analisi del concetto di concelebrazione eucaristica nel concilio Vaticano II e nella riforma liturgica postconciliare," *EL* 96 (1982) 3–56; P.J.F. Baldovin, "Concelebration: A Problem of Symbolic Roles in the Church," *Worship* 59 (1985) 32–47; L. Prat, "La

participation of the faithful,[18] helped to make them aware that the eucharistic celebration is not a private activity proper to the priest, but an action of the entire, hierarchically ordered Church, which is the integral or complete subject of the eucharistic celebration.[19]

In the Church of the early centuries concelebration was the usual way of celebrating; a trace of that practice remains in the Byzantine liturgy, which does not distinguish between celebration and concelebration but calls them both *synaxis* (literally, "gathering" or "assembly" for public worship). The historical development of the Roman liturgy saw concelebration fall into disuse and survive only in the rite of ordinations; it is difficult to determine the explanation for this eclipse, because there was surely a whole series of contributing causes, the influence of which is difficult to assess, even if the determining factor was the development of the theology of priestly ministry.

Concelebration takes place when, with a single priest presiding, who should ideally be the bishop, other priests form a circle around him at the altar and with him proclaim some parts of the anaphora, according to a preestablished plan.[20] The sections which the concelebrants recite together with the principal celebrant, or presider at the eucharistic celebration, are recited chorally,[21] although there should be nothing choral about the concelebration, in the sense that the presider is always a single priest.[22]

---

concelebración," *Phase* 25 (1985) 251–53; P. Tirot, "La concélébration et la tradition de l'Eglise," *EL* 101 (1987) 33–59.

[18] So much so that concelebration is prohibited in Masses with children, that is, with Masses that most fully convey the pastoral role of the liturgy.

[19] "Concelebration, which is a good way *(opportune)* of demonstrating the unity of the priesthood, has remained within the church, both east and west, until now" (SC 57.1; p. 842).

[20] According to present norms, the presiding priest says the Preface, then all join in reciting the first epiclesis, the account of institution, and the anamnesis with the offering and epiclesis; the recitation of the intercessions is assigned to two of the concelebrants. After the doxology the people respond with "Amen."

[21] The word "chorally" describes what is actually being done, but not the norm, since the Missal says that the concelebrants are to recite the passages of the Eucharistic Prayer "in a softer voice" *(submissa voce)*, so that "the principal celebrant's voice stands out clearly. In this way the congregation should be able to hear the text without difficulty" *(General Instruction of the Roman Missal,* 170). [The *General Instruction* can be found in the Sacramentary or in *Documents on the Liturgy 1963–1979. Conciliar, Papal, and Curial Texts,* ed. International Commission on English in the Liturgy (Collegeville: The Liturgical Press, 1982) document 206, pp. 465–533.]

[22] The confusion between concelebration and co-presidency is one of the most widespread errors in this area. There is never a co-presidency; in fact, the

Concelebration has always been practiced in the Church, but the same cannot be said of the present rite, which cannot claim an equally constant attestation in the tradition. The reason is that the present rite, with the communal recitation of some parts of the Canon, had its origin in *Ordo romanus* III,[23] which in turn complemented *Ordo romanus* I.[24]

The "communal" recitation of the Canon presupposes that the text of the Canon is already fixed and that its redaction has been fully stabilized. This already gives us a chronological indication, of at least a general kind, since there could be no communal recitation in the time when the presider was still free to improvise during the Eucharistic Prayer. The earliest instance of concelebration is the one described in the *Apostolic Tradition,* a work that is attributed to Hippolytus and would therefore have been composed at the beginning of the third century. The bishop, who has just been ordained, receives the gifts of bread and wine from the deacons and then begins his improvised Eucharistic Prayer. The bishop alone says the anaphora, but the entire presbyterate takes part, since all, standing in silence, extend their hands over the gifts when the bishop does.[25] This is a silent concelebration in which the only sign that the presbyters are concelebrating is their extended hands. This is the basis of the (optional) gesture of the presbyters during the recitation of the Lord's words; it is therefore a gesture indicating participation, and not an epicletic gesture, as an exaggerated theological conception of the epiclesis would have it.[26] In fact, it is not even a pointing gesture, since it is in any case not possible to state its function when it is thus interpreted.[27]

---

concelebrants, just like all the faithful participating, have a presider over them, the priest who takes the part of principal concelebrant.

[23] *Les Ordines romani du haut moyen âge* II, ed. M. Andrieu (SSL 23; Louvain, 1960) 131.

[24] *Ordo romanus* I is from the first half of the eighth century; *Ordo romanus* III was a supplement for certain occasions, and therefore the dating is rather elastic. *Ordo* III in its entirety was completed before the end of the eighth century; the first part, which contains the rubrics for concelebration, can therefore be regarded as contemporaneous with *Ordo* I (ibid., 127 and 51).

[25] Hippolytus, *Traditio apostolica,* cap. 4; text in *La Tradition apostolique de saint Hippolyte. Essai de reconstitution,* ed. B. Botte (LQF 39; Münster: Aschendorff, 1963) 11.

[26] Historically, the epiclesis has always been a text containing a special reference to the proclamation of the divine names; it may be accompanied by special gestures, but it is the text that is described as epicletic.

[27] It is in fact impossible to determine either what is being pointed to or whether anything at all is being pointed to: The account of institution is addressed to God

The practice of silent concelebration is still attested in the first part of the eighth century in *Ordo romanus* I. This describes a solemn concelebration of the cardinals with the pope four times a year; the concelebrants do not join their voices to that of the pope and they do not pronounce any words of the Canon. They do not even extend their hands, as in the *Apostolic Tradition* of Hippolytus; their participation is expressed by the fact that they hold in their hands the offerings on the corporal.[28]

A change occurs a few years later in *Ordo romanus* III: The cardinals now recite the Canon along with the pope.[29] It must be noted, however, that the change occurs without any particular significance being assigned to it. The rubric neither emphasizes nor explains the change, but simply records it.

From this information it can be concluded that there is no difference between silent concelebration and concelebration with the joint recitation of some parts of the anaphora. In 1965, A. Franquesa himself, the secretary of the commission that composed the ritual of concelebration, had some stern words to say about this rite, on the basis of the historical data.[30] I think that his assessment is still valid, especially since it is the only rite that can win the agreement of the eucharistic theology which holds the field today.[31]

---

the Father, to whom the entire anaphora is addressed. I think that the disagreement among theologians of the liturgy as to whether the gesture is epicletic or one of pointing must finally end with the recognition that it is neither the one nor the other.

[28] There are two recensions of this *Ordo*. Ms. Sangallense 614 is the only one that gives the short or early recension; it says: "When they have finished, the pontiff arises alone for the Canon *(surgit pontifex solus in canone)*." The long recension is identical, except for the addition of *et intrat:* "The pontiff arises alone and enters into the Canon" *(Les Ordines romani* 2, no. 88, p. 95).

[29] Ibid., no. 1 (p. 131).

[30] See A. Franquesa, "La concelebrazione nelle communità sacerdotali," in *Concelebrazione. Dottrina e pastorale* (Brescia: Queriniana, 1965) 187: "As I said, this rite, without being either the earliest or the most authentic, has a venerable tradition behind it in the Roman liturgy; it is coherent with the present theology of the liturgy and does not at all stand in the way of possible future adaptations, if the authority of the Church comes some day to think that such adaptations will fit better with a more communal and more hierarchical vision of the Eucharist."

[31] For the sake of completeness I ought to mention a distinction classical among the theologians. Concelebration may be either sacramental or ceremonial. In the former, all the priests pronounce the words of consecration, in the second they stand in silence. It is a clever distinction that drew its force from theological

The difference between the Oriental conception of concelebration and the Latin has been well described by Dom Lanne: "Among the Orientals the ecclesiological significance of the rite has always been to the fore, whereas among the Latins concelebration seemed to have become associated, as the centuries passed, chiefly with the ordination of a new priest."[32] Another great difference may be noted: Among the Orientals concelebration expresses the hierarchical structure of the Church, its "vertical" unity,[33] and the bishop is therefore the presider, whereas among the Westerners it expresses more the sharing of the one priesthood by all the concelebrants,[34] with the result that the presidency at the concelebration is assigned to any priest whatsoever, independently of his function in the Church.[35]

In the liturgical tradition the eucharistic celebration is a celebration of the entire Church, from which it follows that concelebration "is above all a manifestation of the local Church."[36] And again: "Concelebration looks beyond the unity of the priesthood and manifests in a special way the unity of the Church, the hierarchical unity of the people of God, who are also the body of Christ."[37]

In concluding, it is worth citing this important observation of R. Taft: "Presbyterate is a common ministry whose purpose is service, not a personal privilege entailing individual prerogatives and designed to satisfy personal devotional needs."[38] If, therefore, concelebration is to

---

developments before the council, but it has no support in tradition, as Dom Botte says: "A purely ceremonial concelebration that has no sacramental value is a myth from which we must free ourselves. It has no support in tradition"; see his article, "Note historique sur la concélébration dans l'Eglise ancienne," *MD*, no. 35 (1953) 21.

[32] E. Lanne, "La concelebrazione nella tradizione delle Chiese orientiali," in *Concelebrazione* (note 30, above), 18.

[33] Ibid., 21.

[34] In Latin theology the eucharistic celebration is seen in close connection with the "power to consecrate"; concelebration therefore shows chiefly the unity of the priesthood which the ministers express by their single consecration.

[35] In religious communities of priests we even find the presidential role being taken by turn.

[36] Lanne (note 32, above), 20.

[37] Ibid.

[38] R. Taft, "Praise in the Desert: The Coptic Monastic Office Yesterday and Today," *Worship* 56 (1982) 536. See also idem, *"Ex oriente lux?* Some Reflections in Eucharistic Celebration," *Worship* 54 (1980) 308–25; and "The Frequency of the Eucharist throughout History," in *Can We Always Celebrate the Eucharist?* ed. M. Collins and D. Power (Concilium, 1982, no. 152, 13–24).

manifest the unity of the priesthood and the sacrifice, as well as the unity of the entire people of God,[39] the historical data compel us to say that concelebration is not a synchronized collective celebration of as many Masses as there are celebrants, but the celebration of a single Mass, said in unity by all the concelebrants under a single presider.

[39] *General Instruction of the Roman Missal*, 153.

Chapter 16

The Implementation of the Liturgical Reform

1. THE REFORM OF THE ORDER OF MASS[1]

The new Order of Mass[2] was promulgated in 1969, along with the important *General Instruction*. This latter document is both doctrinal and pastoral, for its purpose is to describe all the elements needed for a correct celebration, while it also successfully enriches the norms for celebration (the rubrics) with the relevant theological explanations.[3] The first typical edition of the Roman Missal was published in 1972.[4]

---

[1] See C. Braga, "Punti qualificanti della *Institutio generalis Missalis Romani*," in *Liturgia opera divina e umana. Studi sulla riforma liturgica offerti a S. E. Mons. Annibale Bignini in occasione dell suo 70 compleanno*, ed. P. Jounel and others (Bibliotheca Ephemerides Liturgicae. Subsidia 26; Rome: CLV–Edizioni liturgiche, 1982) 243–61. The documents and preparatory schemas on the reform of the Order of Mass have been published by E. Mazza, *Le odierne preghiere eucaristiche* 2. *Testi e documenti editi e inediti* (Liturgia e vita 2; Bologna: Edizioni Dehoniane, 1984; 2nd ed., 1991). [This second volume was not translated into English, as the first was.—Tr.]

[2] Continuity with the Tridentine reform was ensured through dialogue with the preceding reform of the Missal (*Missal* of Pius V, 1570). From the latter there was taken over, as a heritage, the intention of returning to the ancient patristic norm: "In setting forth its decrees for the revision of the Order of Mass, Vatican Council II directed, among other things, that some rites be restored 'to the vigor they had in the tradition of the Fathers'; this is a quotation from the Apostolic Constitution *Quo primum* of 1570, by which St. Pius V promulgated the Tridentine Missal" (*General Instruction of the Roman Missal*, "Introduction," 6. Translated in *Documents on the Liturgy 1963–1979. Conciliar, Papal, and Curial Texts*, ed. International Commission on the Liturgy in English [Collegeville: The Liturgical Press, 1982] no. 1381, p. 467).

[3] It thus supersedes the Amalarian method of allegorical explanation, for which there had previously been no alternative.

[4] The second edition was promulgated in 1975.

Among the various models for celebration is Mass with a congregation, and this is the basic model, the point of reference for all the others.[5]

1.1. The Structure of the Order of Mass[6]

The rite of Mass is divided into several parts: entrance rites, Liturgy of the Word, Liturgy of the Eucharist, and conclusion. The entrance rites begin with the opening song, which is sung by the entire congregation and serves to unite the assembly in a single action in which they are of one heart and one soul. This song is followed by the greeting of the celebrant who in this way begins his dialogue with the assembly over which he is presiding.

The penitential act arose in the Middle Ages and is monastic and devotional in origin; before the reform of Paul VI it was an action of the priest and ministers alone, but after the reform, by an express decision of Paul VI, it has become a rite of the entire gathered assembly. In this act God is asked to forgive the sins of all, and the priest asks God to accept this prayer and grant forgiveness. Immediately after the introduction of this act there was a great deal of debate about whether the absolution given by the priest is or is not a sacramental absolution; the reply was always negative: This rite is not to be confused with the sacrament of penance.[7] After the penitential act the *Gloria* is sung; originally a Christmas hymn, it is now used also on feasts and Sundays, except in Advent and Lent. The entrance rites end[8] with the collect, a prayer that should convey the meaning and circumstances of this particular liturgical gathering of people who

[5] Other "kinds" of Mass, such as Mass without a congregation or Mass for particular groups or Mass with children, were to be prepared as adaptations of the basic model, Mass with a participating congregation.

[6] See R. Cabié, *The Eucharist*, trans. M. J. O'Connell (Collegeville: The Liturgical Press, 1986). This is volume 2 of *The Church at Prayer*, ed. A.-G. Martimort.

[7] Since the absolution is not sacramental, this rite has come to be undervalued to some extent. We must realize, however, that it is still a liturgical rite: If a person is truly contrite and converted in God's sight, and if the entire hierarchically organized assembly asks God to forgive, it is not possible to think and act as if nothing has happened.

[8] The entrance rites are, objectively, too long in relation to the other parts of the celebration. For this reason it was decided that in alternative formularies of the penitential act the *Kyrie eleison* should be changed so that there would not be three introductory songs in a row (entrance song; Lord, have mercy; and *Gloria*). For the same reason, the penitential act may be omitted in Masses with children.

have come together to obey Christ's command: "Do this in remembrance of me."

The Liturgy of the Word consists of readings, two on weekdays and three on Sundays, the last of them being taken from the Gospels. The readings are separated by a psalm, understood as a responsory song, and the gospel is preceded by the singing of the Allelujah,[9] which is repeated after the proclamation or singing of a biblical verse. The readings are followed by a homily.[10]

In the homily the role of the priest is that of a prophet who proclaims the word of God to the people. This understanding was characteristic of early Christianity, which saw in the bishop one who spoke by divine inspiration.[11] The homily may not, therefore, be simply a moral exhortation or a more or less detailed exegesis of the biblical text. The homily reflects a twofold fidelity: to God and to his people, a fidelity expressed in the bishop's own faithfulness to the biblical text. In fact, it is by using typology that the bishop applies to the Church the readings that have been proclaimed, and this is how the biblical text, or letter, becomes a living word. The homily is one of the moments is which the bishop fulfills his role as *Typus Christi*.

Where the *type* is fulfilled, *truth* is born, and this is why the missal, and the tradition that inspired the missal, says that in the liturgy Christ speaks to his people.[12] The final rite of the Liturgy of the Word is the universal prayer or Prayer of the Faithful,[13] in which the assembly prays to the Father for the needs of the Church, the civil community, and the entire world.

Because of the typological character of the liturgy of the word we can conclude that this liturgy, too, belongs in the sphere of the sacramental.

---

[9] When it cannot be sung, it may be omitted.

[10] This discourse, like all the liturgical texts, derives its norms from tradition (which in turn produced the norms in the Missal) and should have a precise and well-defined structure and function. By this I mean that the homily is not an extempore liturgical text, but a composition that follows a model.

[11] The best documented work on the various kinds of homily and the various homiletical methods is A. Olivar, *La predicación cristiana antiqua* (Biblioteca Herder. Sección de teología e filosofía 189; Barcelona–New York: Herder, 1991).

[12] See the Constitution *Sacrosanctum concilium* on the Sacred Liturgy 7 (*Documents,* no. 7).

[13] The term "faithful" refers to the baptized and is therefore to be understood in opposition not to the clergy but to the unbaptized.

The Eucharistic Liturgy begins with the preparation of the gifts.[14] The priest accompanies the placing of the bread and wine on the altar, that is, before God, with two prayers drawn from the *Didache* and slightly adapted.[15] There is nothing "offertorial" about this action;[16] nonetheless, the name "offertory" continues to be given to the song accompanying the procession of the gifts which the faithful are offering and which are being brought to the altar.[17] The term "offering," then, is to be understood of the action of the faithful who have contributed the gifts, and not of the action of the priest as he arranges the bread and wine on the altar. The preparation of the gifts concludes with the prayer over the offerings, which usually has a sacrificial theme in order to emphasize the fact that the bread and wine offered by the faithful are becoming the sacrifice of the Church, the Body of Christ.

The preparation of the gifts is followed by the Eucharistic Prayer with its introductory dialogue that helps to put the assembly in the proper interior attitude. For the Eucharistic Prayers, see section 2, below. At this point I want only to stress the point that the reform of the Order of Mass introduced an important novelty into the Roman Eucharist, namely, the acclamation of the faithful at the anamnesis. After repeating the command of Christ: "Do this in remembrance of me," the priest proclaims: "The mystery of faith!" The faithful reply: "Christ has died, Christ is risen, Christ will come again." It is odd that the memorial acclamation is addressed to the Son, whereas the anaphora in its entirety is addressed to the Father.[18]

[14] For a good explanation of this part of the Mass see N. K. Rasmussen, "Les rites de la préparation du pain et du vin," *MD*, no. 100 (1969) 44–58.

[15] These prayers may be said in silence or aloud; if they are said aloud, a response of the faithful is provided.

[16] Before the reform of Paul VI this part of the liturgy was called the "offertory," but now every element suggesting an offering has been eliminated and therefore the name of the rite has also been changed. It was decided that the theme of offering should be peculiar to the anaphora, in which, after the anamnesis, "the bread of life and the cup of eternal salvation" are offered. For the history of the offertorial character of what is now the "preparation of the gifts" see J.-B. Molin, "Depuis quand le mot offertoire sert-il à désigner une partie de la messe?" *EL* 77 (1963) 357–80.

[17] It was the faithful, and not someone representing them, who used to bring the bread and wine to the altar, along with other offerings from nature, to the accompaniment of singing by the entire assembly.

[18] Motives of a devotional kind may have been behind this decision.

After the trinitarian doxology at the end of the anaphora come the Communion rites. The first of these is the Our Father, which is sung by the entire congregation; in this setting the prayer has a penitential character due to the embolism ("Deliver us, O Lord") which develops the words "but deliver us from evil." The doxology from the *Didache* has been added to the end of the embolism: "For the kingdom, the power, and the glory are yours, now and for ever." Finally, preceded by a prayer asking the Lord for the gift of peace ("Lord Jesus Christ"), there is an invitation to the faithful to exchange the kiss of peace. The liturgical use of the kiss of peace has been traced back to Paul who in his letters tells the faithful to greet one another with a holy kiss.[19] Since the letters were read publicly to the faithful in their liturgical gatherings it is permissible to suppose that at the end of the reading, when the exhortation to greet one another with a kiss appeared, the faithful followed Paul's invitation. That is how the kiss of peace became the concluding rite of the Liturgy of the Word.

In our day the kiss of peace has a different location and has become a penitential rite preparatory to Communion. For this reason, it has been linked to the sacrificial character of the Eucharist and therefore with the command of Christ: "So when you are offering your gift at the altar, if you remember that your brother or sister has something against you, leave your gift there before the altar and go; first be reconciled to your brother or sister, and then come and offer your gift."[20]

This penitential preparation is followed by the rite of the breaking of the bread, which is accompanied by its own song ("Lamb of God"): The breaking is a functional action required in order to distribute the eucharistic bread to the faithful, and it is a symbolic action because it goes back to what Jesus did at the Last Supper. The correspondence is not simply external. Since the action of breaking is one of the gestures constitutive of the imitation of Jesus' supper, it follows that it actualizes, typologically, the gesture of Jesus in the upper room. It may therefore be said that at this moment it is Christ himself who breaks the bread for his Church.

[19] For example: "Greet all the brothers and sisters with a holy kiss. I solemnly command you by the Lord that this letter be read to all of them. The grace of our Lord Jesus Christ be with you" (1 Thess 5:26-28).

[20] Matthew 5:23-24. The exchange of peace at the end of the prayer of the faithful has a different meaning: In this case it seals the prayer and does not have a penitential function.

The distribution of Communion is accompanied by a song, the Communion song, which is usually a psalm or a hymn of praise and thanksgiving to God for the deeds he has done in history. The rite of Communion consists of giving the bread, with the accompanying formula, "The body of Christ."[21] In keeping with tradition the believer replies, "Amen," and takes the eucharistic bread.[22] The minister does the same with the cup, using the words "The blood of Christ,"[23] to which the believer answers "Amen." The importance of the action of giving and receiving Communion must be emphasized: It is a gesture corresponding to that of Jesus at the Last Supper and is therefore the typological actualization of the latter.[24] After Communion there may follow a moment of silence, unless it has been preferred to have this before Communion.[25]

At the end of the Communion rites the priest summons the faithful to prayer and, after a moment of silence, recites the Postcommunion prayer. This is a very important text, which, unfortunately, has become greatly impoverished in the Western liturgy as compared with the ancient formulas attested in the Eastern liturgies. Today the Roman texts are very restrained and have two basic elements: a reference to the eucharistic action just completed and a petition for blessing and grace for life after the liturgy and even a request for everlasting life.

The Eucharistic Liturgy ends with a final greeting of the celebrant, a blessing of the people, and the formula of dismissal, which is pronounced by the deacon. To the accompaniment of song the gathering breaks up and the faithful leave the place of celebration.

---

[21] The faithful may receive Communion either in the hand or in the mouth.

[22] Communion may be received in the hand or directly in the mouth; it is for the individual believer, by his or her approach, to determine the manner.

[23] The *General Instruction* suggests that the faithful receive under both species whenever the law allows. Access of the laity to the cup was restored by *Sacrosanctum concilium* 55 for a few specific cases. In successive phases the cases were increased until the permission became very broad. This broadening of the norm has not been matched by a corresponding broadening of practice.

[24] The tradition does not allow Communion to be left on the altar and the individual believer to take it independently; there must be the action of giving and receiving.

[25] This time of silence is not to be confused with the devotional practice of thanksgiving after the Communion. The latter had an extraliturgical origin.

2. THE REFORM OF THE EUCHARISTIC PRAYER

Nothing is said in the Constitution on the Sacred Liturgy about new Eucharistic Prayers, and such a possibility was never even mentioned during the discussion of this document at Vatican II. The Roman Church had known but a single Eucharistic Prayer, the Roman Canon, a text which had received its definitive formulation between the end of the fourth century and the seventh century and which had undergone no significant changes since the time of Pope Gregory the Great (d. 604).

The problem of the Eucharistic Prayer did arise during the work of Vatican Council II. The publication of valuable studies made known the treasures in the ancient anaphoras, especially the Eastern anaphoras, and showed that even the central part of the Mass, that is, the Eucharistic Prayer, could be a time of great participation. As a result, the practice grew, especially in the Low Countries, of freely composing anaphoras and improvising texts;[26] unfortunately, not all the texts were of high quality.[27]

In order to meet this need of the Church and, at the same time, to ensure the Church's control of the eucharistic anaphora, Pope Paul VI decided to authorize the *Consilium ad exsequendam constitutionem de sacra liturgia* (Commission for Implementing the Constitution on the Sacred Liturgy) to prepare two or three new Eucharistic Prayers: "The present anaphora is to be left unchanged; two or three anaphoras for use at particular specified times are to be composed or looked for."[28] The result was the preparation of three new texts that took their place alongside the Roman Canon. Let us look in turn at each of the Eucharistic Prayers in the Missal of Paul VI.

2.1. The Roman Canon[29]

This text was left unchanged, as befitted a monument of the liturgical tradition, apart from a few minor alterations such as the shortening

---

[26] In comparison, the Roman Canon was a loser, being remote in time and therefore not useful for prayer by reason of its themes and language and its length and structure. The text of the Canon was seen as an obstacle to the active participation that had become the goal of the reform.

[27] Above all, they did not follow the traditional models of the various liturgical families; sometimes they indulged in devotional themes, at other times they did not lack expressive references to the political world.

[28] Cited in A. Bugnini, *The Reform of the Liturgy 1948–1975*, trans. M. J. O'Connell (Collegeville: The Liturgical Press, 1990) 450.

[29] For a commentary on the Roman Canon see B. Botte, *Le canon de la messe romaine. Edition critique* (Textes et études liturgiques 2; Louvain, 1935); B. Botte and

of the lists of saints and the elimination of the clausulas "Through Christ our Lord. Amen" at the end of the various units making up the Canon.[30] We need only recall here that this text lacks a thanksgiving of its own; the preface is variable, and whereas there were only ten prefaces in the Gregorian Sacramentary, there are over a hundred in the second edition of the Missal of Paul VI. Also to be emphasized here is that the Roman Canon in its entirety is a lengthy intercession, based entirely on the theme of offering and sacrifice.[31]

Within this intercession the account of the Last Supper has been inserted; it stands out there like a rite within a rite and focuses all the attention of the faithful on itself. Immediately after the anamnesis and the offering of the bread and wine comes a prayer in which God is asked to accept and be pleased with the sacrifice, as he was pleased with the sacrifices of Abel, Abraham, and Melchizedek.[32] An angel[33] will carry the Church's offering to the heavenly altar and God the Father, and he in turn will send down the gift of his blessing. We do not know how to describe this blessing, which can be given numerous interpretations. In my opinion, it is better to let the word remain

---

Chr. Mohrmann, *L'ordinaire de la messe* (Etudes liturgiques 2; Paris–Louvain, 1953); J. A. Jungmann, *The Mass of the Roman Rite: Its Origins and Development (Missarum Sollemnia)*, trans. F. A. Brunner (2 vols.; New York: Benziger, 1951 and 1955); M. Righetti, *Manuale di storia liturgica 3. La messa* (Milan: Ancora, 1966); E. Mazza, *The Eucharistic Prayers of the Roman Rite*, trans. M. J. O'Connell (New York: Pueblo, 1986) chapter 3.

[30] These clausulas were introduced in the Middle Ages.

[31] It is difficult to use this Eucharistic Prayer precisely because it is simply a lengthy plea, or intercession, for the offering of the sacrifice. This does not mean that the Roman Canon is not to be used any longer in the liturgical celebration; it means only that we must keep in mind that a Eucharistic Prayer needs to be prayed, and therefore that we must decide whether a particular eucharistic assembly is capable of expressing its own prayer by means of the Roman Canon.

[32] The worship which these three individuals offered to God is the model, the *typus*, of the worship being offered in the Church's eucharistic action.

[33] There is nothing to suggest that this angel is Christ. The introduction of an angel is to be explained in light of the Jewish sources from which the text derives, and not on the basis of the theology of eucharistic realism with which people try to explain the eucharistic rite in its entirety. The angel, therefore, is simply a heavenly angel whose role is to ensure the connection between the heavenly liturgy and the earthly liturgy. The role of the angel who offers the prayers to God in the Qumran liturgy is well documented: see C. Newsom, *Songs of the Sabbath Sacrifice* (Harvard Semitic Studies 27; Atlanta: Scholars Press, 1985), and D. C. Allison, Jr., "The Silence of Angels: Reflections on the Songs of the Sabbath Sacrifice," *Revue de Qumrân* 13 (1988) (= *Mémorial Jean Carmignac*) 189–97.

general and polyvalent; we may also think that "blessing" refers to the Holy Spirit.[34]

Both the account of institution and the doxology as found in the Roman Canon remain the same in all the Eucharistic Prayers of the Roman Rite.

2.2. Eucharistic Prayer II[35]

The text of the second Eucharistic Prayer in the Missal of Paul VI is not a new composition. Except for a few differences which I shall point out in a moment, this prayer derives verbatim from the anaphoral text in the *Apostolic Tradition,* which has been attributed to Hippolytus; if this attribution is accepted and if this Hippolytus can be identified with the Roman priest of that name, the work would date from 215–220. The anaphora of Hippolytus is the earliest that has come down to us, so much so that at the beginning of the present century P. Cagin thought it was an apostolic text.

This source text has undergone some modifications. The language of the thanksgiving has been corrected and better adapted to the present-day mentality. To the end of the thanksgiving the *Sanctus* has been added, and in order that this in turn might be properly linked with the account of institution, a short transitional passage was needed; in keeping with the non-Roman Western tradition, this takes its name from its opening words *Vere sanctus* ("Holy indeed"). This prayer has, however, been changed into an invocation of the Father that he would send the Holy Spirit to sanctify the bread and wine so that they may become the Body and Blood of Christ.

The *Vere sanctus* is thus an epiclesis which, since it comes before the account of institution, is called a first or consecratory epiclesis. This

---

[34] In his Letter to Elpidius of Volterra, 7 (PL 59:143), Pope Gelasius asked: "At the consecration of the divine mystery, how can the heavenly Spirit who has been invoked come if the priest who prays for his presence is himself condemnable because full of sinful actions?" This text forces us to ask whether a pneumatological epiclesis ever existed in the Roman Canon. The answer is negative: All the evidence excludes such an epiclesis. The only point in the Canon to which Gelasius could be referring is the prayer, the end of which speaks of God's blessing coming down from heaven. In my opinion, Gelasius may have understood the descent of this blessing as the descent of the Holy Spirit.

[35] B. Botte, "La seconda preghiera eucaristica," in *Le nuove preghiere eucaristiche* (Parola per l'assemblea festiva 1; Brescia: Queriniana, 1969) 27–33; Mazza, *The Eucharistic Prayers of the Roman Rite,* chapter 3.

second designation is, however, too closely connected with theology to be applicable to a liturgical text.

This second Eucharistic Prayer has a thanksgiving of which the theme has been derived from the Easter homilies of the second century. The second epiclesis is very important; it is taken directly from the epiclesis in the anaphora of Hippolytus and is built on the theme of unity: God is asked that those who will eat of the one bread and drink from the one cup may become one body through the action of the Holy Spirit. The intercessions are the final element that has been added, in order to complete the anaphoral pattern that was chosen as a model for the new texts: the pattern of the Antiochene anaphora.

We have already seen that the theme of unity, which is proper to the epiclesis, is one that is also present in the *Didache* and that Paul had transformed (1 Cor 19:16-17) so as to express the nature and fruit of the Eucharist as a sacrament. From there the theme of unity passed into the anaphora of Hippolytus and then into that of Basil. The Eucharist as sacrament of the unity of the Church found its best formulation in the homilies of Augustine of Hippo. The other eastern anaphoras did not inherit this theme, thereby showing that they derived from a different tradition, whereas the second anaphora in the Missal of Paul VI, deriving as it does from that of Hippolytus is in continuity with the archaic vein of thought (Paul, the *Didache*) on the Eucharist as sacrament of unity.

The second epiclesis of the second Eucharistic Prayer combines these three elements: sacramental Communion, the Holy Spirit, and the gift of unity.[36] While being the Lord's Supper or the eating of the Body and Blood of Christ, the Eucharist is at the same time a sacrament of the Holy Spirit and sacrament of the unity of the body of Christ that is the Church. In fact, it is precisely by the action of the Holy Spirit that the Eucharist is a sacrament of the unity of Christ's body, the Church.

---

[36] From this it can be seen how insofar as the choices made in the liturgical reform of Vatican II were connected with the liturgical texts of the early Church, they produced solutions very different from those of the medieval period when it came to the various kinds of eating: sacramental, spiritual, sacramental-and-spiritual.

2.3. Eucharistic Prayer III[37]

This text is the most direct answer to the difficulty found in using the Roman Canon. In fact, the authors of this anaphora, while following the usual pattern of the Antiochene anaphora, composed the text using the sacrificial themes proper to the Roman Canon, in order that these might not be completely forgotten. The Preface and Sanctus are followed by the *Vere sanctus*, which, before coming to the epicletic theme, continues the story of God's works that was begun in the Preface.[38] Its themes are two: (a) God gathers his people around him; and (b) the cultic action, proper to a people in the presence of God, consists in the offering of the sacrifice of praise, that is, the hymn of thanksgiving that rises from the hearts of the gathered faithful. After the anamnesis, the theme of the offering of the sacramental bread and wine to God is expanded and becomes a prayer that God may accept and be pleased with the offering of the Church.[39] Next comes the Communion epiclesis, or sanctificatory epiclesis, asking that those who receive Communion may be brought into unity. This text borrows the theme of unity, not from the anaphora of Hippolytus (as Eucharistic Prayer II does) but from the anaphora of Basil,[40] which bears the clear mark of Acts 4:32.[41]

2.4. Eucharistic Prayer IV[42]

This text was not included in the initial plan for new anaphoras. The first draft of these anaphoras did indeed include three texts, but they were: the second Eucharistic Prayer, which was molded on the anaphora of Hippolytus; the third Eucharistic Prayer, thought of as a

[37] L. Bouyer, "La terza preghiera eucaristica," in *Le nuove preghiere eucaristiche* (Parola per l'assemblea festiva 1; Brescia: Queriniana, 1969) 39–50; Mazza, *The Eucharistic Prayers of the Roman Rite*, chapter 4.

[38] Like the Roman Canon, this anaphora lacks a preface of its own.

[39] This is an important theme that reached Christianity from Old Testament worship and has no specific place in the sacramental theology and pastoral practice of our century; I think, therefore, that it was introduced solely out of fidelity to the sources.

[40] ". . . for the sanctification of body, soul, and spirit, so that we may become a single body and a single spirit" (Hänggi-Pahl, 352).

[41] "The whole group of those who believed were of one heart and soul, and no one claimed private ownership of any possessions, but everything they owned was held in common."

[42] J. Gelineau, "La quarta preghiera eucaristica," in *Le nuove preghiere eucaristiche* (Parola per l'assemblea festiva 1; Brescia: Queriniana, 1969) 51–68; Mazza, *The Eucharistic Prayers of the Roman Rite*, chapter 6.

rewriting of the Roman Canon with a different structure; and, finally, the anaphora of Basil.[43] However, the anaphora of Basil was not accepted because it had the prayer for the transformation of the gifts in what we know as the Communion epiclesis, which, as in the usual Antiochene outline, came after the account of institution. Because of the failure of the anaphora of Basil the commission considered that it was authorized to compose a new text which, while following the logic of the oriental anaphoras, did not have the problems associated with the Basilian Eucharist. In the course of a single day, Father Gelineau prepared a text as a basis on which others would work in a series of revisions.

The anaphora begins with a short hymn of praise celebrating the glory of God: All of creation praises God, and the human being, who has become the voice of the rest of creation, interprets this cosmic praise. This theme leads into the singing of the *Sanctus,* after which begins the narrative of God's works, starting with creation and reaching as far as the Old Testament dispensation, the dispensation of the covenant. The sin of humanity is recalled, and the prayer says that God has not abandoned the human race to the grip of sin but has come to the aid of all.

The renewal of the covenant is mentioned, with the entire Old Testament economy being interpreted as a divine pedagogy leading humanity to a great hope, the hope of salvation. The text then moves on to the New Testament economy, recounting the coming of Christ into the world and his work for humanity. The plan of life which Christ has given to human beings is formulated according to the anaphora of Basil: Human beings are to learn to live no longer for themselves but for Christ, who died and rose from the dead for them.[44] The thanksgiving gives way to the first epiclesis, which is constructed in the usual manner, and this in turn leads to the account of institution by way of a citation of John 13:1, which is the Johannine introduction to the Last Supper.[45] At the end of the anaphora come the intercessions,

[43] L. Bouyer had prepared a text drawn from the anaphora of Basil, but with a good revision of the intercessions, which in the original had been overly long.

[44] The basis for this is in 2 Corinthians 5:15: "And he died for all, so that those who live might live no longer for themselves, but for him who died and was raised for them."

[45] "Before the festival of the Passover, Jesus knew that his hour had come to depart from this world and go to the Father. Having loved his own who were in the world, he loved them to the end."

in which a vast horizon is opened up: we pray to God there in light of the problems and needs of the entire world.

Like the epicleses we have seen, that of the fourth Eucharistic Prayer has unity as its theme. We must therefore conclude that the liturgical reform of Paul VI made this theological and liturgical datum into a program: The Eucharist is the sacrament of unity.[46]

2.5. The Eucharistic Prayers for Masses with Children[47]

In utterances on liturgical reform ever since the first Synod of Bishops (1967), various bishops had expressed the desire of their respective episcopal conferences that special adaptations be made for Masses with children. Thus began a journey that would lead to the promulgation of the *Directory for Masses with Children*,[48] which was published on November 1, 1973. This document shows an awareness that the problem of Eucharistic Prayers for children was already a real one, but the solution would be given only later on. On November 1, 1974, three new anaphoras for Masses with children were promulgated, with their own *Praenotanda* (Introduction), for use in the episcopal conferences that had requested them. The reason why they were published only in a booklet reserved to the episcopal conferences that requested them was that these prayers were, and still are, *ad experimentum*.

A child is not a miniature adult, but is different from the adult. The recognition of this difference is the basis of the principles set down in the *Directory*, which was complemented by the *Praenotanda* accompanying the Eucharistic Prayers. The thematic content and the structure of the three anaphoras are consistent with the principles set down in the *Directory* and the *Praenotanda*. The texts contain a change that is important for the structure of the anaphoras: the introduction of numerous acclamations which are intended to help the children to participate better in the mystery of faith through the Eucharistic Prayers. The first Eucharistic Prayer contains, within the thanksgiving, three acclamations obtained by breaking down the *Sanctus* into its three constitutive themes. Thus the structure is entirely new. At least in this instance there is an exception to the Antiochene structure of the Roman anaphoras.

---

[46] As we saw, this theme was characteristic of the eucharistic celebration at its beginnings, but it was completely transformed in medieval theology.

[47] Mazza, *The Eucharistic Prayers of the Roman Rite*, chapter 8.

[48] The title deliberately reads "with children," and not "of children" or "for children."

Another very important change occurs in the anamnesis. This is divided into two phases. The first derives from the non-Roman Western liturgies and describes the Eucharist as an act of obedience to Christ's command. The second describes the eucharistic celebration as a proclamation, which is the typical form of the anamnesis in the Alexandrian liturgy, but is also well documented in the West; the biblical basis for it is 1 Corinthians 11:26. By way of this change the reform of Paul VI introduces two other theologies of the Mass, alongside the theology of the memorial: The conception of the Mass as a proclamation of the death and resurrection of the Lord, and the conception of the Mass as an act of obedience to and imitation of what the Lord did at the Last Supper.

Furthermore, the three anaphoras for children introduce a new expression at the end of the account of institution: "Then he said to them"; it comes between the words over the cup and the command of Christ. This innovation serves to lay greater emphasis on the idea contained in the anamnesis. In fact, the clearer separation of the command from the words over the cup fosters a closer unity between the command and the anamnesis.[49]

2.6. The Eucharistic Prayers for Masses of Reconciliation[50]

There are two Eucharistic Prayers "of reconciliation" and their origin was connected with a very specific event: Holy Year 1975. These were published together with the three anaphoras for Masses with children and are "experimental" texts given to the episcopal conferences that had requested them. The Holy Year has always had a penitential purpose and has always been associated with the sacrament of reconciliation. Holy Year 1975 was connected with the theme of "reconciliation," precisely because the present-day Rite of Penance had chosen this theological emphasis: reconciliation with God is connected with reconciliation with one's brothers and sisters in the Church.

---

[49] Following the same logic, another change was introduced into the first of the three anaphoras: "The place for the acclamation of the faithful at the end of the consecration has been slightly changed. This is done for pedagogical reasons. In order that the children may clearly understand the connection between the words of the Lord, *Do this in memory of me,* and the anamnesis by the priest celebrant, the acclamation, whether of memorial or of praise, is not made until after the anamnesis has been recited" (Introduction, 19; in *Documents on the Liturgy 1963–1979,* no. 2017).

[50] Mazza, *The Eucharistic Prayers of the Roman Rite,* chapter 7.

The Eucharistic Prayers follow closely this theme of reconciliation,[51] but reconciliation with the brothers and sisters seems to have been the main focus of attention for the drafters of both texts, since these are very like each other. There is but one slight difference: The language of the second anaphora is lively, modern, and immediately under-standable. An anaphora is a text that is meant to be proclaimed, and it must be said that from this point of view the second anaphora is a quite successful text.

2.7. Eucharistic Prayers "for Various Needs"[52]

The document which the Congregation for Divine Worship pub-lished in 1973 on the Eucharistic Prayers determined that the four Eucharistic Prayers of the Missal were enough, but it assured its readers that in particular circumstances it might be possible to obtain approval of other new texts.[53] For this reason, approval was given of a Eucharistic Prayer on occasion of the Swiss Synod of 1972; it con-sisted of a basic text with four possible variants[54] and was for the

[51] The texts "shed light on aspects of reconciliation, insofar as they may be the object of thanksgiving" (Introduction, 1, in *Documents on the Liturgy 1963–1979*, no. 2024).

[52] Mazza, *The Eucharistic Prayers of the Roman Rite*, chapter 7; Congregation for Divine Worship and the Discipline of the Sacraments, "Prex eucharistica quae in Missis pro variis necessitatibus adhiberi potest," *Notitiae* 27 (1991) 388–431. See the description of this prayer and its history in A. Hänggi, "Das Hochgebet 'Synode '72' für die Kirche in der Schweiz," ibid., 436–59; C. Maggioni, "Coordinate spazio-temporali della preghiera eucaristica 'Synode '72,'" ibid., 460–79; P. De Clerck, "La revision de la prière eucharistique 'suisse,'" *MD*, no. 191 (1992) 61–68; idem, "Epi-clèse et formulation du Mystère eucharistique. Brèves réflexions sur le language liturgique à partir de la prière eucharistique 'suisse,'" in *Gratias Agamus, Studien zum eucharistischen Hochgebet. Für Balthasar Fischer*, ed. A. Heinz and H. Rennings (Freiburg–Basel–Vienna: Herder, 1992) 53–59; E. Mazza, "La preghiera eucaristica 'Per varie necessità,'" *Liturgia*, no. 96 (1993) 872–83.

[53] *Litterae circulares ad conferentiarum episcopalium praesides de precibus eucharisticis*, no. 6, in *Notitiae* 84 (1973) 193–201.

[54] The text is composed of a fixed section and a variable part that allows for four alternate formularies. The preface and the prayer of intercession are variable; the rest of the anaphora is fixed. There is therefore a close unity between the fixed part and the variable parts of this text, so much so that the variable parts seem to be only four different ways of formulating the same theme. For this reason, the text is not usable with the other prefaces of the Roman Missal, because the thematic synthesis would then be missing. The titles of the four variable formularies are: (A) God Leads His Church; (B) Jesus, our Way; (C) Jesus, Model of Love; (D) The Church on the Way to Unity.

exclusive use of Switzerland. Its use was later extended to other episcopal conferences that requested it. Now this Eucharistic Prayer "for
the Swiss Synod" has a new title: "For Various Needs," and has been
placed in the Roman Missal among the formularies of "Masses and
Prayers for Various Needs and Occasions,"[55] for use especially in
these celebrations.

The theme of "the way" is present in the *Post-Sanctus*,[56] in Preface
A (the first of the four variable texts), and in Preface B, which says:
"Christ, your living Word, is the way that leads us to you." In the fixed
text of the anaphora, in the "commendation of the sacrifice," there is
another reference to the "way": "Christ who . . . by his sacrifice has
opened for us the way to you." And again at the end of the intercessions, before the doxology: "And grant that at the end of our pilgrimage we too may reach the eternal dwelling where you await us."

Because of the frequent occurrence of this theme in the fixed text I
would be inclined to say that it is the fundamental and constitutive
theme of the anaphoras. On the one hand, the theme is very much in
tune with contemporary culture, which often conceives of life as a
journey through time and history, and on the other hand, it is also
very biblical. The text is aware of this, and in fact Preface A begins
with the image of the Israelites wandering in the wilderness. The
new Israel, the Church, is spoken of in these same lines as the typological actuation of that image. God led his people and now accompanies the Church as it advances toward the kingdom of God. The
sequence of themes is carefully chosen: from Israel to the Church and
from the Church to human beings who wander the paths of time.
Since we are now in the thanksgiving section of the Eucharistic
Prayer, the kingdom is described as perfect joy.

Joy is what every human being desires and seeks. Through these
expressions, then, the anaphora is linked to an existential experience:
the fundamental need felt by every human being. The kingdom of
God is the answer to every human need and has its place in the logic
followed by the theology of prayer in Matthew: "Strive first for the
kingdom of God and his righteousness, and all these things will be

[55] *Prex eucharistica quae in missis pro variis necessitatibus adhiberi potest. Decretum*
(Prot. CD 511/91).

[56] "Sustain us always on our way"; the *Post-Sanctus* is a section of the fixed text
that fits in with all four variable texts.

given to you as well."[57] The image of Israel in the wilderness is a pregnant one, for a wandering people is a people that has no well-defined goal and can be compared to life itself, which is often a search for meaning amid attempts in numerous directions and a variety of experiences. In this situation, the starting point contains a program: God does not leave us alone on the journey. Thus the anaphora speaks of his "mighty arm," which is a synonym for the effectiveness of his interventions. It follows that God is the one who constantly sustains us on our journey.[58] Salvation, moreover, is "a journeying in faith and in hope,"[59] in order to reach the eternal dwelling where God awaits humanity.[60] At this point, the text is inspired by the parable of the prodigal son,[61] which is a good reflection of the journey of human life. On the way of salvation the faithful ask God: "Make us open and available to the brothers and sisters whom we meet[62] on our journey."[63]

In this anaphora "for various needs" it is not the language alone that is attuned to the culture of present-day human beings; so too are its mentality, its theological concepts, and its religious sentiments, or, in short, the spirit of the prayer.

In ending, I must say that we cannot be surprised that this text should be among the most frequently used of the Missal and among those that awaken the fullest agreement in the faithful and are heard not distractedly but with participation. I do not mean to say that there is nothing open to criticism in this prayer or that its theology is always good. I mean to say that despite its defects[64] the text promotes prayer, and it is this that makes it easy to pray.

---

[57] John 6:33. See R. Guelly, G. Lafon, P.-J. Labarrière, A. Vergote, and J.-P. Jossua, *La prière du chrétien* (Publications des Facultés universitaires Saint-Louis 2; Brussels: Facultés universitaires Saint-Louis, 1981) 118.

[58] Preface D.

[59] Fixed text.

[60] Ibid.

[61] Luke 15:11ff.

[62] This is the theme of the parable of the Good Samaritan: Luke 10:30ff.

[63] Intercessions B.

[64] The first defect is that it is an anaphora based on a theme. Then, too, we must criticize the text of the epiclesis, which has been replaced by decree of the Congregation for Divine Worship, the new one being similar to the epiclesis of the other Roman anaphoras. But even in its defects the anaphora reflects the religious culture and spirituality of the average Christian.

When all is said and done, the fundamental purpose of every Eucharistic Prayer is to be a prayer. When a text succeeds in being this, its functional role is assured.[65]

[65] The thing that puts life into an anaphora is not its theology nor its citations, whether of the Bible or archaic anaphoras or the great texts of the tradition; if an anaphora is not successful as a prayer text, because it is inspired by a praying soul, it will never be effectively prayed, even if it be praiseworthy for its relationship to the sources. The euchology (minor and major) of the Missal is often more concerned with theological content than with the spirit of prayer.

Chapter 17

The Parts of the Eucharistic Prayer

1. THE PREFACE

The Preface is the first part of the anaphora and comes immediately after the introductory dialogue.

If we look at the Eucharistic Prayer in its origin, we realize that thanksgiving occupies the greatest part of the text and constitutes the very nature of the prayer. This fact is quite clear both in the Jewish texts that were at the origin of the Eucharist and in the archaic Christian texts; we need only look at the *Birkat ha-Mazon*, the Eucharist in chapter 10 of the *Didache*, or the Eucharist in Book 7 of the *Apostolic Constitutions*. Later on, as the Christian liturgy developed, supplication and petition made to God grew to the point of being the most important element; the Roman Canon and the Alexandrian anaphora are the clearest examples of this tendency, which is present, however, in all the liturgical families. The character of the texts in the Missal is the direct result of the historical development of the anaphora.

1.1. Importance of the Preface

The importance of the Preface derives from the command of Jesus: "Do this in memory of me." What did Jesus do? He took bread, gave thanks, broke the bread, and gave it to his disciples, saying. . . . He did the same for the cup. If the Eucharist of the Church is an imitation of the action of Jesus and an act of obedience to his command, then the preface imitates Christ's act of thanksgiving. Because of the Preface, and due to its development in the course of history, the anaphora becomes the carrying out of Christ's command. All this shows the primary importance of the thanksgiving, or Preface, in the Eucharistic

Prayer. Today, nonetheless, the Preface is regarded as simply the beginning of the Eucharistic Prayer, and not its principal part.[1]

1.2. *Object of the Thanksgiving*

On its journey through history the anaphora grew progressively longer. In the archaic eucharistic texts the thanksgivings are very brief: Thanks is offered for the mystery of salvation, which is formulated in a very simple and basic way; the text says only in what the salvation consists which God has accomplished through Christ. As time passes, the texts begin to describe salvation more fully in dependence on the professions of faith, which contemplate the entire work of God. The bipartite nature of some archaic professions of faith explains why the paleoanaphoral texts do not yet have a trinitarian character.[2]

Another major stage in development brought in the paschal theme.[3] When this enters the anaphora, we see the section reserved for thanksgiving, that is, the Preface, acquiring a narrative character and greater amplitude, for, in fact, the entire history of salvation is told. This characteristic is quite visible in the anaphoras of Hippolytus, Basil (Byzantine recension), and the *Apostolic Constitutions* (Book 8).

The paschal theme passes directly into the Missal of Paul VI in the second and fourth Eucharistic Prayers. These paschal traits were already present in the Missal of Pius V, in the form of the Prefaces for the Passion, for Easter, and so on. The use of these texts, whether Prefaces or entire anaphoras, serves to bring out the paschal nature of the Eucharist that is present in every eucharistic celebration, regardless of the liturgical season.

[1] Even in the classical anaphoras from the second half of the fourth century, the Preface is no longer seen as the most important part of the anaphora or Eucharistic Prayer. In the Latin tradition, the principal part is that containing the Lord's words over the bread and wine, while in the Oriental tradition the principal part is the epiclesis. These different assessments depend on the different interpretive criteria applied to the Eucharistic Prayer.

[2] The reference to the Spirit acquired a place in the anaphora as an afterthought, because of the increasing importance of trinitarian doctrine in the Church.

[3] This theme was taken over from the ancient liturgy for the Asian Easter, in which commemoration was made of the pasch–passion of Christ. The text of the celebration commemorated the entire mystery of salvation in its historical trajectory, beginning with creation and at last reaching, via the Old Testament stages (thought of as advance announcements), the incarnation and death of Christ. This last was the focus of the celebration because it was the fulfillment of the ancient Passover. After recounting the various phases of redemption in Christ, the text ended with the ascension.

The distinctive trait of the Roman liturgy was that it had variable Prefaces; this has remained true, despite the addition of new anaphoras that have a fixed thanksgiving. These variable Prefaces are a vestige of the ancient creativity that made it possible to have proper texts for every kind of Mass.

I cannot dwell here on the content of the thanksgiving in the individual Prefaces; their numbers are too great. Each of them gives thanks for some particular facet of the history of salvation. Sometimes it is the feast or the liturgical season that becomes the theme of the thanksgiving. But even when the liturgical feast being celebrated is not concerned directly with Christ but with, for example, the saints, the preface is always structured theocentrically.

Despite the plurality of texts, which is a characteristic trait of the Roman liturgy, and regardless of the degree of their literary success, the Prefaces are at one in that the reality being described is always the gift of God: creation and the redemption which he has wrought.

1.3. To Praise, Thank, and Give[4]

The thanksgiving commemorates and tells of God's gift; God is praised and his gift is praised in a single interior movement, since the gift is a revelation and manifestation of the giver. The gift is a means to an encounter of persons and serves to establish this relationship. It is not just any relationship, but one governed by particular laws inherent in the gift itself. This is the logic of giving. To praise the gift is to declare it pleasing and accepted: To accept the gift means to remain committed to the giver.

A gift has three main characteristics:[5] (1) To establish a relationship, a gift "has" to be given. That is, a gift is a necessity in human relationships, for without it these relationships deteriorate, and fellowship becomes impossible. (2) A gift cannot be refused; a refusal amounts to an insult, because it is the rejection of a positive relationship with the giver, that is, of communion with him. A gift is not neutral: It either creates or breaks a relationship. (3) When a gift is accepted, there is created in the recipient an interior bond that gives rise to an urgent invitation to give a gift in return. In this exchange, the recipient himself becomes a giver.

[4] On the Eucharist from the viewpoint of gift, see Mazza, *The Eucharistic Prayers of the Roman Rite*, 44–47.

[5] See Marcel Mauss, *The Gift. Forms and Functions of Exchange in Archaic Societies*, trans. I. Cunnison (New York, 1967).

In the Preface, thanksgiving rises from human beings to God and is their response, their gift in return for the divine gift.

God's gift is redemption, which crowns his gift of creation. In the presence of this gift, human beings are incapable of giving an equal gift in return, and when the gift transcends the ability of the recipient to give in return, the only possible response is gratitude; in our case, thanksgiving and praise. The Syrian tradition shows its clear awareness of this situation when it says: "We, too, your servants, thank you . . . because you have bestowed on us your great kindness, for which there is no repayment."[6] And again: "And for all this favor toward us we offer you glory and honor in your holy Church before your altar of propitiation."[7]

1.4. Useful for Salvation

The Latin text of the Roman Preface says it is *dignum, iustum, aequum,* and *salutare* to give thanks. The translation of *aequum* as "our duty" does not capture the richness of the Latin word, which signifies a relationship of "parity": In this liturgical text, therefore *aequum* means that thanksgiving is an appropriate gift in return for the divine gift.

Turning from juridical to theological language, we must conclude that the situation created by the human response of thanksgiving is one of communion. The Preface describes all this with the word *salutare*. If the source of this Latin text was the Alexandrian anaphora,[8] the translation should reflect the Greek text which says at this point "useful to our souls."[9]

To these remarks I must add that by reason of its objective contents the Preface takes the form of a true and proper profession of faith. It follows that the classical theme of justification through faith has a really special relationship with this part of the anaphora.

---

[6] Hänggi-Pahl, 377.

[7] Ibid., 412.

[8] We saw that there are good reasons for maintaining the Alexandrine origin of the Roman Canon; furthermore, the term *salutare* ("helpful toward salvation") at the beginning of the Roman Prefaces has no equivalent in any anaphoral tradition except the Alexandrian, which has *exôpheles* ("useful [to our souls]").

[9] Hänggi-Pahl, 102.

2. THE *SANCTUS*

The *Sanctus* became part of the Roman Eucharistic Prayer only in the first half of the fifth century;[10] all in all, this was a fairly late period, inasmuch as by then the text of the Roman Canon had become fixed and was regarded as a text possessing great authority.

There exist two fundamental types of *Sanctus*: the Alexandrian[11] and the Antiochene. The *Sanctus* of the Roman Eucharist derives from the Antiochene liturgy[12] and has two parts: (a) the *Sanctus* true and proper, consisting of the acclamation from Isaiah 6:3;[13] and (b) the *Benedictus*, a christological acclamation taken from Matthew 21:9.[14] The *Sanctus* has been given a christological interpretation and a trinitarian interpretation, and this in both the East and the West. These differing interpretations may be due to the presence, in the text of the *Sanctus*, of a theological section, namely the acclamation from Isaiah 6:3, and a christological part, namely, the acclamation from Matthew 21:9.

The text of the *Sanctus* passed from Jewish use to Christian use at a very early time, since it is cited in the Apocalypse of John and in the

[10] The *Sacramentarium Veronense* has preserved texts of noteworthy antiquity, among which are several Prefaces that have no *Sanctus,* although they are recognizable as Prefaces because they end with the clausula *Per,* which is an abbreviation for *Per Christum Dominum nostrum.* The *Supplementum Anianense* to the Gregorian Sacramentary likewise has Prefaces without a *Sanctus.* Another valuable testimony on the subject is provided by the "Arian" texts published by Cardinal Angelo Mai; they, too, lack the *Sanctus.*

[11] In the Alexandrian tradition, the *Sanctus* consisted of only the first part, the citation of Isaiah 6:3, and lacked the *Benedictus;* this was the earliest form taken by the *Sanctus* in the Eucharist. This early state can be seen in the testimonies of Eusebius of Caesarea, the *Mystagogical Catecheses* of Cyril of Jerusalem, and, above all, the *Ritual* used in the Church of Theodore of Mopsuestia. In the latter, too, that is, in the archaic stage of the Syrian liturgy, the *Benedictus* was unknown, and the *Sanctus* consisted solely of the acclamation from Isaiah 6:3.

[12] P.-M. Gy, "Le Sanctus romain et les anaphores orientales," in *Mélanges liturgiques. Offerts au R. P. Dom Bernard Botte* (Louvain, 1972) 167–74.

[13] "In the year that King Uzziah died, I saw the Lord sitting on a throne, high and lofty; and the hem of his robe filled the temple. Seraphs were in attendance above him; each had six wings: with two they covered their faces, and with two they covered their feet, and with two they flew. And one called to another and said: 'Holy, holy, holy is the Lord of hosts; the whole earth is full of his glory.' The pivots on the thresholds shook at the voices of those who called, and the house filled with smoke" (Isa 6:1-5).

[14] "The crowds that went ahead of him and that followed were shouting, 'Hosanna to the Son of David! Blessed is the one who comes in the name of the Lord! Hosanna in the highest heaven!'" (Matt 21:9).

letter of Clement to the Corinthians.[15] In order to understand the passage, we must refer back to its use in the Jewish liturgy, since the *Sanctus* originated in the Jerusalem Temple and is to be explained by reference to the vicissitudes which the temple experienced. In the beginning, the *Sanctus* referred simply to the angelic liturgy. Under pressure from apocalyptic thought the idea took shape that the true temple is located in heaven and, consequently, that true worship likewise had to be a heavenly worship, such as is assured to God by his court of angels. On the other hand, the theology of the temple, whether in a Canaanite setting or in a Yahwist setting, always maintained that the temple is connected with the heavenly dwelling of God, the kind of connection being specified in various ways. From this thinking came the idea, in turn, that the value of the earthly liturgy depended on its conformity to the heavenly liturgy.

All this yielded the idea that the liturgy celebrated on earth should be a reflection of the angelic liturgy, a true copy of it. This meant the need of having on earth the same hymns that were being sung in the heavenly temple. Isaiah's vision seemed to have been given precisely to satisfy this need, with the result that the acclamation in Isaiah became part of morning prayers, which were one of the key parts of Jewish worship.

We do not know where and why the Jewish text of the *Sanctus* became so important to Christians that it was introduced into the anaphora, especially when we take into account the fact that the *Sanctus* had no connection with the Jewish liturgy for meals, in which the Christian Eucharist originated. It is likely that the introduction took place in Syria, since the *Ritual* followed by Theodore of Mopsuestia attests to an anaphora that is wholly focused on the *Sanctus* and is full of Jewish thinking and the Jewish logic of the angelic liturgy. The *Sanctus* entered the Christian anaphora while retaining its original Jewish significance; in fact, both in Theodore and in the catechetical homilies of Cyril, the *Sanctus* is viewed as having a sanctifying value. Theodore explains the sanctifying power of the Eucharist by linking the eucharistic bread with the burning coal that purified the lips of Isaiah.[16] Cyril is even clearer in a passage that attributes sanctifying

[15] Revelation 4:8; Clement of Rome, *Letter to the Corinthians* 34.6, ed. A. Jaubert (SC 167; Paris: Cerf, 1971) 158.

[16] *Les homélies catéchétiques de Théodore de Mopsueste* (ST 145; Vatican City: Vatican Apostolic Library, 1949) 595.

power to the participation in the angelic liturgy that is expressed by the *Sanctus:* "We say this doxology, which was given to us by the seraphim, in order that by sharing this hymn we may be associated with the heavenly hosts. Next, after being ourselves sanctified by these spiritual hymns, we pray that God, the friend of human beings, would send the Holy Spirit on the gifts placed here. . . ."[17]

The liturgical reform of Vatican II shortened the list of angelic choirs in the introduction to the *Sanctus.* The reason is that, given the difficulty inherent in angelology as such, it is not easy today to speak of a heavenly court, much less of an angelic liturgy. Nor is it easy to speak of the angelic hymn having a sanctifying power.

Despite all these problems and difficulties, the liturgy today still has the *Sanctus,* nor has anyone ever thought of eliminating this hymn from the anaphora.

3. THE ACCOUNT OF INSTITUTION

3.1. Origin of the Account of Institution

The account of the Last Supper, which serves as an account of institution, is at the center of the anaphoras that took form in the fourth century and have existed down to our time.

The origin of this part of the Eucharistic Prayer is to be sought in the Jewish liturgy. As we saw at the beginning of this book, in the treatise *Berakoth* the rabbis ask whence comes the obligation to give thanks at meals, and they find the answer in Deuteronomy 8:10: "You shall eat your fill and bless the Lord for the good land that he has given you."[18] The prayer of thanksgiving at the end of meals (*Birkat ha-Mazon*) was an extempore text that followed a certain pattern; yet in the various extempore texts the verse just cited (Deut 8:10) appears, usually at the end of the second strophe, before the strophe containing the petition or prayer of intercession for Jerusalem. The account of institution was subsequently christianized and, in consequence, instead of Deuteronomy 8:10, new biblical texts were introduced that functioned as an account of institution: Malachi 1:11 (the Eucharist as

[17] Cyril of Jerusalem, *Catéchèses mystagogiques* 5.6–7, ed. A. Piédagnel (SC 126bis; Paris: Cerf, 1988) 154.

[18] "Where does it appear that the blessing of food is contained in the Law? When it was said: 'When you have eaten and are filled, you will bless.'" In *Il Trattato delle Benedizioni (Berakot) del Talmud babilonese,* ed. S. Cavalletti (Classici delle religioni; Turin, 1968) 322.

sacrifice), Isaiah 6:3 (the Eucharist as worship that imitates the heavenly liturgy), 1 Corinthians 11:26 (the Eucharist as proclamation of the death of Christ), and, finally, the account of the Last Supper, formed by combining the four New Testament accounts.

It was in this way that the account of institution became part of the thanksgiving at meals and from there entered the Christian Eucharist.

3.2. Definition of the Account of Institution

According to the definition given by Caesare Giraudo, the account of institution is the theological source of the liturgy being celebrated.[19] In other words, it is the theological reason for this liturgy and the sufficient reason for it. God is told of his own institutive action as a way of expressing our obedience and our fidelity to his command.[20]

3.3. Consecration and Account of Institution

In 1969, when the new *Order of Mass* was published, the *General Instruction of the Roman Missal*[21] spoke only of the "Account of Institution," whereas in the new edition of 1972 it spoke of the "Account of Institution and Consecration." This change shows what the problem is in this section of the Eucharistic Prayer. It is that when we speak of the account of the supper it is always difficult to decide which description to use: "account of institution" or "consecration."

In their explanations of the liturgy, known as their "mystagogical catecheses," the Fathers of the Church developed a method which enabled them to answer the question just asked. For they said that two levels, two different planes, irreducible to each other, must be distinguished in the liturgy. (1) The first plane consists of the rite as such, that is, of what falls under the control of the senses; the rite is made up of visible gestures and objects, words and sounds, colors, odors, and sensations. All these elements of the *rite* have their proper names which serve to designate things in their visibility and tangibil-

[19] "A privileged passage of scripture which the praying community perceives as the theological foundation of the petition around which the formulary of prayer is constructed" (C. Giraudo, *La struttura letteraria della preghiera eucaristica* [AnBib 92; Rome: Biblical Institute Press, 1981] 386).

[20] It also helps those praying before God to be aware of the reason for their obedience and, above all, to take stock of his command. Furthermore, it is from obedience to the divine command that this and other blessings willed by God acquire their ability to sanctify.

[21] See no. 55b of the *General Introduction to the Roman Missal*.

ity, that is, as objects of sense perception. (2) The second plane consists of the relationship between the rite and the saving event. This is an ontological relationship that is the deeper, the true nature of the liturgical rite. This relationship constitutes the sacramentality of the rite and is the direct foundation and sufficient reason of its efficacy.

Every part of the rite may therefore be regarded and described from two different points of view: that of sense knowledge of the rite and that of knowledge by faith. Both of these knowledges are true, each in its own sphere; they complement one another, and neither can replace the other or be a substitute for it. The difference between the two levels of knowledge (a distinction typical of Platonism) explains why each of these two ways of knowing becomes false when it claims to know something outside the object proper to it.[22] I shall now apply this principle to the question raised about the account of institution.

From the viewpoint of direct experience, that is, of textual analysis, the account of institution is a section of the anaphora in which the actions and words of Jesus at the Last Supper are recounted to the Father. From this point of view there is nothing in the account of institution that lets us think of a consecration. In fact, the text does not speak to God of the action now being performed but of the action which Christ did at the Last Supper;[23] it speaks not of the present but of the past, and the account is not addressed to the bread and wine but to God the Father in heaven. From the viewpoint of textual criticism, these are the facts about the account of the Supper. On the basis of a literary analysis of the text, then, we should speak of an account of institution and not of a consecration.

But literary analysis does not tell the whole story about the account of the Last Supper; there is another dimension, which transcends experience and which is made accessible by the patristic method which I just cited. A reading of the text by the typological method cancels out the temporal and spiritual distance separating today's rite from the historical saving event that took place once and for all in Christ.

The event in question is the Last Supper which Jesus celebrated in the upper room. As a result, it is as if the Mass and the Last Supper of

[22] Indeed, the traits proper to one level cannot be applied to the other; there is here a kind of non-"communication of properties" (communicatio idiomatum).

[23] The text is speaking not of "this" bread and "this" wine, but of "that" bread and "that" wine; that is, it is speaking not of the bread and wine that are "now" on the altar, but of the bread and wine that were "at that time" on the table at the Last Supper of Jesus, and of which he said that they were his Body and Blood.

Jesus were contemporaneous and were identified with each other, the one being completely superimposed on the other.[24] At the Last Supper Jesus said the words "This is my body" and "This is the cup of my blood." In the Mass the priest repeats the same words. According to the patristic principle in question, the spatiotemporal gap is as it were annulled, and the words of the priest become fully identical with the words uttered by Jesus at the Last Supper. The words of Jesus at the Last Supper are present again in the words of the priest. In fact, since the priest is the *typus* of Christ,[25] the words of the priest are no longer his own but are solely those of Christ, and have the efficacy proper to the word of Christ. According to typology, the account of the Supper is a consecration.

We can therefore conclude that from the literary point of view the account of the Last Supper in the anaphora is an account of institution, while from the theological viewpoint it is a consecration.

Thus the Catholic tradition on consecration originates in, and takes its logic from, biblical typology as applied to the account of institution.

4. ANAMNESIS AND OFFERING

4.1. *Anamnesis*

This term designates the part of the Eucharistic Prayer that comes immediately after the account of institution and refers to the command: "Do this in memory of me." The Church responds to this command with the anamnesis and says: "Mindful therefore of his death and resurrection, we offer you, Lord, the bread of life and the cup of salvation."[26]

The faithful are caught up in the action of remembering; they are remembering the death and resurrection of Christ and are offering the bread and wine to the Father. Remembering is a state of mind; offering is the action performed by those who are "remembering." If we want a clear vision of the Roman tradition regarding the relationship between the anamnesis and the sacrifice, we need to refer to the Latin

[24] On the method of typology as applied to the liturgy see E. Mazza, "Les raisons et la méthode des catéchèses mystagogiques de la fin du quatrième siècle," in *La prédication liturgique et les commentaires de la liturgie*, ed. A.-M. Triacca and A. Pistoia (Bibliotheca Ephemerides Liturgicae. Subsidia 65; Rome: Edizioni liturgiche, 1992) 154–76.

[25] In the medieval period *typus Christi* became *in persona Christi*.

[26] Eucharistic Prayer II, according to the Latin text.

text of the Roman Canon: "Mindful, therefore, of the blessed passion . . . , we, your ministers and your holy people, offer to your supreme Majesty a pure victim, a holy victim, a spotless victim, the holy bread of everlasting life and the cup of everlasting salvation." In this passage, the subjects of the action are remembering, and the action described is the offering of sacrifice.

4.2. The Offering of the Sacrifice

The reader may fail to grasp the importance that the Roman Canon assigns to the offering of the sacrifice, this latter being something much more comprehensive than the offering of bread and wine, for in the tradition which the Alexandrian liturgy and the Roman liturgy share, sacrifice is synonymous with worship.

The Old Testament gives a great deal of space to sacrifice and sacrificial worship and to the development of this religious practice, since sacrifice was part of the history of salvation for a number of reasons, depending on the period of time and the kind of sacrifice. At the coming of Christ all Old Testament realities reached their fulfillment; there is no longer a lamb, no longer a holocaust, but only Christ, who is their "truth" (veritas). It is by reason of this typological relationship that the "truth" of the Old Testament is found in Christ[27] and, consequently, that there continue to exist in him a series of Old Testament points of contact which now subsist only as an empty "shadow" (umbra) because the veritas has completely evacuated them.[28]

All this is accurately reflected in the vocabulary used, and this is why the death of Christ is described as a sacrifice[29] and why, analogously

[27] There is between the Old Testament and Christ a typological relationship by reason of which the Old Testament participates in the New.

[28] The Alexandrian anaphora, in fidelity to its sources, explicitly cites Malachi 1:11 and makes it the key text, defining the Eucharist as the fulfillment of the prophecy of Malachi. The oldest Prefaces of the Roman Canon, on the other hand, while expressing the same idea, no longer cite Malachi directly; they prefer to speak of the "sacrifice of praise," alluding to Hebrews 13:15: "Through him, then, let us continually offer a sacrifice of praise to God, that is, the fruit of lips that confess his name." We have here a careful development of the theme, which, while remaining consistent with its origin and with that conception of sacrifice, regards the citation of Malachi 1:11 as inadequate.

[29] "He has appeared once for all at the end of the age to remove sin by the sacrifice of himself" (Heb 9:26).

and in the same context, the Christian's prayer[30] and charity[31] are also described as sacrifices. All these are called sacrifices because they are the *veritas* of the ancient sacrifices; at the same time, they are realities that in fulfilling the types also completely transcend them. Strictly speaking, then, we should say that the Christian Eucharist does not belong in any of the categories of ancient sacrifice, whether classical or Old Testamental, because in fulfilling these it transcends them all and is not reducible to them.[32]

The Eucharist is related to the ancient sacrifices as "antitype" to "type," or "truth" to "figure"; the "antitype" is the basis for defining the "type," and the "truth" for defining the "figure," and not the other way around. Redemption, then, has a properly cultic component[33] which the tradition has described in the word "sacrifice."

5. THE EPICLESIS

It is always difficult to deal with the epiclesis because the purely liturgical data concerning it get mixed up with the theological aspects and with the disputes that then arise.

From the liturgical point of view the epiclesis is a text, located after the anamnesis and offering, that asks that the eucharistic liturgy may be fruitful for those who take part in it. This was the original character of the eucharistic epiclesis. Its theme then is the same as that of

[30] "Through him, then, let us continually offer a sacrifice of praise to God, that is, the fruit of lips that confess his name" (Heb 13:15).

[31] "Do not neglect to do good and to share what you have, for such sacrifices are pleasing to God" (Heb 13:16).

[32] Although the two may at first sight seem very close, my typological interpretation of sacrifice has nothing in common with the antisacrificial interpretation of Christianity developed by R. Girard, *Delle cose nascoste fin dalla fondazione del mondo* (Saggi 24; Milan: Adelphi, 1983).

[33] This theology of sacrifice was followed from the beginnings of Christianity, as is clearly shown by the passages cited from the Letter to the Hebrews, but it did not stop there. The Eucharist has been described as a sacrifice ever since the *Didache*, with the aid of the citation from the prophet Malachi, according to whom the Savior will make clean once again the sacrifice of the people: "See, I am sending my messenger to prepare the way before me, and the Lord whom you seek will suddenly come to his temple. The messenger of the covenant, in whom you delight—indeed, he is coming. . . . He will sit as a refiner and purifier of silver, and he will purify the descendants of Levi and refine them like gold and silver, until they present offerings to God in righteousness. Then the offering of Judah and Jerusalem will be pleasing to the Lord as in the days of old and as in former years" (Mal 3:1-4).

the intercessions, except for those intended in the prayer: Instead of praying for the entire universal Church, the prayer of the epiclesis is only for those who partake of the Body and Blood of Christ during this liturgy. In the epiclesis, then, the rite moves on to intercession for the assembly, which, no less than the universal body in the intercessions, is likewise described as "the Church," in keeping with ancient liturgical custom that goes back straight to 1 Corinthians 11:17. Beginning in 1 Corinthians 10:17, attention shifts from the Church universal to the concrete assembly that is celebrating the Eucharist. Indeed, it is under the influence of this passage of Paul that there is a shift from the intercession in *Didache* 9 to the prayer for the assembly in *Apostolic Constitutions* 7.25. We may therefore say that the theology of the epiclesis originated in the desire to highlight the theological value of the assembly. This datum is brought out clearly in the Pauline doctrine of the Church as the body of Christ.

In a second phase, the name of the Holy Spirit was given a place in the anaphora, and to him was attributed the fruit of the Eucharist: unification into oneness, into a single body. This fruit, the unity of the Church, had already been attributed to the Holy Spirit in the baptismal theology of Paul: "In the one Spirit we were all baptized into one body" (1 Cor 12:13). The conclusion was soon drawn: Through their sharing in the one loaf the faithful form a single body, because the Holy Spirit is at work in them. Thus the christological and the pneumatological aspects of the Eucharist are fused to ensure the fruit of redemption to those who participate in the Eucharist. The faithful are thus conformed to Christ by the working of his Spirit.

In the epiclesis the Father is asked to send the Spirit, so that the Eucharist may be fruitful for all those who share in it, that is, for the assembly that eats the holy bread and drinks the cup of salvation.[34]

---

[34] At a later time, a second part was added to the epiclesis; this part has the bread and wine as its object. That is, the Father is asked to send the Holy Spirit not only on "us" but also on the "holy gifts," in order that these may be changed into the Body and Blood of his Son. This is what is known as the "consecratory" part of the epiclesis. It is in light of this aspect especially that the epiclesis is famous, that is, as the prayer which, in the East, has a consecratory function. In the Latin Church, on the other hand, a different part of the anaphora has this function, namely, the account of institution. In the recent liturgical reform it was decided that the pattern of the new anaphoral texts should follow that of the Antiochene anaphora, except for the "consecratory" part of the epiclesis, which was to be placed before the account of institution.

In the intercessions, on the other hand, the prayer is that the entire Church may bear the fruit of the eucharistic celebration, but the intercessions contain no invocation for the sending of the Holy Spirit.

6. THE INTERCESSIONS

The intercessions are not to be regarded as an unimportant part of the Eucharistic Prayer simply because they are too like the prayer of the faithful and too unlike the supposedly more important parts of the anaphora. In fact, when seen in light of its origins, the theme of the intercessions is the theme of the Church and redemption. God is implicitly being asked to grant the Church the salvation brought by Jesus, since the petition is for unification and entrance into the kingdom: "Bring your Church together from the ends of the earth into your kingdom."[35] The proclamation of the kingdom of God is the heart of the message of Jesus, and St. John, too, describes the salvation wrought by Jesus as consisting in reunification and unity: "Jesus was about to die for the nation, and not for the nation only, but to gather into one the dispersed children of God" (John 11:51-52). The theme of the intercessions is, then, the theme of the eucharistic celebration as such: the redemption gained by Christ and manifested in unity.

The entire history of the Eucharistic Prayer makes it clear that the theme of the intercessions is a sacrificial theme in the proper sense, since the intercessions present the universal Church to the Father at the moment when this Church is engaged in the celebration of the eucharistic sacrifice and drawing fruit from it. This is why we pray here for[36] all those who are in the Church, whether living or dead. The intercessions are structured as a pyramid: First we pray for the pope, then for the bishop and for all the bishops,[37] for all the clergy,[38] and for the entire people that God has redeemed.[39]

7. THE DOXOLOGY

At the end of the anaphora, after the intercessions for the living and the dead, comes the doxology, or praise of God. The formula is the

---

[35] *Didache* 9.4.

[36] It should be noted that in these texts there is no real difference between prayer "with" and praying "for."

[37] Roman Canon.

[38] Eucharistic Prayer II.

[39] Eucharistic Prayer III. This expression does not seem to designate the entire people of God but the faithful as an order distinct from the clergy.

same for all the Latin anaphoras, and is taken from the Roman Canon. The doxology voices faith in the Trinity: "Through Christ, with Christ, in Christ, all honor and glory to you, God, the Almighty Father, in the oneness of the Holy Spirit, through endless ages." The entire congregation replies: "Amen."

The "Amen" of the faithful is very important, because it ratifies the anaphora uttered by the priest. The final "Amen" is as it were a seal on the celebration of the Eucharist, which is by definition the sacrament of the unity of the Church. Since the "Amen" of the faithful shows that in the celebration there is a complete identification of the gathered congregation and the priest, we may conclude that the priest is truly the voice of the Church.

Chapter 18

The Last Supper and the Church's Eucharist

1. THE METHOD OF STUDY

Historical investigation into the testimonies of the liturgical texts and of some Church Fathers has provided us with some conclusions, two of which are especially important: (a) the eucharistic celebration is an *imitation* of the Last Supper; (b) by the word "imitation" is meant not an external, purely ritual resemblance, but a certain identity of nature: The Eucharist has the Last Supper as its referent. The history of the rite thus tells us that if we are to know what the Eucharist is, we must know what it was that Jesus celebrated at the Last Supper.

It follows that the Eucharist can be correctly known only through an analysis of the New Testament accounts. Xavier Léon-Dufour has rightly stressed this point: "What is given to us Christians of a later time is not directly an event but a text that reports the event and interprets it in the process. In any and every quest of historical knowledge students of the past have access to the 'facts' only through accounts."[1] We must therefore ask what the New Testament says about the actions of Jesus at the Last Supper: what he ordered others to do, and the nature of these realities.

The change of perspective is profitable because it allows us to place at the center of the discussion not simply the bread and wine but the entire ritual meal celebrated by Jesus in the upper room.[2] When Christ said: "Do this in remembrance of me," the demonstrative pronoun "this" referred to the entire liturgy of the Last Supper.

[1] X. Léon-Dufour, *Sharing the Eucharistic Bread. The Witness of the New Testament*, trans. M. J. O'Connell (New York: Paulist, 1987) 157.

[2] We need to ask, first of all, what the eucharistic meal is that Jesus celebrated and asked others to celebrate and, secondly, why it is necessary to eat that bread and that wine. The answer is known from the accounts in the Gospels: because that bread is the Body of Christ and that cup is the Blood of Christ. The nature of the bread and wine of the Eucharist is therefore to be known from the entire eucharistic

2. THE LITURGY OF THE CHURCH AND THE LAST SUPPER

Beginning with the very first testimonies, the Church's liturgy is seen as an act of obedience to the command of Christ, "Do this in remembrance of me," and as an imitation of the liturgical supper of Jesus in the upper room before he suffered. The imitation has always taken place on two levels: (a) on the level of rite, and in fact the archaic liturgical celebrations display a strong ritual resemblance to the Last Supper; (b) on the level of the ontological nature of the celebration, and in fact everything that Jesus said regarding the Last Supper is applied to the Eucharist by the Church; the testimonies we have studied are in agreement in asserting the ontological correspondence between the Eucharist of the Church and the Last Supper, between the bread and wine of the Church and the bread and wine of Jesus in the upper room. The Church has always described the bread and wine of its own liturgical celebration in the same words that are used of the bread and wine of the Last Supper: the Body and the Blood of Christ.

As we have seen, the ontology of the imitation has its place in the Platonic culture that was widespread in the patristic period of early Christianity. In this ontology, the Last Supper is the type and the Church's Eucharist is the image.

Since the image participates ontologically in the type, everything belonging to the nature of the Last Supper also belongs, by participation, to the nature of the Church's Eucharist.[3] Let us now look at the Last Supper in order to grasp its characteristics and nature; these characteristics will also belong, by participation, to the Church's Eucharist.

3. THE LAST SUPPER

3.1. The Prophetic Character of the Last Supper[4]

At the beginning of this treatise we already noted that Jesus is a Jew who at the Last Supper is performing a Jewish rite. But it is not

---

meal. The words over the bread and those over the cup are never separated, for any reason whatsoever, from the command to eat the bread and drink the wine, since it is this eating and drinking to which the command itself refers. This is the proper order among the questions which the investigator must ask if he is to have an answer that is consistent with the data at his disposal.

[3] I am speaking of the nature of the eucharistic celebration as a celebration, in its completeness, and not simply of the nature of the bread and the wine.

[4] On this point see the extensive discussion in D. Mosco, *Riscoprire l'eucaristia. Le dimensioni teologiche dell'ultima cena* (Cinisello Balsamo [Milan]: Edizioni San Paolo, 1993) 44ff.

enough to say just that; there is more, for there is an important difference that needs to be pointed out, since not everything about the
Supper is reducible to the Jewish rite.

At the Last Supper there are certain objects: the bread, the wine, the
table, the place of the celebration. There are rites: the rite of the bread
and the rite of the cup. There are gestures: the gestures of taking the
bread and of distributing it, and the same for the wine. There are
words[5] and prayers: the prayers of thanksgiving which Jesus recites
during the rite of the bread and the rite of the cup, and the words
with which he offers the bread and wine to the disciples so that they
may eat and drink. The general framework and ritual structure of the
Supper come from the Jewish liturgy, but the behavior of Jesus does
not. His gestures and his words are something new that is not reducible to the Jewish ritual.

The New Testament accounts are not greatly concerned to make
known the elements of the Jewish ritual, because they take it for
granted that everyone is familiar with them. Their concern is to make
clear the novel elements—gestures and words—in the action of Jesus.
This is the most important thing.

The gestures and words of Jesus change the Last Supper into a prophetic action and an announcement: The Last Supper is a parable
and prophecy of the Cross. Contrary to the usage of that time, the
giving of the bread and wine to the disciples is accompanied by some
explanatory words; this underscores the importance of the gift being
given and makes us think of the actions of the prophets. As a matter
of fact, the actions of the prophets were often accompanied by explanatory words,[6] precisely because they were prophetic actions.[7] The
prophetic character of the gestures and words of Jesus turns the supper into a presage of the Cross; all this is part of the self-revelation of
Jesus as master of his own destiny. In a stricter sense, by foretelling
the Cross, he completes the revelation of the life that springs from his
own death;[8] in fact, to eat is to be nourished, and, for the Bible, to be

[5] It is important to see that we have here not only the words of Christ but also
his actions and gestures. We apply to them the same standard that we apply to
his words; it is, in fact, a classic understanding of prophets that they can proclaim
God's will either by speaking it or by doing it.

[6] See Ezekiel 12:8-16, 19f.; 21:12; 37:19-28.

[7] H. Schürmann, *Comment Jésus a-t-il vécu sa mort?* (Lectio divina, 93; Paris: Cerf,
1977) 96.

[8] Léon-Dufour, *Sharing the Eucharistic Bread*, 138.

nourished means that life is being maintained and renewed.[9] Food gives life.

3.2. *A Supper of Communion*

We must now emphasize another meaningful gesture: the sending around of the one cup to all those present, in contrast to the common practice of having each person drink from his own cup.[10] It was an exception for the head of the family, who was presiding at table, to pass his own cup for others to drink from it; such an action signified a special relationship of communion and predilection. Heinz Schürmann concludes from it that in giving his disciples the bread and the cup, Jesus intended to mediate (or simply to suggest) a special blessing. Following a similar line of thought, Xavier Léon-Dufour points out that by the gesture of giving Jesus shows that his life is being communicated:[11] "In saying what he did over the bread and the cup Jesus expressed the meaning of his self-giving unto death; he enables those who share his meal to receive the act by which he saves the world and to share in his sacrifice."[12]

If the Last Supper is a farewell meal and belongs in the literary genre of the testamentary account, we must use this as a criterion for evaluating the gestures and words of Jesus: "Testamentary literature shows the farewell meal as being an act of communion with the testator and a meaningful bond of communion among the testatees."[13]

3.3. *The Announcement of the Cross and the Announcement of Life*

The gestures and words of Jesus refer to the events of Calvary because it is there that they become concrete reality. The words about the "body given" and the "blood shed" refer directly to the cross. The gesture with which Jesus presents the bread and cup to the disciples is the gesture of one who gives, and the explanatory words have for their purpose to explain this gift. Through the gift of the bread-body and the cup-blood he intended to mediate, or simply to suggest, a special blessing.[14] What is this blessing? Calvary is the special blessing

[9] Ibid., 123.

[10] H. Schürmann, "Jesus' Words in the Light of His Actions at the Last Supper," *The Breaking of Bread*, ed. P. Benoit, R. E. Murphy, and B. Van Iersel = Concilium, 1969, no. 40, 125; at greater length, idem, *Comment Jésus* (note 7, above) 99f.

[11] Léon-Dufour, *Sharing the Eucharistic Bread*, 198.

[12] Ibid., 115.

[13] Ibid., 245.

[14] Schürmann, *Comment Jésus*, 100.

in question, that is, his death as the supreme witness *(martyria)* to his mission.

Nevertheless, since to eat is to live, this gift is also connected with life; penetrating more deeply, we must say that this gift is connected with the death of Christ insofar as this death has salvific value.[15] By giving the bread and wine, Jesus showed that salvation comes through his very death;[16] in other words, that the reign of God will come, not despite, but because of his death.[17] If there is here an announcement of the kingdom, then the farewell meal has a specific eschatological connotation, since the kingdom of God is essentially eschatological. To drink the cup which Jesus offers to the disciples means to share in the salvation and the eschatological covenant which are accomplished by the imminent death of Jesus. Finally, the Last Supper is an *active sign* of the eschatological feast[18] in the kingdom of God.[19]

At the Last Supper the disciples are not being presented with information about events that will take place on Calvary; these events are already in motion and present at the Supper, and the disciples are experiencing them. H. Schürmann puts it very well when he says that the Supper is "a symbolic action anticipating his imminent death, an *ôt* rather in the manner of the Old Testament prophets. But here it is not really a case of prophesying the future; prophesied future is proffered as a gift. . . . The sign is in the gift, the gift is not the effect of the sign."[20]

Xavier Léon-Dufour adopts the same perspective: Jesus "anticipates symbolically both his death and the increased life it will bring to his disciples."[21] And again: "Symbolic words or gestures are not simple announcements of what is to come; in them a reality is being enacted before our eyes, a reality that *is* and *is not* the thing said or done.[22] In the

---

[15] Ibid., 104.

[16] A.-L. Descamps, "Cénacle et calvaire. Les vues de H. Schürmann," *Revue théologique de Louvain* 10 (1979) 344.

[17] Ibid., 345.

[18] In the Bible the kingdom of God is often symbolized by a banquet.

[19] Schürmann, *Comment Jésus*, 103ff.

[20] Schürmann, "Le parole di Gesù" (note 10, above) 130–31.

[21] Léon-Dufour, *Sharing the Eucharistic Bread*, 66.

[22] There is a difference between the action of Jesus and that of the prophets of the Old Testament. The action of the Old Testament prophet provides only a framework for the action of Jesus, the efficacy of which surpasses that of the prophetic *ôt*, since it derives from the fact that Jesus is the very Word of God made flesh. In saying this, I am following the approach taken by John Chrysostom in

actions and words of the Supper Jesus is 'expressing' his death, he is 'experiencing' it,"[23] and in this is associating his disciples with himself.

We may therefore conclude that for the disciples their sharing in the Supper of the Lord is much more than simply sharing a meal. Everything refers to something that lies outside the meal itself and becomes concrete elsewhere, on Calvary; participation in the events of Calvary becomes possible for the disciples only through the feast.[24]

3.4. The Explanatory Words

As he extends the bread to the disciples, Jesus explains the gesture and the invitation to eat of it: "Take and eat of this, all of you; this is my body."[25]

In biblical anthropology, the word "body" designates the whole person, and not simply the physical element, as in the modern languages. Just as the devout Jew is nourished by the gifts of the land, which is a sign of divine election, so the disciples are invited, all of

---

his homily on *The Betrayal of Judas:* It is the word of God, the word of Jesus at the Supper, that guarantees that the relationship between Supper and Cross is a real, even if symbolic one, and not a simple allegory.

[23] Léon-Dufour, *Sharing the Eucharistic Bread*, 188.

[24] No one can share and participate in the death of another person: each person is alone with himself or herself. This incommunicability can be overcome only by gestures that are part of communication through symbols. Calvary is therefore a personal event, peculiar to Jesus; the Supper is the bridge and link connecting the disciples with Calvary; the disciples experience Calvary at the Supper.

[25] It cannot be agreed that the separation of the bread from the cup represents the death of Jesus. This explanation was a common one in the Middle Ages and was already present in some Fathers of the Church, such as Theodore of Mopsuestia. The theory cannot be maintained because in the New Testament there is question not so much of a separation of the bread from the wine as of a separation between two rites; it is the nature of the rite of the bread, with its connected prayers, to be separate from the rite of the wine. The two rites come into being as separate and independent, since they are separated by the course of the Supper; there is nothing about the rite of the cup that recalls and requires the rite of the bread. The same is to be said of the rite of the bread, which has nothing in it that refers to the rite of the cup. It follows that the meaning of the rite of the bread can exist as complete and self-sufficient, independently of the rite of the cup. Consequently, it cannot be said that the word "body" and the word "blood" are to be interpreted as if they formed a pair, the pair consisting of "body and blood." In the Bible, this pair signifies the human person in its totality. As we saw at the beginning of the present book, it is only in the Matthew/Mark tradition that the two rites are placed side by side and are thus able to take on a meaning that is due to their reciprocal relationship.

them together, to derive their nourishment from the presence of Jesus. In addition, "body" carries the nuance of a weakness that is proper to creatures, and thus brings out well the attitude of Jesus in his relationships with others. In the Bible, "body" can also signify a corpse,[26] and therefore "the word's range of meanings suggest two alternative lines of interpretation: the person in relation to the universe, or the person as destined to die."[27] If we bear in mind the Pauline addition "which is for you,"[28] and the Lukan variation "given for you,"[29] we must conclude that "when Jesus speaks of 'my body,' he is referring to his life that is given even to the point of accepting death, but in a sacrifice that is personal."[30]

"For you": In Greek the words used in the tradition of Paul and Luke are *hyper hymôn*. There has been a great deal of debate about these words, inasmuch as the opinion is widespread that they point to the sacrifices celebrated in the Old Testament and refer directly to the doctrine of vicarious satisfaction. Xavier Léon-Dufour provides a careful discussion of the problem and concludes the *hyper* cannot be given this meaning without doing violence to the text. Only in Philemon 13 (and perhaps in 1 Corinthians 15:29 and 2 Corinthians 5:14) does *hyper* mean "in place of"; this is too weak a philological support for the doctrine of vicarious satisfaction. I refer the reader to Léon-Dufour's carefully argued demonstration[31] and limit myself to accepting his conclusion. According to his analysis, *hyper hymon* means only "in your favor." Here is how he rewords the language of Christ at the Last Supper: "'I give myself as food so that you may live'; such is the sense, in context, of *hyper* ('for,' 'in favor of') since human beings eat in order to have life."[32]

---

[26] It is worth noting that throughout the biblical world bread had a sacral meaning that was connected with life: Bread sustains life. For this reason it was the place of relationship with God, so that when the devout Jew ate, he was bound to bless God for the gift received. In the same setting at the Last Supper, however, the central reality is not the bread but the person of Jesus, who is the source of life because of the special relationship with others which he himself has established, to the point of dying for them. Life is the key theme, but life comes through the death of Jesus.

[27] Léon-Dufour, *Sharing the Eucharistic Bread*, 119.

[28] 1 Corinthians 11:24.

[29] Luke 22:19.

[30] Léon-Dufour, *Sharing the Eucharistic Bread*, 120.

[31] Ibid., 120–23.

[32] Ibid., 123. "A corollary needs to be stated explicitly. In the words over the bread Jesus is not announcing that he accepts death as a 'means' of salvation; he

Having inspected the words over the bread, let us move on to those over the cup. In the Bible, "cup" has many metaphorical meanings. It can signify the destiny of a person,[33] or the trials he must weather[34] or the punishment he must endure.[35] In addition, a cup is used in worship and recalls the sacrificial rites. It is not useless to recall that what is said in the liturgy is not "This is my blood," but "This is the cup of my blood." The cup is not just any container but an aid to drinking; and wine is a sign of the joy which God gives to human beings.[36] In Paul the cup is described in technical language as the "cup of blessing,"[37] that is, the cup that is connected with the prayer of thanksgiving. "Cup of the covenant" is an expression taken from Exodus 24:4-8, but with one important change. In Exodus, it is the Lord, or God, who concludes the covenant with Israel; at the Last Supper it is Jesus who concludes it and concludes it by means of his own Blood.[38] Jesus is the one who concludes the covenant and, at the same time, he is the means by which it is concluded.[39]

The words over the cup speak of "blood that is poured out." Blood is closely related to violent death: "To shed blood is to destroy the bearer of life and therefore life itself."[40] The cross is in the foreground, and the shedding of blood is the specific action that describes a crucifixion; in the background, however, there is also the adjective "my," attached to the blood that is poured out. Jesus seals the covenant by dying, but a covenant with a dead person is meaningless and foreign to the logic of covenant in Israel. Furthermore, this covenant is "eternal." It is

---

is announcing rather that as a result of his fidelity unto death to God and human beings he will be present to his followers by becoming their food and giving them life through himself" (ibid.).

[33] Mark 10:38ff.

[34] Mark 14:36.

[35] Revelation 14:10.

[36] At solemn festive meals, and especially at the Passover meal, wine is obligatory.

[37] 1 Corinthians 10:16.

[38] We must bear two points in mind: (1) The cup at the Supper contains the blood that will be shed on the cross, and the covenant is said to be made in the blood of Jesus, the blood which, in fact, will be shed only on the cross. (2) From the cross Jesus gives his Spirit (John 19:30) and, as the risen Lord, will continue to communicate it as the typical post-Easter gift (John 7:39; 16:7, 20, 22ff.). It is on the cross, therefore, that he seals the new covenant (Heb 9:18-20), which is characterized precisely by the gift of the Spirit (see Jer 31:31-34).

[39] The covenant that was made by the Lord in Exodus is here the new and everlasting covenant made by Jesus, the Lord, in his own blood.

[40] J. Behm, "Haima," *TDNT* 1:173.

therefore necessary that Jesus be alive, even after the defeat of death, if he is to be able to be eternally a partner in the covenant and to retain his part in it.

Behind the death, then, the resurrection is already making its appearance.

The cup is "poured out."[41] This word here can point only to the bloody death, since it does not match the technical term used in worship: "sprinkle."[42] Only Matthew says that the blood is poured out "for the forgiveness of sins"; this simply makes explicit the theme of the covenant,[43] namely, that Israel must be cleansed of its sins and walk in the ways of the Lord.

We have seen that the theme of the "blood poured out" is at the center of the explanatory words over the cup. In the Old Testament, blood is life: the locus of life and the means of transmitting life. Because of this connection with life, blood is regarded as sacred (Lev 17:11, 14; Deut 12:23). If we wanted to translate the words over the cup into contemporary language, we would have to say that Jesus hands the disciples, not a cup of blood, but a cup of life used up entirely and unrestrictedly for them, to the point of accepting death.

Jesus could not have uttered a clearer prophecy of the Cross than he does by his words over the cup.

4. CONCLUSION

I have now explained the prophetic and symbolic character of the Last Supper as an announcement and prophecy of the Cross, but an announcement possessing an eschatological connotation in which the

[41] *For you and for all.* At the Jewish Passover meal, those present asked for a blessing on Israel and called down the divine wrath on Israel's enemies. Jesus, however, acknowledges no boundaries or enmities. He embraces all. He thus makes himself the single focal point at which all others must take their stand in order to receive blessing. Only the Lord has such a status. Indirectly, these words, too, allude to the resurrection.

[42] The word "sprinkle" has no place at the Supper, since the disciples are not asked to sprinkle the blood of Christ on an altar but simply to drink it: "There is question not of the purification gained from expiatory sacrifices through the sprinkling of the sacrificial blood, but of a drink and therefore of increased life" (Léon-Dufour, *Sharing the Eucharistic Bread,* 143).

[43] A covenant with God supposes a communion with him who is by definition the Holy One. The covenant in the blood of Christ is new and eternal. This means that sin has been removed from the world by his blood. But who can forgive sins except God? The forgiveness of sins announces the coming of the eschatological reign of God (Matt 9:2-6). All this is directly connected with the cup.

theme of the resurrection is present though hidden. From this it follows that the Last Supper has, first and foremost, a figural character as representation of the Lord's Cross.

Since the Eucharist of the Church is an imitation of, that is, a participation in, the Last Supper, it follows that all the characteristics of the Last Supper, those which we have been explaining, must also be predicated of the Church's Eucharist. When, therefore, we continue to use the same gestures and words out of obedience to the command of Christ, we share in the same parable and the same announcement that Jesus Christ made. It follows that the eucharistic celebration is a figure of the passion because of its relationship with the Last Supper, of which it is a participation.

Because of the rules of methodology which they follow, studies of the liturgy should end by bringing to light the way in which the rite is a sign of the reality being celebrated. In the case of the eucharistic celebration, the sign[44] is a complex of elements. Beginning with the New Testament, the liturgical tradition has carefully handed on the list of these elements by recounting the actions of Jesus in the upper room: He took bread, broke it, gave thanks, saying, and so on; he took the cup, gave thanks, gave it, saying, and so on. In other words, it is all of these elements, taken together and brought together in a coherent way in the celebration, that make the eucharistic celebration the antitype of the Last Supper.

The liturgical practice of Christianity maintains that the Eucharist is a sign of the cross; this figural character is due to its relationship with the Last Supper and is to be described in the classical language of sacramentality that was developed in the patristic period through the application of biblical typology to the liturgy. Thus the Church's Eucharist, insofar as it is a meal, is to be described as a figure, form, likeness, and imitation (or "sacrament") of the cross because of its ritual and ontological correspondence to the Last Supper.

In conclusion, if we wish to sum up in a few words what the Eucharist is in this figural perspective, we can only cite Paul: "As often as you eat this bread and drink the cup, you proclaim the Lord's death until he comes" (1 Cor 11:26). The verb "proclaim" *(kataggellô)* is perfectly in place in this passage in which its function is to describe the "sacramental" relationship that exists between the Supper and the Cross.

---

[44] I use the word "sign" to signify that which establishes and defines the conformity of the Church's Eucharist with the Last Supper; the conformity is to be understood as both ritual and ontological.

Appendix

Jewish Texts and Very Early Eucharistic Prayers

QIDDUSH (BLESSING BEFORE A MEAL)

1.1. Blessing over the cup

(In a low voice) "And there was evening and there was morning: *(aloud)* the sixth day. And on the seventh day God ended the work he had done, and on the seventh day ceased from all the work he had done. And God blessed the seventh day and sanctified it, because on it he had ceased from all the work that God had done in creating" (Gen 1:31–2:3).

Blessed are you, Lord our God, king of the world, who create the fruit of the vine.

Blessed are you, Lord our God, king of the world, who has sanctified us with his precepts and has been pleased with us; and in loving kindness has given us his holy Sabbath as an inheritance, to be a memorial of the work of creation, for that is the day which began the holy convocations, a memorial of the departure from Egypt. We are the ones you have chosen, we the ones whom you have sanctified from among all the peoples, and in loving kindness you have given us your holy Sabbath as an inheritance. Blessed are you, Lord, who sanctify the Sabbath.

1.2. Blessing over the bread

Blessed are you, Lord our God, king of the world, who make bread come forth from the earth.

BLESSING AFTER A MEAL *(BIRKAT HA-MAZON)*

The blessing after a meal consists in four (originally three) blessings that refer, in order, to the entire world, the land of Israel, and Jerusalem. I give here the Palestinian recension, from the Genizeh, as reproduced by L. Finkelstein, "The birkat ha-mazon," *JQR* 19 (1928–29) 236–62. On the basis of this and other witnesses Finkelstein reconstructs a hypothetical "original" version. I prefer, however, to keep to a documented text.

2.1. *He who nourishes* (ha-zan)

Blessed are you, Lord our God, king of the world, who nourish the entire world in kindness, grace, and mercy. He gives food to all flesh, because his favor toward us and his great kindness are everlasting. For the sake of his great name, no good thing has ever been lacking to us nor ever will be, because he nourishes and feeds all. Blessed are you, Lord, who nourish all.

2.2. *Blessing of the land* (Birkat ha-arez)

We thank you, Lord our God, because you have given us as an inheritance a desirable, good, and spacious land, the covenant and the Torah, life and peace. For all these we thank you and bless your great and holy Name, eternally and always. Blessed are you, Lord, for the land and for food.

2.3. *Blessing of Jerusalem* (Birkat Jerushalajim)

Have mercy, Lord our God, on Israel your people, on Jerusalem your city, on the house of David, your anointed one, and on the great and holy house upon which your Name has been invoked. Hasten to restore the kingdom of the house of David to its place in our time. Rebuild Jerusalem quickly; restore us to its midst and give us joy in it. Blessed are you, Lord, who in your mercy rebuild Jerusalem. Amen.

DIDACHE

9.1. With regard to the Eucharist, give thanks in this manner:

2. First, over the cup: "We thank you, our Father, for the holy vine of David your servant, which you have revealed through Jesus your servant. Glory be yours through all ages! Amen."

3. Over the (broken) bread: "We thank you, our Father, for the life and the knowledge which you have revealed to us through Jesus your servant. Glory be yours through all ages!

4. "Just as this (bread) was broken, scattered on the hills and gathered and became one, so may your Church be gathered from the ends of the earth into your kingdom. Yours is glory and power through all ages. Amen."

5. Let no one eat or drink of your Eucharist unless they have been baptized in the name of the Lord. For the Lord says in this regard: "Do not give holy things to dogs."

10.1 After you have been satisfied, give thanks in this way:

2. "We thank you, holy Father, for your holy name which you have made to dwell in our hearts, and for the knowledge and the immortality which you have revealed to us through Jesus your servant. Glory be yours through all ages!

3. "Almighty Lord, you have created everything through your name; you have given food and drink to (the children of) mortals for their enjoyment, so that they might give you thanks, but to us you have given a spiritual food and drink and eternal life through Jesus your servant. 4. For all these things we thank you, because you are mighty. To you be glory through all ages. Amen.

5. "Be mindful, Lord, of your Church: deliver it from every evil and make it perfect in love of you. And gather it, a sanctified Church, from the four winds into your kingdom which you have prepared for it. For yours is the kingdom and the glory for all ages.

6. "Let grace come and this world pass away. Hosanna to the Son of David.

"If any are holy, let them draw near; if any are not, let them be converted.

"Maranatha. Amen."

7. Let the prophets give thanks as they wish.

14.1. On the day of the Lord, the Lord's day, when you have gathered, break the bread and give thanks, confessing your failures, in order that your sacrifice may be pure. 2. Anyone having a quarrel with his brother is not to gather with you until he has been reconciled, in order that your sacrifice may not be profaned. 3. For this is the word of the Lord for every time and every place: "Offer me a pure sacrifice, for I am a great king—says the Lord—and my Name is wonderful among the nations."

APOSTOLIC CONSTITUTIONS 7.25.1–26.6

25.1. As faithful and grateful servants, then, give thanks at all times through the Eucharist, in these words: 2. "We thank you, our Father, for the life which you have made known to us through Jesus your servant. For him you have created all things and take care of all things.

You commanded him to become a human being for our salvation; you allowed him to suffer and die; you raised him up, glorified him, and made him sit at your right hand. Through him, too, you announced to us the resurrection of the dead.

3. "Almighty Lord, eternal God, just as that which has been scattered and then gathered together becomes a single loaf, so too gather your Church from the ends of the earth into your kingdom. 4. We also thank you, our Father, for the precious blood of Jesus Christ that was poured out for us, and for the precious body, these antitypes of which we accomplish, for he himself ordained that we should proclaim his death. Through him may glory be yours through all ages. Amen."

4. Let none eat who have not been initiated, but only those who have been baptized into the death of the Lord. 6. If anyone not initiated should conceal his state and share in the Eucharist, he will eat eternal condemnation, because though not sharing faith in Christ, he has shared in these things that are forbidden him, and he will be punished. 7. If anyone participates through ignorance, teach him the rudiments and initiate him quickly, so that he may not continue in contempt.

26.1. After Communion give thanks in this way: 2. "We thank you, God, Father of Jesus our Savior, for your holy name, which you have made to dwell [to set up its tent] in us, and for the knowledge, faith, charity, and immortality which you have given us through Jesus your servant. 3. Lord, almighty God, God of all things, you have created the world and all that is in it, and have sown your law in our hearts, and have prepared nourishment for mortals. God of our holy and blameless fathers, Abraham, Isaac, and Jacob, your faithful servants; mighty God, faithful and true and truthful, who do not deceive with your promises and who sent Jesus, your Christ, to earth in order to live among mortals as a mortal, as God the Logos and a human being, and to destroy error to its every root: so now, in the same way, be mindful through him of your holy Church which you have acquired through the precious blood of your Christ, and deliver it from every evil, make it perfect in your love and your truth, and gather us all into your kingdom which you have prepared for it.

5. "Maranatha. Hosanna to the Son of David. Blessed is he who comes in the name of the Lord, for God the Lord has shown himself to us in the flesh."

6. If any are holy, let them approach. If any are not, let them become holy through conversion. Agree, then, with your presbyters in giving thanks.

STRASBOURG PAPYRUS

It is truly right and just, holy and fitting, and for the salvation of our souls, O Master, Lord, God, Father almighty, that we should praise you, celebrate you, give you thanks, confess you openly, night and day, with mouth *(stoma)* never quiet and lips that do not fall still and heart never silent, for you made heaven and earth, the seas, the springs, the rivers, the lakes, and all that is in them, and you made human beings in your image and likeness. You made everything through your wisdom, through the true light of your Only-begotten Son, our Lord and God and Savior, Jesus Christ.

Through him we give you thanks and offer to you, with him and the Holy Spirit, this spiritual *(logikên)* sacrifice, this bloodless worship, which all the nations offer to you from the rising of the sun to its setting, from the North to the South, for great is your name among all the nations, and in every place incense and a pure sacrifice are offered to your holy name.

Over this sacrifice and offering we pray and beseech you: Be mindful of your holy and one, catholic, and apostolic Church, that reaches from end to end of the earth, of all your peoples and all your flocks. Place the peace of heaven in our hearts, but grant us also peace in this life. Grant that the king of the earth may have thoughts of peace toward us and toward your holy name. Give peace to the governor . . . the military orders, the princes, the senate, the council, and our kindred, and arrange that our coming in and going out may be peaceful.

Go before our brothers who are journeying in various places; deign to be yourself their companion on sea and land, and bring them safely back to their (dear ones). Send your rains; give joy to the face of the earth; show us your fruits for seed and harvest; keep the crops sound and safe: for the poor among your people, for all of us who call upon your holy name, for all who hope in you. Grant peace to the souls of those who have fallen asleep; be mindful of the souls of those whose names we utter and of those whose names we do not utter, and be mindful also of our holy orthodox fathers in every place and of the bishops, and grant us to have part and inheritance in the community of your holy prophets, apostles, and martyrs, because of their authority. And accept this prayer on your holy heavenly altar and deign. . . .

Grant to them the spiritual gifts, through the Lord and our Savior, through whom glory is yours for endless ages.

ANAPHORA ATTRIBUTED TO HIPPOLYTUS

We give you thanks, O God, through your beloved servant, Jesus Christ, whom you have sent to us in these last times as savior and redeemer and messenger of your will, who is your inseparable word, through whom you made everything and who was pleasing to you. You sent him from heaven into the womb of a virgin, and, having been conceived in the womb he took flesh and showed himself to you as a son, born of the Holy Spirit and the virgin.

Fulfilling your will and winning for you a holy people, he stretched out his hands in the time of suffering in order by suffering to set free those who had believed in you.

When he was to be handed over to voluntary suffering in order to cast off death and break the chains of the devil and trample upon hell and enlighten the just and establish a fixed time and make known the resurrection, taking bread, giving thanks, he said: "Take and eat, this is my body which is broken for you."

So too the cup, saying: "This is my blood which will be shed for you. When you do this, make remembrance of me."

Mindful, therefore, of his death and resurrection, we offer you the bread and the cup, giving thanks to you because you have made us worthy to stand before you and serve you [= to celebrate worship in your honor].

And we ask you to send your Holy Spirit on the offering of the holy Church. Gathering them into unity, grant to all those who participate in the holy "mysteries" [or: to all the saints who participate], through the fullness of the Holy Spirit, the confirmation of their faith in the truth, that we may praise and glorify you through your servant, Jesus Christ, through whom glory and honor are yours . . . in your holy Church, both now and through endless ages. Amen.

MARTYRDOM OF POLYCARP

13.1. Events developed rather speedily, quicker than the time it takes to tell you of them; the crowd very quickly gathered pieces of wood and dry branches from the shops and the baths; the Jews in particular, with their customary ill-will, contributed to what was happening. 2. When the pyre was ready, [Polycarp], having removed all his garments and having removed his belt, sought also to remove his shoes, something he himself had never done until this moment, because someone of his faithful always hastened to do it in order to gaze at his body, for even before his martyrdom he had been adorned in every way by the uprightness of his way of life. 3. In a moment, then, there was set around him everything that goes into (arming/building) a pyre. When they were about to nail him to it as well, he said: "Leave me as I am: he who enables me to endure the fire will also enable me to resist (remain) unmoved in it without the insurance of your nails."

14.1. Therefore they did not nail him, but did bind him. After placing his hands behind him and having been thus bound, like a ram chosen from a numerous flock as an offering, and when he had been made ready like a holocaust pleasing to God, he raised his eyes to heaven and said:

"Lord God almighty, Father of your beloved and blessed Son Jesus Christ, through whom we have received knowledge of you, God of the angels and the powers and of all creation and of the entire race of the just, who live in your presence:

2. "I bless you, because you have made me worthy this day and this hour to enter into the number of the martyrs [who have shared] in the cup of your Christ, for the resurrection of eternal life of the soul and the body, in the incorruptibility [that comes from] the Holy Spirit.

"May I be received among them today in your presence as a rich and pleasing sacrifice, as you have arranged, made known, and ful-filled, God truthful and true.

3. "For this and for all things I praise you, I bless you, I glorify you through the eternal and high priest, Jesus Christ, your beloved Son, through whom is glory given to you, along with himself and the Holy Spirit, now and through endless ages. Amen."

15.1. When he had lifted up his Amen and had finished his prayer, those assigned lit the fire, and a great flame shot up; we saw a mir-acle, those of us to whom it was granted to see: we were preserved in order to tell others what happened. 2. In fact, the fire took on the shape of a vault, like the sail of a ship when the wind swells it, and, like a wall, surrounded the body of the martyr, and he was in the midst, not as flesh to be burned, but as bread to be baked or as gold and silver to be refined in a crucible. And we were conscious of so sweet a fragrance, as when incense or some other precious perfume wafts its odor.

16.1. Finally, when the wicked saw that his body could not be consumed by the fire, they ordered the executioner to thrust his dagger (into his breast). And when this was done, a dove came out, and a gush of blood great enough to extinguish the fire and cause the entire crowd to marvel that such a difference should exist between unbelievers and the elect. 2. For he too, the wondrous Polycarp, had become one of them, after having been during our lifetime an apostolic teacher and prophetic bishop of the Catholic Church of Smyrna. For every word that came from his mouth had to be, and will have to be, fulfilled.

ALEXANDRIAN ANAPHORA OF BASIL

The priest in a loud voice: The Lord (be) with you.
People: And with your spirit.
Priest: Let us have our hearts on high.
People: We have (lifted) them to the Lord.
Priest: Let us give thanks to the Lord.
People: (It is) right and just.
Priest: (It is) truly right and just, right and just, right and just.

Beginning of the sacrifice

You who are Master of reality, Lord, God of truth, who exist before the ages and govern throughout the ages; who dwell in the heights of heaven throughout the ages, gazing down on lowly things; you who have made heaven and earth and sea and everything that is in them. The Father of our Lord and God and Savior, Jesus Christ, through whom you made all things, those visible and those invisible. Who sit upon the throne of your holy glory in your kingdom; who are adored by every holy power.
Deacon: Stand up, you who are seated.
Priest: Near him are standing the angels, archangels, principalities and powers, thrones and dominations and powers.
Deacon: Look to the East.
Priest: Those who stand around you, the cherubim with their many eyes, the seraphim with their six wings, who extol you throughout the universe, shout their acclamation and say:
People: Holy, Holy, Holy, Lord Sabaoth.
Deacon: Let us be attentive.
Priest: Holy, Holy, Holy indeed are you, Lord our God who formed us and placed us in the garden of delights. When we had violated

your command because of the serpent's deceit and had lost eternal life and were far from the garden of delights, you did not spurn us to the end, but in every way you watched over us always through your holy prophets, and you showed us, who were sitting in darkness and in the shadow of death, that there was an end of these days through your only-begotten Son, our Lord and God and Savior Jesus Christ. He, having taken flesh by the Holy Spirit and from our holy Lady, Mary Mother of God and ever virgin, and living his life in the midst of humanity, showed us the way of salvation by giving us a new, heavenly birth from water and the Spirit. He made us a chosen people for himself, he sanctified us in your Holy Spirit. He loved his own who were in the world and gave himself as a ransom for the death that reigned over us and in which we were held fast, being corrupted by sin. Having descended through the cross in Hades, he rose from the dead on the third day and, having ascended to heaven, sits at your right hand, Father. He has fixed the day of recompense on which having (once) manifested himself, he will judge the earth with justice and will repay each one according to his own deeds.

People: According to your mercy, Lord, and not "according to our sins."

Priest: He left us this great mystery of mercy. When he was about to hand himself over to death for the life of the world,—

People: Let us believe!—he took bread in his holy, venerable, and blessed hands; lifting his gaze toward the heights of heaven to you, his Father, our God, and God of the universe, and having given thanks,— *People:* Amen!—having blessed,—*People:* Amen!—having sanctified,— *People:* Amen!—having broken (the bread), he gave it to his holy disciples and apostles, saying: "Take, eat, this is my body, broken and distributed for the forgiveness of sins. Do this in remembrance *(anamnêsi)* of me. In the same way also the cup, after having supped, having mixed the wine with water, and having given thanks,—*People:* Amen!—having blessed,—*People:* Amen!—having sanctified,—*People:* Amen!—having tasted it, he gave it again to his holy disciples and apostles, saying: "Take, drink of this, all of you, this is my blood, the blood of the new covenant, shed for you and for all for the forgiveness of sins. Do this in remembrance *(anamnêsi)* of me. For, every time you eat of this bread and drink of this cup, you proclaim my death and you confess my resurrection and my ascension until I come again."

People: Amen, amen, amen, "we proclaim your death, Lord, we confess your resurrection and ascension."

Priest: We, too, therefore, mindful of his holy passion, his resurrection from the dead, his ascension into heaven, and his sitting at your right hand, God and Father, and his glorious and awesome second coming, we offer you, from your gifts, what is yours, in every way and for everything and in everything.

People: We praise you, we bless you, "we give you thanks, Lord, and we pray you, our God."

Deacon: Bow down to God in fear.

Priest, to himself: And we pray you and we invoke you, kind and good Lord, we who are sinners and your unworthy servants, and we worship you for the kindness of your goodness, in order that your Holy Spirit may come upon us, your servants, and upon these gifts set before you, and may sanctify them and manifest the Holy of Holies.

Deacon: Let us be attentive.

People: Amen!

Priest, aloud: And make this bread become the holy body of the same Lord and God and our Savior Jesus Christ for the forgiveness of sins and for the eternal life of those who partake of it.

People: Amen!

Priest: And this cup the precious blood of the new covenant of the same Lord and God and our Savior Jesus Christ for forgiveness and for the eternal life of those who partake of it.

People: Amen! Kyrie eleison *(three times).*

Priest: And make us worthy, Lord, to partake of the holy mysteries for the sanctification of soul and of body, and (partake) of the Holy Spirit, that we may be/become a single body and a single spirit and may have part and obtain the reward with the saints who from the beginning have pleased you.

Remember, Lord, your holy, one, catholic Church and grant peace to her whom you acquired with the precious blood of your Christ.

First of all, Lord, remember our holy father archbishop, Abba *N.,* pope and patriarch of the great city of Alexandria, whom you have given to your holy Churches; (keep him) safe in peace, honored, in good health, that he may correctly explain the doctrine of truth and may feed your flock in peace.

Remember, Lord, the orthodox presbyters and the entire diaconate and of the ministers, of all those who (are/live) in virginity, and of all your most faithful people.

Remember us, Lord, and have mercy on us all in the same way and once and for all.

People: Have pity on us, God, Father, the Almighty.

Priest: Have pity on us, God, the Almighty *(three times).*

People: Kyrie eleison *(three times).*

Priest: Remember, Lord, the safety of this city of ours and of those who dwell therein in the faith of God.

Remember, Lord, the weather and the fruits of the soil.

Remember, Lord, the rain and the seeds in the soil.

Remember, Lord, the orderly flooding of the river waters.

Gladden the face of the earth once again and renew it, fill its furrows, multiply its crops. For our sake, prepare it for the sowing and the harvest, and bless us now with every blessing. Manage our lives. Bless the course of the year in your kindness, for the sake of the poor among your people, the widow and the orphan, the stranger and the foreigner, and all of us who hope in you whose name we invoke. For the eyes of all look to you with hope, and you give them food in due season. Do with us according to your goodness and give food to all flesh. Fill our heart with joy and gladness, in order that, having always enough for ourselves in everything, we may abound in every good work, so as to do your holy will.

People: Kyrie eleison.

Priest: Remember, Lord, those who offer you these precious gifts, for whose sake, through whom, and for whom they have brought them, and grant to all of them the heavenly reward.

For, Lord, the command of your only-begotten Son is that we be at one in the memory of your saints. Again, Lord, deign remember those who pleased you from the beginning, the holy fathers, patriarchs, apostles, prophets, preachers, evangelists, martyrs, confessors, and every just spirit that died in the faith of Christ.

Especially the most holy, most glorious, immaculate, supremely blessed one, Mary, our Lady, Mother of God and ever virgin.

The holy, glorious prophet, precursor, baptist, and martyr, John.

Saint Stephen, first deacon and first martyr.

And our holy, blessed father Mark, the apostle and evangelist, and, among the saints, of our holy father Basil, the wonderworker.

Holy *N.,* whose memory we celebrate today, and the whole choir of your saints, through whose prayers and intercessions you have mercy on us, and save us for the sake of your saint, whose name is invoked over us.

The deacon reads the diptychs.

Priest, to himself: In the same way, remember also, Lord, all those in the priestly order who have already fallen asleep, and those in the lay state; make worthy of rest the souls of all who are in the bosom of our holy fathers Abraham, Isaac, and Jacob. Be near them and lead them to a grassy place, near calm waters in the garden of delights, and from this drive out all suffering, sadness, and groaning in the splendor of your saints.

After the diptychs the priest says: Grant peace to those souls whom you have taken, and make them worthy of the kingdom of heaven. Preserve in the faith us also who dwell here, and lead us on/show us the way to your kingdom. Grant us your peace always, in order that, through this and in everything, your most holy and honored and blessed name, and Christ Jesus, and the Holy Spirit may be glorified, exalted, hymned, blessed, and sanctified.

People: So it was . . .

BYZANTINE ANAPHORA OF BASIL

Priest: The grace of our Lord Jesus Christ and the love *(agapê)* of God the Father and the communion of the Holy Spirit be with all of you.

People: And with your spirit.

Priest: Let us lift up our hearts.

People: We have (lifted) them to the Lord.

Priest: Let us give thanks to the Lord.

People: (It is) right and just.

The priest enters into this holy anaphora: Lord of everything, Lord, almighty and adorable God the Father, (it is) indeed right and just, and suited to the greatness of your holiness, to praise you, hymn you, bless you, adore you, give you thanks, glorify you, the only one true God, and offer you this our spiritual worship with a contrite heart and in a spirit of humiliation. For it is you who have given us the knowledge of your truth, you who would be capable yourself of expressing your powers, rendering audible all your praises, and telling all of your wonders in every age, O Lord, Lord of all things, Lord of heaven and earth and the whole creation, visible and invisible, who sit on a throne of glory and gaze into the abysses, who are without beginning, invisible, incomprehensible, indescribable, immutable, Father of our Lord Jesus Christ, the great God and Savior in whom we hope, who is the image of your goodness, seal of identical form who in himself shows us you, the Father; (who is) the living Word, true God, Wisdom before the ages, life, sanctification, power, true light, by whom the Holy Spirit has been manifested, the Spirit of truth, grace of adoption, pledge of the future truth, first fruits of the eternal blessings,

318

life-giving power, fount of sanctification by whom the whole creation that is spiritual and capable of knowledge is rendered strong and worships you and raises to you an everlasting doxology, in order that the whole assemblage of things may serve you. Indeed, praise is given to you by the angels, archangels, thrones, dominations, principalities, authorities, powers, and the cherubim with their many eyes, the seraphim who encircle you, each with six wings: with two they cover their faces, with two their feet, with two they fly as they cry one to another, with unceasing voices and with endless praises,

Aloud: who sing the hymn of victory, acclaiming, crying out, and saying:

People: Holy, Holy, Holy, Lord Sabaoth, heaven and earth are filled with your glory; hosanna in the highest. Blessed is he who comes in the name of the Lord; hosanna in the highest.

Priest in a low voice: Together with these blessed powers, O kind Lord, we sinners, too, cry out and say: You are holy indeed, and most holy, and there is no measuring the greatness of your holiness, and (you are) holy in all your works, for in justice and true judgment you have given us everything. After forming man by taking the mud of the ground and honoring it with your image, O God, you placed him in the garden of delights and announced eternal life for him and the enjoyment of the eternal blessings if he observed your commands. But when he did not obey the true God who had created him, but was seduced by the deceit of the serpent and became mortal as a result of his own sins, you, O God, in your just judgment, exiled him from the garden in this world, and you changed him back into the earth from which he had been taken. But you prepared salvation for him through a new birth, that (which is) in your own Christ.

You did not in fact scorn your creature, for the sake of the end for which you had made him, O Good One, nor did you forget the work of your hands, but, in the bowels of your mercy, you turned your gaze to him in many ways, and you sent him the prophets, and you did mighty things through your saints who pleased you from generation to generation, and you spoke to us through the mouth of your servants the prophets, telling us in advance of the salvation that would be close at hand. You gave us a law as a help, you set angels as watchmen. When the fullness of time came, you spoke to us in your own Son, through whom you also made the ages: He who is the splendor of glory, the image of your substance, who sustains everything by uttering your power, and who did not think his equality with you, God and Father, a booty (to be grasped), but, being God before the ages, he was seen on earth. He bound himself to humanity, and, taking flesh of a holy virgin, emptied himself by taking the condition of a slave, becoming like to our wretched body, and this in order to conform us to the image of his glory. Since sin entered the world through a man and, through sin, death, your only-begotten Son, who is in the bosom of his God and Father, was pleased to be born of a woman, the holy Mother of God, Mary ever virgin, to be subject to the law, to condemn sin in his flesh, in order that those who are dead in Adam may be made alive in your Christ. While he was a citizen of this world, he gave the precepts of salvation and distanced us from the error of idols; he led us to the knowledge of the true God and Father who acquired us for himself as a chosen people, a royal priesthood, a holy race. After cleansing us in water and sanctifying us in the Holy Spirit, he gave himself as a ransom from the death in which we had been held through the corruption of sin.

Descending through the cross into Hades, in order to fill everything with himself, he put an end to the pains of death. He rose on the third day and showed all flesh the way through the resurrection of the dead, since it was not possible for the author of life to be overcome by corruption. He became the first fruits of those who had fallen asleep, the first-born of the dead, in order that he might in every way be superior in all things, and, having ascended to heaven, he took his seat at the right hand of your greatness in heaven, whence he will come to render to each one according to his works. He left us as a memorial of his passion these things which we offer to you according to his command. For when he was about to go to a voluntary, glorious, and life-giving death, on the night in which he gave himself up for the salvation of the world, he took bread into his holy and venerable hands and, having shown it to you, God and Father, having given thanks, having blessed, sanctified, and broken (the bread), he gave it to his holy disciples and apostles, saying:

"Take, eat, this is my body broken for you for the forgiveness of sins." In the same way, having taken the cup, the fruit of the vine, having mixed it (with water), having given thanks, blessed, and sanctified (it), he gave it to his holy disciples and apostles, saying:

"Drink of this, all, this is my blood, shed for you and for many for the forgiveness of sins: do this in remembrance of me. For every time you eat of this bread and drink of this cup, you proclaim my death and confess my resurrection."

We too, therefore, Lord, mindful of his saving passion, the life-giving Cross, the three days in the tomb, the resurrection from the dead, the ascension into heaven, the sitting at your right hand, O God and Father, and of his glorious and terrible Second Coming,

Aloud: offering to you what is yours, in everything and through everything.

People: We praise you, we bless you, we give you thanks, Lord, and we pray you, our God.

Priest: Therefore, holy Lord, we too, sinners and your unworthy servants whom you have made worthy to serve at your holy altar—not because of our justice, for we have done nothing good on earth, but because of your mercy and your compassion which you have generously poured out upon us—we approach your holy altar with confidence and, having placed before you these antitypes of the holy body and blood of your Christ, we pray you and call upon you, Holy of Holies, that in your kindness and goodness your Holy Spirit may come upon us and on the gifts set before you, to bless them and sanctify them and show *(he signs the holy gifts three times, saying:)* this bread (to be) the precious body of our Lord and God and Savior Jesus Christ. Amen.

This cup (to be) the precious blood of our Lord and God and Savior Jesus Christ. Amen. Shed for the life of the world. Amen.

Prayer: Unite all of us, who partake of a single loaf and a single cup, each with the others in the Communion of the one Holy Spirit, and let no one of us partake of the holy body and blood of your Christ for judgment or condemnation, but in order that we may find mercy and grace with all the saints who have pleased you from the beginning, with the first fathers, ancestors, patriarchs, prophets, apostles, preachers, evangelists, martyrs, confessors, doctors, and every holy spirit who has died in the faith.

Aloud: Most especially with our most holy, unstained, supremely blessed Lady, Mary, Mother of God and ever virgin.

After the deacon has read the diptychs, the priest prays: Let us remember St. John, precursor and baptist, St. *N.*, and all your saints, due to whose prayers you visit us, Lord. And remember all those who have fallen asleep in the hope of resurrection to everlasting life, and grant them rest where the light of your countenance is turned to them. We also pray: Remember, Lord, your holy, catholic, apostolic Church, which (is) from one end of the earth to the other, and grant peace to her whom you won for yourself through the precious blood of your Christ, and strengthen this holy house until the end of time.

Remember, Lord, those who have brought these gifts, and those for whom and through whom and for whose sake they have offered them.

Remember, Lord, those who bear fruit and those who do good works in your holy Churches, those who are mindful of the poor; fill them with abundant heavenly gifts; give them heavenly things in place of earthly, eternal in place of temporal, incorruptible in place of corruptible.

Remember, Lord, those in lonely places, on the mountains, in caves, and in holes in the earth.

Remember, Lord, those who pass their lives in virginity, devotion, and purity of life.

Remember, Lord, our most devout and faithful king, whom you have thought it right should reign over the land. Ring him with the shield of truth, with the shield of kindness; cast your shadow on his head in time of war, make his arm strong, and exalt his right hand; make his realm stable, make subject to him all the barbarian peoples who want war, give him support and the peace that cannot be taken away; inspire his heart with good thoughts for your Church and for all your people, so that in his peace we may live a peaceful and quiet life, in piety and dignity.

Remember, Lord, every authority and power and our brothers who are in the palace and in every army. Preserve the good in goodness and make the wicked good in good will. Remember, Lord, the people standing here and those who are absent for good reasons, and have mercy on them and us in your great mercy. Fill their storerooms with every good thing, preserve them united in peace and harmony, nourish the children, instruct the adolescents, strengthen the elderly, support the faint-hearted, gather the scattered, bring back those who are in error, and unite them all to your holy, catholic, and apostolic Church. Deliver those who are tormented by unclean spirits, sail with those at sea, travel with those on journeys, defend widows, protect orphans, free prisoners, cure the sick. (Remember) those in the courts, in the mines, in exile, in bitter slavery, in every affliction, in need and in difficulty. Remember also, Lord, all those in need of your great mercy and those who love us and those who hate us, and those who have asked us, unworthy though we are, to pray for them.

And remember your entire holy people, Lord, and pour out on all of them your abundant mercy; grant to all the salvation for which they pray. And do you yourself, O God, remember those whom we fail to remember because of our ignorance or forgetfulness or because the names are so many, for you know the age and name of each of them, you know each of them from their mother's womb. You, O Lord, are the help of those who ask, the hope of the despairing, the rescuer of those tossed by storms, harbor for sailors, physician of the sick. Be yourself everything to all, you who know each one and their prayers and their homes and their needs.

And, Lord, deliver this flock and every city and region from hunger, pestilence, earthquake, flood, fire, sword, invasion by foreigners, and civil war.

Above all, Lord, remember our father and bishop N., whom you have given to your holy Churches; (keep him) safe in peace, honored, in good health, long-lived, that he may correctly explain the teaching of your truth.

"And" the diptychs of the living "are read."

Remember, Lord, the entire episcopate of the orthodox who correctly explain the teaching of your truth.

Remember, Lord, in the multitude of your mercies, my unworthy self; forgive me all my sins, voluntary and involuntary, and do not, because of my sins, deny the grace of your Holy Spirit to the gifts set before you.

Remember, Lord, the presbyterate, the diaconate in Christ, and the entire priestly order, and do not cast off any of us who stand around your holy altar.

Look upon us with kindness, Lord, show yourself to us in your abundant mercy, grant us weather that is temperate and useful, give the earth right rains for the crops, bless the course of the year with your kindness. Let divisions in the Church cease, let turmoil among the nations cease. In the power of your Holy Spirit, quickly put an end to the rebellions of heretics. Receive us all into your kingdom as children of the light and children of the day; receive us into your peace and grant us your love *(agapê)*, Lord our God, for you have given us all things.

Aloud: And grant us that with one voice and one heart we may glorify and raise up praises to your holy and exalted name, Father and Son and Holy Spirit, now and always and through endless ages.

People: Amen.

Abbreviations

AnBib	Analecta Biblica
ACW	Ancient Christian Writers
BGPTM	Beiträge zur Geschichte der Philosophie und Theologie des Mitteralters
CCL	Corpus Christianorum, Series Latina
CCLContMed	Corpus Christianorum, Series Latina, Continuatio Medievalis Charlesworth *The Old Testament Pseudepigrapha.* Ed. J. H. Charlesworth. 2 vols. New York: Doubleday, 1983 and 1985
CSEL	Corpus Scriptorum Ecclesiasticorum Latinorum
DACL	*Dictionnaire d'archéologie chrétienne et de liturgie*
DSp	*Dictionnaire de spiritualité*
DTC	*Dictionnaire de théologie catholique*
EL	*Ephemerides Liturgicae*
Greg	*Gregorianum*
Hänggi-Pahl	*Prex Eucharistica. Textus e variis liturgiis antiquioribus selecti.* Ed. Anton Hänggi and Irmgard Pahl. Spicilegium Friburgense 12. Fribourg, Suisse: Editions universitaires, 1968.
Hill	St. Augustine. *Sermons.* Trans. E. Hill. 10 vols. The Works of Saint Augustine. A Translation for the Twenty-First Century, Part III. Brooklyn, N.Y. (later: New Rochelle, N.Y., and then Hyde Park, N.Y.): New City Press, 1990–95.
Irén	*Irénikon*
JQR	*Jewish Quarterly Review*
JTS	*Journal of Theological Studies*

LQF	Liturgiegeschichtliche Quellen und Forschungen
MD	*La Maison-Dieu*
Mus	*Le Muséon*
NRT	*Nouvelle revue théologique*
OC	*Oriens Christianus*
OCA	Orientalia Christiana Analecta
OCP	*Orientalia Christiana Periodica*
OS	*L'Orient syrien*
POC	*Proche-Orient chrétien*
RB	*Revue biblique*
REJ	*Revue des études juives*
RevSR	*Revue des sciences religieuses*
RSPT	*Revue des sciences philosophiques et théologiques*
RSR	*Recherches de science religieuse*
RTAM	*Recherches de théologie ancienne et médiévale*
SC	Sources chrétiennes
SE	*Sacris Erudiri*
SSL	Spicilegium Sacrum Lovaniense
ST	Studi e testi
TU	Texte und Untersuchungen
ZKT	*Zeitschrift für katholische Theologie*

Bibliography

Allison, D. C., Jr. "The Silence of Angels: Reflections on the Songs of the Sabbath Sacrifice." *Revue de Qumrân* 13 (1988) 189–97. = *Mémorial Jean Carmignac.*

Amalarius of Metz. *Amalarii episcopi Opera liturgica omnia.* Ed. I. M. Hanssens. 3 vols. ST 138–140. Vatican City: Vatican Apostolic Library, 1948–50.

Atti e passioni dei martiri. Ed. A.A.R. Bastiaensen and others. Scrittori greci e latini. Milan: Fondazione Lorenzo Valla and Arnaldo Mondadori Editore, 1987.

Audet, J.-P. "Literary Forms and Contents of a Normal *Eucharistia* in the First Century." *Studia Evangelica.* Ed. K. Aland and F. L. Cross. TU 18. Berlin, 1959, 643–62.

_____. "Esquisse du genre littéraire de la 'bénédiction' juive et de l'"eucharistie' chrétienne." *RB* 65 (1958) 371–99.

_____. "Genre littéraire et formes cultuelles de l'Eucharistie. 'Nova et Vetera.'" *EL* 80 (1966) 352–85.

_____. "Le sacré et le profan. Leur situation en christianisme." *NRT* 79 (1957) 33–61.

Augustine of Hippo. *Sermons pour la Pâque.* SC 116. Paris: Cerf, 1966.

Baldovin, J. F. "Concelebration: A Problem of Symbolic Roles in the Church." *Worship* 59 (1985) 32–47.

Baumstark, A. "Das 'Problem' des römischen Messkanons: eine Retractatio auf geistesgeschichtlichem Hintergrund." *EL* 53 (1939) 204–43.

Bazelaire, L. de. "Communion spirituelle." *DSp* 2 (1937) col. 1300.

Behm, J., and E. Würthwein. "Metanoeô-Metanoia." *TDNT* 4:975–89. Benedict VIII. *Epistulae et decreta.* PL 139:1579–1638.

Beran, J. "De ordine missae secundum Tertulliani 'Apologeticum.'" *Miscellanea liturgica in honorem L. Cuniberti Mohlberg* 2. Bibliotheca Ephemerides Liturgicae 23. Rome: Edizioni liturgiche, 1949, 3–32.

Betti, U. "La ragione della permanenza di Cristo nell'eucaristia: una soluzione teologica dimenticata." *Studi francescani* 50 (1953) 151–68.

Boismard, M.-E., and A. Lamouille. *Synopse des Quatre Evangiles* III. *L'évangile de Jean.* Paris: Cerf, 1977.

Botte, B. "La seconda preghiera eucaristica." *Le nuove preghiere eucaristiche.* Parola per l'assemblea festiva 1. Brescia: Queriniana, 1963, 27–33.

____. "Les anaphores syriennes orientales." *Eucharisties d'Orient et d'Occident.* Ed. B. Botte, et al. Lex orandi 46–47. Paris: Cerf, 1970. II, 7–24.

____. "Die Wendung 'astare coram te et tibi ministrare' im eucharistischen Hochgebet II." *Bibel und Liturgie* 49 (1976) 101–4.

____. "L'anaphore chaldéenne des Apôtres." *OCP* 15 (1949) 259–76.

____. "L'épiclèse dans les liturgies syriennes orientales." *SE* 6 (1954) 49–72.

____. "L'épiclèse de l'anaphore d'Hippolyte." *RTAM* 14 (1947) 241–51.

____. "L'Esprit-Saint et l'Eglise dans la 'Tradition apostolique' de Saint Hippolyte." *Didaskalia* 2 (1972) 221–33.

____. *Le canon de la messe romaine, Edition critique.* Textes et études liturgiques, 2. Louvain, 1935.

____. "Les plus anciennes collections canoniques." *OS* 5 (1960) 331–50.

____. "Note historique sur la concélébration dans l'Eglise ancienne." *MD*, no. 35 (1953) 21.

____. "Problèmes de l'anaphore syrienne des Apôtres Addai et Mari." *OS* 10 (1965) 89–106.

____. "Tradition apostolique et canon romain." *MD*, no. 87 (1966) 52–61.

Botte, B., and Ch. Mohrmann. *L'ordinaire de la messe.* Etudes liturgiques 2. Paris-Louvain, 1953.

Bouhot, J.-P. *Ratramne de Corbie. Histoire littéraire et controverses doctrinales.* Paris: Etudes augustiniennes, 1976.

Bouyer, L. "La terza pregiera eucaristica." *Le nuove preghiere eucaristiche.* Parola per l'assemblea festiva 1. Brescia: Queriniana, 1969, 39–50.

Bradley, R. "Backgrounds of the Title 'Speculum' in Medieval Literature." *Speculum* 29 (1954) 100–15.

Braga, C. "Punti qualificanti della 'Institutio generalis Missalis Romani.'" *Liturgia opera divina et humana. Studi sulla riforma liturgica offerti a S. E. Mons. Annibale Bugnini in occasione del suo 70 compleanno.* Ed. P. Jounel, and others. Bibliotheca Ephemerides Liturgicae. Subsidia 26. Rome: CLV–Edizioni liturgiche, 1982, 243–61.

Brown, P. *The Cult of the Saints. Its Rise and Function in Latin Christianity.* Chicago: University of Chicago Press, 1981.

Brunner, P. "Zur Lehre vom Gottesdienst der im Namen Jesu versammelten Gemeinde." *Leiturgia. Handbuch des evangelischen Gottesdienstes* I. Kassel, 1954.

Bugnini, A. *The Reform of the Liturgy: 1948–1975.* Trans. M. J. O'Connell. Collegeville: The Liturgical Press, 1990.

Buis, P., and J. Leclercq. *Le Deutéronome*. Sources Bibliques. Paris: Gabalda, 1963.

Cabié, R. *The Eucharist*. Trans. M. J. O'Connell. Collegeville: The Liturgical Press, 1986. = *The Church at Prayer*. Ed. A.-G. Martimort and others. Vol. II.

Cacitti, R. *Grande Sabato. Il contesto pasquale quartodecimano nella formazione della teologia del martirio*. Studia patristica mediolanensia 19. Milan: Vita e Pensiero, 1994.

Cadier, J. "La prière eucharistique de Calvin." *Eucharisties d'Orient et d'Occident*. Ed. B. Botte and others. Lex orandi 46–47. Paris: Cerf, 1970. I, 171–80.

Calvin, J. *Opera quae extant omnia*. Brunschwig, 1863–1903.

Canon missae romanae. Pars prior: Traditio textus. Ed. L. Eizenhöfer. Collectanea Anselmiana. Rerum ecclesiasticarum documenta. Series minor: Subsidia studiorum 1. Rome, 1954.

Cantalamessa, R. "Cristo immagine di Dio nelle discussioni teologiche del quarto secolo." *Teologia, liturgia, storia. Miscellanea in onore di Carlo Manziana*. Ed. C. Ghidelli. Brescia: Queriniana, 1977, 29–38.

_____. "Cristo immagine di Dio." *La cristologia in S. Paolo*. Atti della 23 settimana biblica. Brescia: Paideia, 1976, 269–87.

_____. *L'omelia "In S. Pascha" dello Pseudo-Ippolito di Roma. Ricerche sulla teologia dell'Asia minore nella seconda metà del II secolo*. Pubblicazioni dell'Università cattolica del S. Cuore. Contributi. Series terza. Scienze filologiche e letteratura 16. Milan: Vita e Pensiero, 1967.

_____. *La pasqua nella chiesa antica*. Traditio christiana 3. Turin: SEI, 1978.

Capitani, O. "Motivi di spiritualità cluniacense e realismo eucaristico in Odone di Cluny." *Spiritualità cluniacense*. Convegni del Centro di studi sulla spiritualità medievale. Todi: Accademia tudertina, 1960, 150–57. Complete text in: *Bullettino dell'Istituto storico italianao per il Medio Evo e Archivio Muratoriano* 71 (1959) 1–18.

_____. "Studi per Berengario di Tours: Introduzione." Ibid., 69 (1957) 71–88.

Casel, O. *Faites ceci en mémoire de moi*. Lex orandi 34. Paris: Cerf, 1962.

_____. *The Mystery of Christian Worship and Other Writings*. Ed. B. Neuheuser. Westminster, Md.: Newman, 1962.

Cazelles, H. "L'Anaphore et l'Ancien Testament." *Eucharisties d'Orient et d'Occident*. Ed. B. Botte, et al. Lex orandi, 46–47. Paris: Cerf, 1970. I, 11–22.

_____. "Eucharistie, bénédiction et sacrifice dans l'Ancien Testament." *MD*, no. 123 (1975) 7–28.

Cerfaux, L. *The Church in the Theology of St. Paul*. Trans. G. Webb and A. Walker. New York: Herder & Herder, 1959.

Clement of Rome. *Epître aux Corinthiens*. Ed. A. Jaubert. SC 167. Paris: Cerf, 1971.

Coena Domini I. *Die Abendmahlsliturgie der Reformationskirchen im 16./17. Jahrhundert*. Ed. I. Pahl. Spicilegium friburgense 29. Fribourg: Universitätsverlag, 1983.

Colombo, G. "La transustanzione." *Teologia* 20 (1995) 8–33.

____. "Per il trattato sull'Eucaristia." *Teologia* 13 (1988) 95–131; 14 (1989) 105–37.

Concilia Africae A. 345–A. 525. Ed. C. Munier. CCL 149. Turnhout: Brepols, 1974.

Concilii Tridentini Acta. Pars III, Vol. I: *Acta Concilii bononiensia a Massarello conscripta*. Ed. T. Freudenberger. Concilium Tridentinum. Nova collectio edidit Societas Goerresiana. Tomus VI, Actorum Pars III, Vol. I. Freiburg im B.: Herder, 1950.

Conciliorum oecumenicorum decreta. Ed. G. Alberigo and others. Bologna: Istituto per le scienze religiose, 1973. Latin text and English translation in *Decrees of the Ecumenical Councils*. English ed.: N. P. Tanner, S.J. 2 vols. London: Sheed & Ward; Washington, D.C.: Georgetown University Press, 1990.

Congar, Y. "L'Ecclesia' ou communauté chrétienne, sujet intégral de l'action liturgique." *La liturgia après Vatican II. Bilan, études, prospective*. Ed. J.-P. Jossua and Y. Congar. Unam sanctam 66. Paris: Cerf, 1967, 241–82.

____. *A History of Theology*. Ed. and trans. H. Guthrie. Garden City, N.Y.: Doubleday, 1968. = "Theologie." *DTC* 15/1, cols. 341–502.

Congregation for Divine Worship and the Discipline of the Sacraments. "Prex eucharistica quae in Missis pro variis necessitatibus adhiberi potest." *Notitiae* 27 (1991) 388–431.

Connolly, R. H. "Sixth-Century Fragments of an East-Syrian Anaphora." *OC* 12–14 (1925) 99–128.

Les Constitutions apostoliques. Livres III et VI and *Livres VII et VIII*. Ed. M. Metzer. SC 329 and 336. Paris: Cerf, 1986 and 1987.

Costecalde, C. B. *Aux origines du sacré biblique*. Paris: Letouzey et Ané, 1986.

Councils and Ecclesiastical Documents Relating to Great Britain and Ireland. Ed. A. W. Hadden and W. Stubbs. Vol. 3. Oxford, 1871.

Councils and Synods. Ed. F. Powicke and C. Cheney. Oxford, 1964.

Cristiani, M. "Il *Liber Officialis* di Amalario de Metz e la dottrina del *Corpus triforme*." *Culto christiano—Politica imperiale carolingia*. Convegni del Centro di studi sulla spiritualità medievale, Università degli studi di Perugia, 18. Todi, 1979, 121–67.

____. "La controversia eucaristica nella cultura del secolo IX." *Studi medievali*, 3rd series, 9 (1968) 167–233.

Cuming, G. J. "The Early Eucharistic Liturgies in Recent Research." *The Sacrifice of Praise. Studies on the Themes of Thanksgiving and Redemption in the Central*

Prayers of the Eucharistic and Baptismal Liturgies. In Honour of A. H. Couratin. Ed. B. D. Spinks. Bibliotheca Ephemerides Liturgicae. Subsidia 19. Rome: CLV–Edizioni liturgiche, 1981, 65–69.

———. "The Shape of the Anaphora." *Studia patristica XX.* Ed. E. A. Livingstone. TU. Kalamazoo–Louvain, 1989, 333–45.

———. "*Di'euches logou,*" *JTS* 31 (1980) 80–82.

———. "Four Very Early Anaphoras." *Worship* 58 (1984) 168–72.

Cutrone, E. J. "The Liturgical Setting of the Institution Narrative in the Early East Syrian Tradition." *Time and Community. In Honor of Thomas Julian Talley.* Ed. J. N. Alexander. NPM Studies in Church Music and Liturgy. Washington, D.C.: Pastoral Press, 1990, 105–14.

Cyprian of Carthage. *Saint Cyprien. Correspondance.* 2 vols. Ed. L. Bayard. Collection des Universités de France. Publiée sous le patronage de l'Association Guillaume Budé. Paris: Les Belles Lettres, 1962 and 1961 . ET: *The Letters of St. Cyprian of Carthage.* Trans. G. W. Clarke. 4 vols. ACW 43–44, 46–47. New York: Newman, 1984–89.

———. *Sancti Cypriani Episcopi Opera.* CCL 3 and 3A. Turnhout: Brepols, 1972 and 1976.

Cyril of Jerusalem. *Cyrille de Jérusalem. Catéchèses mystagogiques.* Ed. A. Piédagnel. SC 126bis. Paris: Cerf, 1990.

Dalmais, I.-H. "La liturgie alexandrine et ses relations avec les autres liturgies." *Liturgie de l'église particulière et liturgie de l'église universelle.* Ed. A. M. Triacca and A. Pistoia. Bibliotheca Ephemerides Liturgicae. Subsidia 7. Rome: Edizioni liturgiche, 1976.

Daniélou, J. "Figure et événement chez Méliton de Sardes." *Neotestamentica et patristica. Festgabe O. Cullmann.* Leiden, 1062, 282–92.

———. *From Shadows to Reality. Studies in the Biblical Typology of the Fathers.* Trans. W. Hibberd. Westminster, Md.: Newman, 1960.

———. *Platonisme et théologie mystique. Essai sur la doctrine spirituelle de saint Grégoire de Nysse.* Paris, 1954.

De Baciocchi, J. *L'Eucharistie.* Le mystère chrétien. Théologie sacramentaire 3. Tournai: Desclée, 1964.

De Clerck. "Epiclèse et formulation du Mystère eucharistique. Brèves réflexions sur le langage liturgique à partir de la prière eucharistique du Synode suisse." *Gratias agamus. Studien zum eucharistichen Hochgebet. Für Balthasar Fischer.* Ed. A. Heinz and H. Rennings. Freiburg–Basel–Vienna: Herder, 1972, 53–59.

———. *La "Prière universelle" dans les liturgies latines anciennes. Témoignages patristiques et textes liturgiques.* LQF 62. Münster: Aschendorff, 1977.

____. "La revision de la prière eucharistique 'suisse.'" *MD*, no. 191 (1992) 61–68.

____. *"Les orandi, lex credendi.* Sens originel et avatars historiques d'un adage équivoque." *Questions liturgiques* 59 (1978) 193–212.

De dedicatione ecclesiae hujius sancti Maioris nostri monasterii. PL 151:273–76.

Deiss, L. *Springtime of the Liturgy. Liturgical Texts of the First Four Centuries.* Trans. M. J. O'Connell. Collegeville: The Liturgical Press, 1979.

Deléani, S. *Christum sequi. Etude d'un thème dans l'oeuvre de saint Cyprien.* Paris: Etudes augustiniennes, 1979.

De Lubac, H. "Souvenirs (1940–1945)." *Alexandrina. Hellénisme, judaïsme et christianisme à Alexandrie. Mélanges offerts ay P. Claude Mondésert.* Patrimoines. Paris: Cerf, 1987, 9–13.

____. *Corpus mysticum. L'eucharistie et l'Eglise au moyen âge.* Paris: Aubier, 1949.

____. *Exégèse médiévale. Les quatres sens de l'écriture.* Paris: Aubier, 1959.

De Montcheuil, Y. "La raison de la permanence du Christ sous les espèces eucharistiques d'après S. Bonaventure et S. Thomas." Idem, *Mélanges théologiques.* Paris: Aubier, 1946, 71–82.

De Montclos, J. *Lanfranc et Béranger. La controverse eucharistique du XI siècle.* SSL 37. Leuven, 1971.

De Roten, Ph. "Le vocabulaire mystagogique de Saint Jean Chrysostome." *Mystagogie. pensée liturgique d'aujourd'hui et liturgie ancienne.* Ed. A. M. Triacca and A. Pistoia. Bibliotheca Ephemerides Liturgicae. Subsidia 70. Rome: Edizioni liturgiche, 1993, 115–35.

Descamps, A.-L. "Cénacle et calvaire. Les vues de H. Schürmann." *Revue théologique de Louvain* 10 (1979) 344.

De Vaux, R. *Studies in Old Testament Sacrifice.* Cardiff: University of Wales Press, 1964.

De Watteville, J. *Le sacrifice dans les textes eucharistiques des premiers siècles.* Bibliothèque théologique. Neuchâtel: Delachaux et Niestlé, 1966.

Didascalia et Constitutiones Apostolorum. Ed. F. X. Funk. 2 vols. Paderborn: Schöningh, 1905.

Dix, G. *The Shape of the Liturgy.* London: Adam & Charles Black, 1945.

La doctrine des douze apôtres (Didachè). Ed. W. Rordorf and A. Tuilier. SC 248. Paris: Cerf, 1978.

Documents on the Liturgy 1963–1979. Conciliar, Papal, and Curial Texts. Ed. and trans. Thomas C. O'Brien of the International Commission on English in the Liturgy. Collegeville: The Liturgical Press, 1982.

Dölger, F. G. "Christphoros als Ehrentitel für Märtyrer und Heilige im christlichen Altertum." *Antike und Christentum* 4 (1934) 73–80.

Dubois J., and Lemaître, J. L. *Sources et méthodes de l'hagiographie médiévale.* Histoire. Paris: Cerf, 1993.

Duc, P. *Essai sur l'Expositio missae de Florus de Lyon, suivie d'une édition critique du texte.* Belley, 1937.

Dumoutet, E. *Corpus Domini. Aux sources de la piété eucharistique médiévale.* Paris: Beauchesne, 1942.

———. *Le Christ selon la chair et la vie liturgique au Moyen-Age.* Paris: Beauchesne, 1932.

———. *Le désir de voir l'Hostie et les origines de la dévotion au Saint-Sacrement.* Paris: Beauchesne, 1926.

Early Christian Writings: The Apostolic Fathers. Trans. M. Staniforth. Baltimore: Penguin Books, 1968.

Engberding, H. "Zum anaphorischen Fürbittgebet der Ostsyrischen Liturgie der Apostel Addai(j) und Mar(j)." *OC*, N.S. 41 (1957) 102–24.

Etheria. *Ethérie. Journal de Voyage.* Ed. H. Pétré. SC 21. Paris: Cerf, 1948.

Eusebius of Caesarea. *Histoire Ecclésiastique.* Ed. G. Bardy. Livres V–VII. SC 41. Paris: Cerf, 1955. Livres I–IV. SC 31. Paris: Cerf, 1978.

———. *The History of the Church from Christ to Constantine.* Trans. G. A. Williamson. Baltimore: Penguin Books, 1965.

Falsini, R. "Eucaristia." *Dizionario francescano.* Padua: Edizioni Messagero, 1983. Cols. 519–48.

———. "La *Conformatio* nella liturgia mozarabica." *EL* 72 (1958) 281–91.

———. "La 'trasformazione del corpo e del sangue di Cristo.'" *Studi francescani* 52 (1955) 5–57.

Finkelstein, L. "The Birkat ha-mazon." *JQR* (N.S.) 19 (1928–29) 211–62.

———. "The Development of the Amidah." *JQR* (N.S.) 16 (1925–26) 1–43; 137–70.

Fragomeni, R. N. "Wounded in Extraordinary Depths: Towards a Contemporary Mystagogy." *A Promise of Oresence. Studies in Honor of David N. Power.* Ed. M. Downey and R. N. Fragomeni. Washington, D.C.: Pastoral Press, 1992, 115–37.

Franquesa, A. "La concelebración a los 16 años de su restauración." *Liturgia opera divina e umana. Studi sulla riforma liturgica offerti a S. E. Mons. Annibale Bugnini in occasione del suo 70 compleanno.* Ed. P. Jounel, R. Kaczynski, and G. Pasqualetti. Bibliotheca Ephemerides Liturgicae. Subsidia 26. Rome: Edizioni liturgiche, 1982, 291–306.

Franz, A. *Die Messe im deutschen Mittelalter.* Freiburg im B., 1902.

Frolow, A. *La relique de la vraie croix. Recherches sur le développement d'un culte.* Archives de l'Orient chrétien 7. Paris: Institut français d'études byzantines, 1961.

_____. *Les reliquaires de la vraie croix.* Archives de l'Orient chrétien 8. Paris: Institut français d'études byzantines, 1965.

Galvin, R. J. "Addai and Mari Revisited: The State of the Question." *EL* 87 (1973) 383–414.

Gamber, K. "Das Eucharistiegebet als Epiklese und ein Zitat bei Irenäus." *Ostkirchliche Studien* 29 (1980) 301–5.

Gastoué, A. "Alexandrie, Liturgie." *DACL* 1, cols. 1189–93.

Geary, P. J. *Furta sacra. Theft of Relics in the Central Middle Ages.* Princeton: Princeton University Press, 1990.

Gelineau, J. "La quarta preghiera eucaristica." *Le nuove preghiere eucaristiche. Parola per l'assemblea festiva* 1. Brescia: Queriniana, 1969, 51–68.

Gelston, A. *The Eucharistic Prayer of Addai and Mari.* Oxford: Clarendon Press, 1992.

Gerhards, A. "Entstehung und Entwicklung des eucharistichen Hochgebets im Spiegel der neueren Forschung." *Gratia Agamus. Studien zum eucharistischen Hochgebet. Für Balthasar Fischer.* Ed. A. Heinz and H. Rennings. Freiburg–Basel–Vienna: Herder, 1992, 75–96.

Gerken, A. "Die theologische Intuition des heiligen Franziskus von Assisi." *Wissenschaft und Weisheit* 2 (1982) 2–25.

_____. *Teologia dell'eucaristia.* Teologia 14. Alba: Edizioni paoline, 1977.

Gero, S. "The Eucharistic Doctrine of the Byzantine Iconoclasts and Its Sources." *Byzantinische Zeitschrift* 68 (1975) 4–22.

_____. "The True Image of Christ: Eusebios' Letter to Constantia Reconsidered." *JTS* 32 (1981) 460–70.

Giet, S. *L'énigme de la Didachè.* Publications de la Faculté des Lettres de l'Université de Strasbourg 149. Paris, 1970.

Girard, R. *Delle cose nascoste fin dalla fondazione del mondo.* Saggi 24. Milan: Adelphi, 1983.

Giraudo, C. *La struttura letteraria della preghiera eucaristica. Saggio sulla genesi letteraria di una forma. Toda veterotestamentaria, Beraka giudaica, Anafora cristiana.* AnBib 92. Rome: Biblical Institute Press, 1981.

Goguel, M. *L'eucharistie. Des origines à Justin martyr.* Paris, 1910.

Goodenough, E. R. *Jewish Symbols in the Greco-Roman Period.* New York, 1964.

Goppelt, L. "Typos." *TDNT* 8:346–59.

Gougaud, L. *Dévotions et pratiques ascétiques du Moyen Age*. Collection Pax 21. Paris–Maredsous: Desclée and Lethielleux, 1925.

Le Grand Euchologe du Monastère Blanc. Text copte edité avex traduction française. Ed. E. Lanne. Patrologia Orientalis 28:265–407.

Grant, G. "The Elevation of the Host: A Reaction to Twelfth-Century Heresy." *Theological Studies* 1 (1940) 228–50.

Grass, H. "Luther et la liturgie eucharistique." *Eucharisties d'Orient et d'Occident*. Ed. B. Botte and others. Lex orandi 46–47. Paris: Cerf, 1970. I, 135–50.

Guelly, R., Lafon, G., Labarrière, P. J., Vergote, A., and Jossua, J. P. *La prière du chrétien*. Publications des Facultés universitaires Saint-Louis 22. Brussels: Facultés universitaires Saint-Louis, 1981.

Guillaumont, A. "Philon et les origines du monachisme." *Philon d'Alexandrie*. Colloque de Lyon (11–15 septembre 1966). Paris: Editions du Centre national de la recherche scientifique, 1967, 361–73.

Guitmond of Aversa. *De corpore et sanguine Domini in veritate*. PL 149:1449–50.

Gutwenger, E. "Substanz und Akzident in der Eucharistielehre." *ZKT* 83 (1961) 257–306.

Gy, P.-M. "Doctrine eucharistique de la liturgie romaine dans le haut moyen âge." *La liturgie dans l'histoire*. Ed. P.-M. Gy. Paris: Cerf–St. Paul, 1990, 187–204.

_____. "L'office du Corpus Christi, oeuvre de Saint Thomas d'Aquin." Ibid., 223–45.

_____. "La mystagogie dans la liturgie ancienne et dans la pensée liturgique d'aujourd'hui." *Mystagogie: pensée liturgique d'aujourd'hui et liturgie ancienne*. Ed. A. M. Triacca and A. Pistoia. Bibliotheca Ephemerides Liturgicae. Subsidia 70. Rome: Edizioni liturgiche, 1993, 137–43.

_____. "La relation au Christ dans l'Eucharistie selon S. Bonaventure et S. Thomas d'Aquin." *La liturgie dans l'histoire*, 247–83.

_____. "Prière eucharistique et paroles de la consécration selon les théologiens de Pierre Lombard à Saint Thomas d'Aquin." Ibid., 211–21.

_____. "Avancées du traité de l'eucharistie dans le *Somme* par rapport aux *Sentences*." *RSPT* 77 (1993) 219–28.

_____. "L'eucharistie dans la tradition de la prière et de la doctrine." *MD*, no. 137 (1979) 81–102.

_____. "La notion de validité sacramentelle avant le concile de Trente." *Revue de Droit Canonique* 28 (1978) 192–202. = *Mélanges J. Gaudemet*.

_____. "Le 'Nous' de la prière eucharistique." *MD*, no. 191 (1992) 7–14.

_____. "Le *Sanctus* romain et les anaphores orientales." *Mélanges liturgiques. Offerts au R. P. Dom Bernard Botte*. Louvain, 1972, 167–74.

Hänggi, A. "Das Hochgebet 'Synode '72' für die Kirche in der Schweiz." *Notitiae* 27 (1991) 436–59.

Heinemann, J. *Prayer in the Talmud. Forms and Patterns.* Studia judaica 9. Berlin–New York: de Gruyter, 1977.

Herrmann-Mascard, N. *Les reliques des saints. Formation coutumière d'un droit.* Société d'histoire du droit. Collection d'histoire institutionelle et sociale 6. Paris: Klincksieck, 1975.

Hippolytus of Rome. *La Tradition apostolique de saint Hippolyte. Essai de reconstitution.* Ed. B. Botte. LQF 39. Münster: Aschendorff, 1963.

_____. *Commentaire sur Daniel.* SC 14. Paris: Cerf, 1947.

Hoffman, L. A. "Rabbinic *Berakhah* and Jewish Spirituality." *Asking and Thanking.* Ed. C. Duquoc and C. Florestan. Concilium, 1990, no. 3. London: SCM; Philadelphia: Trinity Press International, 1990, 18–30.

_____. *The Canonization of the Synagogue Service.* Studies in Judaism and Christianity in Antiquity 4. Notre Dame: University of Notre Dame Press, 1979.

Honorius of Autun. *Gemma animae.* PL 172:541–738.

Hruby, K. "La fête de Rosh ha-Shanah." *OS* 13 (1968) 47–71. = *Mémorial Mgr. Gabriel Khouri-Sarkis (1898–1968).* Louvain: Imprimerie orientaliste, 1969, 47–71.

Ignatius of Antioch. *Ignace d'Antioche–Polycarpe de Smyrne. Lettres–Martyre de Polycarpe.* SC 10. Paris: Cerf, 1969.

Imbach, R. "Le traité de l'eucharistie de Thomas d'Aquin et les averroïstes." *RSPT* 77 (1993) 175–94.

Innocent III. *De sacro altaris mysterio.* PL 217:775–914.

Irenaeus of Lyons. *Irénée de Lyon. Contre les herésies, Livre I.* Ed. A. Rousseau and L. Doutreleau. 2 vols. SC 263–64. Paris: Cerf, 1979.

_____. *Irénée de Lyon. Contre les hérésies. Livre II.* Ed. A. Rousseau and L. Doutreleau. 2 vols. SC 293–94. Paris: Cerf, 1979.

_____. *Irénée de Lyon. Contre les hérésies. Livre III.* Ed. A. Rousseau and L. Doutreleau. 2 vols. SC 210–11. Paris: Cerf, 1974.

_____. *Irénée de Lyon. Contre les hérésies. Livre IV.* Ed. A. Rousseau. 2 vols. SC 100. Paris: Cerf, 1965.

_____. *Irénée de Lyon. Contre les hérésies. Livre V.* Ed. Rousseau, L. Doutreleau, and Ch. Mercier. 2 vols. SC 152–53. Paris: Cerf 1969.

Jacob, C. *Arkandisziplin, Allegorese, Mystagogie: ein neuer Zugang zur Theologie des Ambrosius von Mailand.* Athenäums–Monographies. Theologie Theophaneia 32. Frankfurt: Hain, 1990.

____. "Zur Krise der Mystagogie in der Alten Kirche." *Theologie und Philosophie* 66 (1991) 75–89.

Jeremias, J. "Pais theou. D) In the New Testament." *TDNT* 5:700–17

____. *The Eucharistic Words of Jesus.* Trans. N, Perrin. London: SCM, 1966.

Johanny, R. "Cyprian of Carthage." *The Eucharist of the Early Christians.* Ed. R. Johanny. Trans. M. J. O'Connell. New York: Pueblo, 1978, 156–82.

____. "Ignatius of Antioch." Ibid., 48–70.

John Beleth. Summa de ecclesiasticis officiis. Ed. H. Douteil. CCLContMed 41A. Turnhout: Brepols, 1976.

[John Chrysostom.] *Jean Chrysostome. Trois catéchèse baptismales.* Ed. A. Piédagnel and L. Doutreleau. SC 366. Paris: Cerf, 1990.

____. *Jean Chrysostome. Huit catéchèses baptismales inédites.* Ed. A. Wenger. SC 50bis. Paris: Cerf, 1970.

____. *Baptismal Instructions.* Trans. P. W. Harkins. ACW 31. New York: Newman Press, 1963.

Johnson, M. F. "A Note on the Dating of St. Thomas Aquinas' *Expositio super primam et secundam decretalem.*" *RTAM* 59 (1992) 155–65.

Joncas, J. M. "Eucharist Among the Marcosians: A Study of Irenaeus' *Adversus haereses* I, 13, 2." *Questions liturgiques* 71 (1990) 99–111.

Jouassard, G. "Aux origines du culte des martyrs, S. Ignace d'Antioche, Rom IV, 2." *RSR* 39 (1951) 362–67.

Jungmann, J. A. *The Mass of the Roman Rite: Its Origins and Development (Missarum Solemnia).* Trans. F. A. Brunner. 2 vols. New York: Benziger, 1951 and 1955.

Kaczynski, R. *Enchiridion documentorum instaurationis liturgicae* I. Turin, 1976.

Kannengiesser, Ch. "Humanité du Christ. B) La contemplation de l'humanité du Christ." *DSp* 7:1043–49.

Lanne, E. "L'intercession pour l'Eglise dans la Prière Eucharistique." *L'Eglise dans la liturgie.* Ed. A. M. Triacca and A. Pistoia. Bibliotheca Ephemerides Liturgicae. Subsidia 18. Rome: Edizioni liturgiche, 1980, 183–208.

____. "Cherubim et Seraphim. Essai d'interpretation du chapitre X de la *Démonstration* de saint Irenée." *RSR* 43 (1955) 524–35.

____. "L'Eglise une." *Irén* 50 (1977) 46–58.

____. "L'Eglise une dans la prière eucharistique." *Irén* 50 (1977) 326–44, 511–19.

____. "Les anaphores eucharistiques de saint Basile et la communauté ecclésiale." *Irén* 55 (1982) 307–31.

_____. "Les textes de la liturgie eucharistique en dialecte sahidique." *Mus* 68 (1955) 5–16.

Laurance, J. D. *"Priest" as Type of Christ. The Leader of the Eucharist in Salvation History according to Cyprian of Carthage.* American University Studies VII. Theology and Religion 5. New York–Bern–Frankfurt am M.-Nancy: Peter Lang, 1984.

_____. "Le président de l'Eucharistie selon Cyprien de Carthage: un nouvel examen." *MD,* no. 154 (1983) 151–65.

_____. "The Eucharist as the Imitation of Christ." *Theological Studies* 47 (1986) 286–96.

Léon-Dufour, X. *Sharing the Eucharistic Bread. The Witness of the New Testament.* Trans. M. J. O'Connell. New York: Paulist, 1987.

Le Liber Mozarabicus Sacramentorum et les manscrits mozarabes. Ed. M. Férotin. Monumenta ecclesiae liturgica 6. Paris: Firmin–Didot, 1912.

Le Liber Ordinum en usage dans l'église wisigothique et mozarabe d'Espagne du cinquième et onzième siècle. Ed. M. Férotin. Monumenta ecclesiae liturgica 5. Paris: Firmin–Didot, 1904.

Le Liber Pontificalis. Ed. L. Duchesne. I. Paris: Bibliothèque des écoles françaises d'Athènes et de Rome, 1981.

"Litterae circulares ad conferentiarum episcopalium praesides de precibus eucharisticis." *Notitiae* 84 (1973) 193–201.

Macomber, W. F. "The Ancient Form of the Anaphora of the Apostles." *East of Byzantium: Syria and Armenia in the Formative Period.* Washington, D.C., 1982, 73–88.

_____. "A History of the Chaldean Mass." *Worship* 51 (1977) 107–20.

_____. "The Sources for a Study of the Chaldean Mass." *Worship* 51 (1977) 523–36.

_____. "A Theory of the Origins of the Syrian, Maronite and Chaldean Rites." *OCP* 39 (1973) 235–42.

_____. "The Maronite and Chaldean Versions of the Anaphora of the Apostles." *OCP* 37 (1971) 55–84.

_____. "The Oldest Known Text of the Anaphora of the Apostles Addai and Mari." *OCP* 32 (1966) 335–71.

Macy, G. "Berengar's Legacy as Heresiarch." *Auctoritas et Ratio. Studien zu Berengar von Tours.* Ed. P. Ganz, R.B.C. Huigens, and F. Niewöner. Wiesbaden: Harrassowitz, 1990, 47–67.

_____. "Of Mice and Manna: *Quid summit mus?* as a Pastoral Question." *RTAM* 59 (1992) 157–66.

_____. *The Banquet's Wisdom: A Short History of the Theologies of the Lord's Supper.* New York: Paulist, 1992.

_____. *The Theologies of the Eucharist in the Early Scholastic Period. A Study of the Salvific Function of the Sacrament according to the Theologians c. 1080–c. 1220.* Oxford: Clarendon Press, 1984.

Madeja, S. "Analisi del concetto di concelebrazione eucaristica nel concilio Vaticano II e nella riformm liturgica postconciliare." *EL* 96 (1982) 3–56.

Maggioni, C. "Coordinate spazio-temporali della preghiera eucharistica 'Synode '72.'" *Notitiae* 27 (1991) 460–79.

Manns, F. *La prière d'Israèl à l'heure de Jésus.* Studium biblicum franciscanum, Analecta 22. Jerusalem, 1986.

Marston, W. "A Solution to the Enigma of 'Addai and Mari.'" *EL* 103 (1989) 79–91.

Martimort, A.-G. *Les 'Ordines,' les Ordinaires, and les Cérémoniaux.* Typologie des sources du moyen âge occidental 56. Turnhout: Brepols, 1991.

Marzotto, D. *L'unità degli uomini nel Vangelo di Giovanni.* Supplementi alla *Rivista biblica* 9. Brescia: Paideia, 1977.

Masini, P. "Magister Johannes Beleth: ipotesi di una traccia biografica." *EL* 107 (1993) 248–59.

Mauss, M. *Teoria generale della magia ed altri saggi.* Nuova biblioteca scientifica Einaudi 2. Turin: Einaudi, 1965.

Mazza, E. "L'interpretazione del culto nella chiesa antica." *Celebrare il mistero di Cristo. Manuale di liturgia. I. La celebrazione: introduzione alla liturgia cristiana.* Ephemerides liturgicae. Subsidia 73—Studi di liturgia, Nuova serie, 25. Rome: Edizioni liturgiche, 1993, 229–79.

_____. "La liturgia nella basilica di Sant'Ambrogio in epoca medioevale." *La basilica di S. Ambrogio. Il tempio ininterrotto.* Ed. M. L. Gatti Perer. Milan: Vita e pensiero, 1995. I, 295–309.

_____. "Les raisons et la méthode des catéchèses mystagogiques de la fin du quatrième siècle." *La prédication liturgique et les commentaires de la liturgie.* Ed. A. M. Triacca and A. Pistoia. Bibliotheca Ephemerides Liturgicae. Subsidia 65. Rome: Edizioni liturgiche, 1992, 154–76.

_____. "Saint Augustin et la mystagogie." *Mystagogie: pensée liturgique d'aujourd'hui et liturgie ancienne.* Ed. A. M. Triacca and A. Pistoia. Conférences Saint Serge. XXXIXe Semaine d'études liturgiques. Bibliotheca Ephemerides Liturgicae. Subsidia 70. Rome: Edizioni liturgiche, 1993, 201–26.

_____. *L'anafora eucaristica. Studi sulle origini.* Bibliotheca Ephemerides Liturgicae. Subsidia 62. Rome: Edizioni liturgiche, 1992.

____. "La discussione sull'origine dell'anafora eucaristica: una messa a punto." *Rivista di pastorale liturgica* 32, no. 182 (1994, no. 1) 42–54.

____. *Mystagogy. A Theology of Liturgy in the Patristic Age.* Trans. M. J. O'Connell. New York: Pueblo, 1989.

____. "La portata teologica del termine 'mistero.'" *Rivista liturgica* 74 (1987) 321–38.

____. "La structure de l'anaphore alexandrine et antiochienne." *Irén* 67 (1994) 5–40.

____. *The Eucharistic Prayers of the Roman Rite.* Trans. M. J. O'Connell. New York: Pueblo, 1986.

____. "Tempo, memoria, liturgia. Alcuni dati di epoca patristica." *Rivista liturgica* 77 (1990) 414–34.

McCormick-Zirkel, P. "The Ninth-Century Eucharistic Controversy: A Context for the Beginnings of Eucharistic Doctrine in the West." *Worship* 68 (1994) 2–23.

McGrat, A. E. *Il pensiero della riforma. Lutero, Zwingli, Calvino, Bucero.* Piccola biblioteca teologica 24. Turin: Claudiana, 1991.

Mercati, G. "Frammenti liturgici latini da un anonimo ariano del sec. IV/V." Idem, *Antiche reliquie liturgiche ambrosiane e romane. Con un excursus sui frammenti dogmatici ariani del Mai.* ST 7. Rome: Vatican Apostolic Library, 1902, 47–56.

Mettinger, T.N.D. *The Dethronement of Sabaoth. Studies in the Shem and Kabod Theologies.* Coniectanea biblica. Old Testament Series 18. Lund, 1982.

Missale mixtum secundum regulam Beati Isidori dictum Mozarabes. Rome: Typis Joannis Generosi Salomoni, 1755.

Molin, J.-B. "La restauration de la prière universelle." *Liturgia opera divina e umana. Studi sulla riforma liturgica offerti a S. E. Mons. Annibale Bugnini in occasione del suo 70 compleanno.* Ed. P. Jounel, R. Kaczynski, and G. Pasqualetti. Bibliotheca Ephemerides Liturgicae. Subsidia 26. Rome: Edizioni Liturgiche, 1982, 307–17.

____. "Depuis quand le mot offertoire sert-il à designer une partie de la messe?" *EL* 77 (1963) 357–80.

The Monasteries of the Wâde 'n Natrûn. Ed. W. Hauser. Part II: H.G.E. White, *The History of the Monasteries of Nitria and Scetis.* The Metropolitan Museum of Art. Egyptian Expedition. New York, 1932.

Mosso, D. *Riscoprire l'eucaristia. Le dimensioni teologiche dell'ultima cena.* Cinisello Balsamo (Milan): Edizioni San Paolo, 1993.

Murray, Ch. "Art and the Early Church." *JTS* 28 (1977) 303–45.

Nikiprowetzky, V. "Les Suppliants chez Philon d'Alexandrie." *Revue des études juives* 122 (1963) 241–78.

Odo of Sully. *Synodicae constitutiones*. Communia praecepta, can. 23. PL 212:57–68.

The Old Testament Pseudepigrapha. Ed. J. H. Charlesworth. 2 vols. New York: Doubleday, 1983 and 1985.

Olivar, A. *La predicación cristiana antigua*. Biblioteca Herder. Sección de teología y filosofía 189. Barcelona–New York: Herder, 1991.

Les Ordines romani du haut moyen âge. Ed. M. Andrieu. Vol. II: SSL 23. Louvain, 1960. Vol. IV: SSL 28. Louvain, 1965.

[Paschasius Radbert.] *De corpore et sanguine Domini. Epistola ad Fredugardum*. Ed. B. Paulus. CCLContMed 16. Turnhout: Brepols, 1969.

Pépin, J. *La tradition de l'allégorie. De Philon d'Alexandrie à Dante. Etudes historiques*. Paris: Etudes augustiniennes, 1987.

Peterson, E. "Über einige Probleme der Didache-Überlieferung." *Rivista di archeologia cristiana* 27 (1951) 37–68. Reprinted in idem, *Frühkirche, Judentum und Gnosis*. Rome–Freiburg–Vienna, 1959.

Philo of Alexandria. *De vita contemplative*. Ed. F. Daumas and P. Miquel. Les oeuvres de Philon d'Alexandrie 29. Paris: Cerf, 1963.

_____. *De plantatione*. Ed. J. Pouilloux. Les oeuvres de Philon d'Alexandrie 10. Paris: Cerf, 1963.

_____. *The Contemplative Life, The Giants, and Selections*. Trans. D. Winston. The Classics of Western Spirituality. New York: Paulist, 1981.

Picasso, G. "Riti eucaristici nella società altomedievale. Sul significato storico del trattato eucaristico di Pascasio Radberto." *Segni e riti nella chiesa altomedievale occidentale*. Settimane di Studio del Centro italiano di studi sull'Alto Medioevo 22. Spoleto, 1987, 505–32.

_____. "Sicard de Crémone." *DSp* 15 (1990) 810–14.

Pitra, J. B. *Spicilegium Solesmense* I. Paris, 1852, 383–86.

Pizzolato, L. F. *La dottrina esegetica di sant'Ambrogio*. Studia patristica Mediolanensia 9. Milan: Vita e pensiero, 1978.

Plutarch. *Iside e Osiride*. Ed. D. del Corno. Piccola biblioteca 179. Milan: Adelphi, 1985.

Le pontifical romain au moyen âge I. *Le Pontifical romain du XII siècle*. Ed. M. Andrieu. ST 86. Vatican City: Vatican Apostolic Library, 1938.

Le pontifical romain au moyen âge II. *Le Pontifical de la curie romaine au XIII siècle*. Ed. M. Andrieu. ST 87. Vatican City: Vatican Apostolic Library, 1940.

Le pontifical romain au moyen âge III. *Le Pontifical de Guillaume Durand*. Ed. M. Andrieu. ST 88. Vatican City: Vatican Apostolic Library, 1940.

Le Pontifical romano-germanique du Xème siècle. Ed. C. Vogel and R. Elze. ST 226, 227, 269. 3 vols. Vatican City: Vatican Apostolic Library, 1963–72.

Prat, L. "La concelebración." *Phase* 25 (1985) 251–53.

Prex eucharistica. Textus e variis liturgiis antiquioribus selecti. Ed. A. Hänggi and I. Pahl. Spicilegium fribugense 12. Fribourg: Editions universitaires, 1968.

Quasten, J. *Patrology.* I–III. Westminster, Md.: Newman, 1950, 1953, 1960.

Raes, A. "Le Récit de l'institution eucharistique dans l'anaphore chaldéenne et malabare des Apôtres." *OCP* 10 (1944) 216–26.

____. "Les paroles de la consécration dans les anaphores syriennes." *OCP* 3 (1937) 486–504.

Rasmussen, N. K. "Les rites de la préparation du pain et du vin." *MD*, no. 100 (1969) 44–58.

Ratcliff, E. C. "The Original Form of the Anaphora of Addai and Mari." *JTS* 30 (1928–29) 223–32.

Rengstorff, K. H. *Il vangelo secondo Luca.* Nuovo Testamento 3. Brescia: Paideia, 1980.

Rescriptum contra Lanfrancum. Ed. R.B.C. Huygens. CCLContMed 84. Turnhout: Brepols, 1988.

Riaud, J. "Les Thérapeutes d'Alexandrie dans la tradition et dans la recherche critique jusqu'aux découvertes de Qumrân." *Aufstieg und Niedergang der römischen Welt.* Ed. W. Haase. Teil II: Principat. Band 20/2: Religion (Hellenistisches Judentum in römischer Zeit, ausgenommen Philon und Josephus). Berlin–New York: de Gruyter, 1987, 1189–1295.

____. "Thérapeutes." *DSp* 15 (1990) 562–70.

Ricken, F. "L'*homousios* di Nicea come crisi del platonismo cristiano antico." *La storia della cristologia primitiva.* Ed. H. Schlier and others. Studi biblici 75. Brescia: Queriniana, 1986, 89–119.

____. "Die Logoslehre des Eusebios von Caesarea und der Mittelplatonismus." *Theologie und Philosophie* 42 (1967) 321–52.

____. "Zur Rezeption der platonischen Ontologie bei Eusebios von Kaisareia, Areios und Athanasius." *Theologie und Philosophie* 53 (1978) 321–52.

Riggs, J. W. "From Gracious Table to Sacramental Elements. The Traditions–History of *Didache* 9 and 10." *The Second Century* 4 (1984) 83–101.

Righetti, M. *Manuale di storia liturgica.* III. *La messa.* Milan: Ancora, 1966.

Romanoff, P. *Jewish Symbols on Ancient Jewish Coins.* Philadelphia, 1944.

Rordorf, W. "La vigne et le vin dans la tradition juive et chrétienne." Idem, *Liturgie, foi et vie des premiers chrétiens. Etudes patristiques.* Théologie historique 75. Paris: Beauchesne, 1989.

Rupert of Deutz. *Ruperti Tuitensis. Liber de divinis officiis.* Ed. H. Haacke. CCLContMed 7. Turnhout: Brepols, 1967.

Sanchez Caro, J. M. "La anafora de Addai y Mari y la anafora maronita Sarrar: intento de reconstrucción de la fuente primitiva comun." *OCP* 43 (1977) 41–69.

Sartore, D. "L'*Adoratio crucis* come esempio di progressiva drammatizzazione nell'ambito della liturgia." *Dimensioni drammatiche della liturgia medioevale.* Centro di studi sul teatro medioevale e rinascimentale. Atti del 10 Convegno di studio, Viterbo, 31 maggio–2 giugno 1976. Rome: Bulzoni, 1977, 119–25.

_____. "Mistagogia ieri e oggi: alcune pubblicazioni recenti." *Ecclesia orans* 11 (1994) 181–99.

Saxer, V. "Tertullian." *The Eucharist of the Early Christians.* Ed. R. Johanny. New York: Pueblo, 1978, 132–55.

_____. "Figura corporis et sanguinis Domini." *Rivista di archeologia cristiana* 47 (1971) 65–89.

Schaefer, M. M. "Latin Mass Commentaries from the Ninth through the Twelfth Centuries: Chronology and Theology." *Fountain of Life: In Memory of Niels K. Rasmussen, O.P.* Ed. G. Austin. NPM Studies in Church Music and Liturgy. Washington, D.C.: Pastoral Press, 1991, 35–50.

_____. "Twelfth-Century Latin Commentaries on the Mass: The Relationship of the Priest to Christ and to the People." *Studia liturgica* 15 (1982–83) 76–86.

Scherman, Th. "Zur Erklärung der Stelle Epist. ad Eph. 20, 2 des Ignatius von Antiocheia." *Theologische Quartalschrift* 92 (1910) 6–19.

Schillebeeckx, E. *The Eucharist.* Trans. N. D. Smith. New York: Sheed & Ward, 1968.

Schönborn, C. *L'icona di Cristo. Fondamenti teologici.* Saggi teologici 3. Cinisello Balsamo (Milan): San Paolo, 1988.

Schürmann, H. *Comment Jésus a-t-il vécu sa mort?* Lectio divina 93. Paris: Cerf, 1977.

_____. *Der Einsetzungsbericht Lk 22, 19-20.* Münster, 1955.

_____. "Jesus' Words in the Light of His Actions at the Last Supper." *The Breaking of Bread.* Ed. P. Benoit, R. E. Murphy, and B. Van Iersel. = Concilium, 1969, no. 40, 119–31.

Sententie "Dubitatur a quibusdam." In *Das Schrifttum der Schule Anselms von Laon und Wilhelms von Champeaux in deutschen Bibliotheken.* Ed. H. Weisweiler. BGPTM 33/1–2. Münster, 1936.

Sententiae Anselmi. In *Anselms von Laon systematische Sentenzen.* Ed. F. Bliemetzrieder. BGPTM 19/2–3. Münster, 1919.

Sicard of Cremona. *Mitrale seu de Officiis ecclesiasticis summa.* PL 213:13–436.

Songs of the Sabbath Sacrifice: A Critical Edition. Ed. C. Newsom. Harvard Semitic Studies 27. Atlanta, 1985.

Spinks, B. D. *Addai and Mari—The Anaphora of the Apostles. A Text for Students.* Grove Liturgical Studies 24. Bramcote, Nottinghamshire: Grove, 1980.

_____. "Addai and Mari and the Institution Narrative: The Tantalizing Evidence." *EL* 98 (1984) 60–67.

_____. "Eucharistic Offering in the East Syrian Anaphora." *OCP* 50 (1984) 347–71.

_____. "Sacerdoce et offrande dans les *Koushapè* des anaphores syriennes orientales." *MD*, no. 154 (1983) 107–26.

_____. "The Anaphora for India: Some Theological Objections to an Attempt at Inculturation." *EL* 95 (1981) 529–49.

_____. "The Consecratory Epiclesis in the Anaphora of St. James." *Studia liturgica* 11 (1976) 19–38.

_____. "The Jewish Sources for the *Sanctus.*" *Heythrop Journal* 21 (1980) 168–79.

_____. "The Original Form of the Anaphora of the Apostles: A Suggestion in the Light of the Maronite Sharar." *EL* 91 (1977) 146–61.

_____. *The Sanctus in the Eucharistic Prayer.* Cambridge and New York: Cambridge University Press, 1991.

_____. *Worship: Prayers from the East.* Washington, D.C.: Pastoral Press, 1993.

Suárez, F. *De sacramentis,* Pars prima. *Opera omnia* 10. Venice: Ex typographia Malleonina, 1747.

Süss, Th. "L'aspect sacrificiel de la sainte Cène à la lumière de la tradition luthérienne." *Eucharisties d'Orient et d'Occident.* Ed. B. Botte and others. Lex orandi 46–47. Paris: Cerf, 1970. I, 151–70.

Taft, R. *"Ex oriente lux?* Some Reflexions on Eucharistic Celebration." *Worship* 54 (1980) 308–25.

_____. "The Frequency of the Eucharist Throughout History." *Can We Always Celebrate the Eucharist?* Ed. M. Collins and D. Power. = Concilium, 1982, no. 152, 13–24.

Talley, T. J. "De la 'berakah' à l'eucharistie. Une question à réexaminer." *MD*, no. 125 (1976) 11–39.

_____. "Structures des anaphores anciennes et modernes." *MD*, no. 191 (1992) 15–43.

_____. "The Literary Structure of the Eucharistic Prayer." *Worship* 58 (1984) 404–20.

Tertullian. *Q. S. Fl. Tertulliani Opera*. CCL 1–2. Turnhout: Brepols, 1954.

Tertulliano–Cipriano–Agostino. Il Padre Nostro. Ed. V. Grossi. Rome, 1980.

Theodore of Mopsuestia. *Les homélies catéchétiques de Théodore de Mopsueste*. Ed. and trans. R. Tonneau and R. Devreesse. ST 145. Vatican City: Vatican Apostolic Library, 1949.

Thibodeau, T. M. "Les sources du *Rationale* de Guillaume Durand." *Guillaume Durand évêque de Mende (v. 1230–1296). Canoniste, liturgiste et homme politique*. Ed. P.-M. Gy. Actes de la Table Ronde du C.N.R.S., Mende 24–27 mai 1990. Paris: Editions du Centre national de la recherche scientifique, 1992, 143–54.

Thümmel, H. G. "Eusebios 'Brief an Kaiserin Konstania.'" *Klio* 66 (1984) 210–22.

Thurian, M. *The Eucharistic Memorial*. Trans. J. G. Davies. 2 vols. Ecumenical Studies in Worship 7–8. Richmond, Va.: John Knox, 1960.

Tirot, P. "La concélébration et la tradition de l'Eglise." *EL* 101 (1987) 33–59.

Torrel, J.-P. "L'authenticité de l'*Adoro te devote*." *RevSR* 67 (1993) 78–83.

Il Trattato delle Benedizioni (Berakot) del Talmud babilonese. Ed. S. Cavalletti. Classici delle religioni. Turin, 1968.

Turner, C. H. "*Adversaria patristica*. III. *Figura corporis mei* in Tertullian." *JTS* 7 (1906) 595–97.

Vadakkel, J. *The East Syrian Anaphora of Mar Theodore of Mopsuestia. Critical Edition, English Translation and Study*. Vadavathoor Kottayam, India: Oriental Institute of Religious Studies, 1989.

Van de Paverd, F. *Zur Geschichte der Messliturgie in Antiocheia und Konstantinopel gegen Ende des vierten Jahrhunderts. Analyse der Quellen bei Johannes Chrysostomos*. OCA 187. Rome, 1970.

Van den Eynde, D. "*Eucharistia ex duabus rebus constans*. S. Irénée, *Adv. haereses* IV, 18, 5." *Antonianum* 15 (1940) 13–28.

Vanni, U. "*Homoioma* in Paolo." *Greg* 58 (1977) 321–45, 431–70.

Vellian, J. "The Anaphoral Structure of Addai and Mari Compared to the Berakoth Preceding the Shema in the Synagogue Morning Service." *Mus* 85 (1972) 201–23.

Verhelst, S. "L'histoire de la liturgie melkite de saint Jacques. Interprétations anciennes et nouvelles." *POC* 43 (1993) 229–72.

Viaud, G. *Les liturgies des Coptes d'Egypte*. Paris: Librairie d'Amérique et d'Orient A. Maisonneuve, 1978.

Visonà, G. "Pasqua quartodecimana e cronologia evangelica della passione." *EL* 102 (1988) 259–315.

Vööbus, A. *Liturgical Traditions in the Didache*. Papers of the Estonian Theological Society in Exile 16. Stockholm, 1968.

Webb, D. "La liturgie nestorienne des apôtres Addaï et Mari dans la tradition manuscrite." *Eucharisties d'Orient et d'Occident.* Ed. B. Botte and others. Lex orandi 46–47. Paris: Cerf, 1970. II, 25–49.

Wéber, E. H. "L'incidence du traité de l'eucharistie sur la métaphysique de S. Thomas d'Aquin." *RSPT* 77 (1993) 195–218.

Wegman, H.A.J. "Pleidooi voor ein Tekst de Anaphora van de Aposteln Addai en Mari." *Bijdragen* 40 (1979) 15–43.

[William Durandus.] *Guillelmi Duranti Rationale divinorum officiorum, I–IV.* Ed. A. Davril and T. M. Thibodeau. CCLContMed 140. Turnhout: Brepols, 1995.

Wilmart, A. *"Transfigurare." Bulletin d'ancienne littérature et d'archéologie chrétienne* 1 (1911) 282–92.

Yousif, P. *A Classified Bibliography.* Rome, 1990.

____. *L'Eucharistie chez saint Ephrem de Nisibe.* OCA 224. Rome, 1984.

Zanetti, U. "L'Eglise copte." *Seminarium* 27 (1987) 352–63.

____. *Les lectionnaires coptes annuels: Basse-Egypte.* Publications de l'Institut Orientaliste de Louvain 33. Louvain-La-Neuve, 1985.

Index

Account of Institution, 287–90

Addai and Mari, Anaphora of Apostles, 72, 74, 140–41

Ahabhah Rabbah as prayer for peace, 47, 48, 79–80, 83

Alexandrian anaphora, 61–62, 63, 139–40, 291n., 314–18; paleo-anaphora, 39–41, 46–48, 49, 52, 54–55, 60, 65, 66; as origin of Eucharistic Prayer, 65; *Sanctus*, 62, 64, 285n., 295

Altar relics of the saints, 229–31

Altars, church, 225; consecration of, 231

Amalarius of Metz, 162–73; method of, 163–64; Mass as representation of Passion, 164–67; triform Body of Christ, 169–71

Ambrose of Milan, 141, 147, 151–54

Amidah, 79–80

Anamnesis, 290–91

Anaphora of Hippolytus, 50–54, 61, 312

Anaphoras, 39, 277, 280n.

Animal slaughter as ritual, 10; in Deuteronomy, 10–13

Anselm of Laon, 187–88

Antiochene anaphora, 66; structure of, 49–50; *Sanctus* in, 285

Antitype, 90–92

Apologia of Justin, 107–08, 112, 115

Apostolic Constitutions, 35–36, 309–10

Apostolic Tradition of Hippolytus, 50–51

Apparitions, eucharistic, 203

Aristotelian ontology, 204–05

Aristotelianism, 247–48

Augustine, 132n., 155–59; on eucharistic bread, 155–56; on sacramental realism, 156; teaching on Eucharist, 157–59

Basil, Alexandrian anaphora of, 314–18; Byzantine anaphora of, 143, 318–23

Beleth, John, 176

Benedictus, 62

Berengarius, 190–92

Birkat Ha–Mazon, 15–17, 27, 29, 30, 33, 34, 36–37, 52, 60, 61, 78–81, 105, 281, 307–08

Bishop, ministry of, 96–99

Blessings before and after meals, 307–08

Blood of Christ, 34

Body and Blood of Christ, 139, 141–42, 148, 188, 247; in Ignatius, 105–06

Body of Christ, 102, 169–71, 187, 220–22, 253; Church as, 84; devotion to, 195–97; in Bonaventure, 217; in church altars, 227, 228, 229, 230, 231, 233, 235; in Thomas Aquinas, 207

Boismard, M.-B, 87

Bonaventure of Bagnoregio, 215–20; on Body of Christ, 217

Bread, 218n.

Bread and wine, 19, 20n., 105–06, 114, 218n., 302n.; show unity of

Eucharistic Prayer, 210, 273–75; importance of, 20; parts of, 73; in Cyprian, 128–29; reform of, 269–80
Eucharistic Prayer II, 271–72
Eucharistic Prayer III, 273
Eucharistic Prayer IV, 273–74
Eucharistic Prayers for various needs, 277–80
Eucharistic realism, 182–92
Eucharistic rite in 1 Corinthians, 31
Eudes of Sully, 231–32
Eusebius of Caesarea, on Therapeutae, 53; on Eucharist as image of Christ, 145–47

Figura, 186, 191, 192, 207, 209, 217
Figura corporis, in Tertullian, 119–20
Finkelstein, L., 16, 79
Florus of Lyons, 171, 173–74
Franquesa, A., on concelebration, 259

Giet, S., 77
Gift, characteristics of, 283–84
Gilbert of Nocent, 189
Greek Anaphora of James, 66–67
Guitmund of Aversa, 220–21
Gy, Pierre–Marie, 201, 202, 206, 209, 210, 216

Heavenly elements of Eucharist, 112
Hierarchy, 124
Hippolytus, 271, 272; anaphora of, 52, 56–57, 61, 312; and *Apostolic Tradition,* 50–51
Historical method applied to liturgy, 2–3
Holy Spirit, 59
Homily, 265
Honorius of Autun, on the Mass, 175
Hôs, 99
Humanity of Christ, 193–94; devotion to, 223
Hyper hymôn, 303

Ignatius of Antioch, 93–107; on martyrdom, 93–95
Image, Eucharist as, 145–46
Imbach, Ruedi, 206
Imitation of Christ, by Ignatius, 95
Imitation of Last Supper, Eucharist as, 126–27, 142, 297–98, 306
Immortality, medicine of (*see* Medicine of immortality)
Incense placed in altar, 229, 230, 233, 234
Innocent III, Pope, 179
Institution, Account of (*see* Account of Institution)
Intercessions in Eucharistic Prayer, 294
Irenaeus, 57–58; on Eucharist, 111–14
Ivo of Chartres, 176

Jewish ritual meal, 9, 14; rite of festive meal, 29
John, Gospel of, 86; and the *Didache,* 86–88; and unity, 87–88
Justin, on eucharistic celebration, 107–11; *Apologia,* 107–08, 112, 115

Kingdom of God, 278–79
Kiss of peace, 256, 267

Laon, School of, 187, 188, 189, 221
Last Supper, 19, 289, 297–304; prayers at, 19; as model for celebration of the Church, 21; in New Testament, 22–24; ritual of, 22, 26; as Passover meal in Synoptic Gospels, 24–26; in Cyprian, 127–28; as Eucharist, 139; prophetic character of, 298–99
Laurance, John D., 128–29, 133
Léon–Dufour, Xavier, on Last Supper, 297, 300, 301, 303
Levels of church in Ignatius, 98
Liturgy of the Word, 265
Lothar of Segni, 179

Made in the USA
Monee, IL
02 October 2022

15092073R10207